Active Server Pages 3
Developer's Guide

Active Server Pages 3 Developer's Guide

Manuel Alberto Ricart and
Stephen Asbury

M&T Books.
An imprint of IDG Books Worldwide, Inc.

Foster City, CA ◆ Chicago, IL ◆ Indianapolis, IN ◆ New York, NY

Active Server Pages 3 Developer's Guide

Published by
M&T Books
An imprint of IDG Books Worldwide, Inc.
919 E. Hillsdale Blvd., Suite 400
Foster City, CA 94404
www.idgbooks.com (IDG Books Worldwide Web site)

Library of Congress Catalog Card Number: 00-105677

ISBN: 0-7645-4715-1

Printed in the United States of America

10 9 8 7 6 5 4 3 2 1

1B/SV/QX/QQ/FC

Distributed in the United States by IDG Books Worldwide, Inc.

Distributed by CDG Books Canada Inc. for Canada; by Transworld Publishers Limited in the United Kingdom; by IDG Norge Books for Norway; by IDG Sweden Books for Sweden; by IDG Books Australia Publishing Corporation Pty. Ltd. for Australia and New Zealand; by TransQuest Publishers Pte Ltd. for Singapore, Malaysia, Thailand, Indonesia, and Hong Kong; by Gotop Information Inc. for Taiwan; by ICG Muse, Inc. for Japan; by Intersoft for South Africa; by Eyrolles for France; by International Thomson Publishing for Germany, Austria, and Switzerland; by Distribuidora Cuspide for Argentina; by LR International for Brazil; by Galileo Libros for Chile; by Ediciones ZETA S.C.R. Ltda. for Peru; by WS Computer Publishing Corporation, Inc., for the Philippines; by Contemporanea de Ediciones for Venezuela; by Express Computer Distributors for the Caribbean and West Indies; by Micronesia Media Distributor, Inc. for Micronesia; by Chips Computadoras S.A. de C.V. for Mexico; by Editorial Norma de Panama S.A. for Panama; by American Bookshops for Finland.

For general information on IDG Books Worldwide's books in the U.S., please call our Consumer Customer Service department at 800-762-2974. For reseller information, including discounts and premium sales, please call our Reseller Customer Service department at 800-434-3422.

For information on where to purchase IDG Books Worldwide's books outside the U.S., please contact our International Sales department at 317-596-5530 or fax 317-572-4002.

For consumer information on foreign language translations, please contact our Customer Service department at 800-434-3422, fax 317-572-4002, or e-mail rights@idgbooks.com.

For information on licensing foreign or domestic rights, please phone +1-650-653-7098.

For sales inquiries and special prices for bulk quantities, please contact our Order Services department at 800-434-3422 or write to the address above.

For information on using IDG Books Worldwide's books in the classroom or for ordering examination copies, please contact our Educational Sales department at 800-434-2086 or fax 317-572-4005.

For press review copies, author interviews, or other publicity information, please contact our Public Relations department at 650-653-7000 or fax 650-653-7500.

For authorization to photocopy items for corporate, personal, or educational use, please contact Copyright Clearance Center, 222 Rosewood Drive, Danvers, MA 01923, or fax 978-750-4470.

ABOUT IDG BOOKS WORLDWIDE

Welcome to the world of IDG Books Worldwide.

IDG Books Worldwide, Inc., is a subsidiary of International Data Group, the world's largest publisher of computer-related information and the leading global provider of information services on information technology. IDG was founded more than 30 years ago by Patrick J. McGovern and now employs more than 9,000 people worldwide. IDG publishes more than 290 computer publications in over 75 countries. More than 90 million people read one or more IDG publications each month.

Launched in 1990, IDG Books Worldwide is today the #1 publisher of best-selling computer books in the United States. We are proud to have received eight awards from the Computer Press Association in recognition of editorial excellence and three from Computer Currents' First Annual Readers' Choice Awards. Our best-selling *...For Dummies*® series has more than 50 million copies in print with translations in 31 languages. IDG Books Worldwide, through a joint venture with IDG's Hi-Tech Beijing, became the first U.S. publisher to publish a computer book in the People's Republic of China. In record time, IDG Books Worldwide has become the first choice for millions of readers around the world who want to learn how to better manage their businesses.

Our mission is simple: Every one of our books is designed to bring extra value and skill-building instructions to the reader. Our books are written by experts who understand and care about our readers. The knowledge base of our editorial staff comes from years of experience in publishing, education, and journalism — experience we use to produce books to carry us into the new millennium. In short, we care about books, so we attract the best people. We devote special attention to details such as audience, interior design, use of icons, and illustrations. And because we use an efficient process of authoring, editing, and desktop publishing our books electronically, we can spend more time ensuring superior content and less time on the technicalities of making books.

You can count on our commitment to deliver high-quality books at competitive prices on topics you want to read about. At IDG Books Worldwide, we continue in the IDG tradition of delivering quality for more than 30 years. You'll find no better book on a subject than one from IDG Books Worldwide.

John Kilcullen
Chairman and CEO
IDG Books Worldwide, Inc.

*Eighth Annual
Computer Press
Awards 1992*

*Ninth Annual
Computer Press
Awards 1993*

*Tenth Annual
Computer Press
Awards 1994*

*Eleventh Annual
Computer Press
Awards 1995*

IDG is the world's leading IT media, research and exposition company. Founded in 1964, IDG had 1997 revenues of $2.05 billion and has more than 9,000 employees worldwide. IDG offers the widest range of media options that reach IT buyers in 75 countries representing 95% of worldwide IT spending. IDG's diverse product and services portfolio spans six key areas including print publishing, online publishing, expositions and conferences, market research, education and training, and global marketing services. More than 90 million people read one or more of IDG's 290 magazines and newspapers, including IDG's leading global brands — Computerworld, PC World, Network World, Macworld and the Channel World family of publications. IDG Books Worldwide is one of the fastest-growing computer book publishers in the world, with more than 700 titles in 36 languages. The "...For Dummies®" series alone has more than 50 million copies in print. IDG offers online users the largest network of technology-specific Web sites around the world through IDG.net (http://www.idg.net), which comprises more than 225 targeted Web sites in 55 countries worldwide. International Data Corporation (IDC) is the world's largest provider of information technology data, analysis and consulting, with research centers in over 41 countries and more than 400 research analysts worldwide. IDG World Expo is a leading producer of more than 168 globally branded conferences and expositions in 35 countries including E3 (Electronic Entertainment Expo), Macworld Expo, ComNet, Windows World Expo, ICE (Internet Commerce Expo), Agenda, DEMO, and Spotlight. IDG's training subsidiary, ExecuTrain, is the world's largest computer training company, with more than 230 locations worldwide and 785 training courses. IDG Marketing Services helps industry-leading IT companies build international brand recognition by developing global integrated marketing programs via IDG's print, online and exposition products worldwide. Further information about the company can be found at www.idg.com. 1/26/00

Credits

ACQUISITIONS EDITOR
Debra Williams Cauley

PROJECT EDITORS
Terry O'Donnell
Terri Varveris

CONTRIBUTING WRITER
Jeff Niblack

TECHNICAL EDITOR
Jeff Niblack

COPY EDITORS
Gabrielle Chosney
Sarah Kleinman
Jeani Smith

PROOF EDITOR
Neil Romanosky

MEDIA DEVELOPMENT SPECIALIST
Jamie Smith

PERMISSIONS EDITOR
Carmen Krikorian

MEDIA DEVELOPMENT MANAGERS
Stephen Noetzel
Heather Dismore

PROJECT COORDINATORS
Louigene A. Santos
Danette Nurse

GRAPHICS AND PRODUCTION SPECIALISTS
Robert Bihlmayer
Michael Lewis
Victor Pérez-Varela
Ramses Ramirez

QUALITY CONTROL TECHNICIAN
Dina F Quan

DESIGN SPECIALISTS
Kurt Krames
Kippy Thomsen

BOOK DESIGNER
Jim Donohue

ILLUSTRATORS
Mary Jo Weis
Rashell Smith
Karl Brandt

PROOFREADING AND INDEXING
York Production Services

COVER IMAGE
© Noma/Images.com

About the Author

Stephen Asbury is currently an architect and member of the steering committee for BayWeb, a Silicon Valley consulting company. Before its acquisition in April 2000, Stephen was co-founder and CEO/CTO of Paradigm Research, Inc, an Internet technology training company. As the key technology resource for PRI, Stephen designed, developed and delivered curricula for numerous companies including Sun, Active Software, Brio Technology, HP, IBM, SGI, Ford, Starbucks, Chrysler and Netscape. This is Stephen's sixth book on Internet related topics, including Java, CGI, Perl, and Linux. He can be reached at stephen@sasbury.com.

Manuel Alberto Ricart is an architect for Tibco Software, Inc., (http://www.tibco.com) where he can usually be found tinkering with distributed computing technologies all day long. Tibco Software, Inc. is the leading provider of real-time e-Business infrastructure software for Enterprise Application Integration (EAI), Business-to-Business (B2B) Commerce, and Web and Wireless Portals and Alerting.

Alberto has been involved with computers since the later 1970s, when he was introduced to programming on a then state-of-the-art IBM System 32, which had a whopping 32KB of RAM and a tiny hard disk. Since then, he has developed a number of software products for the Macintosh operating system (OS), the NEXTSTEP OS, Java and Enterprise Application Integration products. Alberto holds bachelor's (1987) and master's (1989) degrees from the University of Wisconsin-Milwaukee.

In 1992, Alberto founded a software company, SmartSoft, Inc., that developed a wide range of commercial object-oriented software tools for the NEXTSTEP/OPENSTEP (UNIX) OS. His products were sold worldwide. In 1995, he co-founded a second firm dedicated to building Internet solutions that enabled companies to harness the Internet for business. He has developed custom technologies used by notable companies such as Oshkosh B'Gosh and Warburg Pincus Funds.

For Cheryl,
— Stephen

To Diana, Julisa, Isabella, Viviana and Alejandro: You make it all possible.
— Alberto

Preface

Welcome to the Active Server Pages 3 Developer's Guide. If you are reading this book you are a web developer and are interested in using Active Server Pages (ASP) to developer server-side web applications. Traditionally server-side development has been cumbersome and somewhat painful. With ASP, much of the difficulties are gone and ASP itself is actually quite simple to learn. This simplicity doesn't mean that ASP isn't powerful – quite on the contrary. The simplicity and extensibility of the ASP framework is what makes ASP very powerful and an ideal candidate for developing web-based applications. In many ways, ASP is so extensible that it can be considered to be an application server of sorts, a term typically reserved for other more complex technologies.

The book you hold in your hands focuses on showing you how to develop ASP applications. Our goal is to make your learning of ASP a simple one. On the surface we tend to trivialize some of the issues, because we believe that focusing on the task or technique is better than showing you a long winded example that hides how to solve a problem or implement the technology. You probably already have an application or two that you need to develop. Solid understanding of the principles we show here will allow you to solve your real-world problems without a lot of reading. We have been selective about what we show you. We believe that very few technologies require books that are fatter than 500 pages, if you are like us, you are probably looking for a concise explanation and relevant examples on the topic at hand: Active Server Pages.

Target Audience

Books are written with a target audience in mind. Our audience is anyone that wants to develop web applications with ASP. This means that this book is for you if you are getting started with server-side applications, or if you have developed server-side applications using CGI or some other technology like Server-side JavaScript on a Netscape server. We assume that you know how to markup in HTML, and perhaps have done some client-side scripting.

If you meet the above criteria, some of the information will be familiar so this book will be quick and easy reading for you. This book makes a few assumptions about your qualifications:

◆ You have used a web browser to surf the Internet and have an understanding of the client-server nature of web applications and understand basic concepts like what is an URL.

◆ You have developed HTML pages and have more than a casual understanding of HTML elements (tags) used in the formatting of content. This means that you have marked up your HTML by using a text editor rather than using a high level tool to generate it for you.

◆ Much of the information used by web applications is provided via HTML forms. It is assumed that you have some understanding on how HTML forms are defined, and are at least vaguely familiar with attributes and options of the <FORM> element, so words such as "POST" and "GET" will ring some sort of bell.

◆ Finally and most importantly, ASP involves programming using a scripting language like VBScript or JavaScript (actually you can use others). Scripting *is* programming, and as such it is assumed that you have an understanding of programming concepts like variables, functions, loops and conditionals. While the norm for an ASP book is to show examples using VBScript, most of the examples in the book are shown using JavaScript (JScript), for we believe if you have done any sort of web development like writing client-side scripts, you already know how to program using JavaScript.

If you are not a programmer, this book may not provide all that you need to know. You may want to consider getting a supplemental text on JavaScript programming and learn how to develop client-side scripts prior to getting involved with server-side programming. If you have not programmed with JavaScript or VBScript but have experience with other programming languages such as Java, C/C++, or even BASIC, we have included references on JavaScript and VBScript that will allow you to get up to speed fast in the language features and syntax. However these references don't really teach a non-programmer how to write a program.

What You Need

To make the best use of this book, you need:

◆ Window 2000 with Internet Information Services (IIS) installed. This book focuses on ASP 3.0. However, the bulk of the book will apply to earlier versions.

◆ If you are using an ASP clone, this book will still be useful because we focus on programming issues rather than on server/implementation details.

As for hardware, anything that will run Windows 2000 should be fine. Some sort of a 300MHz Pentium II processor with 64MB should do just fine.

Conventions in This Book

Take a minute to skim this section and learn some of the conventions used throughout this book.

Keyboard conventions

You need to use the keyboard to write your programs. Here's some of the conventions we have used:

CODE
This book contains many small and not so small snippets of VBScript or JavaScript code, as well as complete listings. Each listing appears in a `monospace font`; each line of code occupies a separate line. (We copied these listings directly from our source and pasted them into the word processor to insure that the code you see is code that was tested, and canoperate).

In all cases, code in the listings should run as you see it listed. In some cases, lines that were too long were folded into two or more lines. However, we have done so in a way that is legible and doesn't affect any compilation of the code.

OBJECTS, FUNCTIONS, AND FILENAMES
Typically when referring to an object or class name we have used `monospace font`. This font distinguishes object or class names from other names in the text.

Mouse conventions

If you're reading this book, you're should know how to use your mouse. The mouse terminology, we use is all standard fare: pointing, clicking, right-clicking, dragging, and so on.

What the Icons Mean

Throughout the book, we've used *icons* in the left margin to call your attention to points that are particularly important.

 We use the Note icon to tell you that something is important. It may be a concept to help you master the task at hand or something fundamental for understanding subsequent material.

Tip icons indicate a more efficient way of doing something, or a technique that may not be obvious.

These icons indicate that an example file is on the companion CD-ROM (see Appendix A, "What's on the CD-ROM"). This CD holds all the code examples listed in the book and much more.

We use the Caution icon when the operation that we are describing can cause problems if you're not careful.

We use the Cross Reference icon to refer you to other chapters when we have more to say on a subject.

How This Book Is Organized

This book consists of 21 chapters. In addition, it includes appendixes that provide supplemental information.

While you may choose to read the book in any way that it makes sense to you, it is probably a good idea to read Chapters 1 through10 in order as this is the core of the book and other chapters do build on this knowledge.

In Chapter 1, we get our terms together and differentiate server-side programming with other types of programming you might have done. We explain the basic currency used by web applications and introduce you to ASP architecture. The second chapter introduces the basic components of a web application written using ASP as well as how to embed server-side code into your HTML pages. In Chapter 3, you'll install your webserver and create a simple ASP page to verify that all is running according to plan. Chapter 4 introduces you to the request object where you'll get information about a visitor's request.

Chapter 5 covers the Response object, which allows you to send HTML or other content to the browser. Chapter 6 covers the Application object, which is shared by all visitors to your application. In it you can store values that you want to share between visitors. The Session object, coverd in Chapter 7, represents information about a particular visitor to your application. Values you store in the Session follow the visitor from page to page. Chapter 8 shows you how the Server object provides many utility functions that you can use when developing your scripts. In Chapter 9, you'll see a complete application that (a web based Chat Room). The application is developed and refined showing you most of the things you'll need to do when writing your own applications.

ASP is extensible by installing additional ActiveX components, and Chapter 10 introduces the components that ship with the server. One of the most important ActiveX components provides access to the file system. In Chapter 11, you learn how to use it to read and write files.

All programs will require varying degrees of error handling and debugging. Chapter 12 tells you how to do it in ASP. Chapter 13 shows you how to save your visitor state on a more permanent basis. In Chapter 14, you'll learn how to use ADO to interact with databases.

Chapter 15 provides a more complete example, one that uses a database for storing information. Some pages may interact with more than one resource. In chapter 16, the coverage of transactional scripts show you how to create transactions that span more than one server. Chapter 17 lists all the directives you need to know and how to use server-side includes in your own applications. Chapter 18 overviews the different security options you have in IIS. We also get to brew our own simple access control feature.

Chapter 19 chapter describes the architecture and code for our simple version of a BBS. Numerous Web sites have begun to include forums and bulletin board systems (BBS) that visitors can use to exchange and share information, and you may want to add such a feature to your Web sites as well. From this example you can learn the basic structure so that you have a version, with source code, that you can modify.

To further demonstrate some of the application design and programming methods that make up the Windows Distributed interNet Applications (DNA) architecture, Chapter 20 rewrites the sample online catalog that was discussed in Chapter 15, "A Simple Online Catalog."

Chapter 21 covers some of the basics related to performance tuning by looking at what makes up an HTTP request and some of the more important aspects of Web traffic. Then, we'll introduce two basic performance-tuning methodologies. This chapter will also briefly discuss how to use Microsoft's Web Application Stress tool, which is a free download from `http://webtool.rte.microsoft.com`.

The Appendixes

In addition to the above this book has several appendixes that provide a quick reference to ASP, JavaScript, VBScript, and other topics. Appendix A describes the contents of the CD-ROM that accompanies the back of the book.

Contacting Us

We want your feedback. After you have had a chance to use this book, please take a moment to register this book on the http://my2cents.idgbooks.com Web site. (Details are listed on the my2cents page in the back of this book.) Please don't hesitate to let us know about any chapters that gave you trouble, or where you thought we could have made concepts clearer. Also let us know where we've done a particularly good job.

To provide us, the authors, with feedback, please write to:

asp_book@yahoo.com.

We will read all/any comments/suggestions that you send to us. However, please realize that it is impossible for us to provide you with ASP or Web development technical support.

Have fun reading this book and learning about ASP!

Acknowledgments

First, I would like to thank the "PRI gang," Karen, Mila, Nicole, Richard, Shrinand, Tyler, James and especially Kerry. Sometimes writing takes away from work and I appreciate their dedication in my stead. Thank you to my wife Cheryl. At times a decade of marriage makes me feel old. But I can't think of anyone else I would rather have spent the years with. I am looking forward to many more years together, probably sprinkled with busy nights and weekends writing, but just as precious.

Stephen Asbury

Developing a book is a monumental task. This time the task was made easier with the help provided by my friend Stephen who kept the book and chapters rolling while I was busy with a different project. Additional thanks go to Lisa Swayne who got us the project; Debra Williams Cauley from IDG who we dissuaded to follow our vision on highly focused books; Terri Varveris and Terry O'Donnell for editing and developing the book; and finally Jeff Niblack, who technically reviewed the content for sanity and also contributed Chapter 20 and Appendixes E and G.

Manuel Alberto Ricart

Contents at a Glance

Contents

Chapter 1

Introduction to Web Applications

IN THIS CHAPTER

- ◆ What are Web applications?
- ◆ Web application development issues
- ◆ An overview of Web technology
- ◆ Programming server-side applications
- ◆ Maintaining state in a stateless environment

THIS CHAPTER PROVIDES THE groundwork necessary to put the Active Server Pages (ASP) in perspective: It introduces how Web applications have been built in the past and some of the issues and challenges involved in developing them now. Finally this chapter provides an overview of how ASP differs from the other technologies used to build Web applications. If you have developed CGIs, many of the issues discussed here will be somewhat familiar to you.

What Are Web Applications?

Web applications are very different from traditional desktop applications. Some of the differences are obvious. Instead of running on one machine for a single user, a Web application runs on some server across the network, and instead of serving one user at a time, a Web application serves many users concurrently.

Using the Web as the delivery mechanism for an application provides many benefits. Chief among them are portability and ubiquitous distribution. To access a Web application you only need a capable browser and a network connection. Depending on the problem you are trying to solve, a creative Web application has little, if anything, to envy from the traditional "desktop applications" we are all used to working with. Often the Web application's features are superior to these traditional applications.

Web applications build their user interfaces using HTML, which stands for HyperText Markup Language. HTML provides the structure and the formatting of the interface. Applications that require more advanced capabilities typically add Java applets, weblets (a Java application that controls the browser), application-specific plug-ins (like a mainframe terminal emulator), or some other custom control that provides the extra features needed to solve the problem. The browser empowers any computer with access to the network to use the application. Gone is the need to develop, install, manage, and update different versions of an application for each potential user.

Because of their client-server nature, Web applications can make use of some tricks that aren't available to regular applications. Web applications can off-load functionality to different components. Using client-side scripts embedded into the HTML, a Web application can perform simple data validation and synchronize multiple HTML frames. Additional complexity can be handled with a Java applet or a browser plug-in that can perform additional operations without requiring additional network trips. On the server side, the Web application maintains state information, a *session*, that follows the visitor from page to page. The server also provides the application logic and generates dynamic HTML content that matches a visitor's request. Lastly, additional logic such as data integrity rules can be off-loaded to other resources such as databases and application servers. The end result can be a very distributed application that integrates numerous systems and processes into a coherent whole.

Web Application Development Issues

There are several challenges to developing a Web-based application. A fundamental concept is that Hypertext Transfer Protocol (HTTP), the protocol used by the browser and Web server to communicate, is stateless: when a visitor makes a request from a Web server, the server has no idea who the visitor is, information that the user has previously provided, or where the visitor is going. This is because HTTP doesn't maintain information (a session) between requests. The Web server's only responsibility is to serve the currently requested URL — period. In terms of applications that span multiple pages and provide a certain degree of interactivity, this limitation of HTTP makes it very difficult to implement what we would think of as an "application."

Other seemingly trivial issues, like what constitutes the beginning or the end of an application, are not so trivial in the Web's stateless environment. In a Web application anyone can jump between application pages just by typing, or selecting a bookmark or favorite to, a specific URL. Where does the application start and where does it end? Desktop applications' internal states know this, because they start when you launch them and quit when you exit them. Web applications are very different, and so is the notion of the *application* and where it starts and ends.

Because it is impossible to implement an application without some state maintenance, HTTP has been enhanced to allow Web developers to easily pass and set information between requests made by a visitor's browser. By executing scripts on the server side, the server can figure out where the user has been, and what information should be presented in response.

To implement this or any other custom functionality, you need a server-side program. Such programs are typically written as Common Gateway Interface (CGI) programs. CGIs are programs external to the Web server that process a request made by a visitor and return a result (typically HTML) to the Web server, which then delivers it back to the visitor. CGIs have had the duties of handling requests and interfacing with the Web server and any other system necessary to fulfill the request. CGIs are relatively primitive, as they require that the programmer know all the intricacies of how HTTP requests are handled – items like what characters you need to output to separate the HTTP header from the HTTP body. These nuances, while not difficult to master, distract from the real task of developing a Web application as the programmer wastes time worrying about how to interact with HTTP rather than thinking about the application logic itself.

Second generation technologies, such as ASP, abstract these low-level requirements to the point that the programmer does not need to dwell on these details. In many cases they are implemented transparently as part of processing a request.

Web application frameworks, like ASP, allow for faster and more scalable applications, provide a higher-level toolkit under which to develop these Web applications, relieve the programmer of tedious tasks such as maintaining application state, and allow the use of transactions that span multiple pages. All this simplifies the programmer's task, allowing more time for what is really important – developing the application.

The benefit to programmers is incredible; instead of developing an HTTP application, they only need to worry about implementing the features of their applications. While these abstractions are an incredible aid, it is important to be aware of what the server is actually doing. Having some insight on what the server does, and how it does it, will help you develop simple yet powerful solutions to your own problems. In other words, it is a good idea to understand how it all works under the covers.

Overview of Web Technology

The next few pages introduce the building blocks for Web applications and how the Web server exchanges information with a browser. At the very core of Web technology is the HTTP message. The HTTP message is the unit of communication between the server and the client browser. The server and the client browser exchange information using HTTP messages. HTTP doesn't have anything to do with the content of the information; it just has to do with the way the browser asks for a resource, provides additional data for processing, and provides additional information about itself. HTTP messages originating from the server provide information about the resource that is retrieved, and embedded within the body of the message is the actual content that a browser will display.

Sending HTTP messages

Browsers and servers use HTTP messages to exchange information. An HTTP message can be a *request* sent by a browser or a *response* returned by the Web (or HTTP) server. All HTTP messages have a *header* and a *body*. A message is much like a letter. The header is conceptually similar to the envelope you mail letters in — containing the address of the person the letter is going to — and the body is the actual letter you send. Listing 1-1 shows an example of an HTTP message sent by a browser.

Listing 1-1: An HTTP request message

```
GET /IISSamples/Default/welcome.htm HTTP/1.1
Accept: */*
Accept-Language: en-us
Accept-Encoding: gzip, deflate
User-Agent: Mozilla/4.0 (compatible; MSIE 5.0; Windows NT; DigExt;
    AT&T WNS5.2)
Host: localhost
Connection: Keep-Alive
```

Listing 1-2 shows the response sent by the server.

Listing 1-2: The server's response to the HTTP request message

```
HTTP/1.1 200 OK
Server: Microsoft-IIS/4.0
Date: Thu, 23 Dec 1999 18:26:10 GMT
Content-Type: text/html
Set-Cookie: ASPSESSIONIDQGGGQGOB=ODAEGDFDLHDEGOJOINCIBOBM; path=/
Cache-control: private
Accept-Ranges: bytes
Last-Modified: Sat, 25 Oct 1997 12:31:32 GMT
Content-Length: 4680

<html>
<head>
<title>Welcome To Microsoft Personal Web Server</title>
</head>
<body bgcolor="#FFFFFF" link="#0080FF" vlink="#0080FF"
topmargin="0" leftmargin="0">
...
```

Setting up the HTTP header

The HTTP header contains information that is *never* displayed to the visitor. The header provides information about the request and in some cases additional information to provide a context for the request. In the previous examples, the HTTP header for the request and the response are shown in bold text. This information includes the following items:

◆ The URL/URI of the requested document. A URL is the virtualized address for a resource, providing a way for you to refer to a particular resource available in some machine.

◆ Information about the application that generated the message such as the brand and version of the browser or server that sent the information. This allows the server to better tune the information it sends to match the capabilities of the browser. Browsers typically ignore this information. Other server clients (Web robots, or webbots) use this information to gather statistics about the servers and figure out which is the most popular brand of Web server running on the Internet.

◆ The version of the HTTP protocol supported. This allows the browser and the server to interact in a way they both understand.

◆ The size of the message body (if one was sent), so the browser knows how much data to expect. This is typically used to show the download progress or calculate how much data was sent to the server.

◆ Information about the type/encoding of information contained in the body. Whether the content is HTML or an image or some other document type.

◆ Additional application information, such as cookies. (We'll talk about cookies in more detail later in this chapter.)

◆ Result codes returned from the server. In the example for the server response above, the server returned a result code of 200 with a message of OK. This tells the browser that the request processed correctly.

Using the HTTP body

The HTTP message body contains the actual information sent to the browser or server. If the message was sent to a browser, the browser will typically display this information if it knows how to display it or ask the user to save the information to a file. The HTTP body of a message sent by the server typically contains the HTML returned by the server (basically the Web page the user requested) while the HTTP body of a request made by a browser contains data submitted by the visitor using an HTML form or through a file upload. Note that information sent to the server can also be encoded in the URL, as we'll explain later in this chapter, in which case the information is found on the HTTP header.

In some cases, a message may not contain a body. This happens, for example, when there is an error processing a request or the user submits information via a form that uses URL encoding (GET method in an HTML form), or the user clicks on a link that embeds the information in the URL.

When a server receives a message body or information encoded into the URL of the request, the Web server makes this additional information available to the requested resource. Typically this resource will be a script or program that can use this information in some way, such as a CGI or some derivative technology.

Programming Server-Side Applications

Providing dynamic content is the goal of any Web application. There are many ways to incorporate dynamic content into a Web page. This section discusses some of the more popular methods you can use to include or generate dynamic content for a page.

Server side includes (SSI)

Early in Web development, servers introduced the concept of server side includes or SSI. Server side includes extended HTML to allow the server to perform operations defined in the HTML file itself. Before the HTML file could be sent to the browser, the HTTP server would parse the HTML file looking for SSI tokens or directives, and replace them with the results of the operation specified. Another popular name for SSI is Server Parsed HTML (SHTML).

SSIs are typically used to include the content of additional files into an HTML template (hence their name). Other popular uses of SSI include simple operations like putting the current time into the page. SSI operations are specified right in the HTML file using HTML's comment syntax. HTML comments start with <!-- and end with -->, as shown in this example:

```
<!--#operation option=value option=value -->
```

In this example *operation* is the task the server needs to perform: execute a program or include a file. The operation will typically specify some options and values to use with it, such as the name of the file to include or arguments to pass to a program.

CGI

Early on in the development of Web technology it became obvious that a server should not only accept requests for static data, such as HTML pages, but also allow for a dynamic component that could interact with the information submitted by a user (namely a program) and generate customized HTML based on the user request. So the Common Gateway Interface (CGI) was developed.

CGI is a specification that indicates how to pass information between an HTTP server and the program that will service the request. Because CGI is designed to pass information through environment variables, CGI programs can be written in almost any programming language that can access environment variables. CGIs are typically developed using Perl, C, Python, Tcl, or any other language that can read information from the environment.

While languages such as Perl and Python are very powerful and in many cases make a great choice for developing CGIs, alternative technologies such as Active Server Pages (Microsoft), Server-side JavaScript (Netscape), and others have successfully isolated the Web developer from the CGI mechanics and issues. This has made server-side development much simpler, more elegant, and more powerful.

ISAPI

One of the limitations of CGI is that for every CGI request, the Web server needs to start a new CGI process. While this initially doesn't sound like a big deal, consider a server that receives more than a casual number of requests. Just the overhead of starting a process for each request can kill the Web server and severely strain the resources of the machine. The result is sluggish performance and a Web site that's hard to connect to.

The Internet Server Application Programming Interface (ISAPI) from Microsoft addressed the most limiting aspect of CGI on the Web server, the necessity of launching a new process to service each CGI request. ISAPI and their counterparts (NSAPI from Netscape) allow dynamic-link libraries (DLLs) to be loaded into the same memory space as the server. The server then processes the request by executing code from a DLL. Because code in a DLL runs on the same memory space as the Web server there is no additional process overhead. Another fringe benefit is that the code from the DLL remains resident in the server's memory until explicitly released by the server, so there's no start-and-stop overhead to execute the program, as the program lives in memory. Needless to say, ISAPI applications execute exponentially faster than CGIs, while at the same time making less demands on the server's memory.

ISAPI filters

In addition to ISAPI, Microsoft introduced the concept of ISAPI filters. ISAPI filters are similar to ISAPI libraries, but allow for server customization. By providing ISAPI filters, programmers can affect the way that the Web server processes a request type. ISAPI filters intercept a request and allow the filter to customize the way the server handles the request.

Active Server Pages is implemented using an ISAPI filter (asp.dll). This filter intercepts any server-side scripts contained in a page that has a .asp extension and forwards them to a scripting engine. The script engine processes the scripts and generates results (typically some customized HTML) that then gets combined with any static HTML contained in the ASP page. Results returned from the scripting engine are then sent back to the Web server, which then returns the HTML to the browser.

Maintaining State in a Stateless Environment

To cope with statelessness, pages in a Web application pass data from the browser to the server and back. Here's a list of the different ways that frameworks and programmers have developed for implementing state:

- URL encoding
- HTTP cookies
- Server-side databases
- IP address databases

URL encoding

URL encoding embeds additional information into the requested URL. Here's an example of a URL that contains additional information:

```
http://www.myserver.com/index.asp?somedata=hello
```

This URL provides quite a bit of information:

- The protocol used to access the resource (http)
- The address of the server hosting the resource (www.myserver.com)
- The virtualized name of the resource (index.asp)
- Some additional parameters that the resource should use to process the request (somedata=hello)

The *protocol* specifies how to access the resource (http). The address of the machine storing the resource (www.myserver.com) tells where the resource lives. The virtualized name of the resource (index.html) tells the server which resource you are interested in.

In addition to this basic information, the URL in the previous example includes additional information for the resource to interpret. If the URL contains a question mark (?) followed by a list of parameters the URL encodes information. The information following the question mark is called the *QueryString* because when the server processes this information it places all the information to the right of the question mark in an environment variable called QUERYSTRING).

The parameters passed to the URL, the QueryString, are nothing more than named values. On the left side of an equals sign (=) is the *name* of the parameter; on the right side is its *value*. You can pass multiple parameters by separating them with an ampersand (&). In the previous URL example, a single parameter called *somedata* with a value of *hello* is passed to the resource. This additional information is *URL-encoded* data. Some characters in URL encoding are illegal; for example, the ampersand is used for separating key value pairs. If a value contains an ampersand, the ampersand is encoded into an escape sequence that can be safely added to the URL. Other values that typically get encoded are spaces. Spaces are typically encoded into plus characters (+). Escape sequences start with a percent sign (%) and are followed by two hexadecimal digits. These digits represent the character.

HTTP cookies

HTTP cookies pass information in a similar way to URL-encoded data, but instead of encoding the information into a URL, the information is set in the HTTP header. HTTP cookies are typically sent by a server-side program in response to some request. When a browser receives cookies for a particular site, it becomes responsible for returning them with each future request it makes of the site. Using this information, the server can keep track of a visitor as the visitor moves from page to page. Cookies are not implemented in older browsers, and most modern browsers allow you to turn them off with disastrous consequences for servers and applications that rely on them.

Server-side databases

Instead of encoding large amounts of data into cookies or URLs, some servers assume the burden of maintaining information for the visitor. The problem is that the server has the responsibility of storing the bulk of the information for the visitor. To accomplish this, a server-side scheme uses cookies or URL encoding to embed additional information into the links to allow the server to identify a particular visitor. As the visitor moves from page to page, the cookie or additional information provided in the URL is passed along, and the server can then restore whatever it knows about the user.

IP server-side databases

IP server-side addresses are similar to server-side databases. However, instead of passing some data, they also provide the ability to track visitors based on their IP addresses. However, this mechanism is not very reliable for general Internet use since it assumes that requests from the same IP belong to the same visitor, which is a faulty assumption if the user is visiting from behind a firewall. All visitors behind a firewall share the same IP address. In some cases, such as with intranets, this mechanism is highly effective and avoids the encoding of additional data from the server, allowing for better performance.

Summary

ASP is a replacement platform for CGI. With it you can develop Web applications. It provides an object framework that greatly facilitates the development of Web applications by relieving the programmer of many tasks that CGI programmers must face. ASP provides much better performance than traditional CGI because it is implemented using ISAPI filters. ASP is extensible, allowing you to create and access, from within a server-side script, external Active X components that provide some functionality not built into ASP itself, like accessing a database.

CGI programs run as an external process to the Web server. Basically, when the visitor makes a request to a CGI, the server will set up the environment of the CGI with the information submitted and start the CGI program, which processes the information. Any output generated by the CGI program is returned to the browser, which then displays it. Careful readers should realize that each time a request is made to a CGI program, a new process is launched. Scale this single interaction by a hundred or by thousands of visitors and suddenly, the supported hardware will be too busy to properly handle new requests.

In addition to this, CGI programs have typically been difficult and cumbersome to debug, and simple tasks such as connecting to a database require a variety of APIs and libraries provided by third parties. Active Server Pages addresses these problems and more. For example, ASP applications run as part of the server process. Instead of launching one application per request, requests are connected to a running application that services them. This allows them to scale better to heavier loads.

For the programmer, ASP applications also handle the minutia of keeping track of the visitor. To make development easy, ASP provides several objects that your server-side scripts will interact with. Some of these objects are used to maintain state for each visitor, and for the ASP application as a whole. Others are used for reading information sent by the user and for writing information back to the browser. Instead of a collection of CGI scripts that pass information among themselves, ASP ties all the scripts into a coherent application. The next chapter will introduce you to the main objects in ASP in detail.

Chapter 2

ASP Basic Architecture

IN THIS CHAPTER

- ◆ Web application components
- ◆ ASP scripting support feature
- ◆ The virtual directory
- ◆ How to run your application
- ◆ Life cycle of an ASP application

IN THIS CHAPTER WE'LL take a quick tour of the different components that make a basic ASP application. In the next few chapters we'll elaborate further on the components introduced here. The goal here is to learn what makes an ASP application.

Web Application Components

As you may already know, Web sites are built from many different types of resources. In a similar vein, ASP applications are built from various resources that make up the ASP application. An ASP Web application is made from a number of different types of documents, including the following:

- ◆ **Regular HTML pages:** These pages have the standard .htm or .html extension, and in addition to HTML content, may contain client-side scripts. Client-side scripts execute, as their name implies, on the client – the browser. For purposes of ASP, client-side scripts are no different from HTML; the server will just forward them to the browser, which will then interpret the script and do whatever it is the script does.

◆ **Active Server Pages (or ASP pages):** These pages have an .asp extension. In addition to server-side scripts, ASP pages can contain HTML and client-side scripts. The server-side scripts run and execute on the server. As a result of executing, the script may generate additional HTML content that is incorporated into the HTML portions of the ASP page. This script-generated content is what ASP is all about. Note that the client, the browser, won't ever see any server-side script code because this code never leaves the server; only its results do. Development of ASP pages is the topic of this book.

◆ **Global.asa:** This is a file that ASP applications may have. The global.asa file contains handlers that initialize the application and session environments. We'll describe global.asa in further detail later in this chapter.

◆ **Ancillary resources:** In addition to the above, an ASP application will typically include ancillary resources, such as images (.gif, .jpg/.jpeg, and so on), and layout files (.alx) that are used as a template for the look of a page.

The Virtual Directory: A Web Application

To make an ASP application, you need to place the files making up your application into a special directory called the *virtual directory* (sometimes also called the *application root or virtual root*). A virtual directory is just a directory that has been specially configured by the Web server's administration tools as an application. This directory can contain any of the ASP files and components described earlier. Typically the name of the virtual directory is the name of the application itself.

The virtual directory is important, because it defines a context and a container for an ASP application. It defines which pages belong to the application (the files contained in the virtual directory). If you have multiple ASP pages, the server will maintain visitor sessions between these pages to bridge them into a coherent whole: an *Application*.

ASP in Many Scripting Languages

An interesting feature of the ASP is that its scripting support is externalized. Unlike other environments that require you to develop applications using the languages and tools that they provide, ASP gives you freedom of choice. You can develop ASP applications in any scripting language for which there's support.

ASP enables you to do this because the ASP engine just provides the hooks for loading the required scripting engine (an ActiveX component). The scripting engine, an external control, performs the actual interpreting and running of the script.

When ASP processes a page containing a server-side script, it checks to see if an appropriate scripting engine is available. If it is, it executes the script. The great thing about this is that the ASP actually doesn't care what scripting language you use so long as a scripting engine for your scripting language is available. This is actually a very novel and exciting concept, as it allows developers to focus on learning how to use the provided ASP object framework, rather than on learning how to program in a new scripting environment.

Both Internet Information Server (IIS) and Personal Web Server (PWS) are installed with support for VBScript and JScript (JavaScript). However, because language support is externalized, additional languages can be added from third parties. Obviously, when you're extending functionality via third-party add-ins, some experimentation and testing on your part may be required to ensure that the scripting engine is well behaved and works properly under ASP.

At the time of this writing, a quick search of the Internet revealed third-party support for Perl, Python, REXX and TCL/TK scripting hosts.

ASP provides a number of objects that you'll use when developing your ASP applications. These objects are part of ASP, and not the scripting environment. These objects provide you with a framework that makes it easy for you to develop your Web application. Your scripts, regardless of the scripting language you choose, will be able to work with these objects.

When you access ASP built-in objects through your scripts, it's important to use the capitalization shown in the ASP documentation when naming the objects and methods, regardless of the conventions used by your scripting language to access objects or other entities, such as array elements. Obviously all features provided by your scripting language will work as you would expect when you create your own objects and primitive types. The scripting host will often behave in the right way when you capitalize according to your language conventions; however, Microsoft warns against this. For this reason, we adhere to these conventions in this book, even if the code looks a little strange. Also note that the capitalization of the ASP built-in objects must follow the ASP documentation regardless of your scripting environment's capitalization conventions.

Running Your Application

To run an ASP page, you must live in a virtual directory and it must have an .asp extension. Running scripts on a Web server is by default a security consideration, so the directory where the page runs must provide scripting permissions. If the server doesn't provide privileges for executing scripts, your ASP page will not run.

To execute a script, your browser just requests one of the ASP pages in your Web application. The browser does this the same way it requests any other resource on the Web server: it asks for the resource by URL. If the page has not been accessed recently, your browser will interpret and cache it for future requests. This increases the performance of the server when additional requests for the same page are made.

Embedding server-side scripts

All server-side scripts are executed in the order in which they are defined on the page — that is, from top to bottom. There are two choices for embedding server-side scripts into your page: <SCRIPT> tags and <% ... %>. ASP also understands two other constructs that are used for embedding directives and variables.

EMBEDDING WITH <SCRIPT> TAGS

To differentiate HTML from your script code, you can write your server-side code inside of <SCRIPT> tags. As you may already know, <SCRIPT> tags are also used for client-side scripting. To differentiate between client-side scripts and server-side scripts, you must specify the RUNAT attribute (this is an ASP addition):

```
<SCRIPT LANGUAGE="VBSCRIPT" RUNAT="SERVER">
some code
</SCRIPT>
```

The RUNAT attribute specifies where the script should run. For server-side scripts this attribute will always be set to "SERVER". Client-side scripts may safely omit this attribute, and ASP will just ignore the contents of the script. The LANGUAGE attribute is a standard attribute of the <SCRIPT> tag, and it specifies the language in which the script is written.

EMBEDDING WITH <% ... %>

In addition to the <SCRIPT> tags, ASP also provides the <% ... %> delimiters to mark a section of your page as code. Unlike the <SCRIPT> tag that bounds code using an HTML element (it has both an open and close tag), this form requires that you write your script between these delimiters.

The advantage of this syntax is obvious: You have much less to type. This markup form implies that the enclosing script is to be run on the server, so there's no associated RUNAT attribute; therefore this markup form should only be used for designating scripts that run on the server side:

```
<%
some code
%>
```

The previous example is equivalent to writing the following:

```
<SCRIPT RUNAT="SERVER">
some code
</SCRIPT>
```

EMBEDDING DIRECTIVES AND VARIABLES

In addition to the `<%` and `%>` delimiters, ASP also understands two other special derivative constructs:

♦   `<%=variableName %>` – Use this construct for printing the value of a variable defined in a server script. When ASP encounters this construct, it evaluates the expression enclosed, typically a `variableName`, to its value and replaces the whole construct with this value. You can use this syntax anywhere in your page, so long as you don't nest them inside of `<% ... %>` blocks.

♦   `<%@ directive=value %>` – This construct is used for specifying different preprocessing directives (configuration parameters). Prepossessing directives are evaluated before any scripts code in the ASP page is processed.

When using `<%@ directive %>`, pay close attention. There should be a space following the @ character. Another restriction is that all `<%@ directives %>` must appear as the very first line of the script, which means that multiple directives appear in the same line directive construct separated by commas. as follows:

```
<%@ directive1=value1, directive2=value2,
directive3=value3 %>
```

Not doing this will generate an error.

Because the short <% ... %> delimiters don't really provide you with a place to provide attributes, such as LANGUAGE, which is shown in bold in the following example, you need to set the default scripting language for the page by inserting the following line as the very first line in your page:

```
<%@ LANGUAGE="VBScript" %>
```

The server processes preprocessing directives before your scripts are passed on to the interpreter. Preprocessor directives provide a means by which to configure various server options. After interpreting the LANGUAGE directive, the ASP ISAPI filter will pass all code between <% ... %> in the page to the scripting engine that knows how to interpret the scripting language specified in the directive. If you wanted to use JScript instead of VBScript, provide JScript as the value of the LANGUAGE directive.

We've written most of the examples in this book using JavaScript because we believe that most Web developers already know how to script using JavaScript.

If you failed to specify the LANGUAGE directive for your page, your page would be at the mercy of the server administrator. Whatever default scripting language the administrator sets will be the one the server will attempt to use. To avoid ambiguity and varying server configurations, always explicitly specify the LANGUAGE directive in each of your pages.

One important thing to remember is that when a server-side script executes, the server will process the script and return HTML generated to the client (if any). We discuss this further in the sidebar.

Do You See Your Server-Side Script Code?

When a server-side script executes, the server will process the script and return HTML generated to the client (if any). It is possible that a script doesn't generate any HTML and instead just captures information sent by the visitor or performs some other server-side operation, such as redirecting a visitor to a different URL. The important thing to keep in mind is that the server will *never* send your server-side scripts to the browser; it will only send the results of the script. If you ever see your script code, this means that either the file containing the server-side script doesn't have an .asp extension or your server-side script was not properly embedded into the page.

A SIMPLE ASP PAGE EXAMPLE

Listing 2-1 shows an example of a simple ASP page. Given the little we know, you can already do some interesting things.

Listing 2-1: My first ASP page in VBScript

```
<%@ LANGUAGE="VBSCRIPT" %>
<HTML>
<HEAD>
<TITLE>First Example</TITLE>
</HEAD>

<%
Dim helloMessage
helloMessage = "My First ASP Page!"
%>

<FONT SIZE="24"><%= helloMessage %></FONT>
</BODY>
</HTML>
```

The Listing 2-1 example is very simple; it prints the words "My First ASP Page!" (shown in bold in Listing 2-1) using a font size of 24 points.

The <FONT> tags are deprecated in favor of style sheets, but this is just a simple example.

The first line of the script specifies that any text enclosed by <% and %> should be passed to the VBScript ActiveX scripting host. The second scripting block declares the helloMessage variable (shown in bold in Listing 2-1). This variable is next initialized to the value of our message. Lastly we use the <%= ... %> to print the value of the variable while inside of the <FONT> tag to make it display in a bigger font face.

Because it is possible that you have never scripted using VBScript, which we use in the Listing 2-1 example, don't despair. One of the goals of this book is to show you that you can write ASP without learning VBScript. In fact we assume that you already know how to write scripts using the language of your choice, and so we won't really dedicate much time to explaining programming constructs.

When the server processes the page shown in Listing 2-1, it will send the following output to the browser:

```
<HTML>
<BODY>


<FONT SIZE="24">My First ASP Page!</FONT>
</BODY>
</HTML>
```

Note that all directives and server-side scripts have been removed, as well as the result of executing the script, and the value of the variable was inserted in place of the `<%= helloMessage %>` placeholders (in some places blank lines have been left instead).

For a scripting primer to get you up to speed in VBScript, see Appendix D, "VBScript Syntax." For a scripting primer to get you up to speed in JavaScript, see Appendix C, "JavaScript Syntax."

Listing 2-2 shows the same example using JavaScript.

Listing 2-2: My first ASP Page in JavaScript

```
<%@ LANGUAGE="JScript" %>
<HTML>
<HEAD>
<TITLE>Logo Example</TITLE>
</HEAD>

<%
var helloMessage = "My First ASP Page!";

helloMessage = helloMessage.fontsize(24);
%>

<%= helloMessage %>
</BODY>
</HTML>
```

Similar to the VBScript version, the JavaScript version is embedded into the page using the same `<% ... %>` tags. The syntax of the script (its language) will be very different depending on the language you use for your scripts. One thing to notice here is that we are using the `fontsize()` method — shown in bold in Listing 2-2 — available to JavaScript `String` objects to provide the `<FONT>` tags rather than write them in HTML. Because JavaScript was originally developed for the Web as a means of scripting Web pages, it provides many useful methods for formatting strings using HTML markup.

For completeness sake, we'll show you yet a third version. Listing 2-3 shows you the same example using PerlScript.

Listing 2-3: My first ASP page in PerlScript

```
<%@ LANGUAGE="PerlScript" %>
<HTML>
<BODY>
<%
$helloMessage = "My First ASP Page!";
%>

<FONT SIZE="24"><%= $helloMessage %></FONT>
</BODY>
</HTML>
```

On the surface, PerlScript is not all that different from VBScript (at least not in this trivial example). PerlScript uses Perl to write scripts. If you have written any CGI programs, chances are it was in Perl. Perl is the most popular language for writing CGI. In ASP, the only requirement for running PerlScript is that you have the PerlScript scripting engine installed. The PerlScript engine is an ActiveX scripting engine that plugs into any ActiveX scripting host, including IIS, PWS, IE (Internet Explorer), or WSH (Windows Scripting Host — a tool for writing user scripts).

If you are interested in learning more about PerlScript, please visit `http://www.activestate.com/ActivePerl`. You can also download a current version of PerlScript from links in the above URL.

Arguably, one of the most powerful features of ASP is its independence from scripting languages. It enables Web authors to develop new ASP applications without having to learn how to script in a new language. For most Web authors, JavaScript (JScript) is a great choice since JavaScript is the standard for writing client-side scripts. For people coming from a Visual Basic background it will be VBScript. Perl, Python, or JavaScript are good choices as well for people coming from UNIX.

ASP built-in objects

If you have developed client-side scripts using JavaScript in the past, you will remember that in addition to any core language objects (like `Math` or `String` in JavaScript), the browser environment provided you with an object framework for representing things in a browser (`document`, `form`, `window`, and so on). As you may expect, on server-side scripts you don't have access to those objects. The reason for this is simple: server scripts run on the server, so there's no notion of a form or a browser window on the server, instead there are ways to find out information about a visitor's browser and to access information the visitor submitted via a form. Server-side scripts concern themselves with other types of operations, such as storing shared application data, accessing databases, storing information about a particular visitor as the visitor navigates through the site, or generating HTML for a browser.

In ASP, there are five major objects, which most of your scripts will use at some point. These are:

◆ Application

◆ Session

◆ Request

◆ Response

◆ Server

THE APPLICATION OBJECT

The Application object represents your application. It provides you with a place to store shared data in an application. This object is shared among all visitors accessing the application. This object is created when the application receives its first request, and in it you can store most variable types. Values you store in this object are shared among all users of the application.

THE SESSION OBJECT

The Session object represents a single visitor session. In it you can store information that follows the user from page to page. A *session* is created when the user first visits a page in your application. If the user doesn't return to your application within a certain amount of time (10 minutes by default), the session information is discarded. Session information can also be explicitly destroyed through a script.

THE REQUEST OBJECT

The Request object represents a visitor's request. Whenever a visitor requests a page, a Request object is created. The Request object contains information sent in the HTTP header and body by the browser, including HTTP cookies, form data, and information about a digital certificate used by the client during an SSL (Secure Sockets Layer) request. Arguably, this is the most important object in ASP, because this object enables you to get input into your script. A new Request object is created for each page the user requests. When the current page finishes processing, the Request object is destroyed.

THE RESPONSE OBJECT

The Response object controls how you send information back to the browser. With the Response object, your script can send HTML content, set HTTP cookies, add additional HTTP headers to the response, or redirect the visitor to a different URL. The Response object also allows you to tune how the server returns information to the browser and how long this information may be cached by proxy servers that passed the information between your server and the requesting browser.

THE SERVER OBJECT

The Server object represents the Web server. It provides you with URL and HTML encoding facilities for encoding data into URLs or for converting some characters into their HTML entity counterparts. The Server object also provides you with the ability to find the real path of a resource given a URL. The Server object provides access to some configuration settings, like setting limits on how long the server may process a script before giving up and canceling the operation. One of the most important features of the Server object is that it enables you to create instances of components. *Components* are objects that are not part of ASP, but that you can instantiate from an ActiveX control. Components allow you to add features not originally built into the server, like database access.

ASP Application Life Cycle

As you may have noticed, most of the main objects Application, Session, and Request are created at very specific times. Unlike other environments, ASP implements some rules that determine the life cycle of the "application." These rules establish the starting and ending point of the Web application. These rules are important, as Web applications are typically not very sequential. For one thing, Web applications typically serve multiple visitors at the same time, so the starting and ending point of the application are triggered by the first and last visitor of the application. To deal with individual access, each visitor has his or her own session to access the application. A *session* keeps track of the application's state for one user.

The life cycle of an ASP application is as follows:

1. When the first visitor accesses the application, the application starts and the Application object is created. Additional visitors may start using the already running application (an application is only started once).

2. Each time a visitor starts using the application and storing state information into a session, a session for the visitor is started, and a Session object for the visitor is created.

3. A session will continue to live as long as the visitor continues to access pages in the application. If the user stops accessing the application for a long period of time (10 minutes), the session will time out and end, and the associated Session object will be destroyed.

4. When all user sessions terminate for a particular application, the application terminates, and the Application object is destroyed. The Web server will wait for a new first visitor to arrive and repeat the life cycle again.

Starting and ending points for an application or visitor session are important events in the life cycle of an application. Typically when an application starts it is very useful to initialize the state of the application to some known state. The same is true for a visitor session. Similarly, when a session or application ends we may want to have the opportunity to save the information the application or session stores for a future run of the application.

ASP implements the notion of *events* to let your application perform these tasks in some controlled way. By providing a file called global.asa in the root directory for the ASP application (the one designated as the virtual directory for the application), ASP gives you the opportunity to handle these events appropriately for your application.

The following well-known handlers (or functions) handle the events:

◆ Application_OnStart – This handler is called once when the first page of the application is run by any visitor.

◆ Session_OnStart – This handler is called the first time a visitor runs any page in the application.

◆ Session_OnEnd – This handler is called when the visitor session times out, or the visitor quits your application.

◆ Application_OnEnd – This handler is called when the last visitor session times out or the Web server shuts down.

As you can see, ASP provides a framework that eliminates most of the issues in Web development. This makes it easy for you to focus on what you need to do: develop an application.

Summary

In this chapter you saw how the underlying technology of the Web works. You also saw a brief introduction into the ASP object framework and how it provides order and a life cycle to your application. You also learned how to embed scripts into the page and that these scripts can be written in most popular scripting languages.

In the next few chapters you'll explore the details of each of the major ASP objects, their events, their properties, and their methods.

Chapter 3

Creating a First Application

IN THIS CHAPTER

- ◆ Getting started with Internet Information Services
- ◆ Creating a virtual directory

THIS CHAPTER WALKS YOU through the basics of setting up a virtual directory in which you can put Web files. Basic operations for configuring the virtual directories where you'll place your Web applications follow the same steps no matter which Microsoft server you use. For this chapter, we have only described the Web server included with Windows 2000, as this is the first server to include support for ASP 3.0, the topic of this book.

If you are using a different operating system, the user interface of the tools will vary slightly depending on the version of the software and operating system that you are using. For this book, all screen shots are shown from Windows 2000, so your tools might look slightly different under other environments; however, they will provide similar features. For exact installation and configuration information on such installations, please refer to your Microsoft documentation.

Getting Started with Internet Information Services

Installation of Internet Information Services (IIS) components is typically integrated into the Add/Remove Windows Components option of the Add/Remove Programs tool in Control Panel. Under Windows 2000 you add the software by clicking Start, pointing to Settings, clicking Control Panel, and starting the Add/Remove Programs tool. On the Add/Remove Programs tool, select Add/Remove Windows Components and select Internet Information Services (IIS) on the Windows Components Wizard that starts up. From there follow any instructions the wizard gives you. Note that on Windows 2000 Workstation, Web services will not be installed by default unless you upgraded from Windows NT Workstation 4.0 and had Personal Web Server installed.

By default, when you install IIS, the install program will create a directory called x:\Inetpub in your boot drive where the "default" Web site is installed. The default Web site will provide directories where you can put the files you want to publish over the Web. Typically, when you create an ASP application, you will want to create your own virtual directory to house all the different documents used by your Web application – see the section, "The Virtual Directory: A Web Application" in Chapter 2. This will make it easier for you to manage, and it will reduce the chance of any conflicts between the Web applications that you may inadvertently create by creating an application that nests in another application. Organization also makes life much easier when you have to migrate and distribute portions of your Web site to different machines.

Creating a Virtual Directory

Creating a virtual root or virtual directory is a simple process. There are at least two tools that you can use to perform this task. You can use the Internet Information Services Manager or the Personal Web Manager tool. You can find both of these tools in Windows 2000 by clicking Start → Settings → Control Panel, double-clicking Administrative Tools, and then double-clicking Internet Services Manager or Personal Web Manager. Internet Information Services Manager exposes more configuration settings and allows you to work with other Internet services such as an FTP publishing service. It also uses Microsoft's Management Console, which is an extensible tool for configuring services in your computer. Other operating systems will store similar tools in a different place. Consult your Microsoft documentation for the location and name of these tools.

Using Internet Information Services Manager

After you have located the Internet Information Services Manager tool, you are ready to create a virtual directory. This directory will be where you place all files related to your application. Here's what you need to do:

1. Create a directory anywhere on your disk where you'd like to place your Web application files. This directory need not be in the x:\Inetpub directory tree. As a matter of fact, your files can reside in a directory on a different computer that is accessible by using the directory's Universal Naming Convention (UNC) name or accessible through a network drive.

2. Using the Internet Information Services Manager tool, select the Web site where you want to add the directory. By default, the default Web site is called "Default Web Site," as shown in Figure 3-1.

3. Click on the Action menu, point to New, and click on Virtual Directory, as shown in Figure 3-2. The New Virtual Directory Wizard will start.

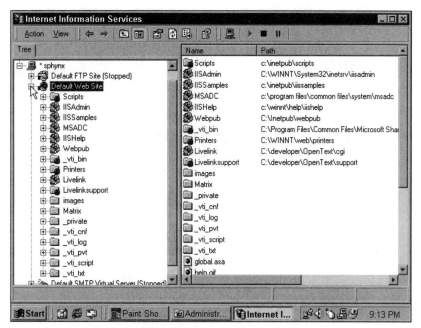

Figure 3-1: Selecting the default Web site

 If you select one of the directories under the default Web site, the virtual directory will be in a different virtual directory. In many cases this is not what you want for reasons that will be revealed when you are learning about the Application and Session objects, which are covered, respectively, in Chapter 6, "The Application Object," and Chapter 7, "The Session Object."

4. Enter the alias name for the virtual directory you want to create (see Figure 3-3). This name is essentially the name of the application and is part of the URL that accesses the Web application. It is a good idea not to have spaces or non-alphanumeric characters in this name. Users will never know or interact with the actual directory name that contains your files.

5. Next, provide the complete path to the physical directory that contains your Web application files. This is the directory that you created in step 1, and it can be anywhere on your disk, or on another computer accessible over the network.

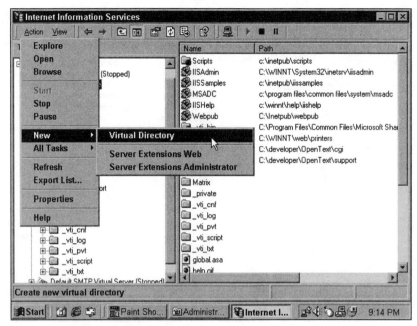

Figure 3-2: Adding a virtual directory

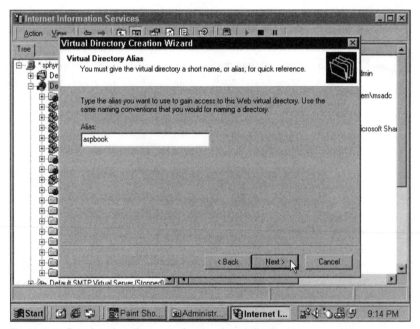

Figure 3-3: Entering the alias name for the virtual directory

6. Specify the permissions for the virtual directory to set its security, as shown in Figure 3-4. By default, the directory should allow visitors to read and run scripts (ASP). The Execute permission allows the server to execute external-type programs, such as .exe files or CGI programs written in Perl or some other language. The Write permission allows visitors to write and modify files and to browse files in the directory by navigating the file system. The Write and Browse options should be disabled because they create security issues for your installation (users can install and modify your scripts and browse files in your application – both of which are probably not a good idea). The Execute option is not really a problem itself, but users will be able to execute programs found in the directory.

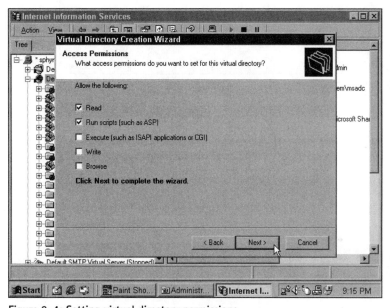

Figure 3-4: Setting virtual directory permissions

After you complete these steps your virtual directory should be ready for you to put some files in it. The right pane of the Internet Information Services Manager lists all the files the virtual directory contains (see Figure 3-5).

You can call up additional settings for the configuration of the virtual directory by right-clicking your virtual directory and choosing properties. The dialog box that opens allows you to see all the settings you specified through the wizard (see Figure 3-6). You can specify additional settings by setting up values on the other tabs. The Documents tab allows you to specify the name of documents (and their order) that will be returned to the visitor if no document name is specified in the URL for your virtual directory. If one of the default names is not found, the directory browsing option is specified, and a listing of all the files in the virtual directory will be generated by the Web server.

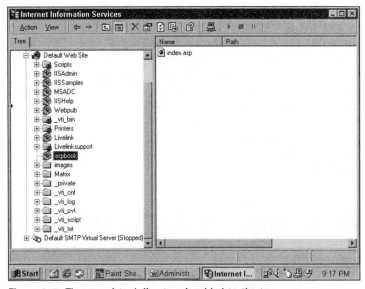

Figure 3-5: The new virtual directory is added to the tree.

The Directory Security option allows you to request authentication prior to accessing the resource. The HTTP Headers and Custom Error tabs allow you to specify custom headers, control the expiration of documents (for controlling caching), provide MIME mappings to different file types, and so on. For additional information on any of these features, use context-sensitive help by clicking on the button marked "Help" and clicking on the item you would like to learn more about.

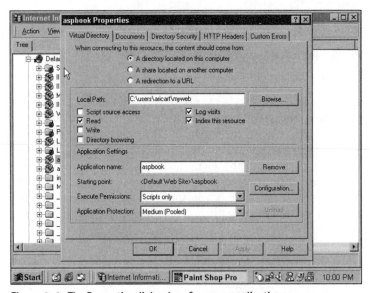

Figure 3-6: The Properties dialog box for your application

Using Personal Web Manager

The Personal Web Manager (PWM) provides a similar interface to the IIS, with the exception that the tool is only able to manage the Web service. Which tool you use to create the virtual directory is a matter of preference. To create a virtual directory using PWS, do the following:

1. Create the physical directory that will house your Web application files. You can create the directory anywhere you'd like.

2. After starting the Personal Web Manager, click Advanced. On the panel that appears click the Add button. This will open a dialog box where you can enter the details about the virtual directory (see Figure 3-7).

3. Enter the full path to your Web directory in the Directory text box, enter the name you would like to use to access your application in the Alias text box, ensure the Read and Scripts check box options are selected, and click OK.

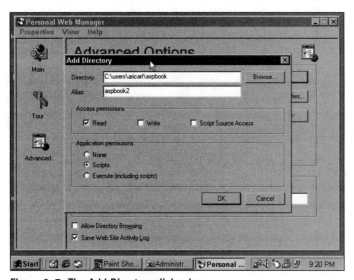

Figure 3-7: The Add Directory dialog box

4. On the Advanced Options panel, the Enable Default Document option allows you to specify the name of the file to return to the browser if the virtual directory is requested without specifying any particular file (that is, `http://localhost/aspbook` versus `http://localhost/aspbook/default.htm`). See Figure 3-8. Make sure your choices match the level of security you require. For example, if one of the default documents is not found and the Allow Directory Browsing option is selected, the Web server will produce a list of all the files found in the directory. This will allow the visitor to pick any file he or she wants, such as yoursecretfile.doc.

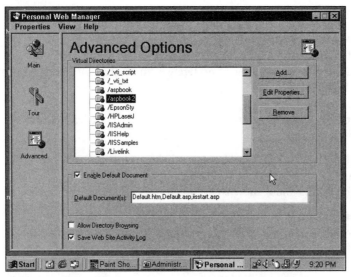

Figure 3-8: Some advanced options have security implications.

Testing your configuration

Once you've created your first virtual directory, you are ready to test it. Using the text editor of your choice — either Notepad or a fancy editor like TextPad, which you can obtain at `http://www.textpad.com` — create a file called index.asp that contains the following ASP program:

```
<%@ LANGUAGE="JScript"%>
<HTML>
<BODY>

<%
var greeting = "Hello World!";
%>

<H1><%= greeting %></H1>
</BODY>
</HTML>
```

You should be able to access the page by entering `http://localhost/aspbook/index.asp`, the URL where you named your virtual directory "aspbook" and your file "index.asp." Note that the Web server performs automatic translation between the alias, the name of the virtual directory, and the physical location of the file, and provides you with the right document. When compared to other Web servers, IIS is very simple to configure as all options have a simple interface for configuration. If you name your document default.asp and you have enabled the

Default Document option for your application, you can enter `http://localhost/aspbook` to show the page. As you try examples in the book or code your own, you'll invariably have to create virtual directories.

Summary

IIS makes configuring a Web service easy without requiring you to remember many configuration parameters. However, improperly configuring your Web server can create a security risk to your computer and your files, so it is imperative that you understand some of the implications of the choices that we listed in this chapter. While the focus of this book is programming ASP and not Web services configuration and administration, we recommend that you browse your Web server's documentation, which you can access by going to your server's start page at `http://localhost` and following the links you find there. The small amount of time you devote to reading over the documentation will pay off.

Chapter 4

The Request Object

IN THIS CHAPTER

◆ Using the Request object to read form data

◆ Using the Request object's properties and collections

MOST COMPUTER PROGRAMS GENERATE a result based on input provided by a user. Web applications are no different; by interacting with the Web page the user provides information that the Web application can use to generate a customized response.

To get up to speed quickly writing Web applications that are somewhat interesting, we'll start by exploring the Request object, as this object is fundamental to how your ASP application gets input. Data sent to a Web application can come from a variety of sources: a form, a link, or a cookie. Most of it will come to your application via an HTML form submission, so we'll begin by taking a look at forms.

Reading Form Data

We begin our look into the Request object by taking a peek at how information is sent from the browser to the server. In Chapter 1, "Introduction to Web Applications," we presented an overview of how the server and browser exchange information. If you have previous experience working with forms, most of the information in this section will be familiar.

An HTML form is what its name suggests, a form that a visitor can fill up with information. HTML provides a variety of controls such as text fields, radio buttons, check boxes, and pop-up menus that the visitor can use to provide input to your Web application. Complete discussion on how to use the various form elements is an HTML topic that is outside of the scope of this book, as we assume that you already know HTML. For information on all the available form controls, take a look at one of the copious HTML resources available.

Form controls are grouped together using the FORM element (tag). The FORM element defines which controls belong to which form and provides the browser with the information it needs for preparing a form submission. When the visitors complete filling in a form, they can send the information back to the server by clicking a submit button. A submit button is a special form element that tells the browser to collect, package, and send the information that the visitors enter to a resource on the server for processing. A single HTML page may define multiple forms; however, only one form can be submitted at a time. Do note that you cannot nest FORM elements.

For definitive information on HTML, you may also want to take a look at http://www.w3.org, as this site is the home of the World Wide Web Consortium. The consortium develops many proposals and recommendations on Web technology, including HTML and XML. Many of these recommendations are ratified into standards. If you want to research a Web-related topic, this is the place to do so.

When a visitor initiates the form submission, the browser packages the information for the server, iterates through each control defined in the form, and collects the name of the control and the value entered into it. The name of the control is used to name the value entered by the visitor so that a program on the server side can access this value by name. Form controls get a name from the NAME attribute of the control. If a form contains the control called "first" and the visitor enters a value of "Chili" into the control, the browser packages the information into a key-value pair that looks like this: "first=Chili". Using this convention a program on the server side can reference this field by name and retrieve the value entered by the visitor. A simple HTML form will look similar to the one shown in Listing 4-1.

Listing 4–1: A simple HTML form

```
<!DOCTYPE html PUBLIC "-//W3C//DTD HTML 3.2//EN">
<HTML>
<HEAD>
<TITLE>FORM</TITLE>
</HEAD>
<BODY>
<FORM METHOD="GET" ACTION="agent.asp">
First Name: <INPUT TYPE="text" NAME="first"><BR>
Last Name: <INPUT TYPE="text" NAME="last"><BR>
Select your favorite colors:<BR><SELECT NAME="colors" MULTIPLE>
    <OPTION>Red</OPTION>
    <OPTION>Blue</OPTION>
    <OPTION>Green</OPTION>
    <OPTION>Yellow</OPTION>
    <OPTION>Purple</OPTION>
    <OPTION>Orange</OPTION>
</SELECT><BR>
<INPUT TYPE="submit" VALUE="Send It!">
</FORM>
</BODY>
</HTML>
```

The HTML form in Listing 4-1 renders three controls: two text fields to capture the first and last name of the visitor and a button used to submit the information in those fields to the server. The fields capturing the first and last name for the visitor have been aptly named *first* and *last*. Note that while server-side programs don't really care what you name a control (as long as it follows proper HTML syntax), some names may cause problems on client-side scripts. The most notorious of these is "name"; you should never name your form controls "name" if you plan to add client-side scripts to your page. If you forget to name the control, the browser more than likely won't include this control in the list of values it sends back.

Details including where the information will be sent (to what URL) and how the data will be sent are provided by attributes of the FORM element; the more important of these are the following:

◆ ACTION – This attribute specifies the URL of the form-processing agent (typically a CGI). In ASP, this attribute will specify the URL of an ASP page that will process the submitted data. In addition to specifying a Web server application, information submitted by a form can be sent directly to an e-mail address; however, this behavior is browser-dependent and outside the scope of this book.

◆ METHOD – This attribute specifies the HTTP method that the browser should use to submit the form data. There are two possible values for this option: GET (the default) and POST. Specifying GET encodes form data into the target URL specified by the ACTION attribute. The POST value encodes the form data into the HTTP body of the request. Typically, you can spot GET requests, because the URL of the requested page will look something like this:

```
http://www.site.com/app/agent.asp?first=Chili&last=Palmer
```

If you look closely you will see that the URL of the ASP page is followed by a question mark and key value pairs matching the form listing above. Note that both fields are included in the submission and are separated by an ampersand (&). If a field name or value contains a character such as a space, an ampersand, or some other special character, these characters are escaped using the URL encoding rules. URL encoding replaces spaces with a plus (+) and other special characters with an escape value that starts with a percent symbol (%) followed by two hexadecimal digits. When the ASP provides you with a value, these special values are returned to their original value.

◆ One concern of using GET versus POST is that CGI expects values that are URL-encoded to be placed in the environment of the form-processing agent. Most operating systems define a limit for the size of the environment space (about 2000 characters, on the average), so a request providing a large amount of data could easily result in exceeding this limit and creating some sort of fatal error condition on the server. When you specify POST the server will pass form information through the standard input stream of the form-processing agent (the program processing the request), so POST requests are not subject to size limitations. Another concern for GET is that URL-encoded values are considered "ugly" by most visitors because the contents of the form are displayed on the browser's location bar. The great advantage of GET over POST is that GET requests can be written to links or bookmarks, providing a way of storing the request data so that it can be resent at a later time. If you're wondering which method to use, your forms should typically specify POST unless you have a good reason not to.

◆ ENCTYPE – This attribute specifies the format used to encode the information for POST requests. The default value is application/x-www-form-urlencoded. Forms can upload the contents of a file as part of the form submission if they use the FILE control. Those forms should specify multipart/form-data instead.

Using the Request object to access form data

Every time your ASP application receives a request it will create a new Request object that contains information about the visitor's request. This object will only survive during processing of the page, so information you want to preserve between pages must be copied elsewhere. When we take a look at the Application and Session objects, we'll show you how to do this. For now we are just interested in processing input sent by the visitor.

For more information on the Application object, see Chapter 6, "The Application Object." For more information on the Session object, see Chapter 7,"The Session Object."

The ASP Request object stores the values that a browser passes to the server during an HTTP request. This includes information sent by the browser in the HTTP header, information sent by the browser as part of the HTTP body, and other information such as X.509 digital certificates used for user authentication.

The Request object provides various collections that store the information the server receives during the request. You can use these collections to read, and in some cases, set values that will affect future requests made by the visitor. Here's the complete list of collections that are available:

♦ QueryString – Stores the value sent, URL encoded as part of a GET request by a form or through a link

♦ Form – Stores the values of form elements sent using POST

♦ Cookies – Stores the value of HTTP cookies sent with the request

♦ ClientCertificate –Obtains information on digital certificates presented by you for authentication during an SSL session (HTTPS)

♦ ServerVariables – Stores a number of variables with information about the server and the request

A collection is a hybrid data structure somewhere between a dictionary (a hash table) and an array. A collection stores values by associating them with a name (a key), which can later be used to retrieve the value. Typically, the keys to the main collections will be the names of

♦ Fields defined in the HTML form that the visitor submits

♦ HTTP server variables

♦ HTTP headers sent by the browser

♦ Cookies that you might have set

The values found in the collections will be values

♦ Provided by the user in the form

♦ Defined by the server

♦ Sent by the browser

♦ Set by your cookies

Typically, most of your scripts will focus on form data submitted by the visitor. In addition to accessing values by a name, collections can also access their elements by index in much the same way that you access array elements. In addition to storing these values, collections typically store other properties like the number of items a collection holds and other collection-specific properties. Most of the ASP server objects provide collections where you can read and store values meaningful to your application or access values such as data submitted via a form, or some other information about some server setting. Collections group-related information together so that it is easy for you to know where to look.

To access a value stored in the Request object you can simply provide the name of the value that you are trying to access, like this:

```
value = Request(keyName)
```

All values that you read from the Request object are in the form of a string, so if you need to use the numeric value represented by the string, you need to perform an appropriate conversion. This is especially true in JavaScript, where the plus (+) operator is overloaded to concatenate strings together.

Listing 4-2 shows an example script for processing the form shown earlier. The lines where the Request object is queried are shown in bold.

Listing 4-2: A script for processing the form shown in Listing 4-1

```
<%@ LANGUAGE="JScript" %>
<!DOCTYPE html PUBLIC "-//W3C//DTD HTML 3.2//EN">
<HTML>
<HEAD>
<TITLE>GET AGENT</TITLE>
</HEAD>
<BODY>
<%
    var first = Request("first");
    var last = Request("last");
    var numberOfColors = Request("colors").Count;

    var fullName = first + " " + last;

    fullName = fullName.bold();

    var colors = "";


    for(var i=1; i <= numberOfColors; i++)
    {
        if(colors != "")
        {
            colors += ", ";
        }

    colors += Request("colors")(i);
    }

    if(colors == "")
    {
        colors = "You don't have any favorite colors";
```

```
    }
    else
    {
        colors = "Your favorite " + numberOfColors + " color(s) are:
 " + colors.bold();
    }

%>

<P>Hello <%=fullName %><BR>
<%= colors %>
</BODY>
</HTML>
```

This trivial example reads the fields containing the *first* and *last* name of the visitor and joins them into a single variable called *fullname*. The complete name gets some additional formatting courtesy of the bold() method available to string objects. The script also stores the number of colors that the user selected in a variable called numberOfColors.

Next the values for the favorite colors are read. Note that the colors variable is initialized to the value of an empty string (""). This will allow us to iterate through the various colors and append values to the string. Note also that if we had *not* initialized the variable to an empty string, the first run through the loop would add the value "undefined" to the variable as the JavaScript environment would evaluate a variable that has not yet been initialized. Another thing to watch out for is that the pattern for the loop is a little different than the pattern most JavaScript developers are used to. When accessing elements in a collection by index, the first index is always one, and the last index equals the number of elements in the array; this differs from JavaScript's arrays where the first element in an array is at index zero and the last element is the number of elements in the array minus one. Because the colors field may contain more than one value, each value is accessed using the collection's list notation: Request("colors")(n) where *n* is the nth element in the list.

After the different values are read, the colors variable is evaluated again to see if its value equals an empty string. If it does, a message stating "You don't have any favorite colors" is written. Otherwise, the list of colors is preceded by a friendlier message, and the actual color list is formatted with the bold attribute. Values stored in the JavaScript variables are incorporated in the HTML by using the <%=variableName%> notation.

Context issues: which value are you reading?

The one gotcha in the Listing 4-2 example is that because the construct doesn't specify which collection to use, ASP will iterate through all the collections in the Request object until it finds a value stored under a matching *keyName*. The order in which ASP searches its collections is well established and has important implications for your scripts. Here's the order used:

1. QueryString

2. Form

3. Cookies

4. ClientCertificate

5. ServerVariables

This search order typically does the right thing and finds the value that you want. However, be aware that there are potential context issues if the *keyName* used to identify a value is duplicated in a collection that is searched earlier. Because ASP will return the first value it finds according to this search order, the value you get back may not be the one you want.

Say for example that your script wants to access a value set by the browser (in the ServerVariables collection) called REMOTE_HOST. The REMOTE_HOST value returns the IP address or the machine name where the visitor came from. If you use the abbreviated form to read the value, most of the time you'll get the value that you expect, the one in the ServerVariables collection. Now suppose that the user submits a form to your script, and one of the fields in the form is (carelessly or unexpectedly) named REMOTE_HOST. Which value do you get? Do you get the one stored in the ServerVariables collection, or do you get the one sent by the form? The answer is the one in the form. To access the value stored in ServerVariables, you need to remove the ambiguity from the script by providing the name of the collection that you want to search, as follows:

```
Request.ServerVariables("REMOTE_HOST")
```

This will limit the search to the collection specified and ensure that you get the value that you really want. This issue will seldom be a problem; however, it is a good idea to protect against this sort of bug by setting project conventions on how to handle this issue. It is probably a good idea to use the short form for processing form data and the long form to process values stored in the Cookies, ClientCertificate, and ServerVariables collections. This way you'll know which value you are retrieving and the code becomes easier to read and maintain for anyone who inherits it. Listing 4-3 provides an example on how to handle the problem.

Listing 4-3: Reading Request values without ambiguity

```
<%@ LANGUAGE="JavaScript"%>
<!DOCTYPE html PUBLIC "-//W3C//DTD HTML 3.2//EN">
<HTML>
<HEAD>
```

```
<TITLE>Get Host</TITLE>
</HEAD>
<BODY>

<%
    function isEmpty(aStr)
    {
        var retVal = false;
        var myStr = aStr + "";

        if(myStr == "" || myStr == "undefined")
            retVal = true;

        return retVal;
    }

    var formRemoteHost;

    if(Request.ServerVariables("REQUEST_METHOD") == "GET")
    {
        formRemoteHost = "" + Request.QueryString("REMOTE_HOST");
    }
    else
    {
        formRemoteHost = "" + Request.Form("REMOTE_HOST");
    }

    if(isEmpty(formRemoteHost))
    {
        formRemoteHost = "You didn't specify a host!";
    }

%>

<P>You say you are visiting from <%=formRemoteHost%><BR>
But you are really visiting from
<%=Request.ServerVariables("REMOTE_HOST")%>
</BODY>
</HTML>
```

The Listing 4-3 example expects to get the name of the visitor's host from a form submission sent by the visitor. The script is generic, so it doesn't assume the type of form used to send the information (POST or GET), as this is easy to figure out by peeking into the REQUEST_METHOD value in the ServerVariables collection. If the method used is GET, we read the value from the QueryString collection. Otherwise we read it from the Form collection. Because the processing agent for the form is not tightly coupled with the form, it is possible that someone will point to or run this page without providing an expected form value for "REMOTE_HOST". If this happens, calls to read the value from the collection using JavaScript won't return the right answer, so we need to test for this condition.

The implementation of JavaScript on IIS has the annoying feature that some expressions are not always evaluated. Specifically, checks to see if a JavaScript variable is undefined or null may not always give the right answer. What is worse, evaluating a value between <%=variable%> constructs won't print anything if the value is undefined or null. Solving this problem is easy once you know its symptoms. So we developed a function called isEmpty() that forces evaluation on string data.

In JavaScript, variables can:

♦ Be initialized to a null value

♦ Be undefined (the variable was never initialized)

♦ Reference an object or some scalar value

The isEmpty() function forces the evaluation of a string by adding to it an empty string (""), which is a less expensive operation than using JavaScript's eval() method. If the variable is null, its new value will be an empty string. If the variable is undefined, the evaluation process converts the undefined type into a string that holds the value of "undefined", enabling us to perform the test we need and provide a meaningful result no matter what.

Using the Request Object's Properties and Collections

In this section you'll find the complete reference to the Request object and how to work with Collections in general. Specifically, we'll look at working with the QueryString and Form collections, including their properties; the Cookies collection, the ClientCertificate collection, and the ServerVariables collection.

The QueryString and Form collections

The QueryString collection stores information sent to the server using a GET request, either from a form with its method set to GET or by the visitor traversing a link that contains URL-encoded information, as in the following link:

```
<A HREF="register.asp?first=Chili&last=Palmer">Register Chili</A>
```

The Form collection contains information sent by the browser using a POST request.

As with all collections, the `QueryString` and `Form` collections provide three properties: `Item`, `Key`, and `Count`. These can be used to read values that the collection stores.

THE COUNT PROPERTY

The `Count` property specifies the number of keys stored in the collection. This property is useful when you want to iterate through items stored in the collection.

```
count = Request.QueryString.Count
count = Request.Form.Count
```

THE ITEM PROPERTY

The `Item` property is used to reference a named item in a collection. The name of the item to access (a string) is provided as an argument, as follows:

```
firstName = Request.QueryString.Item("first")
```

The shorter syntax, `firstName = Request.QueryString("first")`, accomplishes the same result with less typing.

An `Item` property can also specify a `Count` property that can be used to count the number of values stored under a particular key. In the case of form submissions, some controls like the `SELECT` list and `CHECKBOXES` may return multiple values for the same name control. The example that follows reads the number of values stored under the `"colors"` key. Here's a snippet where all the values sent to a form via `POST` and stored under the `"colors"` key are concatenated into a comma-delimited string:

```
var count = Request.Form("colors").Count;
var colors = "";

for(var i=1; i <= count; i++)
{
  if(colors != "")
    colors += ",";
  colors += Request.Form("colors")(i);
}
```

Note that to access individual elements in the multi-valued item you need to provide an index to retrieve the element you want, using the following syntax:

```
value = Request.Form(keyName)(index)
```

In this case *index* is a number between one and the number of elements stored under the *keyName*.

THE KEY PROPERTY

The Key property is used to reference the name of a key that is used to store an item. The keys that you can expect to retrieve here are the names of the form fields that sent data to your application. As an argument you need to pass an index, so typically you will use this property in a loop, as follows:

```
var count = Request.QueryString.Count;
var key;
var list = "";

for(var i=1; i <= count; i++)
{
  key = Request.QueryString.Key(i);
  list += key.bold() + ":" + Request.QueryString(key) + "<BR>");
}
```

Accessing form elements by assuming a position is not a good idea, as this order is determined by the order in which the browser sent them; in some cases this may not match the order defined in the HTML. If your form agent is highly dynamic and multiple forms may point to the same agent, you will want to parse the form for the fields you want first.

The Cookies collection

The Cookies collection represents HTTP cookies that are sent by the browser. A cookie is a piece of data set by your application and stored in the visitor's browser. Whenever the visitor requests a page on your application, the browser returns the cookie back to the application. This allows the application to track users and their preferences over different sessions. Cookies are discussed in detail in Chapter 13, "Application Persistence."

The ClientCertificate collection

The ClientCertificate collection stores information about the digital certificates used by the server and by a client. Digital certificates are used for cryptographic authentication of the visitor and authentication of your Web site. The ClientCertificate collection is discussed in detail in Chapter 18, "Access Control."

The ServerVariables collection

The ServerVariables collection stores a number of informational settings about the server, the browser, and the request made by a client. While your applications may not typically use these variables, having knowledge of them can enable you to develop sophisticated applications that can better respond to requests made by users. Many of these variables will have more than one representation or the value they store may be a component of some other more general variable.

Many of these variables are sent to the server by the browser in the form of HTTP headers; others are defined by the server software. ASP just makes it easy for you to access them by adding them to the ServerVariables collection. We have highlighted some of the more important variables for general use. Note that ASP translates most of this information into objects that are more readily accessible.

As with all collections, this collection has Item, Key, and Count properties. The key values are the names of the defined ServerVariables. (See Table 4-1.) Depending on the HTTP headers sent by the browser, you may see additional variables not listed in Table 4-1.

TABLE 4-1 VARIABLES IN THE SERVERVARIABLES COLLECTION

Variable	Description
ALL_HTTP	Stores all the HTTP headers and associated values sent by the browser in one long string. The header names have been modified from what was sent by the browser. The modification includes starting all header names with "HTTP_" and capitalizing all the header names.
ALL_RAW	Stores all the HTTP headers and associated values sent by the browser in their original state. Compare it to the ALL_HTTP variable.
APPL_MD_PATH	Stores the metabase path for the application. This path is a string in the form of /LM/W3SVC/1/Root/appName, where LM refers to the local machine, W3SVC refers to the World Wide Web Service, 1 refers to the server instance (see the INSTANCE_ID variable), and the appName is an application in relation to the server's virtual path. In this example, appName would be an application that lives on the server's root.
APPL_PHYSICAL_PATH	Stores the physical path to the application, which is the actual path on the server's file system, to the virtual directory that represents the application.
AUTH_USER	Stores the authenticated username supplied by the user.
CERT_COOKIE	Stores a unique ID (a string) for the client's certificate. This ID can be used as a signature for the whole client certificate.

Continued

TABLE 4-1 **VARIABLES IN THE SERVERVARIABLES**
              COLLECTION *(Continued)*

Variable	Description
CERT_FLAGS	A set of flags providing information about the client certificate:
	Bit 0 – if set to 1, the client certificate is present. Bit 1 – if set to 1, Certificate Authority of the client certificate is not recognized by the server.
CERT_ISSUER	Contains the distinguished name (DN) of the client's digital certificate issuer. A DN entry looks like the following: O=My Company, OU=Engineering, CN=Name of the Certificate Owner, and C=USA, where O is the Organization, OU is the organizational unit, CN is the certificate name, and C is a country.
CERT_KEYSIZE	The amount of bits in a certificate key determines how difficult it is to break information encrypted with it. The larger the key, the more difficult it is to break. Longer keys also affect the performance of a server when encrypting data. This variable stores how big, in bits, the key in certificate is. Typically, keys are 128 bits, but smaller and larger sizes are possible. Military grade security can be achieved with a 1024 bit key.
CERT_SECRETSIZE	Number of bits in the server's private key.
CERT_SERIALNUMBER	The serial number field in the client certificate.
CERT_SERVER_ISSUER	The issuer field in the server certificate.
CERT_SERVER_SUBJECT	The subject field in the server certificate.
CERT_SUBJECT	The subject field in the client certificate.
CONTENT_LENGTH	The size of the HTTP body (POST request) sent by the browser in bytes.
CONTENT_TYPE	The MIME type of the data contained by the HTTP body. This setting matches the ENCTYPE attribute set on the form submitting the data. See "Reading Form Data" in this chapter. This field is used by HTTP queries that attach information (GET, POST, and PUT).
GATEWAY_INTERFACE	Specifies the version of CGI specification that the Web server supports.

Variable	Description
HTTP_ACCEPT	Provides information about the MIME types accepted by the requesting browser. This allows a server-side program to match the output it sends to the types the user can view.
HTTP_ACCEPT_ENCODING	Specifies the types of compressed data or encoding that the browser can accept. This can reduce the amount of data the browser needs to download.
HTTP_ACCEPT_LANGUAGE	Specifies the languages the user will accept. This is useful if your content is available in multiple languages.
HTTP_CONNECTION	Specifies if a TCP/IP connection should be reused (Keep-Alive) to send content. First- and second-generation browsers opened one TCP/IP connection per item downloaded. For a single page, multiple connections to the server would need to be established, slowing the download process, as typically the connection process takes longer than sending data. New browsers reuse connections to achieve better performance.
HTTP_COOKIE	Stores the cookie string sent with the request.
HTTP_HOST	The host name of the Web server.
HTTP_REFERER	Stores the URL of a redirected request (where the user came from).
HTTP_USER_AGENT	The brand of browser making the request.
HTTPS	Set to ON if the request was sent using SSL; otherwise, set to OFF.
HTTPS_KEYSIZE	Specifies the number of bits in the SSL connection key size, which is typically 128.
HTTPS_SECRETKEYSIZE	Specifies the number of bits in the server's certificate private key.
HTTPS_SERVER_ISSUER	The issuer field in the server certificate.
HTTPS_SERVER_SUBJECT	The subject field in the server certificate.
INSTANCE_ID	Represents the ID of the server instance to which the query belongs.

Continued

TABLE 4-1 VARIABLES IN THE SERVERVARIABLES COLLECTION *(Continued)*

Variable	Description
INSTANCE_META_PATH	The metabase path for the server instance that is servicing this request in a string using this format: /LM/W3SVC/1, where LM is Local Machine, W3SVC is the Web service, and 1 is the INSTANCE ID.
LOCAL_ADDR	The IP of the Web server where the request came in. If your server is multihomed (has multiple IPs), you can use this information to find out where the request came from. This can be useful if you want to process a request differently depending on where it came from.
LOGON_USER	The Windows account to which the user is logged on.
PATH_INFO	Displays the virtual path to the requested resource (URL path component).
PATH_TRANSLATED	Displays the physical path to the requested resource.
QUERY_STRING	Query information stored in the URL in the request portion of the URL that follows a question mark (?) in the HTTP request.
REMOTE_ADDR	The IP address of the client making the request.
REMOTE_HOST	The host name of the client making the request (if the server cannot resolve this information, its value is the same as REMOTE_ADDR).
REMOTE_USER	Stores the username provided by the user.
REQUEST_METHOD	The method used to make the request — for HTTP this is GET, HEAD, POST, PUT, DELETE, and so on. Refer to the HTTP specification at http://w3.org.
SCRIPT_NAME	The virtual path to the script currently executing.
SERVER_NAME	The server's host name.
SERVER_PORT	The port number to which the current request was sent (the port where the server is listening).
SERVER_PORT_SECURE	If the request is being handled on a secure port, the value of this variable will be 1. Otherwise it will be 0.
SERVER_PROTOCOL	Stores the name and version of the server protocol (protocol/version: HTTP/1.1).

Variable	Description
SERVER_SOFTWARE	Stores the name and version of the HTTP server software.
URL	Stores the base portion of the URL (omits the http://machinename portion in a fully qualified URL).

Listing 4-4 provides an example of a program that loops through all its server variables and generates a list of them. One interesting aspect of this example is that we have broken the program in the middle of the loop, inserted some static HTML to format the table, and inserted some references to the variables in the loop. In ASP this technique is often very useful, as it allows code-generated content to be inserted into an HTML template without disrupting the program flow. The alternative is a lot of string processing to build HTML. This interspersing code and HTML is almost always faster and more straightforward and more ASP-like.

Listing 4-4: Looping through ServerVariables and listing them

```
<%@ LANGUAGE="JScript" %>
<!DOCTYPE html PUBLIC "-//W3C//DTD HTML 3.2//EN">
<HTML>
<HEAD>
<TITLE>ServerVariables</TITLE>
</HEAD>
<BODY>
<TABLE border="1">
<TR><TH>Variable</TH><TH>Description</TH></TR>
<%
    var count = Request.ServerVariables.Count;
    var key;

    for(var i=1; i <= count; i++)
    {

        key = Request.ServerVariables.Key(i);
%>
<TR>
  <TD valign="top"><%=key.bold()%></TD>
  <TD valign="top"><%=Request.ServerVariables(key) + " "%></TD>
</TR>
<%
    }
%>
```

```
</BODY>
</HTML>
```

If you have not worked with HTML for a long time, you will notice that we are adding a non-breaking space ( ) HTML entity to the end of whatever Request.ServerVariables(key) returns. This is to keep the HTML table happy. If a value is not returned by the call, at least it will have a space forcing the browser to properly render the table.

Reading the HTTP body directly

The Request object provides a single method that allows you to read a number of bytes from the HTTP request. This allows your ASP programs to implement file uploads and other interesting solutions. The method signature for the BinaryRead looks like this:

```
safeArray = Request.BinaryRead(byteCount)
```

The byteCount argument specifies the number of bytes to read. Your application may choose to read only a few bytes at a time, or slurp the whole thing at once. You can find out how many bytes your server received by looking at the TotalBytes property of the Request object. The result of this method is a special object called a SafeArray. A SafeArray is a data structure that maintains array-type data; however, it is not a regular array that you can easily manipulate from JavaScript.

 If you call the BinaryRead() method, you cannot make subsequent calls to read the Form collection, as this will result in an error — as the data that the Form collection read will already be exhausted from your call to BinaryRead(). Conversely, you cannot read values from the Form collection and then make calls to BinaryRead(), as a read from the Form collection will exhaust the data in the HTTP body.

We will revisit the BinaryRead() method in Chapter 11, "Reading and Writing Files."

Summary

The Request object is arguably the most important ASP object. In it you can access data sent to you by the visitor and information about the browser making the request. Most of your scripts will focus on processing this information by storing it somewhere, like a database or a file.

Chapter 5

The Response Object

IN THIS CHAPTER

♦ Response methods

♦ Response properties

THE RESPONSE OBJECT, AS its name indicates, allows you to work with responses that your Web application generates. With it you can not only write output to the browser but also control how this information is to be sent to the browser. The Response object gives you control of HTTP headers by letting you use it to set HTTP headers and HTTP cookies. Setting headers allows you to control if and how long a proxy server will cache a document, redirect a visitor's browser to a different page, and many other useful things. This chapter will look at the Response object, its methods, and its properties.

Response Methods

In addition to header manipulation, the Response object also controls how the Web server will buffer content you generate. Output can be sent as you write, or it can be accumulated in a buffer and sent in chunks. If you're using a buffer, the Response object provides methods that allow you to manage the buffer by clearing it or flushing it. The Response object also allows you to terminate script processing on demand. The Response object provides a handful of methods that you can use to do the following:

♦ Write content to the browser

♦ Redirect browsers to a different URL

♦ Add HTTP headers to a response

♦ Write information to the Web server's log files

♦ Manage buffering for generated output

♦ Stop processing of the current page

Writing to the browser

To write text to the browser, you call the Response.Write(String) method. The Write() method takes a string as an argument. The text you write can provide the HTML formatting. Listing 5-1 provides an example of ASP script that contains no HTML formatting in template form. All HTML is provided by the text.

Listing 5-1: Using the Write() method to write text to the browser

```
<%@ LANGUAGE="JScript"%>

<%
  var header = "<HTML>\n<HEAD><TITLE>Writing Text</TITLE>" +
          "</HEAD>\n<BODY>\n";

  var content = "This is some " + "formatted".bold() +
" content.<BR>\n";
  var close = "</BODY>\n</HTML>\n";

  Response.Write(header);
  Response.Write(content);

  for(var i=0; i <= 7; i++)
  {
    Response.Write( i.toString().fontsize(i).bold() + "<BR>\n");
  }

  Response.Write(close);
%>
```

Listing 5-1 uses Response.Write() to generate all output sent to the browser. If you took out the Response.Write() statements, this script would generate absolutely no output. ASP would insert the basic <HTML> and <BODY> tags to inform the visitor's browser that the request was fulfilled. Listing 5-2 shows the output generated.

Listing 5-2: The output generated by the Write() method in Listing 5-1

```
<HTML>
<HEAD><TITLE>Writing Text</TITLE></HEAD>
<BODY>This is some <B>formatted</B> content.<BR>
<B><FONT SIZE="0">0</FONT></B><BR>
<B><FONT SIZE="1">1</FONT></B><BR>
<B><FONT SIZE="2">2</FONT></B><BR>
<B><FONT SIZE="3">3</FONT></B><BR>
<B><FONT SIZE="4">4</FONT></B><BR>
<B><FONT SIZE="5">5</FONT></B><BR>
```

```
<B><FONT SIZE="6">6</FONT></B><BR>
<B><FONT SIZE="7">7</FONT></B><BR>
</BODY>
</HTML>
```

Writing binary data

There might be cases when you need to write binary data to the browser. For example, suppose you load an image from a database and want to send it to the browser. In that case the standard `Write()` method would not work correctly, because some of the binary data would be translated to character data. To write binary data without translation you'd use the `BinaryWrite(byteArray)` method.

Redirecting a visitor

Redirection allows you to forward a visitor to a different page as part of making a request to your application. Redirection can be useful to do the following:

◆ Handle errors, such as missing information in a form or accessing a page within your application out of sequence

◆ Forward the user to a different URL (your application moved)

Browser redirection is handled by setting the Location HTTP header to a different URL. Setting this header in effect tells the browser to ignore the body of the page, and fetch the page at the given URL. If the URL is not fully qualified, it is taken to mean a page relative to the current location. Because redirecting a browser involves setting an HTTP header, your client cannot write any content prior to the redirection. If it does, the server will send the default headers before the content is printed, making it impossible for the redirection to happen. One solution to this problem is to enable ASP to buffer content by setting the Response's `Buffer` property to true (by default, this is set to true). You'll take a closer look at this property later in this chapter.

Listing 5-3 shows an example that uses the Request object to determine the origin of the request. If the request to the application is coming from an external network address (one that has a different IP), the visitor is redirected to a different site. If the address is from the internal network, or originating from the host hosting the services, the visitor is taken to an internal site. While redirection of this kind is useful, note that a real site would also implement security and require a login when accessing the internal site. The login would present more stringent requirements on who can access the page.

Listing 5-3: Using the Request object to determine a request's origin

```
<%@ LANGUAGE="JScript"%>

<%
```

```
   var ourNetwork = "222.200.192.";
   var localhost = "121.0.0.1";

   var remoteIP = Request.ServerVariables("REMOTE_ADDR") + "";

   if(remoteIP.indexOf(ourNetwork) == 0
     || remoteIP.indexOf(localhost) == 0)
   {
       Response.Redirect("http://localhost/aspbook/write.asp");
   }
   else
   {
Response.Redirect("http://www.externalsite.com/
aspbook/write.asp");
   }
  %>
```

TIP
When redirecting to pages within the same server, it is more efficient to use the `Server.Transfer(URL)` method instead. This method avoids the round-trip of sending a redirect to the browser, which then will process the redirect by generating a new request to the provided URL. For more information on the `Transfer` method, see Chapter 8, "The Server Object."

Adding HTTP headers

The `AddHeader()` method is useful for adding your own HTTP headers to your responses. Typically you'll use this feature to set HTTP headers like `CONTENT-TYPE`, which tells the browser the `MIME` type of the content you'll write or some custom header that you want clients to receive. For example, if you want all requests to have the header `CONTENT-COPYRIGHT` set to the name of your company, you can do something like this:

```
<%@ LANGUAGE="JScript"%>

<%
   Response.AddHeader("CONTENT-COPYRIGHT", "My Big Company, Inc.");
%>

<HTML>
<BODY>
```

Some content.
```
</BODY>
</HTML>
```

While the Web server will set this header in all requests, this made-up HTTP header is not very useful, as browsers are not able to do anything with this information. If you wrote your own Web client, you could then parse this information and do what you may with it. A better use of this method is to force a refresh of the current page every some many seconds. Most browsers understand the HTTP Refresh header that causes the browser to re-request the page after the number of seconds specified by the Refresh header has passed. Listing 5-4 provides an example.

Listing 5-4: Re-requesting the page after a one-second refresh

```
<%@ LANGUAGE="JScript"%>

<%
  Response.AddHeader("Refresh", "1");
%>

<HTML>
<BODY>
<%
    Response.Write(new Date());
%>
</BODY>
</HTML>
```

This example reloads the page every second, producing a new printout of the current date and time.

Writing information to the log files

With each request you make of the Web server, the server typically writes an entry specifying when the request was made, the URL of the requested resource, and the IP of the visitor, to name a few. With the AppendToLog() method you can add additional information to the log.

For this method to work, the Extended Logging Properties must include the URI Query option. This option can be enabled by opening the Internet Services Manager console, right-clicking on the Web site entry, and choosing Properties. On the Web Site tab, there is an Enable Logging option (which must be checked) and the Active log format must be set to "W3C Extended Log File Format." To access the extended properties, click on the Properties button that provides access to the Extended Properties tab. Check the URI Stem and URI Query boxes; other choices on what to log are also available.

Lastly, Web server logs are character-delimited files that have fields delimited by a comma and records delimited by a new line. Text that you append to the log should not contain any of these characters. Listing 5-5 provides an example that writes the value of the ID field in the request.

Listing 5-5: Writing the value of an ID field

```
<%@ LANGUAGE="JScript"%>

<HTML>
<BODY>

<%
  var id = Request.QueryString("id") + "";

  Response.AddToLog(id);
  Response.Write("Your id: " + id.bold());
%>

</BODY>
</HTML>
```

Managing output buffering

If your page is using buffering, you have rudimentary control of the buffer. You can clear the buffer and eliminate any content that was previously generated, or you can flush the buffer to the browser. The example shown in Listing 5-6 generates some HTML that is written and cleared from the buffer. Then it generates some more HTML that is sent to the browser. The script creates a small delay by counting to 100000, giving the user a chance to see the words "This will be seen." A second or so later, depending on the speed of the server, the word "Done" is printed. Because output to the browser was flushed, the browser was able to render it before the page completed loading. This capability will depend on the HTML constructs that you use, but can be useful to provide the visitor with feedback (content appearing on the page) as the file loads. If flush() were not used, the user would see the entire page at once, rather than incrementally.

Listing 5-6: Writing and clearing a buffer

```
<%@ LANGUAGE="JScript"%>

<%
  Response.Write("<HTML><BODY>");
  Response.Write("This will not be seen.</BODY></HTML>");
  Response.Clear();
  Response.Write("<HTML><BODY>This will be seen.<BR>\n");
```

```
    Response.Flush();
    for(var i=0; i < 100000; i++);
    Response.Write("Done");
    Response.Write("</BODY></HTML>");
%>
```

Note that the `Clear()` and `Flush()` methods will cause a run-time error if buffering has not been enabled for the page. IIS 5 has buffering enabled by default. Earlier versions have it disabled by default. Another important note is that the `Clear()` method does not clear the HTTP headers.

Stopping processing

The `End()` method stops processing of the current page and sends whatever output is in the buffer to the browser. Any additional script or page processing is not processed. This feature can be very useful to create debug-type messages. Sometimes your ASP page will stop processing at some line for no apparent reason. The following snippet can be used to selectively print out the value of some variable when tracking the problem:

```
<%
Response.Clear();
Response.Write("DEBUG: " + myVariableName + "<BR>";
Response.End();
%>
```

The first line will clear any HTML accumulated for the client, and the second line will output some diagnostic output of your choice. The third line will stop the script and flush the output to the browser.

Response Properties

Response object properties provide you with shortcuts for setting some frequently used headers, many of which can be just as easily set by using the `AddHeader()` method that you saw earlier. The reason why these headers are exposed as properties is that it allows server administrators to set their default values so your scripts don't have to worry about it. Here's a list of what you can control:

- ◆ Turn on/off buffering of content
- ◆ Control caching performed by proxy servers
- ◆ Set the character set used by your document
- ◆ Set the content type (MIME type) of the contents the server is returning

- ◆ Control browser caching for your page

- ◆ Test to see if the browser is still connected to the server

- ◆ Set the PICS (Platform for Internet Content Selection) label control features that limit the type of content that can be downloaded by the browser

- ◆ Set the status value returned by the server in the Status HTTP header; this value indicates if the request was successfully processed or not

Buffer

The `Buffer` property controls if the Web server buffers page output or not. When output is buffered (this is the default on IIS 5), the server doesn't send the response until the page has finished executing, or the `Flush()` or `End()` methods have been called by the script.

Buffering output is the correct thing to do for your application as it allows the server to more efficiently process a request. For pages that generate a lot of output or that take considerable amount of time generating output, buffering can create the illusion of a slow site because the visitor won't see any content on their browser until the entire response has been generated.

To turn buffering off, do the following:

```
<%
    Response.Buffer = false;
%>
```

To turn buffering on, do the following:

```
<%
    Response.Buffer = true;
%>
```

Your scripts should never rely on default values. If the administrator for the server decides to change a default value, your script will break! When you want the buffer on, set it explicitly; this way you don't have any dependencies on some external configuration.

CacheControl

The `CacheControl` property specifies whether a script-generated page is cacheable by a proxy server or not. A proxy server provides Web access to an internal local area network (LAN). The proxy server (a special kind of Web server) makes requests on behalf of browsers in the LAN by retrieving content from sites on the Internet. To increase performance for the LAN and to conserve bandwidth for other purposes, proxy servers typically cache pages they retrieve – in other words, they store pages they retrieve on a local disk and return them when other clients make a request for the same page without further access to the outside network.

Pages generated by scripts are typically not cacheable for a couple of reasons: the page's content depends on some input or context provided by the visitor, and the cached page can contain private information specific to the visitor that should not be shown to others. If you have a script-generated page that only changes at regular intervals, the CacheControl option provides additional information to the proxy server that it can use to determine if the page should be cached or not. Note that setting this property doesn't mean that the page will be cached. Any caching performed by the proxy server depends on that server's configuration.

The options you can assign to this property are the strings Public or Private. To enable caching of the script-generated page, add a line like this to your script:

```
<%
    Response.CacheControl = "Public";
%>
```

To disable caching for a page, provide this line instead:

```
<%
    Response.CacheControl = "Private";
%>
```

The CacheControl property sets an HTTP header on the response page. This requires that you set this property before you write any HTML. If you set this property after any content has been written to the client, the call will result in an error.

Charset

The Charset property appends the name of the character set used by the content you generate. This information is added to the CONTENT-TYPE HTTP header on the response document. This property will append the string that you provide (including a string that is not a valid character set).

```
<%
Response.Charset = "ISO-LATIN-7";
%>
```

Note that the `Charset` property affects the HTTP header, and as with other properties and methods of this kind, any modification performed to such properties must occur before the server outputs any content to the client.

 On IIS 4 and older, you have to access the `Charset` property as if it were a method.

ContentType

The `ContentType` property manipulates the `CONTENT-TYPE` HTTP header. This header tells the browser the `MIME` type of content that is contained in the body of the HTTP message. The browser uses this information to interpret the content in the appropriate way (render images, display text, and so forth). If the browser doesn't provide a content handler for the type specified, it will typically display a Save file dialog box to allow the user to save the file to disk (since it cannot display it). Some of the standard formats used are as follows:

- ◆ text/HTML (HTML document)
- ◆ text/plain (Plain text document)
- ◆ image/GIF (gif image)
- ◆ image/JPEG (jpeg image)

Typically the Web server adds the `CONTENT-TYPE` header automatically when returning a file. The server typically looks at the file extension when serving the file and from that information it provides the appropriate `CONTENT-TYPE` information. If your application retrieves an image in JPEG format from a database and then wants to send the JPEG data to the browser, the Web server will not have access to the extension mapping mechanism (unless you created a temporary-type file and then referenced the file from within your script), so you would have to provide this information manually as follows:

```
<%
    // Load image from a database code omitted.
    Response.ContentType = "image/jpeg";
    Response.BinaryWrite(someimagedata);
%>
```

As stated previously, this information is part of the HTTP header, so it must be set before the HTTP header is sent to the client and before the browser writes any content to the browser.

Expires

The `Expires` property specifies the number of minutes that a browser should cache a document. If the visitor returns to the page before the expiration time, and the page is available on the browser's cache, the browser will reload the page without going out to network. The `Expires` property expresses expiration in terms of minutes, and for complete accuracy requires that clocks in the server and the client be synchronized. To request that a page be cached for a day (48 hours), do this:

```
<%
  Response.Expires = 60 * 48;
%>
```

If the `Expires` property is set multiple times, the browser will pick the shortest expiration time. Setting the property to a zero value may not expire a page if there's a difference between the server and the client's clock time or if there are any time zone differences between the two systems. To force expiration, use a negative number or see the `ExpiresAbsolute` property, which is described next.

ExpiresAbsolute

The `ExpiresAbsolute` property specifies the date and the time when a page cached by a browser expires. If the visitor returns to the page before the expiration time, and the page is available on the browser's cache, the browser will reload the page without going out to the network. The format for the expiration date is as follows:

```
Mon DD, YYYY HH:MM:SS
```

where,

- ◆ `Mon` is the three-letter abbreviation of the month
- ◆ `DD` is the day of the month
- ◆ `YYYY` is the full year
- ◆ `HH` is the hour of the day (in 24 hour format)
- ◆ `MM` is the minute of the hour
- ◆ `SS` is the second in the minute

Listing 5-7 shows an example for a page that sets its expiration to one month from today. Note that the JavaScript Date object will generate a correct date for the month and day of the month values without additional checking or manipulation from the script.

Listing 5–7: Setting expiration to one month from today

```
<%@ LANGUAGE="JScript"%>
<%
  Response.Charset="ISO-LATIN-7";

  function expireNextMonth(d)
  {
      months = new Array("Jan", "Feb", "Mar", "Apr", "May", "Jun",
"Jul", "Aug", "Sep", "Oct", "Nov", "Dec" );

      d.setMonth(d.getMonth() + 1);

      var dateStr = months[d.getMonth()]+ " " + d.getDate() +
              ", "+  d.getFullYear();
      var timeStr = d.getHours() + ":" + d.getMinutes() +
              ":" + d.getSeconds();

      return dateStr + " " + timeStr;
  }
%>
<HTML>
<BODY>

<%
    // expire one month from today
    var expireDate = expireNextMonth(new Date());
    Response.ExpiresAbsolute = expireDate;
    Response.Write("This document will expire on: " + expireDate);
%>

</BODY>
</HTML>
```

IsClientConnected

The IsClientConnected property is a read-only property that returns true or false if the browser is still connected to the server. This property is useful to determine if the browser is still there after a lengthy operation. (See Listing 5-8.)

Listing 5–8: Determining a server–browser connection

```
<%
    var hasMoreWorkToDo = true;

    while(hasMoreWorkToDo)
```

```
    {
        // do something that takes a long time,
        // checking every once in a while if they are
        // still there...
        hasMoreWorkToDo = doWork();

        if(Response.IsClientConnected == false)
        {
            Response.End();
        }
    }

    Response.Write(results);
%>
```

PICS

PICS is the Platform for Internet Content Selection, the World Wide Web Consortium (W3C) – see `http://www.w3.org` – specification that enables metadata to be associated with Internet content. PICS was originally designed to help parents and teachers control what children access on the Internet, but provides a foundation for more general purposes.

PICS enables content providers to self-rate their materials and include third-party ratings in a single label associated with the document. This label can be used by software tools to control access to the page based on a policy set on the visitor's system. This allows the system's manager to limit the type of content that is viewed through their system. The PICS label is composed of the following:

◆ A service identifier

◆ Label options

◆ A rating

The service identifier is a URL that serves as a unique identifier to the rating service used. The rating service will classify pages to different criteria and will provide different rating attributes. Label options provide additional properties about the document being rated, such as the date and time when the document was rated and how long for which this rating remains valid. The rating component is a set of attribute and value pairs that describe the document, in some vocabulary. The attributes (the vocabulary) used in the PICS label will depend on the rating service used. A PICS label in the HTTP header may look something like this:

```
(PICS-1.1 <http://www.someratingservice/v1.0>
by 'John Doe'
```

```
labels on '2000.04.01T14:05-0600'
until '2000.04.02T14:05-0600'
for 'http://www.mysite.com/index.html'"
ratings (interesting 4 informational 4))
```

The above PICS label can be transmitted in one line, and can be made more compact by abbreviating labels to "l," and ratings to "r." Many of the items such as the rated URL can be eliminated if the PICS label refers to the current document:

```
(PICS-1.1 <http://www.someratingservice/v1.0> l r (interesting 4
informational4))
```

Here's an example for a site using RSAC's rating system, which rates for violence (V), sexual content (S), language (L), and nudity (N), so a typical label for a naughty site that uses RSAC's system might look like the following:

```
<%@ LANGUAGE="JScript"%>
<%
  Response.PICS("(PICS-1.1 <http://www.rsac.org/ratingv01.html>
labels on '20000401T00:00-0000' until '20010401T00:00-0000' ratings
(v 4 s 4 l 4 n 4))");
%>

<HTML>
<BODY>
This is a naughty page
</BODY>
</HTML>
```

Following is a similar page, but this one is rated as not containing any offensive materials:

```
<%@ LANGUAGE="JScript"%>
<%
  Response.PICS("(PICS-1.1 <http://www.rsac.org/ratingv01.html>
labels on '20000401T00:00-0000' until '20010401T00:00-0000' ratings
(v 0 s 0 l 0 n 0))");
%>

<HTML>
<BODY>
This page doesn't contain any offensive stuff.
</BODY>
</HTML>
```

While the PICS property is described as a property to agree with Microsoft documentation, this property is in reality a method.

Status

The Status property specifies the result code returned by the Web server after processing a request. These result codes are composed of a three-digit number followed by a string message. Here's a list of some of the standard responses that a server can return:

◆ 100-199 codes are reserved for informational responses

◆ 200-299 codes are reserved for successful responses

◆ 300-399 codes are reserved for redirection (content was moved to a different URL)

◆ 400-499 codes are reserved for errors generated by a client request (document not found)

◆ 500-599 codes are reserved for errors generated by the server, like service is not available due to high volume access

 For a complete list of the most popular error codes, see Appendix F.

The following is an example that sets the status for a request that has been properly fulfilled but with nothing to return to the visitor:

```
<%
Response.Status = "204 NO CONTENT";
%>
```

Response contents collection

The Response object provides the Cookies collection. The collection allows you to add values to the HTTP header that browsers can store on their local disk. On making future requests to your Web site, these values are returned to your site. Cookies are a very important component for HTTP applications, so we have dedicated an entire chapter to their discussion. For more information, please refer to Chapter 13, "Application Persistence."

Summary

The Response object provides you with an easy interface to many powerful and useful functions. With it you can write content, set the content's type, add HTTP headers, and control buffering used by the server. Some of these features, while simple in appearance, are actually quite powerful as they allow you to control performance or create a highly dynamic application.

Chapter 6

The Application Object

IN THIS CHAPTER

- ◆ Shared data and multithreading
- ◆ The lock and unlock application methods
- ◆ Storing shared values in the application
- ◆ Application Contents collection
- ◆ Application events
- ◆ Static objects collection

THE APPLICATION OBJECT REPRESENTS the Web application. An ASP application is literally defined as "a collection of ASP and COM components that share a common directory." This common directory represents the *application*. Sometimes you'll see this directory described as the *application root*. Note that any subdirectories in the application root are part of the same application.

The application root scheme helps the Web server determine the boundaries of an application. Note that a single Web site can define multiple applications; however, it is not a good idea to nest applications, as certain context issues will surface. The Web server creates and maintains a single Application object for each ASP application. The Application object is created when any page in the application root is first requested, and continues to live until the last session ceases to be active, an administrator unloads the application, or the Web server is turned off.

The main purpose of the Application object is to serve as a shared data container. You can add your own variables to the Application object. These values you store here are shared between all the visitors to your application, providing a way for you to share information between application users. In this chapter you will learn how to store values in the Application object. You will also learn about issues that you need to address when storing information that is shared and potentially accessed through several pages at the same time.

Shared Data and Multithreading

Variables in the Application object are by nature global, so when modifying these values it is necessary for a script to obtain exclusive access to the Application by locking it. This is necessary because Web servers are multithreaded and multiple scripts may be modifying the state of the Application object at the same time.

To illustrate the issues of a shared object access in a multithreaded environment, take for instance an application that maintains counters for all individual visitors by domain. The Application object would be a perfect candidate to store this type of information since you would want to be able to access and modify this information from different visitor sessions. Let's say for purposes of this example that two visitors from the same domain access the application at practically the same instant. The pseudocode to update the counter is as follows:

1. Read the counter for the domain of the current visitor.

2. Add one to the value.

3. Set the counter to the new value.

A thread represents an independent execution path in a program; Web servers and many modern applications are often multithreaded. This allows the Web server to process several requests "at the same time." Depending on the hardware, the actual execution of two or more threads won't be at the same time, as really one thread can have access to one processor at any one time. A program called a thread scheduler will run/suspend threads allowing each of the threads a chance to run for a few milliseconds at a time. On machines with multiple processors multiple threads can concurrently execute at the same time. Your concern for all of this is that regardless of your hardware, your code needs to be protected from multiple threads modifying the same data at the same time; your code needs to be *thread-safe*. Take for example the pseudocode above; while it looks harmless, in a multithreaded environment the above code is not thread-safe, as these operations may occur concurrently or interleave. The side effect of this is that data will be lost or corrupted. Here's how the actual scenario of our two visitors could play out:

◆ Thread A reads the counter for the domain "visitor.com," which currently stores the value of one into a local variable.

◆ Thread B reads the counter for the domain "visitor.com" into a local variable. Note that the counter still stores a value of one, as thread A has not yet completed processing the script.

◆ Thread A adds one to the current value (1+1).

◆ Thread B adds one to the current value (1+1).

◆ Thread A sets the counter to the new value of two.

◆ Thread B sets the counter to the new value of two!

In this operation, you can see that whatever thread A contributes is effectively lost. If both visitors had come from different domains, this wouldn't have been a problem because the variables they access would be different. However, this depends on how the code is written. Even if it seems like an unlikely problem, this is a problem that you should always address in your code. As the previous example illustrates, access of shared information must be performed in a controlled way or the information will be meaningless.

 If your application is only reading values, and these values are not changed by multiple users, you don't really need to worry about controlling access of shared information. However, most values stored in the Application object are usually in the form of counters and other values that should use a thread-safe access model.

Application Methods

The Application object provides two methods that you can use to protect the access to shared data: the Lock and Unlock methods. This section takes a look at both of these data-protection methods.

Locking the Application object

The Lock method effectively locks the Application object by blocking other scripts trying to call Lock on the Application object. These other scripts will wait until the holder of the lock releases it. This effectively prevents any other script from accessing or altering values in the Application until the corresponding Unlock method is called, the script times out, or the current script finishes execution (whichever comes first). The Lock method has a simple signature and doesn't take any arguments, as follows:

```
Application.Lock
```

Careful readers will notice that when the Application object is locked, other (well-behaved) scripts trying to obtain a lock on the Application will wait until they get the lock. Locking works by cooperation if all your scripts are well behaved, that is, they lock/unlock the Application object while accessing its values. Then ASP will guarantee that accesses to the Application object are atomic from the script's perspective. This means that instead of the interleaved access between clients as outlined earlier, reading, incrementing, and writing of the values all happen as one unit of work for each script, as listed here:

◆ Read the value for the domain.

◆ Increment the value.

◆ Set the new value.

If two or more scripts want to perform this operation at the same time, only one script at a time will be able to. Other scripts will be temporarily stopped until the current script is finished and the Application object is unlocked.

Because other scripts are effectively stopped for a period of time, always lock or unlock the application as quickly as possible in your script. If you have a long script, one that perhaps takes a considerable amount of time to execute, you will want to make sure that you don't lock the application any longer than you need to or the performance of your server will be reduced, as other scripts will have to wait for a lengthy operation to conclude.

 It is still possible for your scripts to be well behaved and for a rogue script to access and modify the Application object without using the lock mechanism and thus access or modify the Application object and its values in a non-thread-safe way.

Unlocking the Application object

The Unlock method releases the lock on the Application object, allowing other scripts trying to obtain a lock on the application to proceed. Similar to the Lock method, the Unlock method doesn't take any arguments, as you see here:

```
Application.Unlock
```

Storing Shared Values in the Application

To access a property in the Application object, your script will do something like this:

```
Application("key") = value
variable = Application("key")
```

Key is the name of the property you want to access. For VBScript developers this syntax will seem very natural. For JavaScript developers, this syntax will seem strange, as JavaScript allows access to properties directly through the dot (.) operator.

Values stored in the application are actually stored in the Contents collection. We discuss the intricacies of the Contents collection later in this chapter. Listing 6-1 provides an example for accessing a shared property in the Application object using the Lock method.

Listing 6-1: Accessing a shared property in the Application object

```
<%@ LANGUAGE="VBScript"%>
<HTML>
<BODY>

<%
Application.Lock()
previousCount = Application("previousCount")

If isNull(previousCount) Then
    previousCount = 0
End If

Application("previousCount")  = previousCount + 1

Application.Unlock()
%>

<P>This page has been visited by <B><%=previousCount%></B>
visitors, since the application was last restarted.
</BODY>
</HTML>
```

In the Listing 6-1 example, before we access properties in the Application object, we lock it. This will prevent shared access issues, since we are writing and updating shared values. Next, we try to read a property called previousCount from the Application object. If the property does not exist, Application returns null. In our script we test to see if the value of the previousCount variable is null, and if it is, we re-initialize our previousCount variable to zero. Last, we set a new value for the previousCount property in the Application object, by incrementing the count by one.

The syntax for the same script using JavaScript doesn't look much different. The major difference is the way that we test for a null value, as shown in Listing 6-2.

Listing 6-2: Using JavaScript to access a shared property

```
<%@ LANGUAGE="JScript"%>
<HTML>
<BODY>

<%
Application.Lock();
var previousCount = Application("previousCount");

if(previousCount == null)
{
```

```
    previousCount = 0;
}

Application("previousCount")  = previousCount + 1;
Application.Unlock();
%>

<P>This page has been visited by <B><%=previousCount%></B>
visitors, since the application was last restarted.
</BODY>
</HTML>
```

Application Contents Collection

Variables you add to the Application object through the use of scripts are stored in the Contents collection. You can store scalar and most object types in the Application object's Contents collection. You cannot store references to built-in ASP objects such as `Session`, `Request`, `Response`, `Server`, `Application`, or `ObjectContext`. In addition to these built-in objects, JavaScript developers should be aware that you cannot store custom JavaScript objects (including `Object`) in the Application object. The Contents collection has three properties:

- ◆ Item
- ◆ Count
- ◆ Key

The Item property

The `Item` property allows you to access or set a value in the Contents collection. To programmers that are not familiar with VBScript, the Contents collection will seem like a hybrid of a hash table and an array. The `Item` property allows you to access and reference values in the collection by using a name, much like you would in a hash table or by using an index as you would in an array. Here's an example of accessing the Item collection:

```
Application.Contents.Item("key") = value
variable = Application.Contents.Item("key")
```

The `Item` property is the default property of the Contents collection, and the Contents collection is the default collection of the Application object. This is why previously you saw the more concise (and natural) form of the following example to access properties of the Application object:

```
Application("key") = value
variable = Application("key")
```

Note that a third form is also possible, as follows:

```
Application.Contents("key") = value
variable = Application.Contents("key")
```

Finally, you can also access a value in the Items property by specifying an index. The index will depend on when the value was added to the collection, and will always start at index one (1), even if your programming language has arrays that begin with a zero index. This feature exists to enable more dynamic programs to access values when the key is not known during development.

```
Application.Contents(index) = value
variable = Application.Contents(index)
```

The Count property

The Count property of the Contents collection tells you the number of properties stored in the collection. Some dynamic programs may use this property together with the Key property to obtain a list of all the values stored in the Application object. To access the count, just do the following:

```
count = Application.Contents.Count
```

The Key property

The Key property allows you to find the name of a property by index. For each value stored in the Items property there will be an entry in the Key property specifying the name that was used to store the value. Entries in the Key property are accessed by index, so to find the name used to store the first item in the Contents collection, you would write a line of code like the following:

```
PropertyName = Application.Contents.Key(1);
```

Listing 6-3 provides an example that uses these three features to print all the elements stored in the Application object.

Listing 6-3: Using the Item, Count, and Key properties

```
<%@ LANGUAGE="JScript"%>
<HTML>
<BODY>

<%
```

```
var propertyCount = Application.Contents.Count;
var propertyList = "";

if(propertyCount == 0)
{
    propertyList = "No properties defined.";
}
else
{
    for(var i = 1; i <= propertyCount; i++)
    {
        propertyList += Application.Contents.Key(i).bold() + ": "
        + Application.Contents(i) + "<BR>\n";
    }
}

%>
<H1>Properties Currently Defined in the Application Object</H1>
<P><%=propertyList%>

</BODY>
</HTML>
```

The Listing 6-3 example merely gets a count for the number of properties in the `Application.Contents` collection. If items are defined, it loops through all the properties defined, building up an HTML-formatted string that lists the name of the property in bold (using the `String.bold` method) followed by a colon (:) and the value stored in the property.

Application Contents collection methods

Starting with IIS 5.0 and derivative servers, the Application Contents collection provides two methods that you can use for removing items from the collection. You can remove a specific property or all of them. To remove a specific property, use the `Remove(propertyName)` method, as follows:

```
Application.Remove("propertyList")
```

To remove all properties, you use `RemoveAll()`, as follows:

```
Application.RemoveAll()
```

These methods are not present on earlier servers.

Application Events

The Application object can be initialized from scripts found in the global.asa file. The global.asa file allows you to provide code for the `Application_OnStart` and `Application_OnEnd` handlers.

The Application_OnStart event

The `Application_OnStart` event is triggered when the first visitor of the application accesses any page in the application. This handler is called exactly once when the application first starts. Code for this handler executes before any other scripts are run, so this provides you with the ability to initialize or restore the environment of the application between executions. Also, because no script is yet running, you don't have to worry about thread issues. The Web server will look for these scripts in the global.asa file in your application root directory. Your application must provide one and only one global.asa file.

Following is a trivial example of using `Application_OnStart` to initialize the time the application was last started, and as a counter:

```
<SCRIPT LANGUAGE="VBScript" RUNAT="SERVER">
Sub Application_OnStart()
  Application.Contents("appStartDate") = Date
  Application.Contents("pageCounter") = 0
End Sub
</SCRIPT>
```

In JavaScript, you can define the handlers as functions like this:

```
<SCRIPT LANGUAGE="JScript" RUNAT="SERVER">
function Application_OnStart()
{
  Application.Contents("appStartDate") = Date();
  Application.Contents("pageCounter") = 0;
}
</SCRIPT>
```

The Application_OnEnd event

The `Application_OnEnd` event is triggered when the ASP application terminates. An ASP application can terminate for one of four reasons:

◆ The last active user session times out or the user exits the application in such a way that this last session is destroyed.

◆ The administrator turns off the Web service.

◆ The administrator unloads the application.

◆ The administrator shuts down the computer.

If any of these conditions happen, the `Application_OnEnd` event will be triggered. This handler provides you with the opportunity to save any information you have stored in the Application object to a more permanent store such as a file or a database.

Listing 6-4 provides a more advanced example that will write all properties to a file. Many of the details of this example won't be clear until you learn more about files. But in a nutshell, this handler creates an object to access the file system, creates the file `c:\temp\aspstate.txt` (in JavaScript the backslash [\] is the escape character, so it is doubled to provide the backslash), and writes to it the name and value of the properties stored in the collection (one per line), separated by an equals sign (=).

Listing 6-4: Writing all properties to a file

```
<SCRIPT LANGUAGE="VBScript" RUNAT="SERVER">
function Application_OnEnd()
{
  var fso = new ActiveXObject("Scripting.FileSystemObject");
  var stream = fso.CreateTextFile("c:\\temp\\aspstate.txt", true);

  for(var i = 1; i < Application.Contents.Count; i++)
  {
    stream.WriteLine(Application.Contents.Key(i) +
        "=" + Application.Contents(i));
  }

  stream.Close();
}
</SCRIPT>
```

StaticObjects Collection

In addition to the Contents collection, the Application object has a `StaticObjects` collection. The `StaticObjects` collection provides you with a way to access objects added via the `<OBJECT>` tag and an application-level scope.

The `<OBJECT>` tag allows you to create an instance of a component that can be shared with different scopes (`Application`, `Session`, and `Page`), a single instance of such a component is shared in that scope. For example, if you want to access a database connection from multiple scripts, creating an instance of the component and giving it a session scope will allow a single database access component to be available to a single visitor from all ASP pages. Since the Application object is shared by all sessions, very few components should be shared with an Application-level scope.

To make sense of `StaticObjects`, you'll first need to learn how to create components, and learn about some of the components available. You will revisit `StaticObjects` in Chapter 10, "Extending ASP with ActiveX Components."

Summary

The Application object is a shared object where you can store information that all clients of the application can access. Because the Application object is shared and Web servers are multithreaded, you need to ensure that only one script modifies the Application object at any one time. Use of the `Lock` and `Unlock` methods guarantee this. The Application object doesn't provide any built-in properties, and it is a blank object that you can use to store values as you require.

Chapter 7

The Session Object

IN THIS CHAPTER

◆ Using the Session object

◆ Working around multiple server gotchas

◆ Avoiding sessions

SECOND TO THE REQUEST OBJECT, the Session object is arguably the most useful object in ASP. The Session object solves the biggest tedium in web application development: It maintains state for a particular visitor between requests. This chapter is fundamental to all ASP applications.

Using the Session Object

As you know, HTTP is a stateless protocol, so each request is treated independently of one another. Traditionally Web developers have maintained state by using cookies or URL encoding to pass information between pages. ASP doesn't invent a new mechanism to solve this problem; however, the process, from a programmer's perspective, is greatly automated and simplified. Instead of the programmer being responsible for setting cookie values that preserve session information and restoring them as needed, ASP streamlines the process by providing an object that can store values between visitor requests. ASP then performs the necessary chores to ensure that this environment, or session, is restored when the visitor makes further requests.

The Session object basically represents a visitor to your Web application. It maintains any information you store in it. This information can be as simple as an account number or a shopping cart. With it your application knows where your visitors have been and what they have done.

As with all ASP objects there is a life cycle associated with the Session object. Its creation is triggered by one of the following activities:

◆ A new visitor requests a page in an ASP application that defines a `Session_OnStart` handler in its global.asa file.

◆ A new visitor requests an ASP page in an application that uses a global.asa to instantiate an object with a session scope (the `<OBJECT>` tag) (See Chapter 10, "Extending ASP with ActiveX Components.")

79

- ◆ A script on the requested ASP page stores a value in the Session object.

- ◆ ASP receives a request that doesn't contain a valid session ID
  (`Session.SessionID`).

A Session remains valid until:

- ◆ The session times out (by default after 20 minutes of inactivity).

- ◆ The session is abandoned.

- ◆ The visitor exits the browser.

- ◆ The server reboots.

ASP maintains all session information on the server side. When a session is created, the server assigns a session ID to the client. The session ID is a unique identifier (a big number) that gets passed from page to page in the application via an HTTP cookie. This cookie allows the server to create a relationship between the session information that it maintains and a visitor somewhere on the Internet. The cookie component of the session is stored in the visitor's browser, and when the visitor makes additional requests to the application, the browser resends this identifier along with the new request. The Web server then matches the received session identifier and restores the visitor's user session to its previous state, maintaining the illusion of continuity between requests. Your application's server-side scripts have access through this `Session` object to any information you stored for your visitor there.

Session events

Similar to the Application object, creating a Session object is an important event. To allow you to initialize a new session, the global.asa file allows you to define a `Session_OnStart` handler, which gets called when a visitor makes a first request in the application, but before any scripts are run. This event is useful for initializing a session.

When a session times out, the `Session_OnEnd` handler is called (if defined) and the session is discarded. The `Session_OnEnd` handler gives you the opportunity to save session information into a persistent store such as a database or file on the server side. Saving the last state of the application can be useful for restoring the visitor's environment when the visitor returns. When discarded, the server disposes of any resources the Session object might have allocated. Listing 7-1 provides an example.

Listing 7-1: The Session_OnStart and Session_OnEnd handlers

```
<SCRIPT LANGUAGE="JavaScript" RUNAT="SERVER">

function Application_OnStart()
```

```
{
    Application("totalVisitors") = 0;
    Application("totalTime") = 0;
}

function Session_OnStart()
{
    var now = new Date();
    now = now.valueOf();

    Session("startTime") = now;
    Session("lastRequest") = now;
}

function Session_OnEnd()
{
    Application.Lock();

    var totalVisitors = Application("totalVisitors");
    var totalTime = Application("totalTime");
    var visitorTime = Session("lastRequest") - Session("startTime");

    Application("totalVisitors") = totalVisitors + 1;
    Application("totalTime") = totalTime + visitorTime;

    Application.Unlock();
}

</SCRIPT>
```

The Session_OnStart handler shown in Listing 7-1 initializes the Session object so that it stores the current time in milliseconds (the valueOf() method) under the startTime and lastRequest keys. The use of such code can be very useful when validating a request or when keeping track of the amount of time a visitor spends on your site. A typical application will update the value stored under lastRequest on each page in the application.

Note that in the Listing 7-1 example we didn't store a JavaScript Date object. Part of the reason is that on the current releases of IIS and its derivatives, assigning a Date object during the Session_OnStart event gives spurious results. By storing a primitive type, a string, or a number, we don't have such problems, which is more efficient. It is important to point out that assigning a Date object from within ASP pages (not global.asa), works as expected.

The above Session_OnEnd handler calculates the amount of time the visitor spent on the site and stores it in the Application object. The Application object can then be queried at any time for this sort of information using a trivial script like the one shown in Listing 7-2.

Listing 7-2: Querying the Application object

```
<%@ LANGUAGE="JavaScript" %>
<%
var now = new Date();

now = now.valueOf();
Session("lastRequest") = now;
%>

<HTML>
<HEAD>
<TITLE>Application Stats</TITLE>
</HEAD>
<BODY>

<%
var totalVisitors = Application("totalVisitors");
var totalTime = Application("totalTime");
var average = (totalTime/totalVisitors) / 1000;
%>

<B>Total Visitors:</B> <%= totalVisitors %><BR>
<B>Total time spent by visitors:</B> <%= totalTime %><BR>
<B>Average time spent by a visitor:</B> <%= average %> secs.<BR>


</BODY>
</HTML>
```

Storing values in a Session object

Similar to other ASP objects, the Session object has a Contents collection, complete with Item, Key, and Count properties. Similar to the Application object, to add a value to the Session, associate values with a name (a key) that you can use to retrieve the value later. Unlike the Application object, which is shared by all application users, the Session object is unique to each visitor, so no concurrency and threaded issues are present. Here's how you store a value:

```
Session(aName) = value
```

To read the value you reverse the operation:

```
aValue = Session(aName)
```

As with all collections, you can be more specific, and set and retrieve values by specifying the collection's name:

```
Session.Contents(aName) = value
aValue = Session.Contents(aName)
```

You can also use the Item, Key and Count properties to access a value in a collection, query the names of keys used to store values, and get a count of the number of keys stored in the Session, as we have done in previous chapters.

Similar to the Application object, the Session object also has a StaticObjects collection that stores objects added to the application using the <OBJECT> tag that have a session scope. This collection is discussed in detail in Chapter 10, "Extending ASP with ActiveX Components."

Listing 7-3 provides an example of how you read values stored in the Session object. Note that if your page depends on some critical value, you should always verify that the session is still valid, and take appropriate action if an expected value is not defined because the session timed out or was abandoned — this is a good use of the Session_OnStart handler. Listing 7-3 shows an alternative way of dealing with the problem.

Listing 7–3: Reading values in the Session object

```
<%@ LANGUAGE="JavaScript" %>
<%
if(Session("ok") == null)
{
    Response.Redirect("begin.asp");
}
%>

<HTML>
<HEAD>
<TITLE>Accessing A value</TITLE>
</HEAD>
<BODY>
<%
var sessionCount = Session("sessionCount");

Session("sessionCount") = sessionCount + 1;
Response.Write("You have accessed this page: ".bold()
    + sessionCount + " times.");

%>
</BODY>
</HTML>
```

Before outputting any HTML, the script checks to see if the Session object stores a value for the ok key. If it does, the application assumes it is current and properly initialized, and the page outputs a message informing visitors how many times they've viewed this page. If it doesn't store a value for the ok key, the Session object is redirected to a different page for proper initialization. Initialization code is stored in a page called begin.asp, as follows:

```
<%@ LANGUAGE="JavaScript" %>
<%
Session("ok") = true;
Session("sessionCount") = 0;
Response.Redirect("index.asp");
%>
```

Removing values in a Session object

If you are running IIS 5 or one of its derivative servers, in addition to adding properties to the Session collection you can delete them. Deleting the value un-defines its key, making the value inaccessible. To delete existing values in a Session object, you use the Remove method.

```
Session.Contents.Remove(aName)
```

If you would like to remove all values from the Session object, you could also use the RemoveAll() method, as follows:

```
Session.Contents.RemoveAll();
```

Session properties

The Session object provides four properties that control its behavior:

- CodePage
- LCID
- SessionID
- Timeout

THE CODEPAGE PROPERTY

The CodePage property accesses the character set that the server will use to display information generated by the script. A CodePage is a configuration value that you can use to ensure that your scripts generate output that uses appropriate alphanumeric characters for the locale. Unless you are developing multilingual sites, this feature is probably not all that useful to your application.

```
' Read the current codepage
Dim prevousCodePage = Session.CodePage
' Set the code page to American English
Session.CodePage = 1252
```

THE LCID PROPERTY

The `LCID` property sets the locale identifier. This property allows you to control how the server will format elements like dates and times. Instead of hard-coding locale-specific date and time formats, you can let the server apply the correct formatting for you. In addition to controlling how dates and times are formatted, the locale identifier controls the rules used to sort strings. By default, your operating system will set this property to its default value for you, so you don't need to worry about this. However, there might be times when you want your scripts to control how the information is displayed.

Listing 7-4 provides an example that shows how the formatting of date and time information changes depending on the locale identifier.

Listing 7-4: Formatting date and time information with LCID

```
<%@ LANGUAGE="VBScript" %>
<HTML>
<HEAD>
<TITLE>Locale</TITLE>
</HEAD>
<BODY>
<%
Dim date

date = Now

' Set the LCID to US English formatting
Session.LCID = 1033

Response.Write(
  "In the U.S. the date is written like this: "& date &"<BR>")

' Set the LCID for French formatting
Session.LCID = 1036

Response.Write(
  "In France the date is written like this: "& date &"<BR>")

%>
</BODY>
</HTML>
```

Following is the output generated by the script shown in Listing 7-4:

```
In the U.S.A. the date is written like this: 12/20/99 5:34:15 PM
In France the date is written like this: 20/12/99 17:34:15
```

THE SESSIONID PROPERTY

The SessionID allows you to read the session identifier assigned to the current visitor. The browser saves the SessionID identifier until either the user restarts the browser or the Webserver is restarted. This implies that even if the Session object was destroyed because of a time-out, the server will continue to use this SessionID (using a new Session object). The server reuses the SessionID previously assigned to a visitor to minimize the number of cookies sent to the browser.

If the server restarts, it is possible that the SessionID is not unique. For this reason, your application should not rely on the SessionID value as a unique key. SessionID uniqueness is *not* guaranteed between Web server restarts.

The following example displays the SessionID (shown in bold) assigned by the server to your session:

```
<%@ LANGUAGE="VBSCRIPT" %>
<HTML>
<HEAD>
<TITLE>SessionId</TITLE>
</HEAD>
<BODY>
<FONT SIZE="24">Your session id is: <%= Session.SessionID %></FONT>
</BODY>
</HTML>
```

THE TIMEOUT PROPERTY

The Timeout property controls how long the server will maintain a Session object for the visitor. The Timeout property is a shared property of all Session objects in your application, not just the session where a script changed its value.

By default, sessions have a default time-out of 20 minutes. If a visitor does not access the application within 20 minutes of the last request, the session is destroyed. This time-out can be extended or reduced by setting the Session.Timeout property to the number of minutes you'd like the server to maintain state for a visitor, as shown in the following example:

```
Session.Timeout = 5
```

Setting the time-out value to a different value is something that should be done with care, as this property affects the amount of memory the server requires to keep track of visitors. The longer the time-out, the more memory the server will require to maintain sessions. If shorter, a user's session could be prematurely destroyed, even if the user was just busy on a phone call. Making the time-out interval longer could also have adverse effects as the server will have to maintain information longer than it may need to.

The Session method

The session object provides only one method, Abandon(), which allows you to abandon a Session. If your application has an *end* page, a place where the application has gone through a run, and you know that the user won't be back, you can help the server better use its resources by forcefully expiring the session with a call to Session.Abandon().

If not called, the Session object will be abandoned when it times out. Note that calling Session.Abandon() doesn't destroy the session until after all scripts on the current page have been executed, so you can continue to access the Session object until your page has finished processing. Future requests by the same visitor will access a new session. Listing 7-5 illustrates this.

Listing 7-5: Abandoning a session

```
<%@ LANGUAGE="JavaScript" %>
<HTML>
<HEAD>
<TITLE>Abandoning a Session</TITLE>
</HEAD>
<BODY>
<%
Session.Abandon();
var sessionCount = Session("sessionCount");

if(sessionCount == null)
{
    Response.Write("<P>Initializing sessionCount (it was null)");
    sessionCount = 1;
}
Session("sessionCount") = sessionCount + 1;
Response.Write("<P>You have accessed this page: ".bold()
+ sessionCount + " time(s). If you reload the page " +
"the count will revert to 1");
%>
</BODY>
</HTML>
```

When the session is abandoned, it is queued for destruction. However, within the same page, your scripts can continue to access the Session object.

Working Around Multiple Server Gotchas

One way to increase the performance of a Web application is to add more Web servers that can serve up your application. The redundant servers are configured into a cluster. From the visitor's point of view there's only one server; however, all work is distributed between the nodes in the cluster.

The one issue with this type of configuration is that because the Session object for one particular visitor is managed in one particular server, connecting to a different server can create an error for the visitor, as the other servers don't have access to this visitor's session.

The solution to this problem is to guarantee that future requests from the application are redirected to the server holding the session. The best way to deal with this issue is actually related to HTML more than ASP: Your pages must ensure that any URLs or links referenced by your pages, or redirects generated by your scripts, reference each other using relative paths rather than by writing a fully-qualified URL. If you write fully qualified URLs, when you make a request there's no guarantee that you will get a particular server. Another way is to pass information between your pages so that all the information needed to process the request accompanies the request.

Avoiding Sessions

In your own scripts, you can configure the ASP not to create a Session object. You can do this by inserting the following directive as the first line in your page:

```
<%@ EnableSessionState=False %>
```

This will create a sessionless ASP page that will often be more responsive as ASP won't try to create or restore a session for the visitor. Note that you can still access other ASP objects, but the server won't provide a Session object that you can use.

To maintain state, your application will have to revert to using cookies (see Chapter 13, "Application Persistence") or use URL encoding to pass information you would normally store in the Session object. Of the two mechanisms (cookies and URL encoding) both have limitations on the amount of data that you can store. The real implication is the amount of work that your server needs to do to implement your state-saving mechanism and the amount of work that you need to do to maintain state.

URL encoding, as you know, is portable across all browsers, which is a definite advantage over cookies. However, URL encoding requires more network and server resources, as all links in the application need to encode the visitor's information. Therefore, all links in your pages need to be generated by a script, requiring *all* pages in your application to be scripted. Cookies, however, only need to be set when you change the state, and are transmitted once for each page. As usual, there are combinations and variations that you could implement, including passing a cookie to the browser encoding some ID and using a persistent store such as a database to store the details. In many cases the database access may be negligible (if the database is local to the server so no additional networking is required).

While for many applications sessionless may be the way to go, a sessionless page also defeats the biggest benefit provided by ASP, that of maintaining sessions for you.

Summary

The Session object is a blank object that your applications can use to maintain state for the visitor. While the Session object is one of the greatest benefits provided by ASP, there might be some applications that require you to revert back to the world of URL encoding and setting cookies manually to set state. Fear not, these procedures are much easier to do in ASP than they are in other environments, so either way it's easier here.

Chapter 8

The Server Object

IN THIS CHAPTER

- ◆ Server property
- ◆ Server methods

THE SERVER OBJECT, AS its name indicates, represents the Web server. In this spirit, it provides seven utility methods and one property. These properties and methods are core functions that the Web server uses to process client requests. In this chapter you'll see how this object can be used to control your application flow and to generate HTML and URL-encoded strings.

Server Property: ScriptTimeout

The Server object only provides a single property, ScriptTimeout, that specifies the maximum amount of seconds that a script is allowed to run before the server stops it. Note that this time-out does not take effect while a server component is processing – only your script. By default, the ScriptTimeout property is set to 90 seconds.

A related property, AspScriptTimeout, in the metabase controls the minimum setting that can be specified by the ScriptTimeout property. The default AspScriptTimeout in the metabase is 90 seconds. When setting ScriptTimeout to values less than AspScriptTimeout, the AspScriptTimeout property specifies the correct time-out interval.

If you find that the default time-out is not enough to process a particular type of request and your users are experiencing a server time-out, use the ScriptTimeout property to allow more time for your script to execute, as follows:

```
<%@ LANGUAGE="JScript"%>
<HTML>
<BODY>
<%
  Server.ScriptTimeout = 120;
  Response.Write("This page has a timeout of: " +
      Server.ScriptTimeout);
%>
```

```
</BODY>
</HTML>
```

The above example simply sets the ScriptTimeout property and then echoes its value back to the visitor. If the execution of the page would take longer than 120 seconds, the server would kill the script.

Server Methods

While the Server object is skimpy on properties, it more than makes up for this in functionality because of the methods that it provides. These methods are very useful for implementing your own persistence mechanisms, accessing functionality not built into ASP itself, and controlling flow through your application. Here's what you can do using the Server object's methods:

◆ Create instances of ActiveX/COM components.

◆ Execute an ASP file as if it was part of the current page.

◆ Obtain information about the last error that occurred.

◆ Encode characters such as a quote (") to their HTML counterpart.

◆ Map a path specified in a URL to the actual physical path on the system.

◆ Transfer the execution and built-in object's context in the current page to another ASP script.

◆ Create URL encode strings.

Creating components: CreateObject

The single most important feature to ASP is the CreateObject method of the Server object. This method allows you to *instantiate*, create an instance of, an external component (not built into ASP) so that you can interact with it in your scripts. So far you have seen built-in components provided by ASP. Instances of the built-in components are available for you to use in your scripts without any special scripting. Custom components allow you to create scripts that access functionality not directly built into ASP, such as access to files or databases. By creating an instance of a custom component your scripts have unending flexibility; if a component is available, you can use it and interact with it from within your scripts.

While we will explore components in detail in Chapter 10, "Extending ASP with ActiveX Components," Listing 8-1 provides an example of using the Browser Capabilities component. This component can easily provide you with information about the type of browser the visitor is using to make a request. Using this information, your scripts can generate content that is tuned to the specific browser.

In the Listing 8-1 example, we define a simple function to write values back to the browser. The function adds some simple formatting to the provided input by setting the text provided in the *key* argument to bold, and by adding a <BR> tag to the end of the string provided in the *value* argument. Creating the component is done with the CreateObject method, which is shown in bold in Listing 8-1. The name of the component we are creating is MSWC.BrowserType. We then use some of the many methods provided by this object to extract information about the browser, such as its name, version, whether it supports tables, frames, sounds, VBScript, and JavaScript.

Listing 8-1: Testing browser capabilities with the MSWC.BrowserType component

```
<%@ LANGUAGE="JScript"%>
<HTML>
<BODY
<%
  function write(key, value)
  {
    Response.Write(key.bold() + ": " + value + "<BR>");
  }

  var info = Server.CreateObject("MSWC.BrowserType");

  write("Browser", info.browser);
  write("Browser Version", info.version);
  write("Supports Frames", info.frames);
  write("Supports Tables", info.tables);
  write("Plays Sounds", info.backgroundSounds);
  write("Supports VBScripting", info.vbscript);
  write("Supports JavaScript", info.javascript);
%>
</BODY>
</HTML>
```

For an in-depth look at the components and how to use them, please see Chapter 10, "Extending ASP with ActiveX Components."

Treating script pages as procedures: Execute

The Execute method allows you to treat an ASP file as a procedure. It allows you to execute scripts in a separate page as if they were part of the original script. The Execute method takes as an argument a string specifying the location of the ASP file to execute. If an absolute path is provided, the path must be within the same application space.

The Execute method provides you with an alternative to server-side includes, and it allows you to develop your own collection of reusable modules as simple script pages. Parameters passed to the calling ASP page are available from the executed page. Any output generated by the executed page is added to the output generated by the calling page.

Listing 8-2 shows the code for execute1.asp. This example expects to be called with a query string like this: `http://localhost/aspbook/server/execute1.asp?count=10`; the count option is read by the *executed* asp file.

Listing 8-2: Executing another page

```
<%@ LANGUAGE="JScript"%>
<HTML>
<BODY>
<%
Response.Write("output from execute1<BR>");
Server.Execute("execute2.asp");
Response.Write("output from execute1<BR>");
%>
</BODY>
</HTML>
```

Execute2.asp (shown in bold in Listing 8-2) reads the *count* parameter passed through a query string to the URL of execute1.asp (see Listing 8-3).

Listing 8-3: Reading the count parameter

```
<%@ LANGUAGE="JScript"%>
<%
Response.Write("output from execute2<BR>");

var x = Request.QueryString("count");
var str = "";

for(var i=i; i <= x; i++)
{
   str += i + "<BR>\n";
}

Response.Write(str);
Response.Write("output from execute2<BR>");
%>
```

As you can see by the bold line in Listing 8-3, the query string provided to execute1.asp is accessible from execute2.asp, which then counts to the number specified and writes out some output. The output generated is shown in Listing 8-4.

Listing 8-4: Output generated by the script shown in Listing 8-3

```
<HTML>
<BODY>
output from execute1
output from execute2
1
2
3
4
5
6
7
8
9
10
output from execute2
output from execute1
</BODY>
</HTML>
```

Creating your own custom errors page: GetLastError

The `GetLastError` method returns an `ASPError` object that describes the last error that occurred in the script. This mechanism can only be used from within an error-type page. If you have been programming your own ASP pages while reading this book, no doubt you have seen the error report generated by the 500-100.asp page telling you about the reason for your error. The Web server serves this page whenever an error occurs during the processing of script (preprocessing, compiling, or run time). This page makes use of the `GetLastError` method to display additional information about the error that may be useful to you, the developer, to fix. By default this ASP page is located in C:\WINNT\Help\iisHelp\common\500-100.asp.

IIS allows you to define your own error pages that trap these sorts of errors by assigning a custom ASP page to display information about the error. You can easily do this using the Internet Information Services tool and selecting properties on your Web application (or on your Web site), clicking on the Custom Errors tab in the Properties window that appears, and assigning a new URL to the error labeled 500-100. The page you specify here will be sent to the visitor if your script raises a preprocessing, compilation, or run time type error. Listing 8-5 provides an example of an error page. The `GetLastError()` method is shown in bold.

Listing 8-5: A custom error page

```
<%@ LANGUAGE="JScript"%>

<%
function write(key, value)
{
   Response.Write(key.bold() + ": " + value + "<BR>\n");
}

var error = Server.GetLastError();
%>

<HTML>
<BODY>
<%

write("ASPCode", error.ASPCode);
write("Number", error.Number);
write("Source", error.Source);
write("Category", error.Category);
write("File", error.File);
write("Line", error.Line);
write("Column", error.Column);
write("Description", error.Description);
write("ASPDescription", error.ASPDescription);
%>
```

Following is an example of a script that would generate a compilation error:

```
<%@ LANGUAGE="JScript"%>
<%
fr(var i=0; i < 10; i++)
{
   Response.Write(i + "<BR>");
}
%>
```

Note that line 3 in the previous script has an error (`fr` instead of `for`). If the page containing this script is run, our error handling page is executed, producing the following output:

```
ASPCode:
Number: -2146827286
Source: fr(var i=0; i < 10; i++)
Category: Microsoft JScript compilation
```

```
File: /aspbook/server/error.asp
Line: 3
Column: 3
Description: Syntax error
ASPDescription:
```

Encoding HTML: HTMLEncode

As you know, characters such as the greater- and less-than symbols, quotes, ampersands, and so forth are special to HTML. To print these characters in HTML you have to convert these characters to their HTML equivalent escape sequences (>, <, ", and &). The HTMLEncode method simplifies this process for you. If you provide a string that contains these illegal characters, the method will return to you the same string with the illegal characters converted to their appropriate HTML versions, as follows:

```
<%@ LANGUAGE="JScript"%>
<HTML>
<BODY>
<%
var text = "The <BR> tag adds a new line";
text = Server.HTMLEncode(text);
Response.Write(text);
%>
```

The server prints an HTML correct version of the string, without interpreting the <BR> sequence as an HTML break, as follows:

```
</BODY>
</HTML>
<HTML>
<BODY>
The &lt;BR&gt; tag adds a new line
</BODY>
</HTML>
```

This method is especially useful when you are generating content from a database or some other source. By passing this content through this method, you can ensure that any illegal characters are properly mapped to their proper HTML counterparts.

Mapping a resource to a file path: MapPath

The MapPath method converts a URL to the actual file path to the resource on the server. The server performs this operation with every request it handles. Unless you are developing an application that manages a file structure, you probably won't use this feature; however, it is interesting to see how the server does this.

```
<%@ LANGUAGE="JScript"%>
<HTML>
<BODY>
<%
var thisPageURL = Request.ServerVariables("PATH_INFO");
var filePath = Server.MapPath(thisPageURL);

Response.Write("The URL " + thisPageURL +
"<BR> is located: " + filePath );
%>
</BODY>
</HTML>
```

The previous script reads the URL requested by the browser (the URL to this script page) from the server variable PATH_INFO, and it then translates that URL to the actual file on the server using the MapPath method. The result of running this script on my system yields the following result:

```
The URL /aspbook/server/mappath.asp
is located: C:\users\aricart\myweb\server\mappath.asp
```

Note that displaying information to visitors about your Web server's file structure is probably not a good idea. By doing so, you can create a situation where you provide information that could be used for foul play against your system. Using this functionality without exposing the file structure can be very useful in an application that allows a visitor to store files on your server and provides an interface for accessing these files over HTTP.

Transferring to a different script: Transfer

The Transfer method transfers control to a different ASP page. The page's context, values you may have added to the Session or Application objects, are also transferred. If you transfer to a page in a different application, the ASP page will execute as if it was running in the application that contains the call to the Transfer method. Unlike the Execute method, calling Transfer doesn't return you back to the transferring page. The example in Listing 8-6 does the actual transfer. On reaching the Transfer method, execution of the program is transferred to the script, as shown in Listing 8-7.

Listing 8-6: Using the Transfer method

```
<%@ LANGUAGE="JScript"%>

<HTML>
<BODY>
<%
```

```
Session("myInfo") = 12;
Server.Transfer("/aspbook2/transfer2.asp");
%>
</BODY>
</HTML>
```

Listing 8-7: Transferring program execution to the script

```
<%@ LANGUAGE="JScript"%>
<%@ LANGUAGE="JScript"%>
<HTML>
<BODY>
<%
Response.Write("Session.myInfo: " + Session("myInfo"));
%>
</BODY>
</HTML>
```

Note that in this example the first page transfers control to the second after setting up the myInfo value in the Session object. The transfer is actually to a script in a different Web application on the same server. The server transfers the Session object providing a context that allows the script on the second page to access the value set by the first. From the visitor's perspective, the request was serviced by the first page.

Encoding values in HTML: URLEncode

The URLEncode method encodes a string that you provide into its equivalent URL-encoded version. A URL-encoded string can be placed inside of a link. URL encoding works by removing illegal characters such as spaces, ampersands, plus symbols, and so on with their appropriate URL-escaped versions. (See Listing 8-8.)

Listing 8-8: URL encoding strings

```
<%@ LANGUAGE="JScript"%>
<HTML>
<BODY>
<%
  var title = "Active Server Pages 3.0";
  var authors = "Alberto Ricart & Stephen Asbury";

  var encTitle = Server.URLEncode(title);
  var encAuthors = Server.URLEncode(authors);

  var url = "find.asp?title=" + encTitle + "&" +
"authors=" + encAuthors;
%>
```

```
<A HREF=<%=url %>>Click here to find the book</A>
</BODY>
</HTML>
```

The Listing 8-8 script example generates a URL-encoded URL, whose values for the title and authors parameters can be retrieved by another ASP script using the `Request.QueryString()` method. Here's the HTML that the script generates:

```
<HTML>
<BODY>
<A HREF=find.asp?title=Active+Server+Pages+3%2E0&authors=
Alberto+Ricart+%26+Stephen+Asbury>Click here to find the book</A>
</BODY>
</HTML>
```

Note that spaces were translated into plus signs (+); the period in 3.0 was translated into its hexadecimal value, preceded by a percent sign (%); and the ampersand between Ricart and Stephen was also translated to its hexadecimal value. Typical characters that are encoded include: +, <, >, %, ", /, ?, and space. While generally only the previous characters are encoded, *all* characters in the URL could be encoded even if this is not required.

Summary

The Server object provides many utility-type functions that enable you to easily replace standard characters with their HTML counterparts, generate URL-encoded strings, execute and transfer control to a different ASP script, create instances of ActiveX objects, control time-outs, and get additional information about an error in a script. Features like creating instances of ActiveX components and URL encoding strings are fundamental to most of the script pages you'll develop.

Chapter 9

A Prototypical Application

IN THIS CHAPTER

◆ A Web-based chat room

◆ Features to implement

SO FAR YOU HAVE SEEN bits and pieces of how a Web application goes together. Without getting bogged down in a fancy example, it is time to take a look at a simple Web application that puts some of the basic concepts you have learned to work. This chapter will walk you through creating a simple chat room application, including the login process, posting and reading messages, and expiring stale clients.

A Web-based Chat Room

For the application we'll develop a simple chat room–type Web application. A chat room is a place where different visitors meet and interact by typing messages and utterances. Visitors see everyone else's messages and join in a discussion about some topic.

While Web technology can provide an infrastructure for chat rooms, this example is merely that: an example that shows some ASP in action. A real chat room application would probably require the aid of a Java applet to reduce the load of the Web server. Our chat room implementation relies on polling to see new messages. With each poll, the visitor downloads a new page that lists the current utterances from other visitors. The polling is performed every two seconds, and the more visitors on the chat room the more work the Web server will have to perform.

Features to Implement

An example of the completed chat room application in a browser is shown in Figure 9-1. On the left side the visitor enters a message, and the last 25 postings display on the right side. Our chat room will offer the following features:

◆ Users will be required to log in by providing their name. No duplicate names are allowed in the room.

◆ To keep it simple, the application will only keep track of a discrete number of messages. When the maximum number of messages has been reached, the oldest message will be discarded.

◆ Users that are inactive because they left the site will be automatically removed from the chat room.

◆ Utterances of each visitor will be presented in different colors to help distinguish them from other visitors.

◆ For security purposes, the visitor's name will be displayed along with the IP address from their browser.

◆ Visitors will be able to log out of the chat room at will.

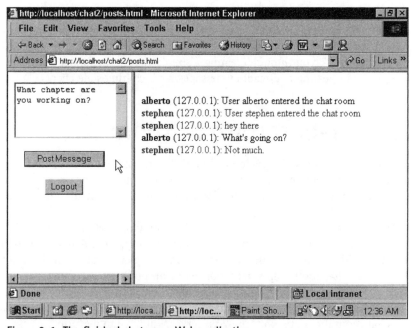

Figure 9-1: The finished chat room Web application

A proof of concept

The first version of this application is somewhat crude. Some of the code is duplicated in different pages. While this may be okay for many little one-shot applications, it doesn't make for very good engineering for the following reasons:

◆ When the implementation changes, all pages in the application will have to be checked to ensure that something was not broken along the way.

◆ Code tends to be messy and hard to reuse.

Once we get the hang of the application, we'll take a second crack at it and make use of some advanced JavaScript features to abstract and generalize the application a little.

Logging into the chat room

Login to the chat room is a straightforward task. We'll develop an HTML form that captures the visitor's login name, processes the input by validating the input, and performs other simple application tasks. Following is the HTML for the form, which is stored in a file named login.html:

```
<HTML>
<BODY>
<CENTER>
<FORM method="POST" action="login.asp">
Login: <INPUT type="text" name="username">
<INPUT type="SUBMIT" value="Enter">
</FORM>
</CENTER>
</BODY>
</HTML>
```

The form has only two controls: a text field called username and a button that displays the word "Enter" on it. When the button is clicked, the contents of the form are packaged by the visitor's browser and sent as arguments to the login.asp URL within the same application. Because the form was designated as a POST form, the user input will be invisible (there's no query string). This will have some implications as to how we read them on the login.asp page.

Next we'll take a look at the login.asp page that will process the input from the login.html form. Following is the code with interspersed commentary:

```
<%@ LANGUAGE="JScript"%>
```

First we define an array of colors. This array will store a list of HTML standard colors. We will use this list to assign a color to the visitor. All of the visitor's utterances will be colored with the assigned color.

```
<%
    var colors = new Array("black", "red", "lime", "blue",
    "magenta", "yellow", "cyan", "teal", "olive", "purple",
    "navy", "green", "maroon", "gray", "silver");
```

Next we define a simple utility function that we'll use to test if a value is empty, null, or undefined. In JavaScript testing, to see if a variable has a value is tricky for a couple of reasons. Unlike other programming languages where if a value has not been assigned the default value is null, in JavaScript a variable that has not been initialized is *undefined*. New versions of JavaScript (ECMAScript) define an undefined type that can be used in an expression to test if the variable is undefined. Alas, ASP's JScript interpreter is not aware of this keyword and thinks that you are referring to an undeclared variable and throws an error. To circumvent this issue we test to see if the variable equals the string "undefined". Since we will use this function in other places, we add tests for null and an empty string.

```
function isSet(val)
{
  var tf = true;

  if(val == "undefined" || val == null || val == "")
  {
    tf = false;
  }

  return tf;
}
```

In our application, we use the username that the user provided as a key on the Application object. To avoid duplicate visitors from using the same name we check to ensure that the value is not defined in the Application object. If the Application object returns a real value, then the key, the username, exists and the new visitor should choose another one. Here's the function that encapsulates this test:

```
function isUnique(username)
{
  return ! isSet(Application(username));
}
```

The Application object will also keep track of a count of visitors to use the application. This number will be used to select a unique color to display the visitor's messages. Note that while this function reads and sets a shared value in the Application object, concurrency handling – calling Lock() and Unlock() – on the application is left for the calling code. This strategy is followed throughout in the application. If there's a concurrency issue that should be handled, the calling code should Lock() and Unlock() as necessary.

```
function getNextID()
  {
    var id = Application("nextID");

    if(isSet(id) == false)
    {
```

```
    id = 1;
  }

  Application("nextID") = id + 1;

  return id;
}
```

Error handling is performed by a function that clears all output that has been collected in the Response buffer, writes an error message, and terminates processing of the page. While this approach is simplistic, it works well. The message can be anything you want, including HTML content, as follows:

```
function handleError(message)
{
  Response.Clear();
  Response.Write(message);
  Response.End();
}
```

Finally we get to our script and process the username entered by the visitor. First we check to see if the current session already defines a username. If it does, the visitor has already logged in and we ignore the new username provided. We then use redirection to send them to a page where they can make a new posting.

```
if(isSet(Session("username")))
{
    Response.Redirect("post.asp");
}
```

 On your version you can use the Transfer method on the Server object. We didn't do this here because this object is new to ASP 3.0 and this would require maintaining separate versions of the chat room for other servers.

If we are still processing this script (the script was not redirected), then we read the information entered by the visitor. We read the value for the username field in the form from the Form collection. We use the Form collection because the contents of the form are submitted using POST. Otherwise, we would have used the QueryString collection.

We validate that the user entered some information. If the form didn't provide a value, we use the handleError() function described earlier to print an error message and terminate the script processing. Note that we add a blank string to whatever is returned from Request.Form("username") because sometimes the value returned by such a call cannot be directly added to an ASP collection, like the Application object. Adding the empty string forces the object to be evaluated as a string and tickles things into working correctly.

```
var username = Request.Form("username") + "";

if(isSet(username) == false)
{
  handleError("Username must not be empty!");
}
```

If the script is still running we have passed most of our validation tests. We now prepare to work with the Application object. Since we will be reading and writing values to this shared object, we need to ensure that other clients are prevented from performing similar modifications while we are working. We use the Lock() method of the Application object to obtain an exclusive right on it. If another client attempts the same code, their script will wait until we complete.

The first test we perform is to see if the username provided by the visitor is unique using the isUnique() function described earlier. If the username is not unique, we first Unlock() the application so others can continue their work, and then use our handleError() function to display a message and terminate the script.

If the username provided by the visitor is unique (it doesn't exist in the Application's Contents collection), we request the next ID using the getNextID() function that was listed earlier. Because the call is operating inside of the Application.Lock() call, we can ensure that no other clients will read and modify the counter while we work with it. After obtaining the next ID, we perform a simple manipulation; we map the id value (an always increasing number) to an index number in the colors array. By using the modulo operator (%) and dividing by the number of elements in the array, we obtain a number between 0 and the greatest index in the array, effectively assigning a number that we can map to a color in the color array. The accessing of the array at that index produces the color name, which we then save in the Application object under the username. After properly setting up this environment, we Unlock() the Application object and redirect the browser to post.asp, which allows the visitor to post a message. This part of the login.asp page is shown in Listing 9-1.

Listing 9-1: Saving the color name and redirecting to post.asp

```
Application.Lock();

if(isUnique(username))
{
  var id = getNextID();
  var index = id % colors.length;
  Session("username") = username;
  Application(username) = colors[index];
```

```
  }
  else
  {
    Application.Unlock();
    handleError("The username: '" + username + "' is in use, please
choose a different one.");
  }

  Application.Unlock();
  Response.Redirect("post.asp");

%>
```

Posting messages

In post.asp we show an alternative way of handling form input. Experienced developers typically combine the HTML form and the ASP page to process the form under the same ASP page. There are some merits to doing it this way. One is that code and form live on the same document. In terms of performance, you may want to keep the HTML form and the ASP in separate documents for a loaded server. The reason for this is that the Web server can serve a static HTML page several times faster than it can serve an ASP page. Think about it. For a plain HTML page, the server basically reads the file from disk and spits it out as quickly as it can. The ASP page, on the other hand, needs to be processed. This takes time. However, sometimes it really doesn't matter that much, and the convenience outweighs the decrease in performance. Listing 9-2 provides the beginning part of the page, and interspersed comments follow.

Listing 9-2: Testing if a value is set, null, or an empty string

```
<%@ LANGUAGE="JScript"%>

<%

  var MAX_POSTS = 25;

  function isSet(val)
  {
    var tf = true;

    if(val == null || val == "undefined" || val == "")
    {
      tf = false;
    }
```

```
    return tf;
}


var username = Session("username");
var wasAnnounced = Session("wasAnnounced");
var newMessage = Request.Form("message") + "";
var wantsLogout = Request.Form("wantsExit");
var senderIP = Request.ServerVariables("REMOTE_ADDR");
```

As in the previous page, we inefficiently duplicate the code for the isSet() function, which we use to test if a value is set or if it contains null or an empty string. We also define a constant called MAX_POSTS that sets the maximum number of posts that the chat room will store. In our case we'll only store the last 25 messages.

Next we read the values for username and wasAnnounced stored in the Session object. The first value is the value entered by the user when they log in. The second value is a flag that allows the program to know if this is the first time the page is loaded. We'll use this flag to write a message telling other visitors when a new visitor enters the chat room.

We then proceed to read values that we expect from a form. The first time the page is loaded, the form won't ever send any information, as the form definition occurs at the end of this page. To provide additional information about the user, we read the REMOTE_ADDR server address so that we can display the IP number where the visitor is visiting.

Next we validate these values. If the username is not set, the user didn't log in, so we redirect them back to the right page. This sort of error should not happen unless the visitor is typing or bookmarking URLs. This test ensures that our program can adjust itself for this possibility. If the username is set, we retrieve the color stored in the Application object under the user's name. You may ask yourself why wouldn't we store the color value in the Session? The answer is we probably should do this. The reason we didn't is that this allows us to easily enhance the chat room to provide a list of current visitors, since this information is stored in the Application object. The more important reason is that we want to ensure unique user names in the session. So long as we need to keep track of the visitors, we might as well store some useful value that we can use.

```
if(isSet(username) == false)
{
    Response.Redirect("login.html");
}
else
{
    color = Application(username);
}
```

The next section of code tests to see if the Session flag wasAnnounced is set. If it is, the visitor has already been announced. Otherwise, we generate a new program-generated post that informs visitors of the new user and updates the wasAnnounced flag so we can ignore this step on the next execution of the page.

```
if(isSet(wasAnnounced) == false)
{
  newMessage = "User " + username + " entered the chat room.";
  Session("wasAnnounced") = true;
}
```

The form provides the user with a control that allows the user to exit the room. If the user clicks the Logout button on the form, the submit button of that form will have the value of "Logout" and we can easily detect when the user wants out. If the user wants out, we reuse the wantsLogout variable to have a true value, and set the current message to be an exit message. Otherwise, we set the value of the flag to false.

```
if(isSet(wantsLogout))
{
  if(wantsLogout == "Logout")
  {
    wantsLogout = true;
    newMessage = "User " + username + " exited the chat room.";
  }
  else
  {
    wantsLogout = false;
  }
}
```

Finally, we check to see if a message was provided by the user (or programmatically set by this page). If no message is set, the portion of the script that actually does the work is ignored. Otherwise, we start the posting operation.

Posting requires that we write a value to a shared value in the Application object. Because we are writing, we need to ensure that the value of this object is not written by anyone else while we complete the operation, so we Lock() the application.

Next we try to read a value from the application stored in the Contents collection under "messages". The "messages" string is a character-delimited string containing the last 25 posts in the application. If we fail to read the string, this is the first time the application is being used, so we initialize the string to an empty string.

```
if(isSet(newMessage))
{
  Application.Lock();
```

```
var messages = Application("messages");

if(isSet(messages) == false)
{
  messages = "";
}
```

Next we use the String's `split()` method to split the string into an array of strings. Splitting will be performed whenever the character sequence "{,}" is found. It is unlikely that a visitor would enter these characters on a message, so this is why we choose them. With a little more work you can remove any tab characters entered as part of the message and use a tab as the message separator. For purposes of this example we have eliminated the validation and escaping of delimiter characters. Given the input "One{,}Two{,}Three" the split method would return an array with three elements storing the values "One", "Two", "Three". Note that our delimiting characters were removed from the string.

Next we get a count of elements in the messages array. If the size of the array is 25 elements or larger, we use the `slice()` method to extract a subarray that copies from index one to the maximum number of elements in the array, effectively getting rid of the first element at index zero.

```
messages = messages.split("{,}");

var size = messages.length;
if(size >= MAX_POSTS)
{
  messages = messages.slice(1);
  size = messages.length;
}
```

After recalculating the number of elements in the messages array, we format the message. The message will contain the name of the user in bold, followed by the IP address where the user is coming from, followed by the message entered into the form. This message is added to the bottom of the array, and the array is converted back into a long string with array elements separated by our delimiter sequence "{,}". The reason we do this is that the various server object collections cannot store JavaScript objects, so we store the array as a string. If we were using VBScript, then we could use an array and forego the `split()`/`join()` ritual.

```
newMessage = username.bold() + " (" + senderIP + "): " +
        newMessage;
newMessage = newMessage.fontcolor(color);

messages[size] = newMessage;

Application("messages") = messages.join("{,}");
```

If the user had requested a logout, the wantsLogout would be set to true. If it were, we would abandon the session, effectively destroying the Session object for the visitor, and redirect the browser to the login page. Finally we Unlock() the application and allow other visitors to do their processing.

```
if(wantsLogout)
{
  Session.Abandon();
  Response.Redirect("login.html");
}

Application.UnLock();
}

%>
```

After the script executes, we print the form using plain HTML to the browser. You can see in Listing 9-3 that our form is really made of two forms. The first is the posting form and it provides a text area and a submit button. The second form, mapped to the same URL, only has a submit button with a value set to "Logout".

Listing 9-3: Printing two forms to the browser

```
<HTML>
<BODY>
<CENTER>
<FORM method="post" action="post.asp">
<TEXTAREA name="message" rows="5" cols="20"
wrap="virtual"></TEXTAREA>
<BR>
<INPUT type="submit" value="Post Message">
</FORM>
<FORM method="post" action="post.asp">
<INPUT type="submit" name="wantsExit" value="Logout">
</FORM>
</CENTER>
</BODY>
</HTML>
```

While this may look like tricky code, it isn't. We rely on the fact that if the script is called with no input, nothing really happens, and the HTML form is printed to the screen. If the form called the script, then we execute the script and perform the posting and finalize the run by reprinting the form to allow the visitor to enter a new posting!

Reading postings

So far we have not seen how we read postings. It would be helpful to understand that our application is running in a frame. To the left side we have the login and posting forms and on the right side we have a list of the current messages. The frameset document looks like the following:

```
<HTML>
<FRAMESET cols="200,*">
<FRAME name="postform" src="post.asp">
<FRAME name="messages" src="messages.asp">
</FRAMESET>
</HTML>
```

Because our post.asp page validates itself, remember that post.asp redirects itself to the login form (login.html) if no username was provided, page management is simplified. Actual display of the messages is performed by another ASP page called messages.asp. Here's the code to messages.asp:

```
<%@ LANGUAGE="JScript"%>

<%
  Response.AddHeader("Refresh", "2");
%>
```

Because HTTP doesn't provide a way to "push" information to a browser, we have to fake the "push" with a "pull." Our browser will reload a page every two seconds. We accomplish this using Response's AddHeader() method. The first argument tells the name of the HTTP header to add, and the second tells the value assigned to it. When the browser loads this page, it will know that in two seconds it should reload the page from the server, essentially displaying information that might have changed since the last request.

To the visitor this looks as if information was updated when someone adds a message in the chat room. But in effect we have a two-to-three second latency between the time of a post and the time we see a new posting. A real chat room would replace this "pull" code with an applet. The applet could open a socket and listen on a known port, and whenever someone adds a new message the applet would update its display. The advantages of such a mechanism would be scalability, as the applet could potentially use a single network transmission (a UDP broadcast, or multicast) to update all clients at once. The other advantage is that updates would only happen if they were necessary. Given the technology focus is ASP, pulling is the only way we can do this, as follows:

```
<HTML>
<BODY>
```

```
<%
  function isSet(val)
  {
    var tf = true;

    if(val == "undefined" || val == null || val == "")
    {
      tf = false;
    }

    return tf;
  }
```

Similar to the other pages, we read the messages entry in the Application object's Contents collection. Note that we are not performing any Lock()/Unlock() here. The reason is because we are not updating the value in any way. Even if someone is in the process of setting a new value, we don't want to wait for this to complete. Any new changes we'll pick up with the next update. This makes the page more responsive and requires less work from the server.

If the chat room has no visitors (we are the first), then we end the processing of the script as there's really nothing to do. Otherwise, we split the message string as we did before and print each message on its own line by appending a <BR> tag at the end, as demonstrated in the portion shown in Listing 9-4.

Listing 9-4: Splitting the message string

```
  var messages = Application("messages");


  if(isSet(messages) == false)
  {
    Response.End();
  }

  messages = messages.split("{,}");

  var size = messages.length;

  for(var i=0; i < size; i++)
  {
    Response.Write(messages[i] + "<BR>\n");
  }

%>

</BODY>
</HTML>
```

As you can see, reading the postings is easy from the code perspective. The work is really performed by the refreshing of the page every two seconds.

Expiring stale clients

One last consideration for our application is what happens when a client disconnects without first logging out. Because our application is keeping track of different usernames, we need to provide some way of cleaning up our application once those sessions expire. The way we handle this is by adding a global.asa file with a Session_OnEnd handler. Note that we have included the code for isSet() in this file as well, as follows:

```
<SCRIPT LANGUAGE="JScript" RUNAT="server">
  var MAX_POSTS = 25;

  function isSet(val)
  {
    var tf = true;

    if(val == null || val == "undefined" || val == "")
    {
      tf = false;
    }

    return tf;
  }
```

Cleanup is performed by the Session_OnEnd handler, which gets called when a session is abandoned or expires on its own. Our handler posts a message using the same techniques that we showed earlier, so some of the code will be familiar. The handler is shown in Listing 9-5.

Listing 9-5: Cleaning up a session

```
function Session_OnEnd()
{
  var username = Session("username");
  var color = Application(username);
  var message = "User " + username + "'s session terminated.";

  Application.Lock();

  var messages = Application("messages");
  if(isSet(messages) == false)
  {
    messages = "";
  }
```

```
messages = messages.split("{,}");

var size = messages.length;
if(size >= MAX_POSTS)
{
   messages = messages.slice(1);
   size = messages.length;
}

message = username.bold() + ": " + message;
message = message.fontcolor(color);

messages[size] = message;

Application("messages") = messages.join("{,}");
```

After posting a message, we clean the Application object's Contents collection by calling its `Remove` method. This essentially destroys a reference to the user, thus cleaning our application of stale entries.

```
Application.Contents.Remove(username);

Application.UnLock();
}
```

The `Session_OnStart()` handler will get called the first time the Session object is accessed on the application. This handler simply sets the Session's time-out to one minute instead of the default ten minutes. While one minute may seem short, remember that the messages.asp page refreshes every two seconds, effectively resetting the timer forever so long as the visitor's browser is focused on the site.

```
function Session_OnStart()
{
   Session.Timeout = 1;
}

</SCRIPT>
```

A better version

While the version we listed works fine, there are some issues with it. First, there's duplication of code. Change one thing, and there are many other things that you need to check to ensure that you didn't break anything. The other issue is a matter of style. The operations for logging in, adding messages, and logging out could be easily encapsulated into an object, as shown in Listing 9-6. Doing so would simplify the pages to extracting form data and calling methods on a custom object. This approach is much less cluttered and feels better. The following subsections show what our pages would look like if the functionality of the chat room was black boxed to an object.

Listing 9-6: The custom chat room object

```jscript
<SCRIPT LANGUAGE="JScript" RUNAT="server">

function isSet(val)
{
    var tf = true;

    if(val == "undefined" || val == null || val == "")
    {
        tf = false;
    }

    return tf;
}

function handleError(message)
{
    Response.Clear();
    Response.Write(message);
    Response.End();
}

function getMessages()
{
    var messageStr = Application("messages");

    if(isSet(messageStr) == false)
    {
        messageStr = "";
    }

    this.messages = messageStr.split("\n");

    return this.messages;
}

function addMessage(newMessage)
{

    Application.Lock();
```

```
    this.getMessages();

    newMessage = newMessage.split("\n");
    newMessage = newMessage.join("<BR>");

    newMessage = this.username.bold() + " (" +
    Request.ServerVariables("REMOTE_ADDR") +
      "): " + newMessage;

    newMessage = newMessage.fontcolor(this.usercolor);


    var size = this.messages.length;

    if(size >= this.MAX_POSTS)
    {
        this.messages = this.messages.slice(1);
        size = this.messages.length;
    }

    this.messages[size] = newMessage;

    Application("messages") = this.messages.join("\n");

    Application.Unlock();
}

function login()
{
    Application.Lock();

    if(isSet(Application(this.username)))
    {
        Application.Unlock();
        this.handleError(this.username + " is already registered");
    }

    var id = this.getNextID();
    var index = id % this.colors.length;

    Session("username") = this.username;
    Application(this.username) = this.colors[index];
    this.usercolor = this.colors[index];

    this.addMessage("User " + this.username +
```

```
        " entered the chat room");

        Application.Unlock();
}

function logout()
{
    this.addMessage("User " + this.username +
    " has left the chat room");

    Application.Lock();

    Application.Contents.Remove(this.username);

    Application.Unlock();

    Session.Abandon();
}

function getColor(username)
{
    return this.usercolor;
}



function getNextID()
{
    var id = Application("nextID");

    if(isSet(id) == false)
    {
        id = 0;
    }

    Application("nextID") = id + 1;

    return id;
}


function printMessages()
{
    var html = "";
```

```
var entries = this.getMessages();

for(var i=0; i < entries.length; i++)
{
    html += entries[i] + "<BR>\n";
}

Response.Write(html);
}
```

All the references to `this` that you see in the functions shown in Listing 9-6 imply properties that are defined as part of the object, the object being *messaged*. The way you define a custom object is to create a function named after the object and then define a series of properties by starting the property name with `this`, as shown in Listing 9-7. This blesses the property as part of the object rather than as a variable. Adding methods to the object is just a matter of saying `this.methodName = function`, where `methodName` is the name of the method the user will use to call the method, and `functionName` is the name the method maps to (note that the parentheses are not provided).

Listing 9-7: Defining object properties

```
function ChatRoom(username)
{
    this.messages = null;
    this.username = username;
    this.usercolor = null;
    this.MAX_POSTS = 25;
    this.colors = new Array("black", "red", "lime",
      "blue", "magenta", "teal", "olive", "purple",
      "navy", "green", "maroon");


    this.isSet = isSet;
    this.handleError = handleError;
    this.login = login;
    this.logout = logout;
    this.getNextID = getNextID;
    this.getMessages = getMessages;
    this.printMessages = printMessages;
    this.addMessage = addMessage;
    this.getColor = getColor;

    if(isSet(username))
    {
        this.usercolor = Application(username);
```

```
    }
}
```

```
</SCRIPT>
```

The simple abstraction of making a ChatRoom object makes all the difference in the world when it comes time to maintain and manage the application. The interface for the different functionality was a collection of disparate scripts. This was messy. Our new version is now an object with a nice and tidy API.

The great benefit of this abstraction is obvious on the script listings that follow. Most scripts are minimal because the object takes care of everything. This is just an example, but it comes closer to what your ASP code should look like, and will allow you to maintain simplicity, clarity, and generality in your code, which is a good thing.

THE LOGIN PAGE: LOGIN.HTML

The login page is shown in Listing 9-8.

Listing 9-8: The login page

```html
<HTML>
<BODY>
<CENTER>
<FORM method="POST" action="login.asp">
Login: <INPUT type="text" name="username">
<INPUT type="SUBMIT" value="Enter">
</FORM>
</CENTER>
</BODY>
</HTML>
```

The login.asp is shown in Listing 9-9.

Listing 9-9: The login.asp page

```
<%@ LANGUAGE="JScript"%>

<!-- #include file="ChatRoom.js" -->

<%
  var username = Request.Form("username") + "";

  if(isSet(Session("username")))
  {
    Response.Redirect("post.asp");
  }
```

```
if(isSet(username) == false)
{
  handleError("Username must not be empty!");
}

var room = new ChatRoom(username);
room.login();

Response.Redirect("post.asp");
```

```
%>
```

The post.asp page is shown in Listing 9-10.

Listing 9-10: The post.asp page

```
<%@ LANGUAGE="JScript"%>

<!-- #include file="ChatRoom.js" -->

<%

  var room = null;
  var username = Session("username");
  var newMessage = Request.Form("message") + "";
  var wantsExit = Request.Form("wantsExit");


  if(isSet(username) == false)
  {
    Response.Redirect("login.html");
  }
  else
  {
    room = new ChatRoom(username);
  }

  if(isSet(wantsExit))
  {
    if(wantsExit == "Logout")
    {
      room.logout();
      Response.Redirect("login.html");
    }
  }
```

```
  if(isSet(newMessage))
  {
    room.addMessage(newMessage);
  }

%>



<HTML>
<BODY>
<CENTER>
<FORM method="post" action="post.asp">
<TEXTAREA name="message" rows="5" cols="20"
wrap="virtual"></TEXTAREA>
<BR>
<INPUT type="submit" value="Post Message">
</FORM>
<FORM method="post" action="post.asp">
<INPUT type="submit" name="wantsExit" value="Logout">
</FORM>
</CENTER>
</BODY>
</HTML>
```

THE MESSAGE PAGE: MESSAGES.ASP

The message page is shown in Listing 9-11.

Listing 9–11: The message page

```
<%@ LANGUAGE="JScript"%>

<%
  Response.AddHeader("Refresh", "2");
%>

<!-- #include file="ChatRoom.js" -->

<HTML>
<BODY bgcolor="white">
<%

  var room = new ChatRoom(null);

  room.printMessages();

%>
```

```
</BODY>
</HTML>
```

THE POST FORM: POSTS.HTML
The post form is shown in Listing 9-12.

Listing 9-12: The post form

```
<html>
<head>
<title></title>
</head>
<frameset cols="200,*">
<frame name="postform" src="post.asp">
<frame name="messages" src="messages.asp">
</frameset>
</html>
```

USING GLOBAL.ASA TO CLEAN UP
The global.asa page is shown in Listing 9-13.

Listing 9-13: The global.asa page

```
<SCRIPT LANGUAGE="JScript" RUNAT="server">

function Session_OnEnd()
{
  var username = Session("username");

  Application.Lock();
  Application.Contents.Remove(username);
  Application.UnLock();
}

function Session_OnStart()
{
  Session.Timeout = 1;
}

</SCRIPT>
```

Much better! All duplicated code has been hidden from view and made into a nice package that is easy to maintain. A server-side include makes sure that the definition for the custom object called ChatRoom is in-lined into every page (<!-- #include file="ChatRoom.js" -->).

Summary

This simple application exercised many different aspects of an ASP application, including error handling, dynamic content generation, cleanup, form input, input validation, and many other things. It also provided insight into what an ASP application looks like when you first develop it, and what it can look like if you put a couple more hours into it. The initial prototype is how we would have developed it. After understanding the problem, we packaged the solution and made it more abstract and reusable.

Chapter 10

Extending ASP with ActiveX Components

IN THIS CHAPTER

♦ Creating objects

♦ Installable components

♦ Finding and installing components

THE ACTIVE SERVER PAGES designers wanted the basic programmer interface to be simple to learn and unencumbered by non-Web information. They also wanted to provide access to non-Web functionality and make the standard extensible. To accomplish these goals, the designers defined some built-in objects, like the Server and Application, to deal with Web-specific functionality. All other programmer resources are defined via ActiveX components. Using the ActiveX standard, Microsoft made it easy for programmers to extend their Active Server Pages to support as yet unthought-of functionality.

In this chapter we will discuss how to access ActiveX components from your ASPs. We will include examples for the components that come with IIS and how to add new components that you write or download.

Creating Objects

Microsoft includes a number of components with IIS and the Personal Web Server (PWS). These include the components that implement useful and reusable functionality as well as file and database access. These components will be discussed in this chapter. File access will be discussed in Chapter 11, "Reading and Writing Files," while database access is saved for Chapter 14, "Database Access in Active Server Pages." You can also create your own components using Visual Basic, Visual C++, and Visual J++. Creating your own components is an advanced task and is really worthy of a book by itself. However, there are a number of components available on the Web, and later in this chapter we will discuss how to install components once they are created.

Developers use a component's class name to create it. There are two ways to perform this creation process. First, you can use the Server's `CreateObject`   125 method. This will create an object within the context of a single page. For example, to create a Tools object in JavaScript, use the following code:

```
var tools;

tools = Server.CreateObject("MSWC.Tools");
```

or to create a Tools object in VBScript, use the following code:

```
Set tools = Server.CreateObject("MSWC.Tools")
```

The second object-creation method is to use the <OBJECT> tags in your global.asa file. The <OBJECT> tag creates objects for a specified scope, and makes the object you create available to multiple pages. In other words, the <OBJECT> tag lets you share objects between pages. The formal syntax for the <OBJECT> tag is the following:

```
<OBJECT RUNAT=Server SCOPE=Scope ID=Identifier
{PROGID="progID"|CLASSID="ClassID"}>
```

Each of the parameters in this example is described in Table 10-1.

TABLE 10-1 OBJECT TAG PARAMETERS

Parameter	Description
RUNAT	Always SERVER.
SCOPE	Where the object is available, either SESSION or APPLICATION.
ID	The name used to access the object in ASPs.
PROGID	A name-based identifier for the object type. This will include a vendor code, such as MSWC.Tools.
CLASSID	A unique class identifier, such as Clsid:8AD3067A-B3FC-11CF-A560-00A0C9081C21.

Notice that if the scope is set to SESSION, pages for a particular user's session have access to the object. If the scope is APPLICATION, all the pages in the application will share the object. For example, if we add the following code to our global.asa file:

```
<OBJECT
RUNAT=Server
```

```
SCOPE=Application
ID=adRotator
PROGID="MSWC.AdRotator">
</OBJECT>
```

then the ASPs in the context of that application can access the adRotator object, by name, as if it were a built-in object.

```
adRotator.GetAdvertisement("adrotator.cfg")
```

In general, objects that store persistent information should be shared, while objects that are used for simple tasks can be created on a per-page basis. However, keep in mind that it does take resources to create objects, so sharing them can improve performance. On the other hand, shared data may need to be protected using the Application locking mechanism.

Installable Components

Microsoft includes a number of components with IIS and PWS. These are called the *installable components* in the documentation, but are really preinstalled. You should be able to access these components by their class name as listed in Table 10-2.

TABLE **10-2 PROVIDED COMPONENTS**

Name	Class Name	Description
Ad Rotator	MSWC.AdRotator	Uses a configuration file to rotate through a list of images.
Browser Capabilities	MSWC.BrowserType	Provides information about the visitor's browser.
Content Linking	MSWC.NextLink	Uses a configuration file to create a set of ordered links, like a table of contents for a book.
Content Rotator	MSWC.ContentRotator	Uses a configuration file to rotate through a list of text and HTML items.

Continued

TABLE **10-2 PROVIDED COMPONENTS** *(Continued)*

Name	Class Name	Description
Counters	MSWC.Counters	Maintains a set of developer-named counters.
Logging	MSWC.IISLog	Provides access to the Web server logs.
MyInfo	MSWC.MyInfo	Uses an XML file to support server-wide identification information.
PageCounter	MSWC.PageCounter	Counts the number of times a page is accessed.
Permissions	MSWC.PermissionChecker	Can be used to check if a page is accessible by the current user.
Status	MSWC.Status	Provides information about the Web server's status (Macintosh only).
Tools	MSWC.Tools	General tools for ASP developers.

Each of the components listed in Table 10-2 is discussed in this section.

Ad Rotator

The Ad Rotator component, formally named MSWC.AdRotator, can be used to iterate across a set of images or ads. As users access a page using the Ad Rotator component, a different image is displayed, based on a simple algorithm. Each image may include a link that the user can click on to learn more about the ad.

To get an idea of how to use the Ad Rotator component, Listing 10-1 displays a single advertisement at the top of an HTML page. Using the GetAdvertisement method returns the appropriate HTML to display the ad, including any <A> tags needed to define links. Notice that you pass in a relative path to the configuration file when you call GetAdvertisement.

You will find the images used in the Listing 10-1 example on the CD-ROM.

Listing 10-1: Using the Ad Rotator component

```
<%@ LANGUAGE="JAVASCRIPT" %>

<html>
<head>
<title>Using the AdRotator</title>
</head>
<body>
<%
var adRotator;

adRotator = Server.CreateObject("MSWC.AdRotator");

%>
Brought to you by our sponsor:<BR>
<%= adRotator.GetAdvertisement("adrotator.cfg") %>
</body>
</html>
```

The ads to enumerate are defined in a configuration file called the Rotator Schedule File. This schedule is a simple text file with entries of the following form:

```
adURL
adHomePage
text
impressions
```

The adURL entry is either an absolute or relative URL to the image for the ad. If a relative URL is used, it should be relative to the ASP that is creating the Ad Rotator. The adHomePage should either be a URL for information about the product, or a dash character (–) to indicate there is no link for that ad. The text field can be used to provide a text version of the ad, in case the client doesn't support images.

The algorithm for choosing the ad to display is based on the impressions value. This value should be a number from 0 to 10,000. All the ads in a file are compared to each other based on this weighting factor and displayed appropriately. For example, if there are two ads, each with a weight of 1, the default, they should display approximately the same number of times. If there are three ads ranked 20, 30, and 50, the one ranked 20 should be displayed about 20 percent of the time. Ads ranked 0 will not be displayed.

The sum of all the impressions values in a schedule file cannot exceed 10,000.

At the top of the configuration file can be four optional values: REDIRECT, WIDTH, HEIGHT, and BORDER.

The REDIRECT value is used to indicate the URL that all the images are linked to. If no value is provided, the images will link to the page they appear on. However, the link includes a query string with a single value called url that contains the URL in the configuration file. For example, if the file contains an ad for http://www.pri.com, and appears on the page ads.asp, then by default the link will be ads.asp?url=http://www.pri.com. You can create your own page to handle this link. Your page might also count the number of times an ad is selected or provide some other sort of information. For our example, we created the following page to redirect the client to the URL for the product.

```
<%@ LANGUAGE="JAVASCRIPT" %>
<%
    Response.Redirect(Request.QueryString("url")) %>
%>
```

The WIDTH and HEIGHT values define the size of the ads. By default, ads are banner sized, 440x60 pixels. But you can assign new values with these two global values.

The last global value is BORDER, which is used to indicate if a line should be drawn around the ads. The default is 1, for a one-pixel border. Setting it to 0 will turn off the border.

An * is used to separate the global values from the ads. If no global values are used, then the * should appear alone on the first line.

The file in Listing 10-2 was used to generate the ad.

Listing 10-2: The file that generates the ad

```
REDIRECT adredir.asp
WIDTH 113
HEIGHT 140
BORDER 1
*
images/linuxidiots.gif
http://www.amazon.com/exec/obidos/ASIN/
0789721961/qid=946856346/sr=1-2/103-0136868-0172657
Complete Idiot's Guide to Linux 2nd Edition
10
images/cgihowto.gif
http://www.amazon.com/exec/obidos/ASIN/
```

```
157169028X/qid=946856503/sr=1-1/103-0136868-0172657
CGI How-To
10
images/ejava.gif
http://www.amazon.com/exec/obidos/ASIN/
0471327565/qid=946856503/sr=1-2/103-0136868-0172657
Developing Enterprise Java Applications
10
images/perlhowto.gif
http://www.amazon.com/exec/obidos/ASIN/
1571691189/qid=946856503/sr=1-3/103-0136868-0172657
Perl 5 How-To
10
```

All these ads have the same impressions weighting. We also changed the size to account for a non-banner style of ad.

Browser Capabilities

The Browser Capabilities component, formally called `MSWC.BrowserType`, is used to learn about the client. To use this component, simply create it and use the properties listed in Table 10-3 to learn about the client.

TABLE 10-3 BROWSER TYPE PROPERTIES

Property	Description
Browser	The type of browser
Platform	The platform the browser is running on
Version	The browser's version
Frames	Whether the browser supports frames
Tables	Whether the browser supports tables
BackgroundSounds	Whether the browser supports background sounds
ActiveXControls	Whether the browser supports ActiveX controls
JavaApplets	Whether the browser supports Java applets
VBScript	Whether the browser supports VBScript
JavaScript	Whether the browser supports JavaScript

For example, the page shown in Listing 10-3 displays these properties in a table, first checking that tables are supported. If tables are not supported, then the information is displayed in text form.

Listing 10-3: Displaying properties in a table

```
<%@ LANGUAGE="JAVASCRIPT" %>

<html>
<head>
<title>Using the BrowserCapabilities</title>
</head>
<body>
<%
var bCap;

bCap = Server.CreateObject("MSWC.BrowserType");

if(bCap.tables)
{
%>
    <table border=1>
    <tr><td>Browser</td><td><%= bCap.browser  %></td></tr>
    <tr><td>Version</td><td><%= bCap.version  %></td></tr>
    <tr><td>Supports Frames</td>
            <td><%= bCap.frames  %></td></tr>
    <tr><td>Supports Tables</td>
            <td><%= bCap.tables  %></td>
        </tr>
    <tr><td>Supports BackgroundSounds</td>
            <td><%= bCap.BackgroundSounds  %></td></tr>
    <tr><td>Supports VBScript</td>
            <td><%= bCap.vbscript  %></td></tr>
    <tr><td>Supports JavaScript</td>
            <td><%= bCap.javascript  %></td></tr>
    </table>
<%
}
else
{
%>
    Browser: <%= bCap.browser  %>
    Version</td><td><%= bCap.version  %>
    Supports Frames: <%= bCap.frames  %>
    Supports Tables: <%= bCap.tables  %>
    Supports BackgroundSounds: <%= bCap.BackgroundSounds  %>
```

```
      Supports VBScript: <%= bCap.vbscript  %>
      Supports JavaScript: <%= bCap.javascript  %>
<%
}
%>
</body>
</html>
```

When accessed, this ASP will display a page like the one shown in Figure 10-1.

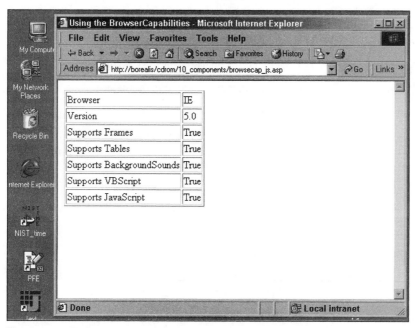

Figure 10-1: The browser type properties displayed in a table

All the information that the BrowserType component has access to is configured in a file called browsecap.ini. This file contains information about various browsers and must be kept up to date as new browsers are released. Commercial versions of the Browser Capabilities component are available and can provide more extensive, up-to-date information. For the most recent version of the browsecap.ini file visit the Microsoft Web site.

Content Linker

You may have seen or created Web sites that have a collection of ordered pages. These pages act like a book or presentation where the user can move forward and backward through the information. To help implement this type of page, Microsoft provides a component called the Content Linker, or MSWC.NextLink. Like the Ad Rotator, the Content Linker uses a configuration file.

There are a number of methods for accessing the set of links defined in the ContentLink configuration file. These are described in Table 10-4. Unless otherwise specified, all these methods take a path to the configuration file as an argument.

TABLE 10-4 CONTENT LINKER METHODS

Method	Description
GetListCount	Returns the total number of pages listed in the configuration file.
GetListIndex	Returns the index for the current page.
GetNextDescription	Returns the description for the next page.
GetNextURL	Returns the URL for the next page.
GetNthDescription	Returns the description for the nth page, where *n* is one of the arguments, along with the configuration file.
GetNthURL	Returns the URL for the nth page, where *n* is one of the arguments, along with the configuration file.
GetPreviousDescription	Returns the description for the previous page.
GetPreviousURL	Returns the URL for the previous page.

To demonstrate how you can use the Content Linker, we have created a number of ASPs. First, there is the configuration file. This file contains the relative URL and a description for each link. These two fields must be separated by a tab. You can also add a third field, using a second tab that contains a comment.

```
page1.asp    First Page
page2.asp    Second Page
page3.asp    Third Page
```

This configuration file refers to three pages in a single directory. The first page, page1.asp, displays a link to the next page in the list, as shown in Listing 10-4. Notice that the page actually checks to see if it is the first page, and will display a link to the previous page if the configuration file is changed. This page, and the others in this example, uses <A> tags to create links from the URLs, but you could also use them in FORMs, or as part of JavaScripted buttons on the client.

All of the pages for the Listing 10-4 example are provided on the CD-ROM.

Listing 10-4: The page1.asp with a link to the next page

```
<%@ LANGUAGE="JAVASCRIPT" %>

<html>
<head>
<title>Page 1</title>
</head>
<body>
<h1>Page One</h1>
<%
var linker;

linker = Server.CreateObject("MSWC.NextLink");

if(linker.GetListIndex("contentlink.cfg") > 1)
{
%>
    <a href="<%= linker.GetPreviousURL("contentlink.cfg") %>">
    Previous
    </a>
<%
}
%>

<a href="<%= linker.GetNextURL("contentlink.cfg") %>">Next</a>
</body>
</html>
```

The second (see Listing 10-5) and third pages display both Next and Previous links. If you click Next on the last page, you will be directed to the first page, like in a ring structure.

Listing 10-5: The second page, with Next and Previous links

```
<%@ LANGUAGE="JAVASCRIPT" %>

<html>
<head>
<title>Page 2</title>
```

```
</head>
<body>
<h1>Page Two</h1>
<%
var linker;

linker = Server.CreateObject("MSWC.NextLink");
%>

<a href="<%= linker.GetPreviousURL("contentlink.cfg") %>">
Previous</a>

<a href="<%= linker.GetNextURL("contentlink.cfg") %>">
Next</a>
</body>
</html>
```

Next we created an ASP called contentlink_js.asp, as shown in Listing 10-6. This page displays a list of the links in the configuration file. Files are indexed from 1, which is familiar to VBScript programmers, but will be unusual to JavaScript programmers.

 The pages linked to in the Listing 10-6 example are provided on the CD-ROM in a directory called content.

Listing 10-6: The contentlink_js.asp, with configuration file links

```
<%@ LANGUAGE="JAVASCRIPT" %>

<html>
<head>
<title>Using the ContentLink Component</title>
</head>
<body>
<%
var linker;
var i,max;

linker = Server.CreateObject("MSWC.NextLink");

max = linker.GetListCount("content/contentlink.cfg")
%>
```

```
There are <%=max%> links:<br>
<%
//Note indexes are from 1 -> Count
for(i=1;i<=max;i++)
{
%>

    <a href=
     "content/<%= linker.GetNthURL("content/contentlink.cfg",i) %>">
    <%= linker.GetNthDescription ("content/contentlink.cfg",i) %>
    </a>
    <br>
<%
}
%>
</body>
</html>
```

Displaying contentlink_js.asp will result in a page like the one shown in Figure 10-2.

Figure 10-2: Content Linker test page

As you can see, this content link component can be a useful way of managing a set of ordered pages.

Content Rotator

The Content Rotator provided with IIS 5.0, `MSWC.ContentRotator`, is very similar to the Ad Rotator. Rather than displaying images, it displays text and HTML. As a result, the configuration file is different, but using it is basically the same. You might use the Content Rotator for a tip of the day, or some other message that you want to display on your site.

To create a configuration file for the Content Rotator, use the `%%` combination to indicate a new piece of content, numbers for the weighting, and `//` for comments. For example, the following file contains three content entries:

```
%% 2
You are what you eat
%% 2
A penny <em>saved</em>, is a penny <em>earned</em>
%% //no weight, default to 1
Don't count your chickens<br>
before they hatch
```

The first entry is weighted at 2, the second is weighted at 2, and the third has no weight, so it defaults to 1. Notice that the `%%` is used to end content and begin the next one. Also, HTML is valid in the content entries.

Listing 10-7 uses the `ChooseContent` method to display one of the items from this configuration file. Like the Ad Rotator, the name of the configuration file is passed to the method. The `GetAllContent` method can be used to display all of the content in the configuration file.

Listing 10-7: Using ChooseContent to display a configuration file item

```
<%@ LANGUAGE="JAVASCRIPT" %>

<html>
<head>
<title>Using the ContentRotator</title>
</head>
<body>
<%
var quoteRotator;

quoteRotator = Server.CreateObject("MSWC.ContentRotator");

%>
Food for thought:<br>
<%= quoteRotator.ChooseContent("quotes.cfg") %>
<br><br>
```

```
A list of all the quotes:<br>
<%= quoteRotator.GetAllContent("quotes.cfg") %>
</body>
</html>
```

The Listing 10-7 example also shows how the GetAllContent property will generate a list of the entire configuration file's contents.

Counters

The Counters component provided with IIS 5.0, MSWC.Counters, stores a list of named counters in a file on the Web server. By using the same names, you can keep a persistent count. Because the counters are named, you can maintain different counts using the same object.

The Counter objects have four methods, which are described in Table 10-5. All these methods take the name of a counter as an argument.

TABLE 10-5 COUNTER COMPONENT METHODS

Method	Description
Get	Gets the current count.
Set	Sets the current count.
Increment	Adds 1 to the current count.
Reset	Sets the current count to 0.

One common mistake would be to create a separate Counter for each count. But you only need one Counter object for all counts; the methods take the name of the count to identify them. Also, Counters are a component that should be shared. You should create a Counter object for your application in the global.asa file using the <OBJECT> tag and simply access it in your ASPs.

For example, the following code was placed in the global.asa file for our next example. It creates a Counter component called counter.

```
<OBJECT
RUNAT=Server
SCOPE=Application
ID=counter
PROGID="MSWC.Counters">
</OBJECT>
```

Then the page shown in Listing 10-8 accesses the counter object created in the global.asa file and increments two different counters based on the contents of the query string. The page will also reset the counters if told to.

Listing 10-8: Accessing the counter object

```
<%@ LANGUAGE="JAVASCRIPT" %>

<html>
<head>
<title>Using the Counter</title>
<%
var special = Request.QueryString("special");

counter.Increment("hits");

if(special == "true")
{
    counter.Increment("special");
}
else if(special == "reset")
{
    counter.Remove("hits");
    counter.Remove("special");
}
%>
</head>
<body>
There have been <%= counter.Get("hits")%> hits.<br>
There have been <%= counter.Get("special")%> special hits.<br>
<br>
<a href="counters_js.asp">Plain Hit</a>
<a href="counters_js.asp?special=true">Special Hit</a>
<a href="counters_js.asp?special=reset">Reset Counts</a>
</body>
</html>
```

The counts that you set using a Counter component are stored on disk. In Windows 2000, they are in the file \WinNT\system32\inetsrv\Data\Counters.txt.

MyInfo

A component called MyInfo, `MSWC.MyInfo`, can be used to store information about the Web server owner. With the Personal Web Server, this component will have default information provided when the Personal Web Server was configured. For IIS, the object starts out empty. In either case, properties of the MyInfo components

you create will be stored in an XML file on the server at \WinNT\system32\inetsrv\
Data\MyInfo.xml on Windows 2000.

You can either assign properties to an object in an ASP, possibly from a configuration page, or in the XML directly. However, if you edit the XML file, you should
do so when the server is not running. Each time the server is shut down, the MyInfo
components in it will save their information to disk, overwriting other changes.

As an example, the following XML file defines three properties. The name of the
property is the name of the tag. The contents of the tags are the values of the properties. These should be plain text values.

```
<XML>
<CompanyName>ASP Masters</>
<CompanyAddress>123 E. West St., Ballo CA, 94949</>
<CompanyPhone>555-1212</>
</XML>
```

Then the page in Listing 10-9 displays them.

Listing 10-9: Displaying MyInfo properties

```
<%@ LANGUAGE="JAVASCRIPT" %>

<html>
<head>
<title>Using the MyInfo Component</title>
</head>
<body>
<%
var myInfo;
myInfo = Server.CreateObject("MSWC.MyInfo");
%>

<table border=1>
<tr><td>Company Name</td><td><%= myInfo.CompanyName%></td></tr>
<tr><td>Company Address</td>
    <td><%= myInfo.CompanyAddress%></td></tr>
<tr><td>Company Phone</td><td><%= myInfo.CompanyPhone%></td></tr>
</table>
</body>
</html>
```

The MyInfo component is a useful way to centralize information such as company
names, as well as to support e-mail addresses and copyright notices. Remember that
if you use a MyInfo object, you can either create it in each ASP, or better yet create a
shared object in the global.asa file.

Page Counter

There are a number of occasions where you may want to keep a count of the number of people who have accessed a particular page. Although the Counters component could be used for this task, you can also use the Page Counter component, formally called `MSWC.PageCounter`.

This object keeps a single count, rather than the multiple named counts of the Counter object. To get the number of hits, you use the Hits method. To increment the count, use `PageHit` and to reset the count, use Reset. Listing 10-10 shows how to maintain and display a simple page count.

Listing 10-10: Maintaining and displaying a page count

```
<%@ LANGUAGE="JAVASCRIPT" %>

<html>
<head>
<title>Using the PageCounter</title>
<%
var pageCounter;

pageCounter = Server.CreateObject("MSWC.PageCounter");
pageCounter.PageHit();
%>
</head>
<body>
There have been <%= pageCounter.Hits()%> hits.
</body>
</html>
```

The running count is made persistent via settings in your registry. These settings are found under `MSWC.PageCounter` in the HKEY_CLASSES_ROOT part of the registry. There are two keys. The `File_Location` key is the path for the file to store the count in. This defaults to hitcnt.cnt in the Windows directory. The `Save_Count` key indicates the number of hits to keep before saving and defaults to 25. By configuring these parameters, you can control how persistent and accurate the page counter will be.

Permissions

IIS supports a number of authentication schemes. When used, these allow the Web server to restrict access to various resources. For example, only members might be allowed into a particular directory.

The Permissions component, called `MSWC.PermissionsChecker`, can be used to test whether the current user can access a particular URL. This lets you as a developer control the links on a page, restricting them to resources that the user actually has access to. Or, you might use this component to test whether the user needs to log in. The `HasAccess` method is used to test a URL or file path, and relies on the Web server to account for any user authentication that has been performed. The page in Listing 10-11 tests both a URL and a file path.

Listing 10-11: Testing a URL and file path

```
<%@ LANGUAGE="JAVASCRIPT" %>

<html>
<head>
<title>Using the PermissionChecker</title>
<%
var checker;

checker = Server.CreateObject("MSWC.PermissionChecker");
%>
</head>
<body>
content/Page1.asp is Accessible:
<%= checker.HasAccess("content/Page1.asp") %>
<br>
c:\content\Page4.html is Accessible:
<%= checker.HasAccess("c:\content\Page4.html") %>
</body>
</html>
```

In this case, we are actually testing whether the file path exists, since you can't access a nonexistent resource. In your pages, you will rely on the server administrator to control permissions for resources and indicate which directories may require checking. Permissions might be set at a Web server level or at a file system level.

Status

The Status component, `MSWC.Status`, provides information about the server. Unfortunately, as of this writing it is only supported on the Macintosh IIS server. However, if you are running this server, you can try out the following page from the CD-ROM to see your server's statistics. This page displays all of the properties and statistics available from the Status object. Note that if you try the page shown in Listing 10-12 on a Windows server, it will indicate that the specified properties are unavailable.

Listing 10-12: Displaying server Information

```
<%@ LANGUAGE="JAVASCRIPT" %>

<html>
```

```
<head>
<title>Using the Status Component</title>
<%
var status;

status = Server.CreateObject("MSWC.Status");
%>
</head>
<body>
Currently, only a Mac Server should return any values other than:
unavailable.<br><br>

<table border=1>
<tr><td>VisitorsSinceStart</td><td><%=status.VisitorsSinceStart()%>
</td></tr>
<tr><td>RequestsSinceStart</td><td><%=status.RequestsSinceStart()%>
</td></tr>
<tr><td>ActiveHTTPSessions</td><td><%=status.ActiveHTTPSessions()%>
</td></tr>
<tr><td>HighHTTPSessions</td><td><%=status.HighHTTPSessions()%>
</td></tr>
<tr><td>ServerVersion</td><td><%=status.ServerVersion()%></td></tr>
<tr><td>StartTime</td><td><%=status.StartTime()%></td></tr>
<tr><td>StartDate</td><td><%=status.StartDate()%></td></tr>
<tr><td>FreeMem</td><td><%=status.FreeMem()%></td></tr>
<tr><td>FreeLowMem</td><td><%=status.FreeLowMem()%></td></tr>
<tr><td>VisitorsToday</td><td><%=status.VisitorsToday()%></td></tr>
<tr><td>RequestsToday</td><td><%=status.RequestsToday()%></td></tr>
<tr><td>BusyConnections</td><td><%=status.BusyConnections()%>
</td></tr>
<tr><td>RefusedConnections</td><td><%=status.RefusedConnections()%>
</td></tr>
<tr><td>Ktransferred</td><td><%=status.Ktransferred()%></td></tr>
<tr><td>TotalRequests </td><td><%=status.TotalRequests ()%>
</td></tr>
<tr><td>CurrentThreads</td><td><%=status.CurrentThreads()%>
</td></tr>
<tr><td>AvailableThreads</td><td><%=status.AvailableThreads()%>
</td></tr>
<tr><td>RecentVisitors</td><td><%=status.RecentVisitors()%></td>
</tr>
<tr><td>PopularPages</td><td><%=status.PopularPages()%></td></tr>
</table>
</body>
</html>
```

Tools

The Tools component installed with IIS5, MSWC.Tools, provides five utility methods for developers. These are described in Table 10-6.

TABLE 10-6 TOOLS COMPONENT METHODS

Method	Description
FileExists	Tests if the provided URL represents a real resource.
Owner	Tests if the current user is also the Web site owner.
PluginExists	Tests for the existence of a server plug-in, and only works on a Macintosh server.
ProcessForm	Processes the data from a form based on a template file.
Random	Generates a random integer between –32768 and 32767.

Listing 10-13 shows how you can use these methods in your pages.

Listing 10-13: Using Tools component methods

```
<%@ LANGUAGE="JAVASCRIPT" %>

<html>
<head>
<title>Using the Tools Component</title>
<%
var tools;

tools = Server.CreateObject("MSWC.Tools");
%>
</head>
<body>
Does tools_js.asp exist: <%= tools.FileExists("tools_js.asp")%><br>
Am I the site owner: <%= tools.Owner()%><br>
Random Integer: <%=tools.Random()%>
wait a second and press reload to change.<br>
</body>
</html>
```

That concludes the components provided with IIS, other than the file and database access components that will be discussed later. As you can see, they provide a wide range of functionality. However, there is a lot more to do than what we have mentioned so far. For that, you may need to get a component from the Web or a commercial vendor.

Finding and Installing Components

Numerous components are available on the Web. These range from managing e-mail, to calculating GUIDs, to accessing LDAP servers. Basically, everything that somebody might need. There are even components for generating graphics from data or drawing commands. Check out the Microsoft site, or simply search for Active Server Pages on your favorite search engine, to locate ASP components. You might also try the following sites:

◆ www.activeserverpages.com

◆ www.aspdeveloper.net

but there are many more. Think of these as jumping-off points.

The components that you find on the Web will fall into one of three categories: commercial, shareware, or free. The commercial components require you to buy them. The shareware components are also bought, but usually provide a reasonable evaluation time for testing them. The free components are, of course, free, but rarely offer support.

Regardless of how you get a component, you will need to install it. The file you get will be a .dll file. The first thing you will need to do is install the component before you use it. Also, read any documentation provided with the component to determine its methods and usage.

To install a component, you need to place it in the correct directory and register it with the Web server. First, copy the .dll file to your server's add-ons directory. On Windows 2000 with IIS this is the following path:

```
\winnt\system32\inetsrv
```

To make organization easier, you can create a subdirectory for your custom components. We created one called

```
\winnt\system32\inetsrv\addons
```

Now, open a command line and make the directory containing the .dll current. Run the regsvr32.exe program on your .dll. For example, enter this command at a command prompt:

```
regsvr32 GUIDMKR.dll
```

This should display a message box like the one shown in Figure 10-3. If you get an error, check your spelling and the directory location.

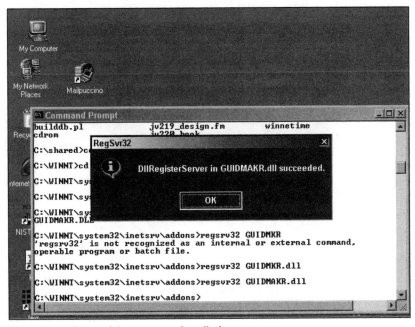

Figure 10-3: Successful component installation

Keep in mind that once you register the component, you will have to re-register it if you move it. Otherwise, it is a simple two-step process. Once installed, use the documented name to create the custom component and use it.

Summary

ActiveX components provide a powerful yet simple way to extend Active Server Pages. You can create components within a page using `Server.CreateObject` or in the global.asa file using `<OBJECT>` tags. In either case, the objects you create will appear to your scripts as normal objects with properties and methods. Using these methods you can access functionality well beyond what is supported by the scripting language itself. For example, an ActiveX component could allow a JavaScript to send e-mail, or a VBScript to access an LDAP server. As a standard component architecture, ActiveX components are widely available and solve the problem of making a simple page development technology like ASP powerful and far reaching.

Chapter 11

Reading and Writing Files

ACCESSING FILES IS A primordial task for computer programs. Using files, you can create simple databases, store information submitted by your users, store preferences settings, and so on. Web applications typically use databases to store information, so the need for files is greatly reduced. In many situations, use of files versus a database makes the site more manageable. Instead of worrying about another component that you must maintain and have available for your application to work, using files can ensure that, so long as your Web site is running, your application can find its data. Another advantage of files over databases for simple applications is that a text file is readable and writeable by using a simple text editor such as Notepad.

The Scripting.FileSystemObject

The `Scripting.FileSystemObject` is your entry point to the file system. This object lets you open and close files. In addition to these basic file operations, you also can access other objects such as `Drive`, `Folder`, and `File`. These additional objects provide most, if not all, the functionality your application will ever require for manipulating and accessing files. To work with the contents of a file, your script must do the following:

1. Create an instance of the Scripting.FileSystemObject.

2. Open a `TextStream`.

3. Read and write data to the `TextStream`.

4. Close the file.

To access information about the file system, your script will:

1. Create an instance of the Scripting.FileSystemObject.

2. Access the drive.

3. Access the folders and files you are interested in.

A complete list of the FileSystemObject's methods is provided in Table 11-1. We will discuss many of these throughout the chapter. These methods deal primarily with files and folders as paths in the file system. Later in the chapter, we see how objects can also be used to represent these entities.

TABLE 11-1 FILESYSTEMOBJECT METHODS

Method	Description
CopyFile	Copies a file from one path to another.
CreateTextFile	Creates a new text file and opens it.
DeleteFile	Deletes the file at a specified path.
FileExists	Returns true if there is a file at the specified path.
MoveFile	Moves a file from one path to another.
OpenTextFile	Opens an existing text file.
CopyFolder	Copies a folder from one path to another.
CreateFolder	Creates a folder at the specified path.
DeleteFolder	Deletes the folder at a specified path.
FolderExists	Returns true if there is a folder at the specified path.
MoveFolder	Moves a folder from one path to another.
BuildPath	Appends a name to a path, if it is necessary.
GetAbsolutePathName	Returns a complete, unambiguous path from one that can contain wild cards (like *, ., and ..).
GetBaseName	Gets the name of the last element in a path, minus the extension.
GetDrive	Returns a drive from its identifier.
GetDriveName	Returns the name of a drive from a path.
GetExtensionName	Returns the extension, if any, for the last element in a file path.

Method	Description
GetFile	Returns the File object for a specific path.
GetFileName	Returns the string name for the last element in a file path that is not a drive.
GetFolder	Returns the Folder object for a specific path.
GetParentFolderName	Returns the string name for the parent of the last element in a file path.
GetSpecialFolder	Returns a Folder object for the special folder specified by a number: 0: Windows 1: System 2: Temp
GetTempName	Returns a temporary, and semi-unique, name for a file. Normally, you would create this file in the temp directory by using the GetSpecialFolder method.

Let's start looking at the FileSystemObject by seeing how we can use it to create, read, and write files.

Opening a Text Stream

To access a file's contents, you must open it. There are two ways to open a file:

- ◆ CreateTextFile
- ◆ OpenTextFile

When you are done working with a file, you must close it using the Close method. Both the CreateTextFile and OpenTextFile methods are similar in that they return a TextStream object that you can use for adding data to a file.

Using the CreateTextFile method

The CreateTextFile method, as its name suggests, creates a new file. Here's the complete method signature:

```
CreateTextFile(filename[, overwrite][, Unicode])
```

The *filename* argument is a string that specifies the name and path of the file to create. If you provide a filename without any path information, the file is created in the same directory as the ASP page running the script. Your script must have permissions to write into the directory, and it is almost always a bad idea, from a security and maintenance perspective, to let your scripts write into the same directory where the programs reside. The best way to use files is to create a specific directory for your Web applications to write to. This makes security and monitoring easier.

The *overwrite* argument is optional. If the value is true, then your script can overwrite any files of the same name. If not provided or set to false, an existing file won't be overwritten.

The *Unicode* argument is also an optional Boolean value. If the value is true, the file is created as a Unicode file. If false or omitted, the file is created as ASCII. Here's an example for creating a file:

```
var fso;
var ts;

fso = Server.CreateObject("Scripting.FileSystemObject");
ts = fso.CreateTextFile("c:\\temp\\afile.txt", true);
fh.Close();
```

This JavaScript code differs from the VBScript version in two ways. First, the Boolean constant for `true` is lowercase. Second, the backslash characters are escaped in JavaScript.

Using the OpenTextFile method

The `OpenTextFile` method, as its name suggests, opens an existing file. This method is more useful than `CreateTextFile`, as it provides you with more control on how the file is opened. Files can be accessed in one of three ways, or *modes*:

- ◆ `ForReading`
- ◆ `ForWriting`
- ◆ `ForAppending`

Files opened for reading (`ForReading`) can be used only for reading. Attempting to use any method to write to the file will fail with an error. Files opened for writing (`ForWriting`) can be used only for writing. If the file exists, any write operation will overwrite its previous contents. Files opened for appending (`ForAppending`) are opened for writing, but unlike the `ForWriting` mode, any write operations are appended to the end of the file.

As you might have guessed, you cannot open a file for both reading and writing at the same time. If your program must write to a file and then read over the file, you must perform this operation by opening the text file twice.

Here's the complete method signature for the `OpenTextFile` method:

```
OpenTextFile(filename[, accessMode][, create][, format])
```

The *filename* argument is a string that specifies the name and path of the file to create. If you provide a filename without any path information, the file is created in the same directory as the ASP page running the script. Note that your script must have permissions to write into the directory, and almost always it is a very bad idea to let your scripts write into the same directory where the programs reside.

The *accessMode* argument is an optional argument. It provides an integer value that specifies the access mode for the file. Specifying 1 means `ForReading`, 2 means `ForWriting`, and 8 means `ForAppending`.

The *create* argument is also an optional Boolean value. It specifies if the file should be created, if it doesn't exist already. The default value for this argument is `false`.

The *format* argument is also an optional integer value. If the value is –2, the file format is assumed to be the default format used by the server. If the value is –1, the file is opened as Unicode. If the value is 0, the file is opened as ASCII (the default). Listing 11-1 provides an example of using the `OpenTextFile` method.

Listing 11-1: Using the OpenTextFile method to build a template

```
var fso;
var ts;

// Constants for the file access modes
var ForWriting = 1;
var ForReading = 2;
var ForAppending = 8;


fso = Server.CreateObject("Scripting.FileSystemObject");
ts = fso.OpenTextFile("c:\\temp\\atempFile", ForWriting, false);

// If the file doesn't exist, it will return a file not found error
// since it specifies false for the create argument.
// To make the program do something useful, we need to call some
// methods to write some data to the file.

// done working with the file
ts.Close();
```

As you can see in Listing 11-1, our program is actually rather boring. What it does is provide a template to build on.

Reading and Writing with a TextStream

Once you have opened text stream, you can use one of the various methods provided to read and write the file. The methods provided by the `TextStream` object are listed in Table 11-2.

TABLE 11–2 TEXTSTREAM METHODS

Method	Description
Close	Closes an open `TextStream` (all open files should be closed!).
Read	Reads the specified number of characters from a `TextStream` and returns a string.
ReadAll	Reads the entire file into a string.
ReadLine	Reads text until it finds a new-line character and returns a string. The returned string does not include the new-line character.
Skip	Skips the specified number of characters when reading from a `TextStream`.
SkipLine	Skips the next line when reading from a `TextStream`.
Write	Writes the specified string to the `TextStream`.
WriteLine	Writes the specified string to the `TextStream`, followed by a new-line character.
WriteBlankLines	Writes the specified number of blank lines to the text stream.

The text stream also has a property called `AtEndOfStream` that will indicate when the program has read all the lines in the stream.

Reading from a TextStream object

Let's look at an example where we read from a text stream. In this case, we have included a text file in the same directory as the ASP. This file, called constitution.txt, contains the text for the U.S. constitution. The ASP simply reads the contents of the file and displays them in an HTML page. When accessed, our example ASP will look like the one shown in Figure 11-1.

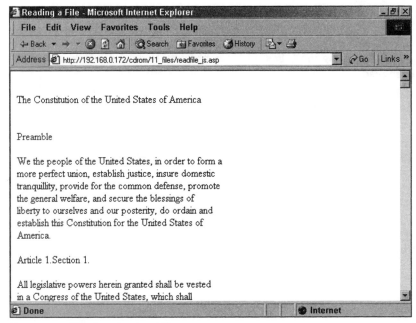

Figure 11-1: The Constitution ASP

The code for this page is quite simple. First, we start the HTML.

```
<%@ LANGUAGE="JAVASCRIPT" %>

<html>
<head>
<title>Reading a File</title>
</head>
<body>
```

The first real code uses the `Server` object to get the real path for the file, since it is in the same directory as the ASP.

```
<%
var myFile;
var ForReading = 1, ForAppending = 8;
var fileStreamObj,textStream;

myFile = Server.MapPath("Constitution.txt");
```

Next, we create a `FileSystemObject` and use it to open the text file. This would generate an error if the file didn't exist.

```
fileStreamObj = Server.CreateObject("Scripting.FileSystemObject");
textStream = fileStreamObj.OpenTextFile(myFile,ForReading,false);
```

The script loops, using the `AtEndOfStream` property to determine when all of the file has been read.

```
while(!textStream.AtEndOfStream)
{
```

Each line is read, and encoded as HTML, before being displayed.

```
    line = textStream.ReadLine();
    line = Server.HTMLEncode(line);
%>

<%= line %><BR>

<%
}
```

When the entire file is displayed, the text stream should be closed.

```
textStream.Close();
%>
```

Finally, the HTML/ASP is closed.

```
</body>
</html>
```

As you can see, reading a file is pretty simple. The one subtle technique that we used is to make sure to check if the stream is at its end before reading any lines. This is implicit in the `while` loop, but you may construct the loop differently. In that case, be sure to check that the stream contains data before trying to read it. Otherwise, you will generate an error.

Writing to a TextStream object

Our next example demonstrates how to write to a text stream. This example takes the data from an HTML form and appends it to a guestbook file. The HTML form is contained in the page entry_js.htm file, which is displayed in Figure 11-2.

As you can see in the figure, the form contains three fields: Name, Company, and Phone. The values of these fields will be stored in our file. The code for this HTML page appears in Listing 11-2. Notice the action is set to writefile_js.asp; this file is discussed below and appears on the CD-ROM.

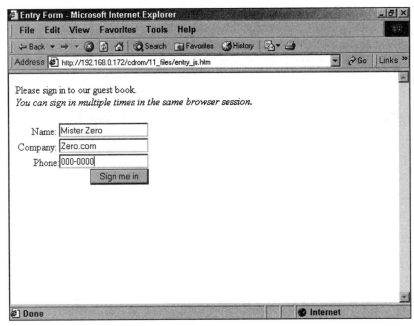

Figure 11-2: An HTML entry form

Listing 11-2: Creating an HTML entry form

```
<HTML>
<HEAD>
<TITLE>Entry Form</TITLE>
</HEAD>
<BODY>

Please sign in to our guest book.<BR>
<EM>You can sign in multiple times in the same browser session.</EM><BR><BR>

<TABLE><TR><TD ALIGN="right">

<FORM METHOD="POST" ACTION="writefile_js.asp">

Name: <INPUT TYPE="text" NAME="user_name"><BR>
Company: <INPUT TYPE="text" NAME="company"><BR>
Phone:<INPUT TYPE="text" NAME="phone"><BR>
<INPUT TYPE="submit" VALUE="Sign me in"><BR>

</FORM>
</TD></TR></TABLE>
</BODY>
</HTML>
```

The ASP for this example performs two tasks. First, the page takes input from the entry form and appends it to a file. Next, the page displays the contents of the guest book, as shown in Figure 11-3. This page demonstrates writing to a file, as well as a more complex example of reading a file. Because the same file is written to and displayed, we will actually open it twice in the same page.

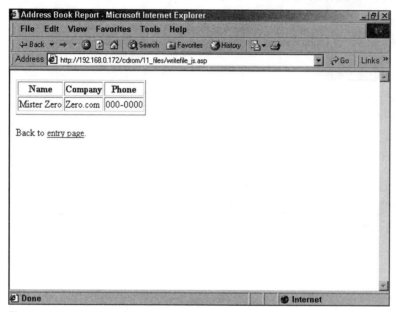

Figure 11-3: A guest book ASP

This page starts with the basic HTML header.

```
<%@ LANGUAGE="JAVASCRIPT" %>

<HTML>
<HEAD> <TITLE>Address Book Report</TITLE>
</HEAD>
<BODY>
```

Variables are declared to store the name of the log/guestbook file and the file system object. We also declared constants to store the ForReading and ForAppending constants. You can also create an include file for these constants.

```
<%
var logFile;
var ForReading = 1, ForAppending = 8;
var fileStreamObj;
```

Then we create the file system object.

```
fileStreamObj = Server.CreateObject("Scripting.FileSystemObject");
```

We then set up the name of the log file. This can be any file that the ASP would have access to. In this case, we are using the temp directory.

```
logFile = "c:\\temp\\book.txt";
```

Next, we check if the page is being called because a form was submitted.

```
if(Request.Form("user_name")!=null)
{
```

If this is a submission, we create a text stream for the file, opening it for appending. This means that the current contents will remain in place. We also indicate that if the file doesn't exist, it should be created.

```
    visitorLog =
        fileStreamObj.OpenTextFile(logFile,ForAppending,true);
```

Next, we write a single line to the file containing the values of the form elements separated by | characters. This is a simplistic format. In a robust solution, you should make sure that the encoding characters are not part of the form data.

```
    visitorLog.WriteLine(Request.Form("user_name") + "|" +
            Request.Form("company") + "|" +
            Request.Form("phone"));
```

After the line is written, we close the file.

```
    visitorLog.Close();

}
%>
```

Next, the ASP displays the contents of the file by splitting the name, company, and phone information into separate strings again and placing them in a table. Begin the table first, and define the header row, as follows:

```
<TABLE border=1>
<TR><TH>Name</TH><TH>Company</TH><TH>Phone</TH></TR>
```

We are going to need variables to hold the current line from the file as we read through it — the name, company, and phone — as well as indices for use when splitting the one line into its three components.

```
<%
var line;
var name;
var company;
var phone;
var index;
var lastIndex;
var fileStreamR,visitorLogR;
```

Make a file system object, or reuse the one above, and create a stream for the log/guestbook file. This time, open the file for reading and don't create it if it isn't there.

```
fileStreamR = Server.CreateObject("Scripting.FileSystemObject");
visitorLogR = fileStreamR.OpenTextFile(logFile,ForReading,false);
```

Loop over the file, reading each line, as follows:

```
while(!visitorLogR.AtEndOfStream)
{
    line = visitorLogR.ReadLine();
```

Look for the first | character on the line and take everything up to that as the name, as shown here:

```
    lastIndex = 0;
    index = line.indexOf("|");
    name = line.substring(0,index);
```

Look for the second | character on the line and take everything from the first pipe up to the second one as the company, as you see here:

```
    lastIndex = index+1;
    index = line.indexOf("|",lastIndex);
    company = line.substring(lastIndex,index);
```

Everything after the second | is the phone. Again, this isn't a foolproof system, because someone could put a | in their name, company, or phone number and mess up the system. In a more robust example, you should use encoding to guarantee that the separator character is not in the strings being separated.

```
    lastIndex = index+1;
    phone = line.substring(lastIndex,line.length);
%>
```

Once we have the information, we put it in a row of the table, as follows:

```
<TR>
<TD> <%= name %> </TD>
<TD> <%= company %> </TD>
<TD> <%= phone %> </TD>
<TR>

<%
}
```

When we are done with the file, we close it, like this:

```
visitorLogR.Close();
%>
```

Then we close the HTML page, as follows:

```
</TABLE><BR>
Back to <A HREF="entry_js.htm">entry page</A>.

</BODY>
</HTML>
```

As you can see, writing to the end of a file is really just a few lines of code. Reading and writing are both limited by the TextStream object to basic operations. At the same time, using separators and other techniques, the complete process of reading a formatted file can be rather complex.

Shared File Issues

In cases where multiple clients may be writing to the same file at the same time, you need to protect the integrity of the file. If you don't use some means of protection, you might have one page writing a line at the same time another page is writing a line to the same file. This can result in numerous unintended results, like one line getting written, while the other isn't, or the lines getting combined.

To protect a shared file, use the Application object's lock method. Lock the application before writing to the file, and unlock it after you close the file. Since locking can affect the performance of your scripts, minimize the time the Application object is locked.

Keep in mind that this is only an issue for writing. If no scripts write to the file, you don't need to worry about locking it. But if even one script writes, all the scripts need to use locking.

 For more information on using the lock and unlock methods, see Chapter 6, "The Application Object."

File Properties

The FileSystemObject also provides access to information about the drives, folders, and files on the server machine. Although we have included this information in the book for completeness, keep in mind that it may be a security problem for you to make this sort of information available on the Web. In particular, you do not want people to be able to browse your entire file system remotely.

To inspect the file system, you will use one of two mechanisms. First, the FileSystemObject has a property called Drives that is a collection of Drive objects. These objects store information about the drives on your computer. The FileSystemObject also has a method called GetDrive that can be used to get a Drive object for a specific identifier, like "c:." The Drive object provides access to its files and folders using the properties listed in Table 11-3.

TABLE 11-3 DRIVE OBJECT PROPERTIES

Property	Description
AvailableSpace	The space available on the drive.
DriveLetter	The letter identifier for the drive.
DriveType	The type of drive: 0: Unknown 1: Removable 2: Fixed 3: Network 4: CD-ROM 5: RAM disk
FileSystem	The type of file system on the drive: FAT, NTFS, or CDFS.
FreeSpace	The amount of free space on the drive.
IsReady	Indicates if the drive is ready or not.

Property	Description
Path	The path for the drive.
RootFolder	A Folder object representing the root folder for the drive.
SerialNumber	The drive's serial number.
ShareName	The name used, if any, for sharing this drive.
TotalSize	The total space on the drive.
VolumeName	Returns the name of the drive.

If you are going to access a drive's property, first check if the drive is ready. If you don't, you will get an error indicating the drive isn't ready.

The example shown in Figure 11-4 shows how you can use the Drives property to display information about all the drives on the server. To run this script, as is, you will need to put a CD in your CD-ROM drive and a floppy disk in your floppy disk drive. If you want to perform a small test of knowledge, use the IsReady property to update the script so that it won't fail if a drive isn't ready. The solution for that version is on the CD-ROM.

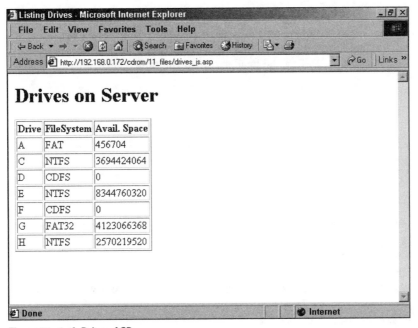

Figure 11-4: A Drives ASP

The JavaScript version of the drives page uses a new object called the `enumerator`. This `enumerator` is used to get to all of the elements in the Drives collection. It has four methods we care about: `atEnd`, `moveFirst`, `item`, and `moveNext`. These are described shortly. Think of the `enumerator` itself as a cursor that moves through the collection providing access to the elements in a sequential order.

First, we start the page off, as follows:

```
<%@ LANGUAGE="JAVASCRIPT" %>

<html>
<head>
<title>Listing Drives</title>
<%
```

Next, we declare variables for the current drive, the Drive collection, the `enumerator`, and the `FileSystemObject`.

```
var fileSystem = Server.CreateObject("Scripting.FileSystemObject");
var drive,drives;
var enumerator;
```

Then we get the collection of drives and create an `enumerator` for it.

```
drives = fileSystem.Drives;
enumerator = new Enumerator(drives);
%>
```

Next, start the HTML. Define the header row of the table that will contain drive information.

```
</head>
<body>
<h1>Drives on Server</h1>
<table border=1>
<tr><th>Drive</th><th>FileSystem</th><th>Avail. Space</th></tr>
<%
```

Then move the `enumerator` to the first element in the collection, as follows:

```
enumerator.moveFirst();
```

Loop, checking each time if the `enumerator` is at the end of the collection, like this:

```
while(!enumerator.atEnd())
{
```

Next, get the current item from the `enumerator`, as follows:

```
    drive = enumerator.item();
%>
```

Display information about the drive in a row of the table. Remember, this will fail if the drive isn't ready.

```
<tr>
<td><%=drive.DriveLetter%></td>
<td><%=drive.FileSystem%></td>
<td><%=drive.AvailableSpace%></td>
</tr>
<%
```

 How could you fix the problem of a drive not being ready? See the CD-ROM for a solution.

Now move the `enumerator` to the next element in the collection. If this is the last one, the `atEnd` method will return `true`.

```
    enumerator.moveNext();
}
%>
```

Close the HTML.

```
</table>
</body>
</html>
```

As you can see, it is pretty easy to get information from the Drive object about a particular drive. The `enumerator` object is an important new tool in your JavaScript toolbox because it is necessary when you want to iterate over collections. The `for-in` syntax will not always work in ASPs. In VBScript, you can use a `For-Each` syntax to accomplish the same task, as shown in Listing 11-3.

Listing 11-3: Using VBScript to list drives

```
<%@ LANGUAGE="VBScript" %>

<html>
<head>
<title>Listing Drives</title>
<%
DIM fileSystem
DIM drive,drives

Set fileSystem = Server.CreateObject("Scripting.FileSystemObject")
Set drives = fileSystem.Drives
%>
</head>
<body>
<h1>Drives on Server</h1>
<table border=1>
<tr><th>Drive</th><th>FileSystem</th><th>Avail. Space</th></tr>
<%
For Each drive In drives
%>
<tr>
<td><%=drive.DriveLetter%></td>
<td><%=drive.FileSystem%></td>
<td><%=drive.AvailableSpace%></td>
</tr>
<%
Next
%>
</table>
</body>
</html>
```

Listing 11-3 shows the same page, but in VBScript. The For-Each loop performs the same job as the enumerator in JavaScript.

You may have noticed from Table 11-3 that the Drive objects provide access to their root folder. This Folder object provides access to the files and folders on the drive. The RootFolder property holds a Folder object. This object has the properties described in Table 11-4.

TABLE 11-4 FOLDER PROPERTIES

Property	Description
Attributes	The attributes associated with this folder. These can be a combination of the following: 0: Normal 1: Read Only 2: Hidden 4: System 8: Volume 16: Directory 32: Archive 64: Alias 128: Compressed
DateCreated	The date the folder was created.
DateLastAccessed	The date for the last time someone accessed the folder.
DateLastModified	The date for the last time someone modified the folder or its contents.
Drive	The drive letter for the drive containing the folder.
IsRootFolder	A Boolean value indicating if this is the root folder for its drive.
Name	The name of the folder.
ParentFolder	The Folder object for the parent of this Folder, which may be null for the RootFolder.
Path	The full path to the folder.
ShortName	The 8.3 version of the folder's name.
ShortPath	The 8.3 version of the folder's path.
Size	The size of the folder and its contents.
SubFolders	A collection of the folders within this folder.

The Folder also has two important collections:

◆ Files

◆ Folders

These are used to recursively access the subfolders and files. From the Folders collection, you can get to the subfolders, as `Folder` objects. From these Folders you can get to others, deeper in the file system. The `Folder` object also has methods to manipulate itself. These are `Copy`, `Delete`, and `Move`. `File` objects are used to represent the files in a folder. These objects have the properties listed in Table 11-5.

TABLE 11-5 FILE OBJECT METHODS

Property	Description
Attributes	The attributes associated with this file. These can be a combination of the following: 0: Normal 1: Read Only 2: Hidden 4: System 8: Volume 16: Directory 32: Archive 64: Alias 128: Compressed
DateCreated	The date the file was created.
DateLastAccessed	The date for the last time someone accessed the file.
DateLastModified	The date for the last time someone modified the file or its contents.
Drive	The drive letter for the drive containing the file.
Name	The name of the file.
ParentFolder	The Folder object for the folder containing this file.
Path	The full path to the file.
ShortName	The 8.3 version of the file's name.
ShortPath	The 8.3 version of the file's path.
Size	The size of the file and its contents.
Type	Information about the file's type.

The `File` object also has four methods, which are listed in Table 11-6.

TABLE 11-6 FILE OBJECT METHODS

Method	Description
Copy	Copies the file to a specified location.
Delete	Deletes the file.
Move	Moves the file to a specified location.
OpenAsTextStream	Opens a text stream for the file.

Notice how the File object can open a text stream on itself. You may want to use this if you are implementing a searching algorithm, or some other ASP that browses the files and looks at their contents. The examples we used previously always knew the path for a file before opening it. This method lets you open a stream on a file without knowing its path ahead of time.

To give you an example of how the File and Folder objects can be used, the page in Listing 11-4 displays information about the files and folders on the C: drive. This page displays two tables, one with folders and one with files.

Start by creating a FileSystemObject and getting to the C: drive. Then get the RootFolder for the C: drive. Use an enumerator to iterate over the files in the root folder and display information about them. Then use a second enumerator to iterate over the folders in the root folder and display information about them. When accessed, this page should look like the one shown in Figure 11-5.

Listing 11-4: Displaying information about files and folders

```
<%@ LANGUAGE="JAVASCRIPT" %>

<html>
<head>
<title>The Root Folder</title>
<%
var fileSystem = Server.CreateObject("Scripting.FileSystemObject");
var drive,root,file,folder;
var enumerator;

drive = fileSystem.GetDrive("c:");
root = drive.RootFolder;
%>
</head>
<body>
<h1>Files on C:</h1>
<table border=1>
```

```
<tr><th>File</th><th>Size</th><th>Date Created</th></tr>
<%
enumerator = new Enumerator(root.Files);
enumerator.moveFirst();

while(!enumerator.atEnd())
{
    file = enumerator.item();
%>
<tr>
<td><%=file.Name%></td>
<td><%=file.Size%></td>
<td><%=file.DateCreated%></td>
</tr>
<%
    enumerator.moveNext();
}
%>
</table>

<h1>Folders on C:</h1>
<table border=1>
<tr><th>File</th><th>Date Created</th></tr>
<%
enumerator = new Enumerator(root.SubFolders);
enumerator.moveFirst();

while(!enumerator.atEnd())
{
    folder = enumerator.item();
%>
<tr>
<td><%=folder.Name%></td>
<td><%=file.DateCreated%></td>
</tr>
<%
    enumerator.moveNext();
}
%>
</table>
</body>
</html>
```

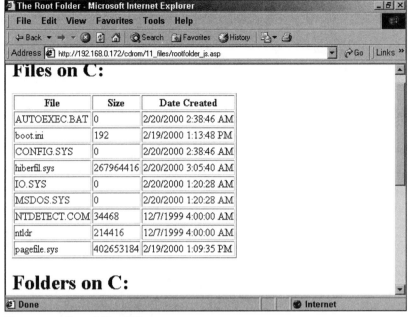

Figure 11-5: Root folder ASP

As you can see, it is pretty easy to browse the file system. The most likely use of these techniques is for searching. It is not a good idea, in general, to display information about your file system to the user.

Summary

File system access in Active Server Pages is controlled and defined by the `FileSystemObject`. Currently, this object restricts reading and writing to text files. Other component providers can extend this functionality and sell ActiveX components that provide access to binary or other files. However, for basic situations, the `FileSystemObject` is more than powerful enough to create file-driven server pages, by providing access to logs, text storage, and non-HTML information.

Chapter 12

Error Handling and Debugging

IN THIS CHAPTER

- Types of errors
- Error handling in VBScript
- Error handling in JavaScript
- Debugging tips

UNFORTUNATELY, ALONG WITH THE power of programming comes the possibility of errors. Of course, programmers rarely cause errors themselves, but users have been known to generate what we call "user errors." When dealing with external components, the file system, networks, and databases, there is also always the problem of some form of system error. As a result, production-level code should deal with the possibility of errors and handling them gracefully when they occur. This chapter takes a look at the types of errors that cause Web servers to send error messages to clients, how these errors are handled in VBScript and JavaScript, and some tips on debugging.

Types of Errors

Usually when we talk about errors, they fall into two major categories: runtime errors, like dividing by zero or trying to access nonexistent data, and I/O errors that occur when reading from a file, database, or some other kind of input/output. If this type of error is not handled, then the ASP engine in the Web server will send a message to the client indicating that the requested page is not available. Although you have probably seen one of these pages before, Figure 12-1 shows the type of error page that the server may produce. You can also configure the Web server to return a different page than this one, resulting in a prettier generic error response.

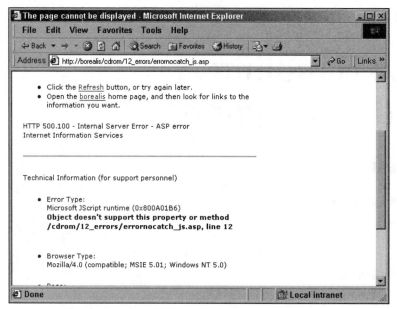

Figure 12-1: A standard error page

When a script handles its own errors, it can return a prettier page, or more useful debugging information. Figure 12-2 shows a possible example of the type of page a script might return.

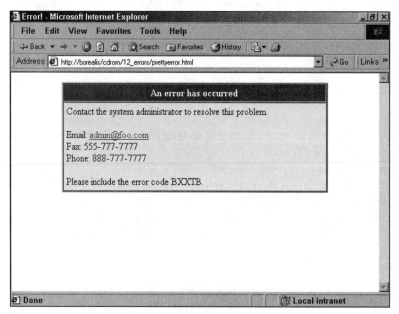

Figure 12-2: A program-generated error page

JavaScript and VBScript use different techniques for dealing with errors. However, both rely on the same basic strategy: perform an action and catch an error if it occurred. This means that the error-handling code is located after the potential error. More importantly, it is up to you to place the code where you want to handle the error. It is possible to execute several lines of code that may generate an error before inserting the code to handle any, or all, of the errors. To handle two possible errors separately, you can use multiple error handlers, as illustrated in Figure 12-3.

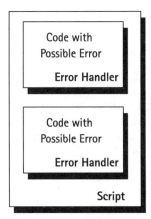

Figure 12-3: Handling multiple errors

The second commonality between VBScript and JavaScript error handling is that errors can be transmitted beyond a procedural boundary. This means that if you call a subroutine that causes an error, your script may still be responsible for handling the error that occurred. This unraveling of subroutine calls as the result of an error is illustrated in Figure 12-4.

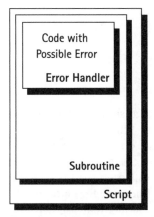

Figure 12-4: Errors in subroutines

Other than these similarities, the VBScript and JavaScript mechanisms for handling errors are quite different. In the next two sections, we will look at the two languages individually, rather than trying to combine our discussion further. In the last section of this chapter, we will discuss some basic ASP debugging techniques.

 ON THE CD   The examples in this section are all available on the CD-ROM. In most cases, general HTML has been removed to focus on the programming. Please refer to the CD-ROM for the complete example.

Error Handling in VBScript

VBScript error handling works by telling the ASP engine to ignore any errors that occur and attempt to continue executing the current script. This means that if an error on one line affects the lines following it, they may also generate an error. To tell the scripting engine to behave this way, include the line

```
On Error Resume Next
```

at the top of your script. This line is self-descriptive; if an error occurs, resume executing on the next line. For example, the following excerpt from errornocheck _vb.asp on the CD-ROM generates an error before and after sending output to the client.

```
On Error Resume Next

DIM x,y,z

x = 0
y = 1

Response.Write("About to divide by zero.<br>")
z = y/x
Response.Write("Divided by zero.<br>")
```

When this page is accessed, both messages are displayed, as shown in Figure 12-5.

By itself, this is a very minimal form of error handling since it really is just a method for ignoring errors, not handling them. To handle errors in VBScript, you have to take advantage of the Err object. When the script engine encounters an error, it stores information about the error in a global object called err, or Err. This Err object is created for you and lives through the entire page. The same Err object will be used to store information about all errors on that page. Scripts that use On Error Resume Next should check Err to see if an error occurred and handle it appropriately.

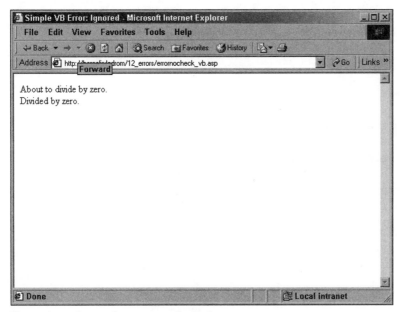

Figure 12-5: Output from errornocheck_vb.asp

The Err object provides properties for learning about what happened. These properties are described in Table 12-1.

TABLE 12-1 ERR OBJECT PROPERTIES

Property	Description
Number	An error code indicating the type of error
Source	The part of the ASP engine that noticed the error, which is often the VBScript runtime
Description	A text description of the error in programmer readable form

For example, in the Listing 12-1 code, an error is generated by treating a number like an object. Immediately after the error occurs, the script checks to see if an error occurred and prints information about it.

Listing 12-1: Treating a number like an object

```
On Error Resume Next

DIM x,y,z
```

```
x = 0
y = 1

z = x.error

If err Then

    Response.Write("Error occurred.<br>")
    Response.Write("<ul>")
    Response.Write("Source: "& err.Source &"<br>")
    Response.Write("Number: "& err.Number &"<br>")
    Response.Write("Description: "& err.Description &"<br>")
    Response.Write("</ul>")
    err.Clear

Else

    Response.Write("No error, z="&z)

End If
```

Placing error-handling code

One disadvantage of this error-handling model is that you need to check for errors whenever they may occur. Because the scripting engine will continue to execute code beyond an error, it is possible for the program's state to change between the time that the error occurred and the Err object was checked. For example, in the Listing 12-2 code, a divide-by-zero error occurs, but other assignments are made before the Err object is checked.

Listing 12-2: Generating a divide-by-zero error

```
On Error Resume Next

DIM x,y,z

x = 0
y = 1

z = 1
z = x/y
z=4
REM Error on the next line
z = y/x
z=5

If err Then
```

```
Response.Write("Error occurred z="& z &"<br>")
Response.Write("<ul>")
Response.Write("Source: "& err.Source &"<br>")
Response.Write("Number: "& err.Number &"<br>")
Response.Write("Description: "& err.Description &"<br>")
Response.Write("</ul>")
err.Clear

Else

Response.Write("No error, z="&z)

End If
```

In this case, a page like the one shown in Figure 12-6 will be displayed. Notice that the value of z has changed to 5, even though this line of code occurred after the error. Also, the Err object knows the last error that occurred, but it wasn't necessarily on the last line executed.

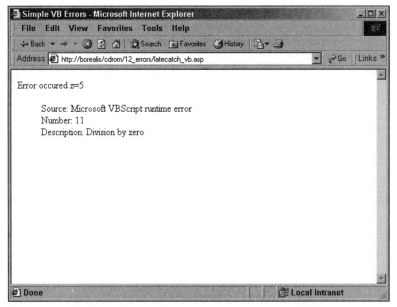

Figure 12-6: Catching the error late

As a programmer this means that the placement of your error-handling code is critically important to your script's behavior. Code placement is even more important when you intend to handle more than one possible error. When multiple errors are possible, you can include multiple checks of the Err object in your code.

However, to make this work, you need to use the Clear method to clean up one error before checking for the next one.

For example, in the Listing 12-3 code there are two places that an error can occur. If an error occurs in the first place, it is handled and the Err object is cleared.

Listing 12-3: Handling and clearing an Err object

```
On Error Resume Next

DIM x,y,z

x = 0
y = 1

z = x.error

If err Then

    Response.Write("Error occurred.<br>")
    Response.Write("<ul>")
    Response.Write("Source: "& err.Source &"<br>")
    Response.Write("Number: "& err.Number &"<br>")
    Response.Write("Description: "& err.Description &"<br>")
    Response.Write("</ul>")
    err.Clear

Else

    Response.Write("No error, z="&z)

End If

Response.Write("<BR>")

z = y/x

If err Then

    Response.Write("Error occurred.<br>")
    Response.Write("<ul>")
    Response.Write("Source: "& err.Source &"<br>")
    Response.Write("Number: "& err.Number &"<br>")
    Response.Write("Description: "& err.Description &"<br>")
    Response.Write("</ul>")
    err.Clear
```

```
Else

    Response.Write("No error, z="&z)

End If
```

If you don't clear the Err object, then an old error can remain stored in the Err object, misleading the script into thinking that an error occurred when it did not. In the next page, shown in Listing 12-4, an error occurs and is handled. But the Err object is not cleared, so when the next check occurs it thinks that an error occurred even though it did not. This will result in a page like the one shown in Figure 12-7, indicating two errors although only one occurred.

Listing 12-4: Generating a mistaken error

```
On Error Resume Next

DIM x,y,z

x = 0
y = 1

z = x.error

If err Then

    Response.Write("Error occurred.<br>")
    Response.Write("<ul>")
    Response.Write("Source: "& err.Source &"<br>")
    Response.Write("Number: "& err.Number &"<br>")
    Response.Write("Description: "& err.Description &"<br>")
    Response.Write("</ul>")

Else

    Response.Write("No error, z="&z)

End If

Response.Write("<BR>")

x = 1
y = 1
REM the next line doesn't create an error
REM but the error wasn't cleared
z = x/y
```

```
If err Then

    Response.Write("Error occurred.<br>")
    Response.Write("<ul>")
    Response.Write("Source: "& err.Source &"<br>")
    Response.Write("Number: "& err.Number &"<br>")
    Response.Write("Description: "& err.Description &"<br>")
    Response.Write("</ul>")
    err.Clear

Else

    Response.Write("No error, z="&z)

End If
```

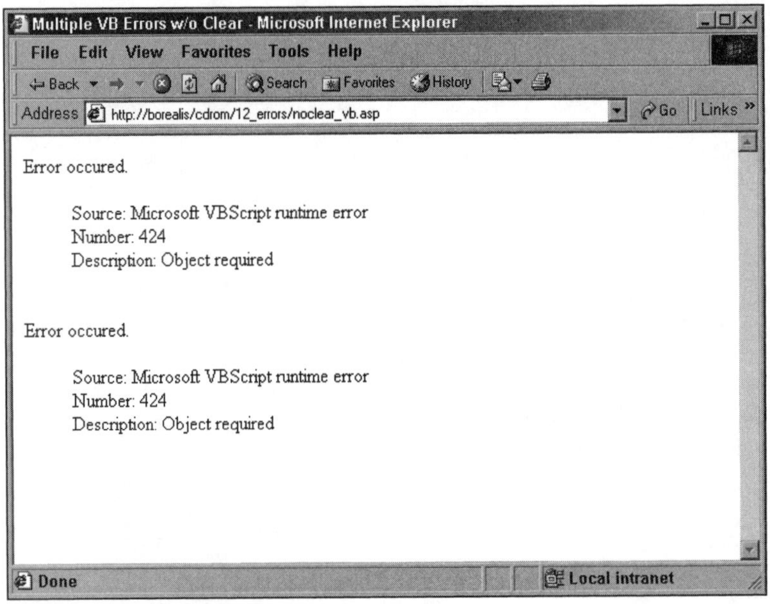

Figure 12-7: Mistaken error

Errors and subroutines

The simplicity of the "resume next" model hits a snag when subroutines are used. By default, each On Error Resume Next is scoped to the script in which it occurs, not including subroutines. This means that if an error occurs in a subroutine, it is up to the caller to handle it. For example, in the Listing 12-5 code, a subroutine called ErrorMaker was defined to generate an error. The script that calls the subroutine handles the error after the error occurs.

Listing 12-5: Defining a subroutine to generate an error

```
On Error Resume Next

Sub ErrorMaker

    DIM x,y,z
    x = 1
    y = 0
    z = x/y

End Sub

Call ErrorMaker

If err Then

    Response.Write("Error occurred in main script.<br>")
    Response.Write("<ul>")
    Response.Write("Source: "& err.Source &"<br>")
    Response.Write("Number: "& err.Number &"<br>")
    Response.Write("Description: "& err.Description &"<br>")
    Response.Write("</ul>")
    err.Clear

Else

    Response.Write("No error in main.")

End If
```

When executed, the Listing 12-5 code will display a page like the one in Figure 12-8.

A caller should not make any assumptions about what happened inside the subroutine that generated an error; that routine may or may not have executed very much code. When you are writing your own subroutines, you may want to handle errors locally, in the routine, rather than requiring the caller to handle problems. In this case, add a call to On Error Resume Next in your subroutine, and handle errors appropriately.

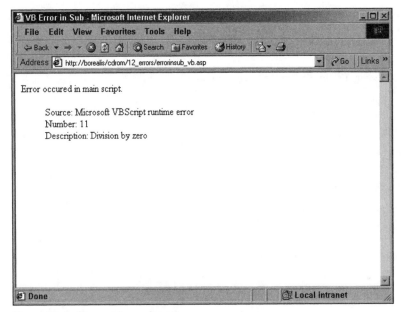

Figure 12-8: An error in a subroutine

The example shown in Listing 12-6 handles an error in a subroutine, and prints a message indicating that the error was handled. The main script, which calls the subroutine, doesn't even know that an error occurred, as shown in Figure 12-9.

Listing 12-6: Handling an error in a subroutine

```
On Error Resume Next

Sub ErrorMaker

REM You must include this in the Subroutine

    On Error Resume Next

    DIM x,y,z
    x = 1
    y = 0
    z = x/y

    If err Then
    Response.Write("Caught Error in Sub.<br>")
    err.Clear
    End If
```

```
End Sub

Call ErrorMaker

If err Then

    Response.Write("Error occurred in main.<br>")
    Response.Write("<ul>")
    Response.Write("Source: "& err.Source &"<br>")
    Response.Write("Number: "& err.Number &"<br>")
    Response.Write("Description: "& err.Description &"<br>")
    Response.Write("</ul>")
    err.Clear

Else

    Response.Write("No error in main.")

End If
```

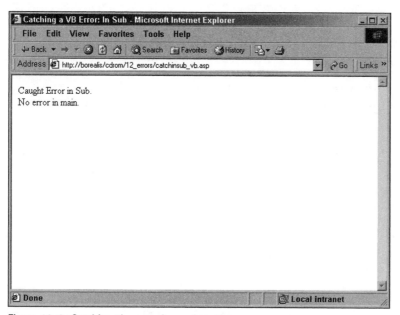

Figure 12-9: Catching the error in a subroutine

In this last example, you can see the absolute necessity of clearing the Err object once an error is handled. Imagine the confusion of trying to handle an error from a subroutine that didn't really exist.

By placing your error handling appropriately, and localizing error handling for subroutines, you should be able to properly manage errors inside your VBScripted Active Server Pages. Keep in mind that VBScript doesn't stop a script on an error when using On Error Resume Next, so it is really up to you as a programmer to take care of problems in scripts where you turn error handling on.

Error Handling in JavaScript

JavaScript uses a different approach to error handling called a try-catch block. A try-catch block works by isolating potential errors and surrounding them with the appropriate error-handling code. The keyword `try` is used to start a block of code, indicated by curly brackets, that isolates the possible error. The keyword `catch` is used to indicate the code to execute if an error occurs in the try block.

 Errors in JavaScript are also called exceptions.

Let's look at an example to see what this means. In the Listing 12-7 code, a script tries to send a message to a number. When this happens, an error is generated.

Listing 12-7: Generating an error by sending a message to a number

```
var x,z;

try
{
    x = 0;
    z = x.error();
    Response.Write("No error, z="+z)
}
catch(err)
{
    Response.Write("Error occurred.<br>");
    Response.Write("<ul>");

    Response.Write("Number: "+err.number+"<br>");
    Response.Write("Description: "+err.description+"<br>");

    Response.Write("</ul>");
}
```

When accessed, this code will display HTML like the page shown in Figure 12-10.

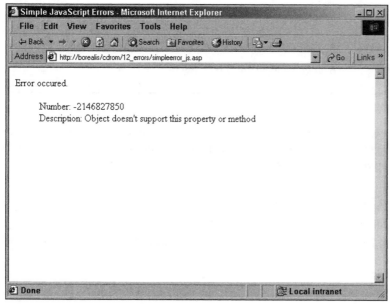

Figure 12-10: Error in JavaScript

As you can see in the figure, the call to `Response.Write` that appears just after the error-generating line is not executed. One of the main differences between VBScript's On Error Resume Next strategy and JavaScript's try-catch blocks is that JavaScript errors stop the normal flow of the program looking for the catch block, whereas the VBScript simply moves to the next line. This means that there may be code in your try block that is never even looked at by the scripting engine. On the other hand, if no error occurs in the try block, then the catch code is ignored.

 You can't have a catch block without a try block.

The second important concept in this example is that an Exception object represents the error. This object has the properties described in Table 12-2.

TABLE 12-2 EXCEPTION OBJECT PROPERTIES

Property	Description
number	An error code indicating the type of error that occurred
description	A programmer-friendly text description of the error

The catch block gets the Exception object as its argument and can name the Exception object anything it wants. In this chapter we normally call the Exception object Err, but you can name it anything, like curException or even just e.

Placing try-catch code

To handle multiple possible errors on a JavaScript ASP, use multiple try-catch combinations. The Listing 12-8 code uses two try-catch constructs to handle two separate possible errors.

Listing 12-8: Using two try-catch constructs

```
var x,z;

try
{
    x = 0;
    z = x.error();
    Response.Write("No error, z="+z)
}
catch(err)
{
    Response.Write("Error occurred.<br>");
    Response.Write("Description: "+err.description+"<br>");
}

Response.Write("<br>");

try
{
    x = 1;
    z = x.error();
    Response.Write("No error, z="+z)
```

```
}
catch(err)
{
    Response.Write("Error occurred.<br>");
    Response.Write("Description: "+err.description+"<br>");
}
```

You can place as many try-catch blocks as necessary to handle the errors you
are planning for. Each try block can contain as little or as much code as you want
to try to execute with the possibility of an Exception object aborting that execution
in favor of the catch block. Try-catch blocks can even be nested inside each other,
as shown in Listing 12-9. The only limitation to this type of nesting is that you
should use a different name for the Exception object in each catch block that is
contained in another catch block.

Listing 12-9: Nesting try-catch blocks

```
var x,z;

try
{
    x = 0;

    try
    {
        x = 0;
        z = x.error();
        Response.Write("No nested error, z="+z)
    }
    catch(err)
    {
        Response.Write("Nested error occurred.<br>");
        Response.Write("Description: "+err.description+"<br>");
    }

    z = x.error();
    Response.Write("No error, z="+z)
}
catch(err)
{
    Response.Write("Error occurred.<br>");
    Response.Write("Description: "+err.description+"<br>");
}
```

When this code is executed within a page, both of the `x.error()` calls generate errors. The inner try-catch code handles the first exception and the outer block handles the second exception.

Exceptions in subroutines

In both VBScript and JavaScript, errors that occur in a subroutine or function will be propagated to the calling code. For example, in the Listing 12-10 code the error generated in the `errorMaker` function is handled in the main script's try-catch block.

Listing 12-10: Generating an error in the errorMaker function

```
var x,z;

x = 0;
z = 0;

function errorMaker()
{
    z = x.error();
}

try
{
    errorMaker()
    Response.Write("No error, z="+z)
}
catch(err)
{
    Response.Write("Error occurred.<br>");
    Response.Write("<ul>");

    Response.Write("Number: "+err.number+"<br>");
    Response.Write("Description: "+err.description+"<br>");

    Response.Write("</ul>");
}
```

However, the subroutines that you write can handle their own errors locally. In the Listing 12-11 example, the `errorMaker` function handles the error and resets the variable z so that it is still usable by the calling code.

Listing 12-11: Handling the errorMaker error in the function

```
var x,z;

x = 0;
z = 0;

function errorMaker()
{
    try
    {
        z = x.error();
    }
    catch(er)
    {
        Response.Write("Caught error in function.<br>");
        z = 5;
    }
}

try
{
    errorMaker()
    Response.Write("No error in main script, z="+z)
}
catch(err)
{
    Response.Write("Error occurred.<br>");
    Response.Write("<ul>");

    Response.Write("Number: "+err.number+"<br>");
    Response.Write("Description: "+err.description+"<br>");

    Response.Write("</ul>");
}
```

When run, the Listing 12-11 example displays a page like the one shown in Figure 12-11.

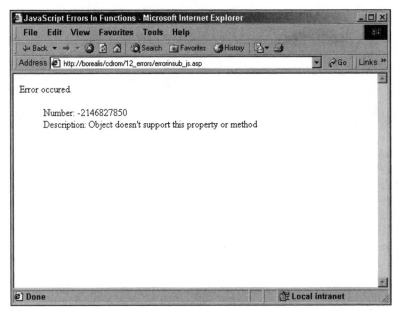

Figure 12-11: Handling an error in a function

Notice how, in this case, the caller is unaware of an error and can continue to execute code normally. Ideally, you will be able to create all of your reusable functions in a way that they handle their own errors, allowing them to propagate to the caller only when absolutely necessary.

Debugging Tips

One of the harder aspects of writing Active Server Pages, or any other Web application, is the debugging. This difficulty arises from the distributed nature of Web programs. Errors occur on the server, but you find out about them on the client. Luckily, the ASP engine provides a number of mechanisms for debugging your pages and correcting any program errors.

Your first line of defense when trying to find and fix errors is the error page that the ASP engine returns. These error pages, like the one shown in Figure 12-12, are sent to the client automatically when a programming error occurs in an ASP, and it is not handled using error handling as described previously. As you can see, an error page indicates the type of error as well as the line on which it occurred.

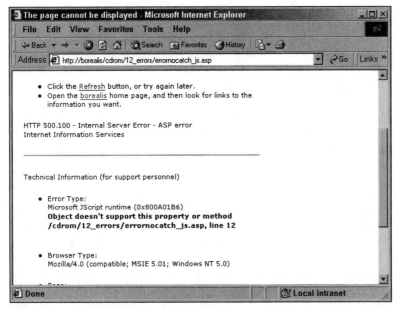

Figure 12-12: A typical ASP error page

Once you have a page that doesn't return any errors, the next step is to make sure that it works properly. If it doesn't, then you need to figure out what and where a problem is occurring. To do this, you first use logic to determine where you think the error is. Then using one or more of the following tools, you can pinpoint and fix the error:

◆ Response.Write

◆ The Log file

◆ Script Debugger

◆ Visual Interdev

Let's look at each of these techniques in turn. Perhaps one of the oldest and most reliable forms of debugging is to put "print" statements in your code. These statements might print values of key variables, or simply indicate a location in the code. Since errors stop normal execution of code, the messages you get, and more important don't get, tell you where a problem is occurring. There are two ways to print messages: `Response.Write` and `Response.AppendToLog`. The first prints messages that are easier to read, but the log should be more reliable in the case of a bad error.

If you use this style of debugging, you will need to combine it with your error-handling code.

Of course, you can also use error handling to find problems. In a large application, you will be combining your error-handling code with your debugging code throughout the development process. You may decide to include logging in all of your exception handling to ensure that your pages track problems throughout their life.

The final two debugging techniques rely on tools. The Microsoft script debugger and Visual Interdev both provide graphical debugging capabilities. These tools allow you to set breakpoints in your code, where the script engine stops execution to allow you to inspect the values of variables. You can also use these tools to step through code, one line at a time, looking for errors.

Part of your ASP applications will be the HTML forms that you submit to ASPs. One technique you may find useful when debugging these forms is to print out all of the contents of the Request object's collections. This may help you find naming problems that cause an ASP to fail.

Summary

By using debugging techniques to remove programming errors from your scripts and error handling to manage runtime errors, you can create reliable Active Server Pages for even the most strenuous corporate applications. Always keep in mind that errors will often occur when the page is trying to access outside resources, like a file or database. Protect code that accesses these resources and respond to errors in a user-friendly manner. For the user, a page saying that the service is unavailable is much more appealing than a runtime error page generated by the scripting engine.

Chapter 13

Application Persistence

IN THIS CHAPTER

- ◆ Cookies
- ◆ Other persistence mechanisms

IN CHAPTER 5 YOU SAW how the Session object can be used to maintain information about the current client session. Although the Session object is a great resource during a client's interaction with the ASP application, it doesn't survive beyond one session. Many applications need some way to store information beyond a single session. For example, a Web site might want to remember each user's client identification number.

In this case, you need to introduce some form of persistence to your application and there are several ways to do this. The first way is with HTTP cookies. These cookies live on the client's computer but are provided to your ASP as needed. The second most common persistence mechanism is to use a file to store information. Finally, many large applications use a database to store information between client sessions.

Cookies

If you have used the Web you have probably heard the term *cookie*. But often this simple concept is treated as an insidious virus to be feared. In reality, a cookie is just a little piece of text stored on your computer. Web applications, on the server, assign cookies to a client. The client's browser stores the cookie in a text file. When the client returns to the same server it forwards the cookie along with any requests. In other words, the cookie becomes a persistent string of text that the client and server share. This relationship between the server and client is shown in Figure 13-1. In this figure you will see that the server sets cookies. This usually happens the first time the client comes to that server. Then the client stores the cookie in a text file. Finally, each time the client returns to the server, the cookie is included in the HTTP message.

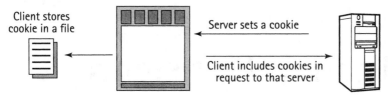

Figure 13-1: HTTP cookies

Since the cookie is stored on the client the server doesn't have to make the association between the data in the cookie and the cookie itself. This relationship between client and data is part of the definition of cookies.

HTTP, the protocol used by the Web server and browser to communicate, breaks messages into two pieces, a header and a body. The header contains named fields, like the content type of a reply or the type of request being made. Cookies rely on the header of an HTTP request and reply for their transport. Transferring the cookies in the header means that the person using the browser won't see the cookie; they are transparent and that's why cookies scare some folks.

What are cookies?

Really, cookies are just some text; they're not very scary at all. The text in a cookie is grouped into key-value pairs. These pairs define a cookie's properties including its:

◆ Name

◆ Data

◆ Expiration

◆ Domain

◆ Path

◆ Security

Let's take a look at each of these in turn. First, the cookie's name and data are just strings of characters. It should not contain white space, colons, semicolons or any other "special" characters. To protect the cookie, the data is often URL-encoded, replacing special characters with hexadecimal codes. The server will use the name to find the cookie, especially in the case where a server uses more than one cookie per client.

The expiration date for a cookie indicates how long the client should keep track of it. If a cookie doesn't have an expiration date, then it will survive as long as the user keeps their browser open. Once they close the browser, the cookie is gone. However, if the cookie has an expiration date, it is stored in a text file by the browser, so that it can persist among the various times that the user runs the browser application.

An expiration date is specified as follows:

```
expiration= Weekday, DD- Mon- YY HH: MM: SS GMT;
```

This format is standardized, and should be used for all cookies.

The domain for a cookie is used to control the servers that receive it. By default the domain for a cookie is the server it came from. For example, if Amazon.com sets a cookie on your computer, then only the server(s) at Amazon.com will receive the cookie with your browser's requests. If you also have a cookie from Barnes and Noble's Web site, it will not be sent to Amazon.com, and neither will know that you have been shopping at their competitor. The form for assigning the domain of a cookie, in the HTTP header, is as follows:

```
domain= pri.com;
```

Domains solve one of the main security concerns for cookies, which is that a cookie's domain prevents crosstalk between servers at different companies. The reasonable concern that some users will have about cookies comes from companies placing ad banners or other resources on their pages that live in different domains. For example, one ad company was recently "outed" for their use of cookies to track the users surfing habits. In this case, the sites that were tracked all used that company's ads on their pages. By commingling the resources for the Web page, they were able to bypass the domain separation provided by the cookie's domain value. Each company displaying the ads could include information in the ad request that would associate the ad's cookie with the user, thus creating a shared tracking mechanism.

A cookie's path constrains the cookie even more. When a path is assigned, the client will restrict the cookie to requests at that path, or a subpath. In other words, it sets a directory on the Web server that the cookie belongs to. To manually assign the path, use the following:

```
serverpath=/;
```

Finally, the cookie can be set to secure. When secured, the cookie will only be sent if the server and client are communicating over a secured socket layer (SSL) connection. This means that the cookie is encrypted, protecting it from prying eyes on the Internet. A cookie is secured by including the following:

```
secure;
```

in the HTTP header field that defines it.

Keep in mind that although cookies can be secured, and limited to a particular domain, they are not foolproof. In general, cookies should be used for customer IDs and other innocuous data, not credit card and social security numbers. Most users consider cookies to be a possible breach of privacy, if not security, and it is up to Web programmers to respect the privacy of their cookie clients.

Limitations on cookies

The mainstream browsers have placed a number of limitations on cookies. These range from restricting the size of a cookie to the number of cookies that a particular domain can assign.

The first limitation on a cookie is that it cannot be more than 4KB in size, including the name and attributes. When you think about it, this allows for a pretty big string of text, and is a limitation that you should avoid even thinking about exceeding. Remember that cookies go back and forth with the client's requests to the server that set them. If you set four 4KB cookies, that's 16KB with each request. If you do exceed this limitation, your cookie will be trimmed to fit.

Next, a domain is only allowed to set 20 separate cookies. In general, most sites use a cookie to store a user ID and store any other information using the file system or a database. The ID is used to look up the client's record in the persistent storage on the server machine. This reduces both the size and number of cookies, while still taking advantage of their implicit relationship with a particular client.

Most browsers will limit the total number of cookies to around 300. This means that at any one time, you will only be storing 300 or fewer cookies on your computer. It also means, as a programmer, that the cookie you set may not be stored on the client's file indefinitely. When either the 20 or 300 cookie limits are exceeded, the least used cookie is deleted from the cookies database.

Also, users can turn off cookies for their browser, and older browsers don't support cookies. Meaning that you, as the programmer, have to plan for the cookie to go missing, or not exist. To handle this situation, most sites support both a cookie-based identification process and a straight login process. After the login occurs, a cookie is set, putting it at the top of the list, and allowing it to be used for other pages during the client's session.

ASP and cookies

Active Server Pages have access to the HTTP cookies that move between the client and server. Cookies are set in the Cookies collection of the Response object. Cookies are read from the Cookies collection in the Request object. Each cookie is represented by a Cookie object that has properties to control the expiration and other configuration parameters. These properties are listed in Table 13-1.

TABLE 13-1 COOKIE OBJECT PROPERTIES

Name	Description	Example
Expires	The date the cookie expires	`January 1, 2000`
Domain	The server the cookie belongs to	`www.pri.com`
Path	The directories on the server with which the cookie is associated	`/marketing`
Secure	Whether the cookie should only be available over secure connections	`True`

Cookie objects in the two Cookies collections are accessed by name. For example, to access a cookie called firstVisit you would use the following code:

```
firstVisit = Request.Cookies("firstVisit");
```

To set this cookie, you would use the following syntax:

```
Response.Cookies("firstVisit") = firstVisit;
```

 These two examples come from the file simplecookie_js.asp.

This ASP also demonstrates another common aspect of cookie programming. When you use cookies, you will encounter two kinds of clients, those with the cookie already, and those without it. This means that the first thing a cookie ASP will probably do is check for the cookie's existence. If the cookie has not been set, then it is initialized. The simplecookie_js.asp example shown in Listing 13-1 uses this technique to display the first time it was visited by each unique user.

Listing 13-1: Initializing a cookie on the first visit

```
<%@ LANGUAGE="JAVASCRIPT" %>
<%
var firstVisit;

firstVisit = Request.Cookies("firstVisit");
```

```
if(!firstVisit || (firstVisit==null) || (firstVisit==""))
{
    firstVisit = (new Date()).toString();
    Response.Cookies("firstVisit") = firstVisit;
}
%>

<html>
<head>
<title>Simple JavaScript Cookie</title>
</head>
<body>
<%
Response.Write("Your first visit was: "+firstVisit);
Response.Write("<br>");
Response.Write("It is currently: "+(new Date()).toString());
%>
</body>
</html>
```

Another technique that this page demonstrates is that cookies should be set at the top of an ASP so that they can be assigned to the HTTP header. If you send HTML before you set the cookie, it may not make it to the client. Depending on your luck, this can be a programming error that doesn't generate any exceptions. As a result, your cookies will just seem to disappear. Be very careful about where you set cookies; always do it first, even if that requires using variables to store data for displaying in the HTML.

Setting properties is just an extension of the syntax from the previous example. The code in Listing 13-2 sets a cookie with a two-month expiration date. As you read the example, note that in JavaScript the Locale string is used to set a cookie's expiration. In VBScript you can set expiration dates using Date objects directly.

Listing 13-2: Setting a cookie with a two-month expiration date

```
<%@ LANGUAGE="JAVASCRIPT" %>
<%
var expire,expireString;
var month,year;

Response.Cookies("twomonths") = "Two months";

expire = new Date();

month = expire.getMonth();
year = expire.getFullYear();
```

```
if(month > 9)
{
    month = (month+2)%12;
    year = year+1;
}
else
{
    month = month+2;
}

expire.setMonth(month);
expire.setFullYear(year);

expireString = expire.toLocaleString();
Response.Cookies("last").Expires = expireString;
%>


<html>
<head>
<title>Expiring JavaScript Cookie</title>
</head>
<body>

<%
Response.Write("The cookie is set.");
%>

</body>
</html>
```

The Listing 13-2 example also uses some logic to account for months near the end of the year. VBScript provides a built-in function for adding time to a date, whereas JavaScript requires you to perform this operation by hand. Of course, you can create reusable functions for this type of operation if you plan to do it a lot.

Multivalued cookies

Remember that there are limits on cookies, both a total limit per client and a limit per domain. The Cookie object can support multiple values so that one cookie can hold more than one piece of data. To access these multiple values, you access each one as an attribute of the cookie, by name. For example, to access the value of the message field in the cookie named "compound use" you would use the following:

```
Request.Cookies("compound")("message")
```

Putting this concept with the previous example, we created the page compound-cookie_js.asp. This page, shown in Listing 13-3, sets two values for a cookie and displays them each time the user accesses the page.

Listing 13-3: Setting two values for a cookie

```
<%@ LANGUAGE="JAVASCRIPT" %>
<%
var cookie;
var first,message;

cookie = Request.Cookies("compound");

if(!cookie || (cookie==null) || (cookie==""))
{
    first = (new Date()).toString();
    message = "Hello";
    Response.Cookies("compound")("firstVisit") = first;
    Response.Cookies("compound")("message") = message;
}
else
{
    message = Request.Cookies("compound")("message");
    first = Request.Cookies("compound")("firstVisit");
}
%>

<html>
<head>
<title>Compound JavaScript Cookie</title>
</head>
<body>
<%
Response.Write("<h1>"+message+"</h1>");
Response.Write("Your first visit was: "+first);
%>

</body>
</html>
```

Although multivalued cookies make it easy to store information in an organized fashion, you should limit your use to applications that require persistence. In general, you will want to use the Session object to store temporary information about a client session. Of course, cookies can be mixed between different server technologies, so they provide a great mechanism for sharing information about a client between ASPs and CGI scripts, or other server programs.

TIP Remember: cookies should be set at the top of your ASP, before any HTML is sent to the client.

Using cookies to manage user logins

One of the places that you have probably run into cookies recently is in managing your login to a Web site. Many of the online stores and magazines require you to register before you use them. Although this registration is usually free, you are required to log in before using the site. Often, your login can be set up as manual or automatic. In other words, you can either type in your username and password each time you go to the site, or you can have your browser "memorize" your identification and send it automatically. The memorization feature for these sites normally uses cookies.

Let's look at a small example that implements this functionality. We will create three ASPs: the first allows you to log in, the second lets you log out, and the third will be used as an example of a page inside the site that requires you to log in before you access it.

When the user tries to access either the logout or test page, the page checks to see if the client's username is stored in a cookie. If the username cookie is not set, the page redirects the client to the login page. As an added bonus, the page tells the login page which page the user was really trying to access. This way, the user will be sent directly to their requested page after they log in.

The login page checks to see if the user is already logged in, and if so, forwards them to either a requested destination, as described above, or to the logout page. Of course, on a real site the login page would direct you to an index page of some sort after a default login. The login page displays a form, which is shown in Figure 13-2, that the user can fill out with their username and password. There is also a check box to indicate if they want the site to "memorize" their identity. This form is submitted to the login page itself; remember it is an ASP so it has access to form elements. If a login is successful, the client's username is stored in a cookie and they are redirected appropriately. If the memorize box is checked, then the cookie has an expiration date assigned to it so that it will be maintained between client sessions.

Let's look at these three pages in turn, starting with the login page.

 ON THE CD The login page is available on the CD-ROM in VBScript and JavaScript. The JavaScript version is called login_js.asp, and it is shown in the next section.

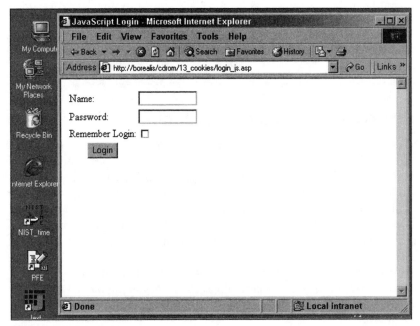

Figure 13-2: A login page

LOGIN PAGE

Start the login page off by declaring any variables that will be used in the page's scripts. In this case, we will store the username, password, remember flag, and requested destination in variables.

```
<%@ LANGUAGE="JAVASCRIPT" %>
<%
var username=null;
var password=null;
var remember=null;
var dest=null;
```

Try to get a cookie called username. This is the cookie we will use to identify the client.

```
username = Request.Cookies("username");
```

If this line returns an undefined value for username, replace the undefined value with null.

```
if((""+username) == "undefined") username = null;
```

See if there is a requested destination in the query string. Other pages on the site will provide this value via the URL. For example, the test page will use a URL of the following form:

```
http://server/login_js.asp?dest=test_js.asp
```

to access the login page. This dest variable may be undefined, null, or empty, but we will check on that later.

```
dest = Request.QueryString("dest");
```

Check to see if the username cookie was empty. If so, try to get the username, password, and remember flag from the form on this page. Notice that this will also set the username variable to null or a similar value if the page was accessed directly rather than through the form.

```
if((username==null) || (username==""))
{
    username = Request.Form("username");
    password = Request.Form("password");
    remember = Request.Form("remember");
```

For this example, allow the user to log in if the username and password match. On a real site, this test will probably require a file or database lookup.

```
    if((username != password)
        &&!eval("\""+username+"\"==\""+password+"\""))
            username=null;
}
```

Again, reset the username if it is undefined, and perform the same test for the dest variable.

```
if((""+username) == "undefined") username = null;
```

```
if((""+dest) == "undefined") dest = null;
```

If the dest variable wasn't set, assign it the default value. We are using a logout page for this example, but you would probably use an index type page in a real application.

```
if((dest==null) || (dest=="")) dest = "logout_js.asp";
```

Now, if the username is not null, or empty, then either it was in the cookie, or it was in the form and the password was okay. In both of these cases we want to redirect the client to the destination page.

```
if((username!=null) && (username!=""))
{
```

First, set the username cookie.

```
    Response.Cookies("username")=username;
```

Now, check the remember flag. If it is on, then set the expiration for the username cookie to one month from now, as shown in Listing 13-4.

Listing 13-4: Setting the expiration for the username cookie

```
    if(remember=="on")
    {
        var expire,expireString;
        var month,year;

        expire = new Date();

        month = expire.getMonth();
        year = expire.getFullYear();

        if(month == 11)
        {
            month = 0;
            year = year+1;
        }
        else
        {
            month = month+1;
        }

        expire.setMonth(month);
        expire.setFullYear(year);
        expireString = expire.toLocaleString();

        Response.Cookies("username").Expires = expireString;
    }
```

Redirect the client to the dest variable. This will either be from the query string or the default.

```
    Response.Redirect(dest);
}
%>
```

If the client wasn't redirected, then they weren't logged in properly. In this case, display the login form.

```
<html>
<head>
<title>JavaScript Login</title>
</head>
<body>
```

In the case that another page pointed the user to this page, there may be a dest value in the query string. Make sure to include the query string shown in Listing 13-5 when pointing the form back to the login page.

Listing 13-5: Defining the login form

```
<form method="POST" action="login_js.asp?dest=<%=dest%>">

<table border=0>
<tr>
<td>Name:</td>
<td><input type="text" name="username" size=12></td>
</tr>
<tr>
<td>Password:</td>
<td><input type="password" name="password" size=12></td>
</tr>
<tr>
<td>Remember Login:</td>
<td><input type="checkbox" name="remember" value="on"></td>
</tr>
<tr colspan=2>
<td><center><input type="submit" value="Login"></center></td>
</tr>
</table>
</form>

</body>
</html>
```

EXAMPLE PAGE

Once this login page is installed, you can update the other pages on the site to require login. The following page displays very little HTML but contains the code necessary to check for user login. (See Listing 13-6.)

 The page discussed in this section is called testlogin_js.asp on the CD-ROM.

Listing 13-6: Checking for user login

```
<%@ LANGUAGE="JAVASCRIPT" %>
<%
```

Start by looking for the username cookie.

```
var username=null;

username = Request.Cookies("username");
if((""+username) == "undefined") username = null;
```

If the cookie is not there, the user is not logged in. Redirect them to the login page, setting the dest value in the query string to make sure that they come back to this page after they log in.

```
if((username==null) || (username==""))
{
    Response.Redirect("login_js.asp?dest=testlogin_js.asp");
}
%>
```

Place the remaining HTML or code after the login test and redirect.

```
<html>
<head>
<title>JavaScript Test Login</title>
</head>
<body>
You are logged in.
</body>
</html>
```

LOGOUT PAGE

On a real site many of the pages might have a button that allows the user to log out. In this case, logging out means that the username cookie is set to "" and the user is redirected to the login page. The following page displays a message to the user and a button that can be used to log out, as shown in Figure 13-3.

Figure 13-3: A logout page

Like the login page shown previously, this page both displays the button that initiates a logout and acts as the target for the form containing the button.

```
<%@ LANGUAGE="JAVASCRIPT" %>
<%
```

First, this page tries to get the username cookie.

```
var username;

username = Request.Cookies("username");
if((""+username) == "undefined") username = null;
```

If the cookie is empty, or the logout button was pressed, then the cookie is set to "" and the client is redirected to the login page. Note that this code does have the side effect that if a user is not logged in and tries to access the page, then they will have their cookie set to "" and be sent to the login page.

```
if((Request.Form("logout") == "logout")
    ||(username==null) || (username==""))
{
    Response.Cookies("username") = "";
    Response.Redirect("login_js.asp");
}
%>
```

The page itself displays a personalized message to the user and a Logout button. On a real site, the username might be used to look up information in the database. Then the database data could be used to personalize the user's experience on the site. (See Listing 13-7.)

Listing 13-7: Defining the logout page

```
<html>
<head>
<title>JavaScript Logout</title>
</head>
<body>

Hi <%=username%>.
<form method="POST" action="logout_js.asp">
<input type="submit" value="Logout">
<input type="hidden" name="logout" value="logout">
</form>

</body>
</html>
```

As you can see, cookies can be used to create a pretty sophisticated user experience with only 50 or so lines of code. If you are working on an e-commerce type of site, or any site that requires personalization, you might consider using this type of code to manage your users and support their login options.

Other Persistence Mechanisms

In Chapter 11 we discussed how you can access files in your Active Server Pages. Files can be a powerful mechanism for storing data that is shared by clients but isn't changed by them. That way, you don't have to worry about locking the files.

One powerful technique that you may want to use is to cache the data from a file in the Application object as part of an `Application_OnStart` script. This will allow the application to access shared information very quickly, while maintaining persistence between Application invocations. Because the data will be in memory, you may want to provide an administrative page to reload the data outside of the OnStart script.

For example, the code in Listing 13-8 loads an address from a file during the `Application_OnStart` script:

Listing 13-8: Loading an address from a file

```
<SCRIPT RUNAT="SERVER" LANGUAGE="JAVASCRIPT">

function Application_OnStart()
{
    var addrFile;
    var ForReading = 1;
    var fileStream;
    var address;

    try
    {
        fileStream =
            Server.CreateObject("Scripting.FileSystemObject");

        addrFile = "c:\\shared\\cdrom\\address.txt";

        file = fileStream.OpenTextFile(addrFile,ForReading,true);

        address = "";

        while(!file.AtEndOfStream)
        {
            address += file.ReadLine();
        }

        file.Close();
    }
    catch(e)
    {
```

```
        address = "";
    }

    Application("Address") = address;
}
</SCRIPT>
```

The address is stored in the Application object for later use. Pages like the following use the data directly, without having to access the file system:

```
<%@ LANGUAGE="JAVASCRIPT" %>

<html>
<head>
<title>Display File Cache: JavaScript</title>
</head>
<body>
The address is:<br>
<%=Application("Address")%>
</body>
</html>
```

These two files are on the CD-ROM, as well as a file called reloadcache_js.asp that shows how you might create a file for the administrator to use to reload the file data.

If you are using VBScript, you may want to use a Dictionary object to store data from a file. This will provide the same effect as a custom object in the JavaScript version. Of course you can also access files directly in your scripts.

The primary persistence mechanism for many large Web sites is a relational database of some sort. Many companies actually use several databases to store all of their data, and use a single Web site to provide an interface on top of these multiple sources. In the next chapter we will discuss how you can access a database and use it to store data for your Active Server Pages.

Summary

If you compare the various persistence mechanisms, databases are probably the best for large amounts of data and data that change a lot. Files are best for medium to small datasets that are primarily read-only. Cookies are best for very small data sets. Cookies have the primary advantage that they relate their data to a specific client, while files and databases require the ASP to know which client is currently accessing them.

By combining these technologies you can create a powerful, information-rich and user-friendly Web site. Typically you'll want to:

◆ Store most of your information on a database or in a file

◆ Set a cookie with the key to the database record

◆ Let the ASP server use cookies to maintain the Session object and use the Session object for your data

As you read through the next chapter, keep in mind how sessions or cookies could be used to augment your database applications.

Chapter 14

Database Access in Active Server Pages

IN THIS CHAPTER

◆ Active Data Objects

◆ How to create the database

◆ Basic database access

◆ Connections

◆ Commands

◆ Advanced RecordSet usage

◆ About the database

◆ Database errors

◆ Transaction basics

◆ Database access tips

IF YOU ARE READING this book it is likely that you, like most Web developers, want to use a database to store data for your Web applications, or access data stored in a database to create your Web pages. If you haven't considered using a database as part of your Web applications, chances are you should. A database is a reliable, organized data storage mechanism that will often improve the performance and maintainability of your Web applications. You can use a database to store customer accounts, user profiles, and just about anything else you want to keep track of, and want to last beyond the execution of a single ASP. In this chapter we will explore how your Active Server Pages can access a relational database server.

Active Data Objects

A database server or database application manages data for you. These programs range in complexity from a simple flat-file database engine like Microsoft Access, to large scalable solutions like Microsoft's SQL server, Oracle, Sybase, and Informix. Depending on your application, you may need a database at either end of

215

this spectrum, or possibly one in the middle, like the semi-freeware database MySQL. Regardless of your needs, you will access databases in the same way from your Active Server Pages. Actually, that's a bit of a lie. You will use the same objects, called Active Data Objects, to access your database, but some of the features will be available or unavailable depending on the database engine. As you read this chapter, keep an eye out for where we indicate a feature that is likely to be database-dependent.

 Since this isn't a book on database technology, for this chapter we assume you have a basic knowledge of database technology. However some of the basics are included as a review and to set the context for other discussions.

There are three main Active Data Objects that you will use to access databases in Active Server Pages: Connection, Command, and RecordSet. These objects are shown in Figure 14-1.

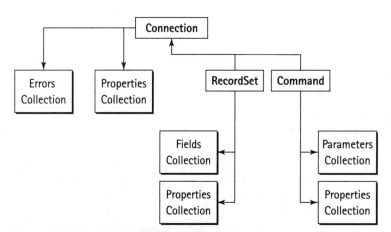

Figure 14-1: The Active Data Objects: Connection, Command, and RecordSet

A Connection object is responsible for working with ODBC and native libraries to communicate with a database. Command objects represent a database command, and the RecordSet is used to read data retrieved from the database. As you progress through the chapter we will discuss each of these objects in turn. But first, let's look at some basic database access techniques.

Creating the Database

The first step before you create a database-powered ASP is to create the database. This entails defining a set of named tables to store your data. Each table consists of rows, or records. A record is a collection of data items, called columns. Each column has a name and a type. For example, you might have a column named student_name that stores a string and another called passport_photo that stores an image. When you design the database, you determine what kind of records you want. The record types correspond to the tables. Then you figure out what data each record should include. That determines the columns. As an example, the database used in the following examples has two tables called `products` and `choices` containing the columns described in Tables 14-1 and 14-2.

TABLE 14-1 PRODUCTS TABLE SCHEMA

Column	Description
id	A short string that uniquely identifies the product
name	The name of the product, as a string
description	A brief description of the product
longDescription	A longer description of the product
msrp	The suggested price, as a double
price	The actual price, as a double

TABLE 14-2 CHOICES TABLE SCHEMA

Column	Description
name	The string name of this choice
choice_id	A number uniquely identifying this choice
score	A numeric score for this choice

After you design the database, you will need to create it. This process is very database-dependent. Regardless of the database, you basically follow a two-step process. First you create the database itself, and then you define the schema. This schema defines the tables and columns. To create the database you might create a file, as in Microsoft Access, or you might run some kind of administration tool. Some database engines, like Access, provide graphical tools for defining the database schema. Other engines expect you to use SQL commands to create the database schema. For the examples in this chapter we created the database schema with an Active Server Page that executes the commands necessary to build the table and columns. Our build script, called build_db.asp, also loads the database with some preliminary data. We have also created a build script called build_db2.asp that creates the same schema on a different datasource. This allows us to create scripts that switch between sources, or use multiple sources.

Once you have a database, the next step is to make it available to your Active Server Pages. The easiest way to do this is to set up an ODBC datasource name, or DSN. Create this DSN using the ODBC control panel or administrator on your computer. When you create the DSN you will configure which database it is associated with and any configuration parameters, as shown in Figure 14-2. For the examples, we created a DSN called asp_devguide for a MySQL database, and another called asp_devguide2, for an MS Access database. These DSNs are used throughout the small examples in this chapter.

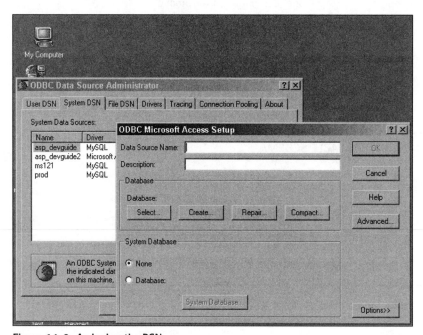

Figure 14-2: Assigning the DSN

Remember that you will be accessing the same objects to access your database regardless of the type of database you use. That makes this DSN an even more important rendezvous point for your ASP and the database. Once you have the database defined, created, and published, you are ready to access it from your ASPs.

Basic Database Access

There are a number of ways to access a database from ASP. Your choice of methods will depend on your ultimate goal. For example, you will access a database differently if you are going to perform multiple operations with the same database connection than you will if you only want to get one table worth of data. As you progress through this chapter, we will discuss a number of the connection and access techniques, but let's start with the simplest one – issuing a database query.

A database query

Suppose that you want to connect to a database and retrieve one table of data. In particular, let's write a program that gets the data from our products table and displays it as an HTML table. To perform this simple operation we can use the ADODB.RecordSet object. RecordSet objects will be the way that we read database data regardless of the access mechanism, so they are a great place to start our discussion.

To use a record set, you first create it using the Server object. In the following line of code, we create a record set and store it in the recordSet variable:

```
var recordSet = Server.CreateObject("ADODB.RecordSet");
```

or in VBScript, it looks like this:

```
Set recordSet = Server.CreateObject("ADODB.RecordSet")
```

Once you have a record set created, you can tell it to perform a query on your database. For example, in the line of code that follows, we use JavaScript to tell our RecordSet object to open a connection to the asp_devguide database and execute the command select * from products.

```
recordSet.Open("select * from products;","DSN=asp_devguide")
```

Notice that we are telling the record set the database source name (DSN) for our database. Later we will see how you could also provide a username and password.

When a record set executes a query, it retrieves the first data record from the query, and stores it in a collection. You access this data by column name. For example, to access the name from the first record, use the following syntax:

```
recordSet("name")
```

Given this first record, the obvious question is how do I get to the next one? The answer is to use the MoveNext method, as follows:

```
recordSet.MoveNext()
```

This will step the record set to the next record in the database table that was queried. Of course, there are a limited number of records, so to check if you are at the last record, you can use the EOF property.

Taking these basics – creating a record set, connecting it to the database, accessing data, and moving through records – let's create a page that displays the name and description for each record in the products table. This example is available on the CD-ROM under the name simplequery_js.asp and simplequery_vb.asp for the JavaScript and VBScript versions, respectively. As with any good ASP, start off by defining the language you are using and begin the HTML for this page to return, as follows:

```
<%@ LANGUAGE="JAVASCRIPT" %>

<html>
<head>
<title>Data From Database</title>
</head>
<body>
<%
```

Next, create the record set, and connect it to the asp_devguide datasource, like this:

```
var recordSet = Server.CreateObject("ADODB.RecordSet")
recordSet.Open("select * from products;","DSN=asp_devguide")
```

Start writing an HTML table with a border size of one, like this:

```
Response.Write("<table border=1>")
```

Now, loop over the records in the products table. Keep looping until we get to the last record by checking the value of recordSet.EOF.

```
while(!recordSet.EOF)
{
```

For each record, write out an HTML table row containing two cells, as follows:

```
Response.Write("<tr>")
Response.Write("<td>")
```

In the first cell, write the name of the current database record, as shown here:

```
Response.Write(recordSet("name"))
```

Close that HTML cell and start the next one, like this:

```
Response.Write("</td>")
Response.Write("<td>")
```

In the second cell, write the description of the current database record, as follows:

```
Response.Write(recordSet("description"))
```

Close the second HTML cell and the row, as follows:

```
Response.Write("</td>")
Response.Write("</tr>")
```

When the row is complete, move to the next one. Be sure to include the following line in your code or your loop will run forever, since the recordSet will always be pointing at the first record in the database.

```
recordSet.MoveNext()
}
```

Conclude the page by closing the HTML table and HTML page, as shown here:

```
Response.Write("</table>")
%>
</body>
</html>
```

That's it. If you install the test database and access this page, you should see an HTML table like the one shown in Figure 14-3.

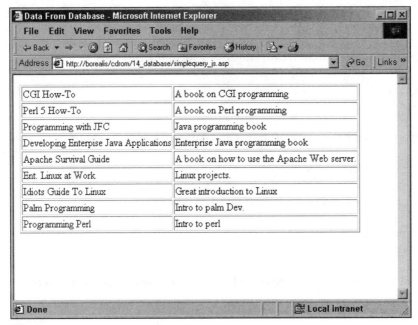

CGI How-To	A book on CGI programming
Perl 5 How-To	A book on Perl programming
Programming with JFC	Java programming book
Developing Enterpise Java Applications	Enterprise Java programming book
Apache Survival Guide	A book on how to use the Apache Web server.
Ent. Linux at Work	Linux projects.
Idiots Guide To Linux	Great introduction to Linux
Palm Programming	Intro to palm Dev.
Programming Perl	Intro to perl

Figure 14-3: The simplequery_js.asp page

As you can see, the syntax for accessing a database is pretty straightforward for the simple case. As you will see in the remainder of this chapter and future examples, a database-enabled ASP can become pretty complex once you add in error handling, multiple record sets, and manipulating as well as viewing data.

TIP

It is very common when using a RecordSet object in a loop to forget the call to MoveNext. This will result in an infinite loop, so keep an eye out.

Dealing with bad data

In fact, there is one simple technique that we need to apply to the current example if we really want it to work right. To motivate this technique, let's think about what happens if there is a product in the database that doesn't have a description. This product will result in different appearances depending on your browser. For example, you might see something like the table shown in Figure 14-4.

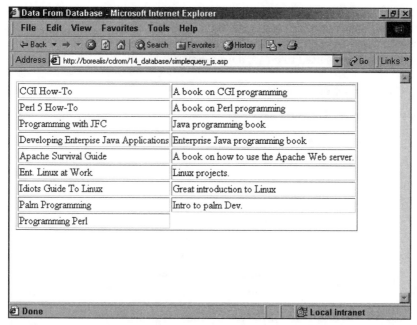

Figure 14-4: Table containing a record with no description

Ideally, the ASP will look the same regardless of the browser used to access it. So we need to do something about this null-valued record property. The easiest way to deal with it is to put a character in the empty cell. You want to use an invisible character, so we chose the non-breaking space, . This results in code that looks like this:

```
if(IsNull(recordSet("name")))
{
        Response.Write(" ")
}
else
{
        Response.Write(recordSet("name"))
}
```

First you check if the value is null, and then you put the right character into the cell. You could also check if the value is "", and put the nonbreaking space in the cell in that case as well.

Of course, these two examples of using a database demonstrate the obvious use of database data as something to display in a table. You can also use database data in other ways on your Active Server Pages. For example, in Listing 14-1, the data from a table called choices is used to create a drop-down list.

Listing 14-1: Creating a drop-down list

```
<%@ LANGUAGE="JAVASCRIPT" %>
<html>
<head>
<title>Dynamic Select List</title>
</head>
<body>
<form>
<%
var choice;
var selectStr;
var recordSet = Server.CreateObject("ADODB.RecordSet");
recordSet.Open("select * from choices;","DSN=asp_devguide");

Response.Write("<select size=1>");

selectStr = "selected";

while(! recordSet.EOF)
{
    choice = recordSet("name");
    Response.Write("<option name='" + choice);
    Response.Write("' " + selectStr + ">");
    Response.Write(choice);
    Response.Write("</option>");
    selectStr = "";
    recordSet.MoveNext();
}

Response.Write("</select>");
%>
</form>
</body>
</html>
```

When you access this page, it will display an HTML page containing a single drop-down list with the first item selected, as shown in Figure 14-5.

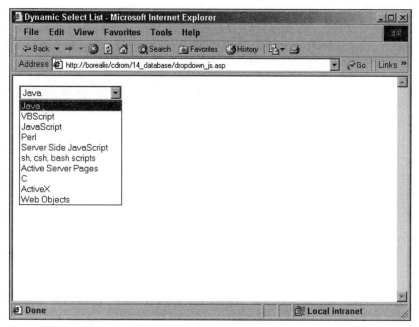

Figure 14-5: A dynamically generated drop-down list

So, basic database access is pretty straightforward. Some of the issues to keep in mind are the following:

◆ Make sure to create and open the record set before using it.

◆ Access the data in a record set by name.

◆ When using a loop to iterate through the data, be sure to move the record set to the next record before beginning the next loop.

◆ By default, record sets can only increment through the data one time.

◆ Use the EOF property to determine when you reach the end of the data.

Keeping these basics in mind, let's take a look at the two objects that support the RecordSet and see how you can create more complex data access applications.

Connections

Underlying each RecordSet object is another ADO called a Connection. A Connection object represents a conduit to a single database. It is possible that your ASP will create connections to more than one database or more than one connection to the same database. As a result, you might want to gain a finer granularity of control over the connection process itself. To gain this control you need to create your connections explicitly instead of letting the RecordSet object create them for you. In other words, if you want to manage the connection, you shouldn't create it by using the following syntax:

```
recordSet.Open("select * from products;","DSN=asp_devguide");
```

as we did in the previous examples. Instead, create an `ADODB.Connection` object and open it as follows:

```
var connection;
connection = Server.CreateObject("ADODB.Connection");
connection.Open("DSN=asp_devguide");
```

This syntax is very similar to the way that you open a RecordSet object. The difference is that you will be able to use this same connection to create multiple record sets, and perform other connection-related operations.

Opening a connection

There are actually a number of ways to open a Connection object. The easiest is the method described previously using a DSN, as follows:

```
connection.Open("DSN=asp_devguide");
```

You can also provide a username and password, as shown here:

```
connection.Open("DSN=asp_devguide;UID=root;PASSWORD=foofighter");
```

and for databases that separate the concept of the DSN and the database, you can specify the database separately, like this:

```
connection.Open("DSN=asp_devguide;DATABASE=devg");
```

It is even possible to create a connection to a database without using a DSN. In this case, you have to provide all of the information that the system will need to find your database, including the provider, filename, datasource, username, and password.

```
connection.Open("DRIVER={Microsoft Access Driver (*.mdb)};"
          +"DBQ=c:\\temp\\aspdev.mdb");
```

 We had to escape the backslash character in JavaScript.

When you open a connection, you are actually assigning one of the Connection object's properties called `connectionstring`. You can set this property manually, and then call the open method with no arguments, as follows:

```
connection.connectionString = "DSN=asp_devguide";
connection.Open();
```

All of these techniques create equivalent Connection objects and can be used inside an ASP or even in the global.asa file.

CREATING A CONNECTION IN THE GLOBAL.ASA FILE

Depending on your situation, you may want to share a single database connection between all of the pages in your application, or for all of the pages that a particular user accesses. For example, you might have a different username and password for each session.

When sharing connections there are a couple things to keep in mind. First, depending on the database and operations that you are performing, you may have to think about corrupting your data. Second, you can often improve overall performance by reducing the number of times that you have to connect to the database. So if you connect once for the entire application, you will probably improve the overall user experience.

The following global.asa file shows how you can use the `Application_OnStart` script to create a shared connection.

```
<SCRIPT RUNAT="SERVER" LANGUAGE="JAVASCRIPT">

function Application_OnStart()
{
    var conn = Server.CreateObject("ADODB.Connection")

    conn.connectionString = "DSN=asp_devguide";
    conn.open();

    Application("dbconn") = conn;
}
</SCRIPT>
```

Since the connection is already created, you can simply access it in your active server pages, skipping the opening step.

CLOSING THE CONNECTION

When you are finished with a Connection object, you should close it to free up any resources that the Web server or database server is using to maintain the connection.

To close the connection, use the `close` method, and then set the variable that stored the connection to null. In JavaScript this means doing the following:

```
connection.close();
connection = null;
```

In VBScript use the following:

```
connection.Close
Set connection = Nothing
```

In general, the server will clean up connections created in a page automatically, but we suggest that you close the connection explicitly to ensure that everything works properly. For connections that you create in the `Application_OnStart` or `Session_OnStart` scripts, use the associated script to close them. For example, use the `Session_OnEnd` script to free up any connections stored in a Session object.

Using a connection to execute SQL

Since a connection represents the fundamental relationship between the database and the ASP, the ADO designers decided to include the ability to execute SQL at the connection level. Keep in mind that executing commands at this level of the model could require application locking to protect any shared connections. Also, you will not be able to access the results of the SQL you invoke at this level, so you will still rely on record sets to get at data using select statements.

To execute a command with a Connection object, use the `execute` method, as shown in Listing 14-2.

Listing 14-2: Using a Connection object to execute a command

```
var database = Server.CreateObject("ADODB.Connection");
database.Open "asp_devguide","asp_dev",""

database.execute("drop table products")

sql = "create table products "
sql = sql & "(id char(12) not null primary key"
sql = sql & ", name varchar(80) null"
sql = sql & ", description varchar(250) null"
sql = sql & ", longDescription long varchar"
sql = sql & ",msrp float null, price float null)"

database.execute(sql)
```

In this case, we are using Execute to drop and re-create a database table. You can also use this technique to execute update, insert, and delete commands as well as stored procedures. For example, in the following example we use the Execute method to call a stored procedure, as follows:

```
var conn = Server.CreateObject("ADODB.Connection");
var recordSet = Server.CreateObject("ADODB.RecordSet");

conn.connectionString = "DSN=asp_devguide2";
conn.open();

conn.execute("deleteAbove(50.0)");
```

For stored procedures the trick is to make sure that you use the correct syntax for your database. In this case, we are really calling a predefined query in an MS Access database. For SQL Server, you might use the following syntax:

```
conn.execute("[call deleteAbove(50.0)]")
```

or something similar.

The Execute method can take one of three arguments. We have just used one so far, the SQL string, but you can also control the execution more precisely with the other arguments. In its full version, Execute is defined as follows:

```
Execute( commandText, numRows, options)
```

The numRows argument is used to return the number of rows affected by the call. This value is returned by reference and is only valid in VBScript. The options flag is one of the values in Table 14-3. The underlying database connectivity library may use this flag to improve performance.

TABLE 14-3 DATABASE COMMAND TYPES

Option	Actual Value	Meaning
adCmdUnknown	0	No prior knowledge is available on the command text. This is the default.
adCmdText	1	The command is a SQL statement of some sort.
adCmdTable	2	The command is the name of a table to associate with a record set.
adCmdStoredProc	4	The command is a stored procedure.

The text names for these options are stored in an include file called Adovbs for VBScript files and Adojavas for JavaScript files. As an example, the code in Listing 14-3 executes a stored procedure and then prints the number of rows affected.

Listing 14-3: Executing a stored procedure

```
<%@ LANGUAGE="VBSCRIPT" %>
<!-- #include file="adovbs.inc" -->
...
Set conn = Server.CreateObject("ADODB.Connection")
Dim numRec

conn.open "DSN=asp_devguide2"
...
conn.execute "deleteAbove(50.0)",numRec,adCmdStoredProc

If numRec = 1 Then
Response.Write("<h2>Deleteted "&numRec&" row.</h2>")
Else
Response.Write("<h2>Deleteted "&numRec&" rows.</h2>")
End If
...
```

Some of the code for this example was removed to save space. The complete example is available on the CD-ROM in the file conn_cmdtype_vb.asp.

Since many of the pages you create will also want to retrieve data, let's go back to the RecordSet object and see how we can use connections with record sets.

Using a connection to create a record set

To create a RecordSet object that uses a specific connection, just replace the connection string from the open method with the Connection object, as follows:

```
var conn = Server.CreateObject("ADODB.Connection");
var recordSet = Server.CreateObject("ADODB.RecordSet");

conn.open("DSN=asp_devguide2");

recordSet.Open("select * from products",conn);
```

You can also set the connection before you open the `recordSet` using the `ActiveConnection` property, like this:

```
var conn = Server.CreateObject("ADODB.Connection");
var recordSet = Server.CreateObject("ADODB.RecordSet");

conn.open("DSN=asp_devguide");

recordSet.ActiveConnection = conn;
recordSet.Open("select * from products;");
```

Once the record set is connected to the database, you can open and close it to reset the command text, as shown in Listing 14-4.

Listing 14-4: Opening and closing the record set

```
var conn = Server.CreateObject("ADODB.Connection");
var recordSet = Server.CreateObject("ADODB.RecordSet");

conn.open("DSN=asp_devguide2");

recordSet.ActiveConnection = conn;
recordSet.Open("select * from products");
...
recordSet.Close();

conn.execute("deleteAbove(50.0)");

recordSet.Open("select * from products",conn);
...
```

This brings us to the following logical question: Can we simultaneously use the same connection with multiple record sets? The answer is, of course.

Using the same connection for multiple record sets

To use the same connection with more than one record set, just create multiple `RecordSet` objects and assign them to the same connection. The example shown in Listing 14-5, which is displayed in a browser in Figure 14-6, creates a record set for the `products` table and another for the `choices` table in our sample database. Then a loop traverses both record sets, as long as they both have records, and displays some of their properties.

Listing 14-5: Creating multiple record sets

```javascript
<%@ LANGUAGE="JAVASCRIPT" %>

<html>
<head>
<title>Data From Database</title>
</head>
<body>
<%

var conn = Server.CreateObject("ADODB.Connection");
var recordSet = Server.CreateObject("ADODB.RecordSet");
var recordSet2 = Server.CreateObject("ADODB.RecordSet");

conn.open("DSN=asp_devguide");

recordSet.ActiveConnection = conn;
recordSet2.ActiveConnection = conn;

recordSet.Open("select * from products;");
recordSet2.Open("select * from choices;");

Response.Write("<table border=1>");

while(!recordSet.EOF && !recordSet2.EOF)
{
    Response.Write("<tr>");

    Response.Write("<td>");
    Response.Write(recordSet("name"));
    Response.Write("</td>");

    Response.Write("<td>");
    Response.Write(recordSet("description"));
    Response.Write("</td>");

    Response.Write("<td>");
    Response.Write(recordSet2("name"));
    Response.Write("</td>");

    Response.Write("</tr>");
```

```
        recordSet.MoveNext();
        recordSet2.MoveNext();
}

Response.Write("</table>");

%>

</body>
</html>
```

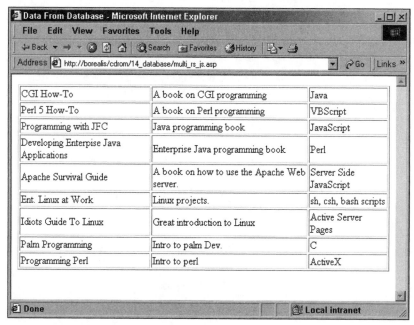

Figure 14-6: Multiple record sets with one connection

The key step to the example shown in Listing 14-5 is indicated in bold, where we set both record sets to use the same `ActiveConnection`. After that, you can treat the record sets independently.

Connection properties

As you are using a Connection object, you may want to control, or query, the configuration used to create the connection. The Connection object provides a number of properties that you can use to get at information about it. These properties are listed in Table 14-4.

TABLE 14-4 CONNECTION PROPERTIES

Property	Description
Attributes	Used to indicate database specific attributes of the connection. The default is 0.
CommandTimeout	Restricts the time, in seconds, that the connection will allow a command to run. The default is 30 seconds.
ConnectionString	The complete string used to connect to the database. This string may include default values for parameters that you did not set. The default is 15 seconds.
ConnectionTimeout	The time, in seconds, that the connection will wait to open its conduit with the database.
CursorLocation	A flag indicating if the cursors used for RecordSets are stored on the server or the client. The value is either AdUseClient (3) or AdUseServer (2).
DefaultDatabase	The default database used by the connection.
IsolationLevel	Controls the transaction level for the connection. It is database-dependent.
Mode	Sets or returns the permissions for accessing a connection.
Provider	The name of the provider library for this connection.
State	Indicates if the connection is open or closed. The value is either AdStateOpen (1) or AdStateClosed (0).
Version	The version of ADO being used.

All of the values in this table that rely on constants can be found in adovbs.inc and adojavas.inc. To get an idea of what these values hold, we created an ASP that connects to two different data sources and prints the properties for each. This page, shown in Listing 14-6, is available on the CD-ROM as connectionprops_js.asp. When we ran it against MySQL and MS Access databases we got the results shown in Figure 14-7. Again, some of the code was repeated and was removed to save space.

Listing 14-6: Connecting to two datasources

```
<%@ LANGUAGE="JAVASCRIPT" %>
<!-- #include file="adojavas.inc" -->

<html>
```

```
<head>
<title>Connection Properties</title>
</head>
<body>
<%

var conn = Server.CreateObject("ADODB.Connection");
var recordSet = Server.CreateObject("ADODB.RecordSet");

conn.connectionString = "DSN=asp_devguide";
conn.open();

recordSet.Open("select * from products;",conn);

Response.Write("<h1>Connection Constants</h1>")
Response.Write("</h3>Cursor Locations:<h3>");
Response.Write("adUseClient ="+adUseClient+"<br>");
Response.Write("adUseServer ="+adUseServer+"<br>");

Response.Write("</h3>State:<h3>");
Response.Write("adStateOpen ="+adStateOpen+"<br>");
Response.Write("adStateClosed ="+adStateClosed+"<br>");

Response.Write("<h1>Connection Properties - 1</h1>");

Response.Write("Attributes = "+conn.Attributes+"<br>");
Response.Write("CommandTimeout = "
               +conn.CommandTimeout+"<br>");
Response.Write("ConnectionTimeout = "
               +conn.ConnectionTimeout+"<br>");
Response.Write("ConnectionString = "
               +conn.ConnectionString+"<br>");
Response.Write("CursorLocation = "
               +conn.CursorLocation+"<br>");
Response.Write("DefaultDatabase = "
               +conn.DefaultDatabase+"<br>");
Response.Write("IsolationLevel = "
               +conn.IsolationLevel+"<br>");
Response.Write("Mode = "+conn.Mode+"<br>");
Response.Write("Provider = "+conn.Provider+"<br>");
Response.Write("State = "+conn.State+"<br>");
Response.Write("Version = "+conn.Version+"<br>");

recordSet.Close();
conn.close();
```

```
conn = null;

var conn = Server.CreateObject("ADODB.Connection");
var recordSet = Server.CreateObject("ADODB.RecordSet");

conn.connectionString = "DSN=asp_devguide2";
conn.open();

recordSet.Open("select * from products;",conn);


...
REM Repeat the Response.Writes for this connection
...

recordSet.Close();
conn.close();
conn = null;

%>

</body>
</html>
```

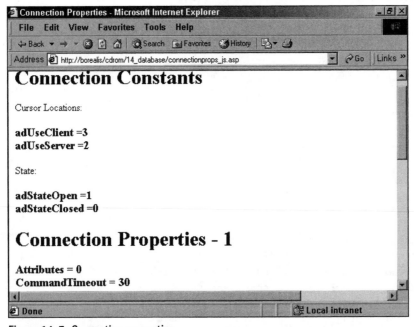

Figure 14-7: Connection properties

In the same way that the Connection object provides the underlying database conduit for a record set, the Command object is used to represent a database command.

Commands

A Command object is used to represent a single operation on the database. For example, a command might be used to represent a query, or an insert statement. Given that description, you might wonder why you need a Command object at all. The answer lies in some of the more advanced uses for ADO. For example, a Command object can be used to create a prepared statement. This type of statement, when supported, will execute more quickly than a regular SQL command. Command objects also support the concept of parameters, where a parameter is a piece of data passed to a SQL command or stored procedure. By using parameters you can insert binary and large text data into a database. Commands can also be used to separate the execution of generic SQL, like creating tables, from the Connection object itself. Creating a Command object is similar to creating the other objects; just use the following:

```
var cmd = Server.CreateObject("ADODB.Command");
```

Once you have the Command object, you can use its properties to set the connection and command text. A complete list of these properties is described in Table 14-5.

TABLE 14–5 COMMAND OBJECT PROPERTIES

Property	Description
ActiveConnection	Set this to the Connection object or connection string that you want to use for this command.
CommandText	The SQL that you want the command to execute.
CommandTimeout	The limit, in seconds, placed on the command running. If the command exceeds this limit, an error is generated.
CommandType	Like the connection command type, this flag can be used to improve performance of the database engine.
Name	The name of the Command object.
Prepared	True/False, indicating if the command should be prepared before being sent to the server.
State	Indicates if the command is open, closed, or executing.

To give you an idea of how you might use these properties, the following snippet of code creates a command from a Connection object and associates a simple query with it:

```
var conn = Server.CreateObject("ADODB.Connection");
var cmd = Server.CreateObject("ADODB.Command");

conn.connectionString = "DSN=asp_devguide";
conn.open();

cmd.ActiveConnection = conn;
cmd.CommandText = "select * from products";
```

Once you have the command, the next step is to execute it. This is as easy as calling the Execute method. This method takes the same arguments as the Connection object's Execute method, but it has the advantage that for SELECT statements it returns a record set. So you can catch the results of the command defined above using the following:

```
var recordSet;
recordSet = cmd.Execute();
```

Then use the record set normally. You can of course use the command to perform an insert operation, like this:

```
var command = Server.CreateObject("ADODB.Command");
command.ActiveConnection = conn;
command.CommandText = "insert into products values"
        +" ('lnx','Idiots Guide to Linux'"
        +",'Introduction to Linux'"
        +",'An introduction to linux for the common man'"
        +",19.99,19.99)";
command.Execute();
```

or call a stored procedure, as shown here:

```
var command = Server.CreateObject("ADODB.Command");
command.ActiveConnection = conn;
command.CommandText = "deleteAbove(50.0)";
command.CommandType = adCmdStoredProc;
command.Execute();
```

These last two uses of the Command object lead us to the question of parameters in general. Both the insert command and the stored procedure accepted parameters of some sort. In the generic case, these parameters could be binary data or large text strings. In either of those cases it is unreasonable to imagine hard coding them into the SQL itself. Also, some stored procedures return data, and we need a way to get to that data outside the record set mechanism.

Parameters

To deal with parameters, ADO provides two types of objects. The Parameters object stores a collection of Parameter objects. Note the subtle distinction in the names of these objects, one is singular and one is plural. Each command has a Parameters object as its Parameters property. So to get to the parameters for a command, use the following:

```
command.Parameters
```

This object provides four methods of interest. These are listed in Table 14-6.

TABLE 14-6 PARAMETERS METHODS

Method	Description
Append	Add a Parameter to the collection.
Delete	Delete a Parameter from the collection.
Item	Returns a Parameter from the collection, either by name or index.
Refresh	Updates the parameter information from the database that this Parameter collection will need to match.

There is also a single property for the Parameters object called Count that indicates the number of parameters in the collection. The elements of the Parameters collection are Parameter objects. These objects have a number of properties, and a single method. The properties are listed in Table 14-7.

TABLE 14-7 PARAMETER PROPERTIES

Property	Description
Attributes	Used to store configuration information.
Direction	Used for input, output, or both. It should be set to adParamInput (1), adParamOutput(2), adParamInputOutput(3), adParamReturnValue(4), or adParamUnknown(0).

Continued

TABLE **14-7 PARAMETER PROPERTIES** *(Continued)*

Property	Description
Name	Assigns a name for the parameter, or it can be used to get the name.
NumericScale	The scale of a numeric value in the parameter.
Precision	The degree of precision to use for numeric values of the parameter.
Size	The maximum size of a text value in the parameter.
Type	The type of parameter, which should be one of the database types listed in Table 14-11, "Database Field Types."
Value	The value of the parameter.

The single method is called AppendChunk, and it can be used to add large text or binary data to a parameter.

To create a parameter you can either ask the Command object to do it for you, or you can create it manually. The example shown in Listing 14-7 sets two parameters for an insert statement. Note that the parameters are indicated in the SQL with question marks (?). The first parameter is created by the Command object, and the second one is created manually.

Listing 14-7: Setting two parameters for an insert statement

```
command.ActiveConnection = conn;
command.CommandText = "insert into products values"
        +" ('devlnx','10 Enterprise Applications for Linux'"
        +",?,?,39.99,39.99)";

param = command.CreateParameter("description"
                ,adVarChar
                ,adParamInput
                ,80
                ,"10 Projects for Linux developers.");

command.Parameters.Append(param);

param = Server.CreateObject("ADODB.Parameter");

param.Name = "longDescription";
```

```
param.Type = adVarChar;
param.Size = 200;
param.Direction = adParamInput;
param.value = "This book provides a number of useful"
                + " techniques for linux developers.";

command.Parameters.Append(param);

command.Execute();
```

To pass a parameter to a stored procedure, you will need to know the appropriate syntax for your database vendor. But you will essentially leave out the arguments and use a parameter instead. For example, the code in Listing 14-8 uses the stored procedure discussed earlier to delete all products with an MSRP greater than 35.0 dollars.

Listing 14-8: A stored procedure for deleting specific products

```
command.ActiveConnection = conn;
command.CommandText = "deleteAbove";
command.CommandType = adCmdStoredProc;

param = Server.CreateObject("ADODB.Parameter");

param.Name = "amount";
param.Type = adDouble;
param.Direction = adParamInput;
param.value = 35.0;

command.Parameters.Append(param);

command.Execute();
```

If you plan to use parameters to get data from a stored procedure, you can either store the objects in variables or retrieve them from the Parameters collection by index or by name.

Large data

To include large text data or binary data in an insert command or stored procedure, you will need to use Command and Parameter objects. First, create a Command and Parameter as described previously. Leave the value blank, and instead use the AppendChunk method to set the value for the parameter. For example, in the code shown in Listing 14-9 we use the contents of a file to set the long description for a product.

Listing 14-9: Setting the long description for a product

```
var conn = Server.CreateObject("ADODB.Connection");
var recordSet = Server.CreateObject("ADODB.RecordSet");
var command = Server.CreateObject("ADODB.Command");
var param = Server.CreateObject("ADODB.Parameter");
var fileSys = Server.CreateObject("Scripting.FileSystemObject");
var file = fileSys.OpenTextFile(Server.MapPath("lnxdev.txt"));

conn.connectionString = "DSN=asp_devguide2";
conn.open();

command.ActiveConnection = conn;
command.CommandText = "insert into products values"
            +" ('devlnx','10 Enterprise Applications for Linux'"
            +",'Project for Linux developers'"
            +",?,39.99,39.99)";

param.Name = "longDescription";
param.Type = adLongVarChar;
param.Size = 4800;
param.Direction = adParamInput;

param.AppendChunk(file.readAll());

file.close();

command.Parameters.Append(param);

command.Execute();
```

In this case we called AppendChunk once, which is indicated in bold, but you can call it repeatedly. Each call will append the data passed into the existing value.

Advanced RecordSet Usage

Up to this point we have relied pretty heavily on SQL to perform the database operations that we wanted to perform. Some of these operations, like finding a subset of records and performing updates, can be managed at a higher level using the RecordSet object.

To access these advanced features, we need to take a closer look at the open method. When we called this method before, we provided a SQL statement and possibly a Connection object. Now let's look at all of the parameters that can be passed into the open method. These are described in Table 14-8, and in the remainder of this section.

TABLE 14-8 RECORDSET OPEN METHOD PARAMETERS

Parameter	Description
Source	Where the data for this RecordSet object is coming from
Connection	The Connection object or DSN to use
CursorType	The kind of RecordSet this is, and whether it supports updates
LockType	How the RecordSet protects data from other database users
Options	Miscellaneous options to control the RecordSet objects. These are similar to the command types in Table 14-5.

Using all of the parameters, you might open a record set with the following:

```
recordSet.open("select * from products",conn
               ,adOpenDynamic,adLockOptimistic,adCmdText);
```

That said, what are the valid values for these parameters? First, there is the data-source. The source for a RecordSet can be one of the following four values:

♦ A database table name

♦ A SQL statement

♦ A stored procedure call

♦ A Command object

If you use a database table name, you are essentially selecting all of the records from that table. With a Command object, the RecordSet will execute the command to get its data. The SQL statement and stored procedure are simply called and the results are used to define the RecordSet.

The second parameter is the connection. This parameter can be a DSN, as we saw at the beginning of the chapter, or a Connection object.

Cursor types

The cursor type defines how the RecordSet can be used to look at the data it represents. Up to this point, the RecordSets that we created could only be used to read the data one time, from top to bottom. Other cursor types allow you to move arbitrarily around in the data. A complete list of cursor types is provided in Table 14-9. The constants used to define the cursors are in the adovbs.inc and adojavas.inc files.

TABLE 14-9 RECORDSET CURSOR TYPES

Cursor Type	Description
adOpenForwardOnly	This is the default cursor type. A RecordSet object with this type of cursor can read through the data one time, forward only. Changes to the data since the RecordSet object was created are ignored.
adOpenKeySet	The RecordSet object can be read forward and backward. You can update data with this type of RecordSet object and you can set bookmarks in the data. You can refresh the RecordSet object to reflect changes made by other database users; although, these updates are not visible automatically.
adOpenDynamic	Allows you to read and write with the RecordSet object. You can navigate forward and backward, but cannot bookmark. Changes to the underlying data are reflected in the RecordSet object automatically.
adOpenStatic	Designed for data that is copied to the client, this type of cursor works on a static copy of the database. Changes are not reflected automatically. Forward and backward navigation is supported.

Depending on your situation you will pick one of these cursor types for your RecordSet. In general, pages that need to display data will just use the default forward-only cursor type. Pages that want to update the database can use key set cursors. You will probably only use a dynamic cursor if you need immediate notification of changes to the data. Similarly, static cursors are designed for situations where the database is disconnected from the server, which is probably not a common occurrence for Active Server Pages. So for now, focus on the first two types.

Keeping the data in sync

If you are using either a key set or static cursor, you can resynchronize it with the database using the ReSync method. This is essentially like executing the command again, only the underlying engine can be smart about how it retrieves the updates.

Moving around in the data

When you create a RecordSet with any CursorType besides the forward-only type, you can move around in the records arbitrarily. There are two methods that move the cursor absolutely in the records. These are MoveFirst and MoveLast. There are two methods that move relative to the current record: MoveNext and MovePrevious.

Finally, the Move method takes a single argument containing the index of the record you want to move to.

While you are moving around you may want to mark a particular record. This is accomplished with bookmarks, which are available for the KeySet and Static cursor types. To create a bookmark, go to the record and get the Bookmark property from the RecordSet, as follows:

```
bmark = recordSet.Bookmark;
```

Then when you want to return to that record, set the property to the value you stored, as follows:

```
recordSet.Bookmark = bmark;
```

 ON THE CD Keep in mind that not all cursors support this feature. For an example that uses bookmarks, see bookmark_js.asp on the CD-ROM.

In most cases you can find how many records there are with the RecordCount property, as follows:

```
recordSet.RecordCount
```

If this value is unavailable, it is set to −1.

Protecting data and lock types

The third parameter for opening a RecordSet is the lock type. There are four lock types. These are listed in Table 14-10.

TABLE 14-10 RECORDSET LOCK TYPES

Lock Type	Description
AdLockReadOnly	The record set is read-only, so the data cannot be changed. As a result, the RecordSet object is thought of as a safe snapshot and no locking occurs.
AdLockPessimistic	Records in the database are locked when a program begins to edit them.

Continued

Lock Type	Description
AdLockOptimistic	Records in the database are locked when you update them, but not while the initial client-side edits are occurring.
adLockBatchOptimistic	Locks multiple records for a batch update, in an optimistic manner.

TABLE **14-10 RECORDSET LOCK TYPES** *(Continued)*

For most situations you can use the default read-only lock to look at data and use the optimistic lock to update data. Only use the pessimistic lock in situations where you don't have to worry about a lot of pages, or clients, waiting to access the database. You might also use the pessimistic lock in a situation where your page changes a lot of data. Note that the main difference is that the pessimistic lock starts protecting a record as soon as you start to update it, while the optimistic lock waits for a signal – the update method – to perform the lock.

Using the record set to update records

You can use a RecordSet to update data in the database. The first step in updating the data is to create the RecordSet. Then find the record you want to update, using MoveNext, or one of the techniques shown in this section. Update the properties that you want to change and call Update. For example, the code in Listing 14-10 updates the prices in our products database by making them 10 percent higher than the MSRP. Then it moves the cursor to the first record to begin displaying them. Notice that we resync the data before getting ready to display it.

Listing 14-10: Updating prices in the Products database

```
var conn = Server.CreateObject("ADODB.Connection");
var recordSet = Server.CreateObject("ADODB.RecordSet");

conn.open("DSN=asp_devguide2");

recordSet.Open("select * from products",conn
               ,adOpenKeyset,adLockOptimistic
               ,adCmdText);

//Raise the prices!
while(!recordSet.EOF)
{
    recordSet("price") = recordSet("msrp")*1.1;
```

```
    recordSet.Update();
    recordSet.MoveNext();
}

recordSet.ReSync();
recordSet.MoveFirst();
```

 The complete text of the Listing 14-10 example is in update_js.asp on the CD-ROM.

In situations where you may want to update multiple records, you can cache up the changes in the RecordSet and then update the database in one operation, or batch. To perform a batch update, use the method UpdateBatch (see Listing 14-11) that lowers the prices by 10 percent. Again we resync the data with the database to prepare for displaying it.

Listing 14-11: Using the UpdateBatch method

```
var conn = Server.CreateObject("ADODB.Connection");
var recordSet = Server.CreateObject("ADODB.RecordSet");

conn.open("DSN=asp_devguide2");

recordSet.Open("select * from products",conn
               ,adOpenKeyset,adLockBatchOptimistic
               ,adCmdText);

//Lower the prices!
while(!recordSet.EOF)
{
    recordSet("price") = recordSet("msrp")*0.9;
    recordSet.MoveNext();
}

recordSet.UpdateBatch();
recordSet.ReSync();
recordSet.MoveFirst();
```

Using these two methods, Update and UpdateBatch, you can use the higher level RecordSet to manage data instead of relying on raw SQL. If you are in the process of updating and want to cancel it, use the method CancelUpdate or CancelBatch. This should reset the RecordSet to the state before you started making changes.

Using the record set to add records

Adding records with a RecordSet object is actually a two-step process. First you create a new local record using AddNew. This creates a virtual record in the record set and positions the record set at this new record. You can then set the values for this record as if you were updating it. Finally, call Update to register the change with the database. Listing 14-12 provides an example that adds a record to the products table.

Listing 14-12: Adding a record to the Products table

```
var conn = Server.CreateObject("ADODB.Connection");
var recordSet = Server.CreateObject("ADODB.RecordSet");

conn.open("DSN=asp_devguide2");

recordSet.Open("select * from products",conn
               ,adOpenKeyset,adLockOptimistic
               ,adCmdText);

recordSet.AddNew();
recordSet("id") = "ms121";
recordSet("name") = "Introduction to Active Server Pages";
recordSet("description") = "Introductory course on ASP";
recordSet("msrp") = 895;
recordSet("price") = 895;
recordSet("longDescription") = "This 2 day courses introduces ASP";
recordSet.Update();
```

Keep in mind that adding records with a RecordSet object is a two-step process. Don't forget to call Update, or your changes won't take effect in the database.

Using the record set to delete records

The final database operation, after select, insert, and update is delete. You can use a RecordSet object to delete records as well as add and update them. This is a three-step process:

1. Find the record you want to delete.

2. Call Delete to remove the record locally.

3. Call Update to save those changes to the database.

The following example deletes the first record from the products table:

```
var conn = Server.CreateObject("ADODB.Connection");
```

```
var recordSet = Server.CreateObject("ADODB.RecordSet");

conn.open("DSN=asp_devguide2");

recordSet.Open("select * from products",conn
               ,adOpenKeyset,adLockOptimistic
               ,adCmdText);

recordSet.Delete();
recordSet.Update();
```

Again, keep in mind that for all of the data manipulation features in RecordSet, you have to call Update to see the changes.

Finding records

The RecordSet object supports basic find capabilities, if you use one of the cursors that supports forward and backward motion. To search for records, call Find with a string indicating the comparison you want to make. If you are comparing a string field, put the string in single quotes. If you are comparing a number field, just include the number. For example, the following example finds a record where price is greater than 45:

```
recordSet.Find("price > 45");
```

The next example finds a record with a price greater than 45 dollars:

```
recordSet.Find("price > 45");
```

To test if your search succeeded, use the EOF property. So in the previous find, we actually wrote the following:

```
recordSet.Find("name = 'Perl 5 How-To'");

if(!recordSet.EOF)
{
    Response.Write("<tr>");

    Response.Write("<td>");
...
```

In general, you want to try to limit the data traveling to and from the database, so you should use where clauses in your SQL instead of finding records once you get them. This will also be more efficient for most databases. However, the find capability is very useful if you cache the data for multiple pages in the Application object, or perform some other operation where you will reuse the RecordSet enough to justify getting all or much of the data.

Filters

In the same way that a Find command can be used to search for a record based on a criterion, the Filter property of a RecordSet can be used to limit the data that it displays. To set a filter, assign a value to the Filter property, as follows:

```
recordSet.Filter = "price < 40.0";
```

To unset the filter, set the property to an empty string "", like this:

```
recordSet.Filter = "";
```

Again, give preference to performing filtering on the database. In some situations, where you already have the RecordSet, filtering is a great way to limit the records displayed. But limit your use, and keep in mind that not all databases will support filtering.

ON THE CD

An example of turning a filter on and off is available on the CD-ROM under the name filter_js.asp.

Multiple record sets

Some queries can return non-rectangular data, or data from multiple database tables. To handle these situations the RecordSet object has a method called NextRecordSet. Call this method to get the next rectangle of data from your query. When no more sets are available, this method will return null. The key steps in this process are highlighted with bold in the code that follows:

```
while(recordSet != null)
{
    Response.Write("<table border=1>")

    . . .

    Response.Write("</table>");

    recordSet = recordSet.NextRecordSet();
}
```

It is easier to think about database data as rectangular, but in some cases, stored procedures will return data that isn't rectangular. When possible, avoid it to decrease the complexity of your code.

Learning About the Database

The next step in investigating database access from Active Server Pages is to look into the information provided to an ASP about the database that you connect to. For example, you might want to find out what the names of the columns in your database are, or discover the types of data in each column. Although you will usually know the schema for your database ahead of time, and therefore the names and types for each column, you may want to create more generic tools that allow you to determine this information at run time.

To learn about the columns accessed by a record set, you can use the record set's Fields collection. This collection contains objects with a name and a type. The name will be the string title for the column in question. The type will be one of the constants listed in Table 14-11. These constants relate a numeric code to a database type.

TABLE 14-11 DATABASE FIELD TYPES

Constant	Value	Description
adBigInt	20	An eight-byte signed integer
adBinary	128	A binary value
adBoolean	11	A boolean value
adBSTR	8	A null-terminated character string (Unicode)
adChar	129	A string value
adCurrency	6	A currency value
adDate	7	A date value
adDBDate	133	A date value (yyyymmdd)
adDBTime	134	A time value (hhmmss)
adDBTimeStamp	135	A date/time stamp
adDecimal	14	Indicates an exact numeric value with a fixed precision
adDouble	5	Indicates a double-precision floating-point value

Continued

TABLE 14-11 DATABASE FIELD TYPES *(Continued)*

Constant	Value	Description
adEmpty	0	Specifies no value
adError	10	A 32-bit error code
adInteger	3	A four-byte signed integer
adLongVarBinary	205	A long binary value
adLongVarChar	201	A long string value
adLongVarWChar	203	A long null-terminated Unicode string value
adNumeric	131	An exact numeric value
adSingle	4	A single-precision floating-point value
adSmallInt	2	A two-byte signed integer
adTinyInt	16	A one-byte signed integer
adUnsignedBigInt	21	An eight-byte unsigned integer
adUnsignedInt	19	A four-byte unsigned integer
adUnsignedSmallInt	18	A two-byte unsigned integer
adUnsignedTinyInt	17	A one-byte unsigned integer
adVarBinary	204	A binary value
adVarChar	200	A string value
adVarWChar	202	A null-terminated Unicode character string
adWChar	130	A null-terminated Unicode character string

You can access these field objects by name, if you know them, or by index. In the case that you use indices, the number of fields is accessed using Count, as follows:

```
recordSet.Open("select * from products;","DSN=asp_devguide");
numFields = recordSet.Fields.Count;
```

Using this collection you can create a page that displays any table, including the types of data for each column. We have created just such a page called using_fields.asp and included it on the CD-ROM. Some of the key parts of the page are an array that we create containing the data in Table 14-11 called TYPES, the code that prints each field name, the code that prints the types, and the code for printing each field in each record. Rather than include the entire page here, we decided to cut out the HTML and the big array definition for TYPES, and will just show the three main sections of code.

First, to access all of the field names, use Fields and the numFields variable, defined previously, as follows:

```
Response.Write("<tr>");
for(i=0;i<numFields;i++)
{
    Response.Write("<th>");
    Response.Write(recordSet.Fields(i).name);
    Response.Write("</th>");
}
Response.Write("</tr>\n");
```

Using this same technique, you can output the types, as follows:

```
Response.Write("<tr>");

for(i=0;i<numFields;i++)
{
    Response.Write("<th>");
    Response.Write(TYPES[recordSet.Fields(i).type]);
    Response.Write("</th>");
}

Response.Write("</tr>\n");
```

And the data for each field, as shown in Listing 14-13.

Listing 14-13: Outputting the data for each field

```
while(!recordSet.EOF)
{
    var field,value;
    Response.Write("<tr>");
    for(i=0;i<numFields;i++)
    {
        field = recordSet.Fields(i).name;
        value = recordSet(field);

        if((value==null) ||(value=="")) value = " ";

        Response.Write("<td>");
        Response.Write(value);
        Response.Write("</td>");
```

```
        }
        Response.Write("</tr>\n");
        recordSet.MoveNext();
}
```

In this case, we have tried to avoid printing nonexistent data and have used local variables to organize the loop. When accessed, this page will look like the one shown in Figure 14-8.

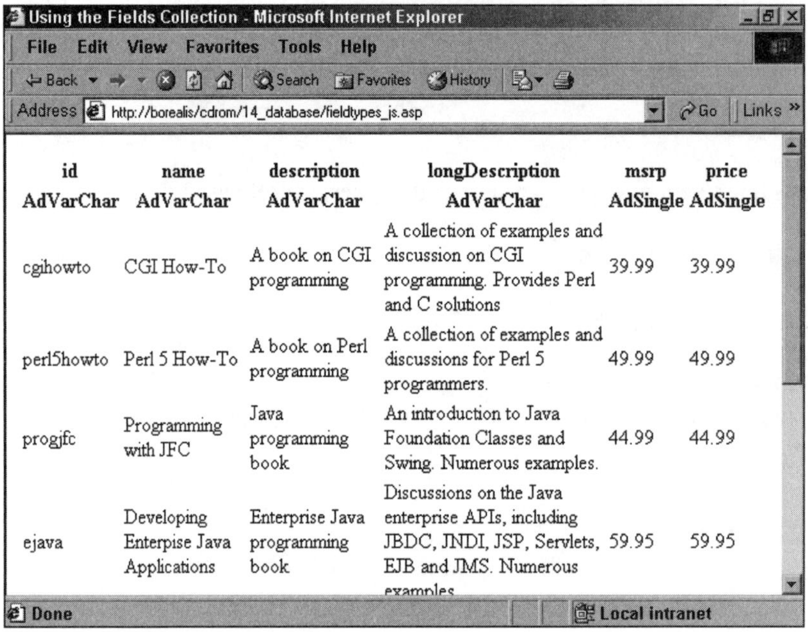

id AdVarChar	name AdVarChar	description AdVarChar	longDescription AdVarChar	msrp AdSingle	price AdSingle
cgihowto	CGI How-To	A book on CGI programming	A collection of examples and discussion on CGI programming. Provides Perl and C solutions	39.99	39.99
perl5howto	Perl 5 How-To	A book on Perl programming	A collection of examples and discussions for Perl 5 programmers.	49.99	49.99
progjfc	Programming with JFC	Java programming book	An introduction to Java Foundation Classes and Swing. Numerous examples.	44.99	44.99
ejava	Developing Enterpise Java Applications	Enterprise Java programming book	Discussions on the Java enterprise APIs, including JBDC, JNDI, JSP, Servlets, EJB and JMS. Numerous examples	59.95	59.95

Figure 14-8: The using_fields.asp page

As well as the Fields collection provided by a RecordSet, the Connection object can provide schema information to your ASPs.

The Connection object provides access to information about your database schema. Since most ASPs don't need to read schema at run time, we will not discuss the complete list of information available here. However, there are a few things you might want to find out about. In particular, you can list the tables and columns for your database, as well as the stored procedures of supported database engines.

To get to the schema, use the Connection's `OpenSchema` method. This takes an argument indicating the type of information you want, and returns a RecordSet object with the information. To find out about the tables use `adSchemaTables`, for columns use `adSchemaColumns`, and for procedures use `adSchemaProcedures`.

Keep in mind that the procedure information is not available in all databases. In fact, schema information in general may be limited.

Once you get the RecordSet containing the information, access it. For tables, you can get the Table_Name and Table_Type. For columns, there is the Column_Name, Column_Default, Data_Type, and Description. For procedures you can get the Procedure_Name, Procedure_Definition, and Description. That is to say, you can ask for these values, but whether they are actually returned it depends on your database.

Listing 14-14 shows how you can use this technique to get information about the tables in your database. The entire version of this page, schema_js.asp, is available on the CD-ROM and when accessed, displays a page like the one shown in Figure 14-9.

Listing 14-14: Getting information about tables

```
var conn = Server.CreateObject("ADODB.Connection");
var recordSet;

conn.open("DSN=asp_devguide2");

recordSet = conn.openSchema(adSchemaTables);

Response.Write("<h1>Tables</h1>");

Response.Write("<table border=1>");

while(!recordSet.EOF)
{
    Response.Write("<tr>");

    Response.Write("<td>");
    Response.Write(recordSet("Table_Name"));
    Response.Write("</td>");

    Response.Write("<td>");
    Response.Write(recordSet("Table_Type"));
    Response.Write("</td>");

    Response.Write("</tr>");

    recordSet.MoveNext();
}

Response.Write("</table>");
```

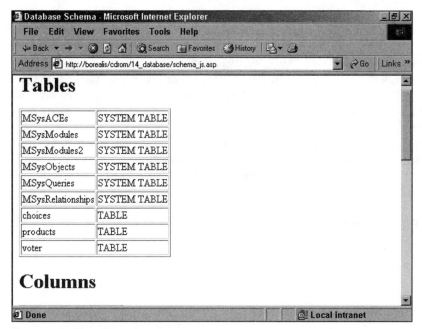

Figure 14-9: The schema_js.asp page

Again, most ASPs know the schema for their database ahead of time, but you never know when you might want to check out what the database is really like in your environment, from an Active Server Page's perspective.

Database Errors

One unfortunate issue with database development is the possibility of errors, either in the connection library, the SQL, or the database itself. You could also add the possibility of errors in the ASP, but just between us, we know those don't really happen.

Dealing with errors will be dependent on the language that you are using to write your Active Server Pages. In JavaScript, you use a try-catch syntax to handle errors gracefully. In this case, an Error object is provided directly to you and you can use it to get the number and description for the error. For example, the following code intentionally tries to use a forward-only cursor to move previous. This generates an error or, in JavaScript terms, throws an exception. The script catches the exception and displays the number and description, as shown in Listing 14-15.

Listing 14-15: A JavaScript Exception model

```
<%@ LANGUAGE="JAVASCRIPT" %>
<!-- #include file="adojavas.inc" -->
```

```
<html>
<head>
<title>Database Errors</title>
</head>
<body>
<%

var conn = Server.CreateObject("ADODB.Connection");
var recordSet = Server.CreateObject("ADODB.RecordSet");

conn.open("DSN=asp_devguide2");
recordSet.Open("select * from products;",conn,adOpenForwardOnly);

try
{
    recordSet.MoveNext();
    recordSet.MovePrevious();
    recordSet.MoveLast();
    recordSet.MoveFirst();
}
catch(err)
{
    Response.Write(err.number + "<br>");
    Response.Write(err.description + "<br>");
}


%>

</body>
</html>
```

One of the nice things about this JavaScript exception model is that you know immediately if an error occurs.

In VBScript there is a different error-handling syntax. Using On Error Resume Next, you can ask the VBScript engine to ignore errors and continue executing. For general errors, the Err object is used to see if an error occurred. For database errors, a special collection has been added to the Connection object. This collection, called Errors, can be used to check if there have been database errors and then to access the information about these errors. Keep in mind that there may be multiple errors in the collection if you don't check for errors very often in your script. To use the Errors collection, check for errors with the Count property, as follows:

```
If conn.Errors.Count > 0 Then
    . . .
```

Then access the errors by index. Each error has the properties listed in Table 14-12. When you are done with the collection, use `Clear` to empty it.

TABLE 14-12 ERROR PROPERTIES

Property	Description
Description	A string describing the error
HelpContext	A long number that can be used to associate the error with a context
HelpFile	The path to the help file for this error
NativeError	The provider-specific error number
Number	The ADO error number
Source	The name of the object that created the error
SQLState	The current state of the connection when the error was generated

Keep in mind that some of these properties don't have a real meaning in an ASP, like `HelpFile`. In Listing 14-16 we try to move previous with a forward-only cursor. This creates an error. Later, when we check for errors, information about each error is printed. The basic error-handling code has been highlighted with bold.

Listing 14-16: Using VBScript to check for errors

```
<%@ LANGUAGE="VBSCRIPT" %>

<html>
<head>
<title>Database Errors</title>
</head>
<body>
<%
On Error Resume Next

Set conn = Server.CreateObject("ADODB.Connection")
Set recordSet = Server.CreateObject("ADODB.RecordSet")

conn.open "DSN=asp_devguide2"
recordSet.Open "select * from products;",conn
```

```
recordSet.MoveNext
recordSet.MovePrevious
recordSet.MoveLast
recordSet.MoveFirst

If conn.Errors.Count > 0 Then

    For Each error in conn.Errors

        Response.Write(error.Number&"<br>")
        Response.Write(error.Description&"<br>")
        Response.Write(error.Source&"<br>")
        Response.Write(error.SQLState&"<br>")
        Response.Write("<br>")

    Next

    conn.Errors.Clear

End If


%>

</body>
</html>
```

Because of the VBScript error-handling design, you will want to check the `Errors.Count` property as often as you think an error may have occurred, or at least at the granularity that you want to handle errors. You certainly don't want to have hundreds of errors before you realize and handle them.

Transaction Basics

In cases where you have a number of operations to perform on the database and you want all of them to succeed or fail, but not have some succeed and some fail, there is the concept of a transaction. Transactions rely on three concepts: the transaction scope, committing, and rolling back. A beginning and an end determine a transaction's scope. The programmer sets the beginning. The end is determined by committing or rolling back the transaction. Committing causes the changes in the scope to happen. Rolling back causes them to be ignored. This relationship is diagrammed in Figure 14-10.

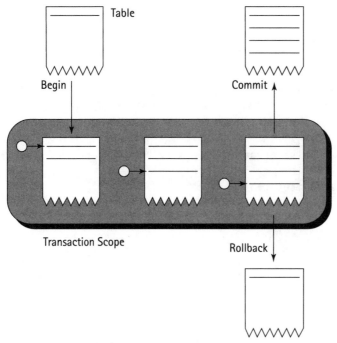

Figure 14-10: Transactions

At the ADO level, transactions are managed by the connection and use a very simple syntax. When you want to protect a block of commands, tell the connection to begin a transaction, as follows:

```
conn.BeginTrans();
```

Then to tell the connection that you want to commit the changes you made to the database, use CommitTrans, as follows:

```
conn.CommitTrans();
```

Finally, if an error occurred and you don't want any of the changes to take place, use RollbackTrans to roll back the transaction, like this:

```
conn.RollbackTrans();
```

As with many of these ADO features, keep in mind that transaction support is database dependent. If this is the case, you will get an error when you try to begin the transaction. Often, you will use error-handling techniques with transactions to determine if a problem occurred and whether you should roll back. (See Listing 14-17.)

Listing 14-17: Determining whether to commit or roll back

```
conn.BeginTrans();

try
{
    //Raise the prices!
    while(!recordSet.EOF)
    {
        recordSet("price") = recordSet("msrp")*1.1;
        recordSet.MoveNext();
    }

    conn.CommitTrans();
}
catch(err)
{
    conn.RollbackTrans();
}
```

Database Access Tips

As you work on your database access pages, keep in mind the following ideas:

- ◆ If necessary, use the connection and command time-outs to support long-running queries.

- ◆ It is very common when using a RecordSet object in a loop to forget the call to MoveNext. This will result in an infinite loop, so keep an eye out.

- ◆ Database records can contain null values. Test your results before assuming that they will display in a user-friendly manner.

- ◆ Most databases require string data in SQL to be in quotes, and numbers to not be in quotes. Be sure to include single quotes (' ') around string literals.

- ◆ Check all input from the client before adding it to the database. Some things to check for include formatting, size, and existence.

- ◆ Since quotes are special to SQL, you may need to check user input for single quote (') characters and remove them before adding the input to your SQL statement.

- ◆ Although you can store connections in a Session object, this could lead to excessive use of resources. Also, it will prevent the ODBC engine from pooling connections.

◆ Use forward-only cursors if you can. This will improve performance.

◆ Use Connection objects to control connections explicitly.

◆ Close connections when you are done, or set the `ActiveConnection` property of a Command or RecordSet object to null.

◆ If you use transactions, keep the scope to a minimum size to improve performance and maintainability.

◆ Use batch updates when possible to improve performance.

◆ Include error handling in your production code.

◆ Rely on the database to filter data when possible. Also, use database performance tuning techniques to improve the performance of your database-enabled Web applications.

◆ If you are using Access with stored procedures, you may get an error that says only `SELECT`, `INSERT`, `UPDATE`, `DELETE`, and `PROCEDURE` operations are supported. This can happen if the query or procedure you are calling is misspelled or not defined, and can be misleading.

◆ Double-check parameters, both their count and type, for stored procedures and parameterized commands.

Summary

As you can see, the ADO library provided to an Active Server Page developer is a simple and powerful tool for accessing databases. Using the Active Data Objects you can connect to a database, perform queries to retrieve data, insert or update data, and even delete data from the central store. The objects also provide access to stored procedures and database schema information.

Now that you see how easy it is to store data in a database, consider adding one at the back end to your Web site if you haven't already. If you are using a database already, the techniques and concepts in this chapter should give you the tools to start connecting your existing databases to your Active Server Pages. From there, you can create a dynamic database-driven Web site.

Chapter 15

A Simple Online Catalog

ONE THING THAT MIGHT help solidify some of the lessons from previous chapters is a larger example that includes a number of pages accessing the same database. For simplicity and familiarity, we choose an online catalog for this example. Our catalog application is discussed in this chapter.

The catalog stores basic information about products and organizes the products into categories. The categories are like file folders in that they do not exist in a tree but simply associate related products. However, unlike its real-world counterpart, a product can be placed in multiple categories.

Users of the online catalog can add and remove categories and add and remove products. They also can search for and inspect products, updating attributes if necessary. Finally, users may browse the categories looking for related products. This is by no means a complete commercial solution. However, it does demonstrate a number of the features of a commercial Web site solution, including keyword searches and very basic form validation. The entire catalog is created with seven ASPs and one HTML page.

Basic Architecture for the Online Catalog

The online catalog is accessed via a main menu. From this page, the user can view a list of the entire contents, search the catalog, browse by category, add categories, or add products. Depending on the users' choices, they will receive a form or set of

263

links that lead them to their next page. Each page in the catalog contains a small menu at the top of the page to let users return to the main menu, or take a shortcut to another page.

Pages that contain forms use a simple programming pattern that associates the code for handling the form with the page itself. For example, the form for adding products is on the page insert_prod.asp. This page is also the form's target. When the user submits the form, the data is sent to insert_prod.asp, handled, and then the user is either redirected to a new page, or the form is redisplayed for the user to correct erroneous information.

The relationship between pages is displayed in Figure 15-1. This diagram does not include the small menus on each page. Instead, it focuses on the main flow experienced by a catalog user.

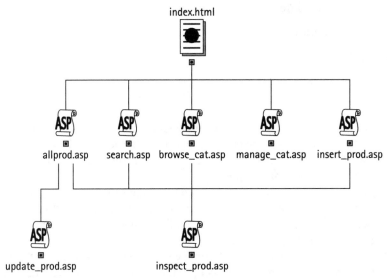

Figure 15-1: Catalog page relationships

Database Schema for the Catalog

Driving the online catalog is a database containing three tables. The products table stores information about the products in the database. It contains the columns described in Table 15-1.

TABLE 15-1 PRODUCTS TABLE

Column Name	Description
id	A unique identifier for the product.
name	The product's name.
description	A short description of the product.
longdescription	A longer, text description of the product.
msrp	The manufacturer's suggested retail price.
price	The actual, current price of the product.

The categories table contains information about the categories defined for the catalog. This table has one row, which is described in Table 15-2.

TABLE 15-2 CATEGORIES TABLE

Column Name	Description
Name	The category's name.

The final table, called prodcat, joins the products and categories. This table contains two columns, which are listed in Table 15-3. These columns relate a product to its categories. Products in more than one category may appear in the table multiple times.

TABLE 15-3 PRODCAT TABLE

Column Name	Description
Catname	The name of the category for this join.
Prodid	The ID of the product being joined.

This schema, along with some default data, is created with the page build_db.asp. This page is available on the CD-ROM. The ODBC datasource for this example will be called asp_devguide.

Main menu

The main menu for the online catalog is created with the HTML shown in Listing 15-1. This page should look like the one shown in Figure 15-2, when displayed in a browser.

Listing 15-1: The main menu for the online catalog

```html
<html>
<head>
<title>Simple Online Catalog</title>
</head>
<body link="006666" vlink="006666">
<center>
<table bgColor=006666 border=2
       cellspacing=1 cellpadding=4 width=450>
<tr><td align="center">
<font color="white"><b>Main Menu</b></font></td></tr>
<tr bgColor=F0F0F0><td align="left">
<a href="allprod.asp">List All Products</a><br>
<a href="search.asp">Search Catalog</a><br>
<a href="browse_cat.asp">Browse Categories</a><br>
<a href="manage_cat.asp">Manage Categories</a><br>
<a href="insert_prod.asp">Add A Product</a>
</td></tr></table>
</center>
</body>
</html>
```

This page also shows the basic color scheme and format used for all of the HTML in this example. We will not be discussing the HTML specifically, so this page provides the easiest lab for discovering how changes in the HTML can affect the appearance of the pages.

In a commercial solution, you probably want to use some sort of style sheet to define the look and feel of your HTML. We decided to bypass style sheets to focus on the ASP aspects of the pages. However, this would lead to unnecessary maintenance in a real-world solution.

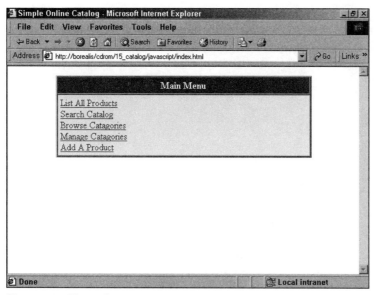

Figure 15-2: The main menu page

Complete catalog

When the user asks to see the complete catalog, the page allprod.asp is displayed. This page, shown in Figure 15-3, displays a list of the products in the products table.

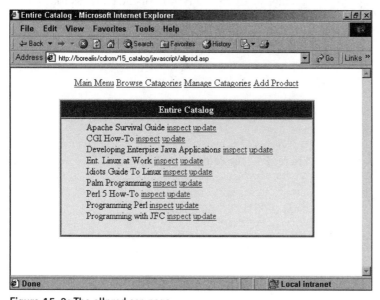

Figure 15-3: The allprod.asp page

Beside each product's name are two links. One link lets you inspect the product to view its attributes. This link goes to the inspect_prod.asp page. The other link goes to the update_prod.asp page that can be used to change the properties for a product. Both these ASPs accept a query string containing the ID of the product to display or update.

Start off the page with the standard language tag and an HTML header, as follows:

```
<%@ LANGUAGE="JAVASCRIPT" %>

<html>
<head>
<title>Entire Catalog</title>
</head>
<body link="006666" vlink="006666">
```

Display a small menu for the user to navigate around the catalog, without always having to return to the main menu, as shown here:

```
<center>
<a href="index.html">Main Menu</a>
<a href="browse_cat.asp">Browse Categories</a>
<a href="manage_cat.asp">Manage Categories</a>
<a href="insert_prod.asp">Add Product</a>
<br><br>
```

The page is displayed in a table, so create the HTML for the table, as follows:

```
<table bgColor=006666 border=2 cellspacing=1 cellpadding=4
width=450>
<tr><td align="center">
<font color="white"><b>Entire Catalog</b></font></td></tr>

<tr bgColor=F0F0F0><td align="left">
<ul>
```

Create a RecordSet object to retrieve the contents of the products table, as follows:

```
<%
var recordSet = Server.CreateObject("ADODB.RecordSet");
var id;
```

Open the record set by selecting all the products, sorted by name, as shown here:

```
recordSet.Open("select * from products order by name;"
                ,"DSN=asp_devguide");
```

Loop over the record set, displaying the name for each product along with the inspect and update links, as shown in Listing 15-2. As always, make sure to include the call to MoveNext or this loop will continue forever. Recall that both the inspection and update pages take a query string containing the ID of the product that they will work on. Create these URLs dynamically based on the data in the record set.

Listing 15-2: Looping over the record set

```
while(!recordSet.EOF)
{
    id = recordSet("id");

    Response.Write(recordSet("name"));
    Response.Write(" <a href='inspect_prod.asp?id=");
    Response.Write(id);
    Response.Write("'>inspect</a>");
    Response.Write(" <a href='update_prod.asp?id=");
    Response.Write(id);
    Response.Write("'>update</a><br>");

    recordSet.MoveNext();
}
```

Close the record set when you are done, as follows:

```
recordSet.Close();
%>
```

Then close the list, table, and HTML page as follows:

```
</ul>
</td></tr>
</table>
</center>

</body>
</html>
```

This is perhaps the simplest ASP in the example, so make sure that you feel comfortable with the basic process of connecting to the database, retrieving data, and displaying it before moving to the more complex pages.

Search page

The search page displays a form containing a number of criteria that can be used to limit the products found. These criteria include a keyword search, price limitations, or category limits. The keyword search looks for a word in the name, description, and longdescription of a product using the SQL "like" syntax.

This is the first page in the example that both contains a form and acts as the target for the form. When displayed via a link, the search page will look like the one shown in Figure 15-4. There are four main elements of the search form: the keyword field, the minimum price field, the maximum price field, and the category list.

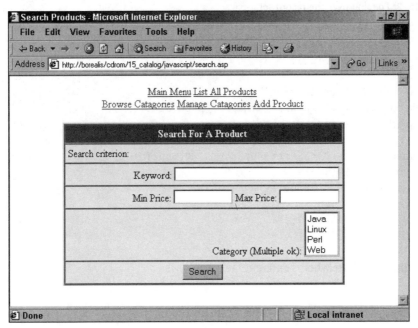

Figure 15-4: The search page

Notice that the page doesn't include any results and is just displaying a form. When the user fills out one of the criteria and submits the search, the page will be redisplayed like the one shown in Figure 15-5.

This page contains links, like the allprod.asp page, that let viewers inspect or update the pages that match their search criterion. The page still can be used to create a new search. Start off the page with the standard language tag, as follows:

```
<%@ LANGUAGE="JAVASCRIPT" %>
<%
```

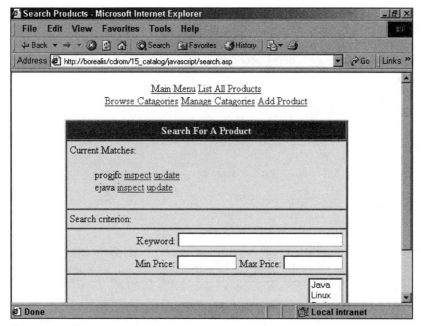

Figure 15-5: A successful search

Next, declare all the variables that will be used for this page. These include the values from the form, a SQL string, the ID of products in the search results, a record set, and a database for searching. The only really interesting variable is the idString. We will use this string to indicate the name of a product ID in the database, because the name in the products table is "id" and the name is "prodid" in the prodcat joining table.

```
var category,keyword,max,min;
var recordSet = Server.CreateObject("ADODB.RecordSet");
var database = Server.CreateObject("ADODB.Connection");
var sql;
var i,max;
var id = null;
var idString=null;
```

Open a connection to the database, as follows:

```
database.Open("asp_devguide","asp_dev","");
```

Try to get the keyword and price data from the form. Remember that the JavaScript/ASP interface requires you to convert the values in a Form collection to strings using concatenation to compare them to `undefined`. We will use these values to determine if the page is being accessed via a link, or if it is handling the form submission.

```
keyword = Request.Form("keyword");
if(("""+keyword) == "undefined") keyword = null;

max = """+Request.Form("max");
if(("""+max) == "undefined") max = null;

min = """+Request.Form("min");
if(("""+min) == "undefined") min = null;
```

If a keyword was provided, do the keyword search. This skips the other criterion but makes this page much easier to write. In a real application, you might provide separate pages for each criterion, or coalesce the results from all three limits.

```
if((keyword != null)&&((""+keyword) != ""))
{
```

Using the keyword, construct a SQL statement containing `where` clauses for the `name`, `description`, and `longdescription`. The `%` in a `like` clause will act as a wild card. So the following SQL should return any products whose `name`, `description`, or `longdescription` contains the keyword.

```
    sql = "select * from products where "
    sql += "name like '%";
    sql += keyword;
    sql += "%' or description like '%";
    sql += keyword;
    sql += "%' or longdescription like '%";
    sql += keyword;
    sql += "%'";
```

Open the record set, thus performing the query. Set the `idString` to `id`, since we are using the products table.

```
    recordSet.Open(sql,database);
    idString = "id";
}
```

If we didn't get a keyword from the form submission, but we got a `min` and `max` price, perform that search. These values will be `""` if they are empty, or undefined (null) if the page is accessed via a link.

```
else if((max != null)&&(min != null)
        &&((""+max) != "")&&((""+min) != ""))
{
```

Limit the `select` statement by the minimum and maximum prices, as follows:

```
sql = "select * from products where "
sql += "(price >= ";
sql += min;
sql += ") and (price <= ";
sql += max;
sql += ")";
```

Open the record set and perform the query. Set the `idString` to `id`, since we are using the products table.

```
recordSet.Open(sql,database);
idString = "id";
}
```

If there was no keyword, and no price restriction, check if the Form collection has a category field containing at least one value. This field actually will be a selection list and could contain multiple values.

```
else if(Request.Form("category").Count > 0)
{
```

Begin creating the `select` statement for the prodcat table, where the category to products map is. Use a loop to add the restrictions for each category selected in the list, as follows:

```
sql = "select * from prodcat where "

max = Request.Form("category").Count;

for(i=1;i<=max;i++)
{
```

Place an or before each category name restriction, except the first one, as follows:

```
    if(i>1) sql += " or ";

    sql += "(catname = '";
    sql += Request.Form("category")(i);
    sql += "')";
  }
```

Open the record set and perform the query. Set the idString to prodid, since we are using the prodcat table.

```
    recordSet.Open(sql,database);
    idString = "prodid";
  }
%>
```

Start the HTML, including the header and the small menu, as shown in Listing 15-3.

Listing 15-3: Starting the HTML for the search page

```
<html>
<head>
<title>Search Products</title>
</head>
<body link="006666" vlink="006666">

<center>
<a href="index.html">Main Menu</a>
<a href="allprod.asp">List All Products</a><br>
<a href="browse_cat.asp">Browse Categories</a>
<a href="manage_cat.asp">Manage Categories</a>
<a href="insert_prod.asp">Add Product</a>
<br><br>
```

Open the form for this page, and point it back to the page itself. Use a post request to distinguish the form submission from any query strings, as follows:

```
<form action="search.asp" method="post">
```

Format the form into a table, for look and feel, as follows:

```
<table bgColor=006666 border=2 cellspacing=1 cellpadding=4 width=450>
<tr><td align="center">
<font color="white"><b>Search For A Product</b></font></td></tr>
```

Check if there was a value assigned to `idString`. If this value is set, then a search was performed. Otherwise, we should just display the form.

```
<%
if(idString != null)
{
%>
<tr bgColor=F0F0F0><td align="left">
Current Matches:<br>
<ul>
<%
```

Iterate through the record set, displaying the ID for each product found. Also, display links to inspect and update the product's data. One possible enhancement for this page would be to use product names rather than IDs. We used IDs to make combining the prodcat and products tables easier.

```
    while(!recordSet.EOF)
    {
        id = recordSet(idString);
        Response.Write(id);
        Response.Write(" <a href='inspect_prod.asp?id=");
        Response.Write(id);
        Response.Write("'>inspect</a>");
        Response.Write(" <a href='update_prod.asp?id=");
        Response.Write(id);
        Response.Write("'>update</a><br>");
        recordSet.MoveNext();
    }
```

Close the record set when you are done with it, as follows:

```
recordSet.Close();
%>
```

Continue the HTML layout, as follows:

```
</ul>
</td></tr>
<%
}
%>

<tr bgColor=F0F0F0><td align="left">
Search criterion:
</td></tr>
```

Define the form containing the search criteria, as follows:

```
<tr bgColor=F0F0F0><td align="right">
Keyword: <input type="text" name="keyword" size=40>
</td></tr>

<tr bgColor=F0F0F0><td align="right">
Min Price: <input type="text" name="min" size=12>
Max Price: <input type="text" name="max" size=12>
</td></tr>

<tr bgColor=F0F0F0><td align="right">
Category (Multiple ok):
```

For the category list, perform a `select` on the categories table, ordering the results by name, as follows:

```
<%
recordSet.Open("select * from categories order by name",database);

Response.Write("<select size=4 name='category' multiple>");
```

Display each category as an option in the list, as follows:

```
while(!recordSet.EOF)
{
    category = recordSet("name");
    Response.Write("<option value='" + category);
    Response.Write("' >");
    Response.Write(category);
    Response.Write("</option>");
    recordSet.MoveNext();
}
```

Close the record set when you are done with it, as follows:

```
recordSet.Close();
```

Complete the HTML formatting, like this:

```
Response.Write("</select>");
%>
</td></tr>

<tr bgColor=F0F0F0><td align="center">
<input type="submit" value="Search">
</td></tr>
</table>
</form>
</center>
<%
```

Close the database connection and the HTML page. You might consider using a shared connection for this application. We created a connection for each page as a convenience, and they act as a reminder about closing connections. You may want to use the global.asa file to create shared connections, thus reducing connection time.

```
database.Close();
%>
</body>
</html>
```

Hopefully, this page gives you some idea of how the same ASP can be used to display a form and respond to the user submitting the form. This basic pattern is a very powerful tool in organizing code and HTML.

Browsing by Category

When users choose to browse by category, they are directed to a page called browse_cat.asp. This page performs two tasks. First it will display a list of categories. Also, if a category name is provided in a query string, the page will display the products in that category. When displaying the categories, each category is a link to the browse_cat.asp with the appropriate query string. For example, using the sample data, the page will look like the one shown in Figure 15-6.

When you select a category, like Java, the products in that category are displayed, as shown in Figure 15-7.

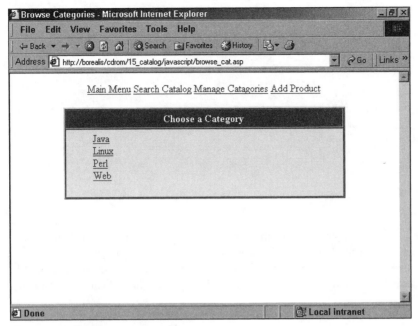

Figure 15-6: The browse category page

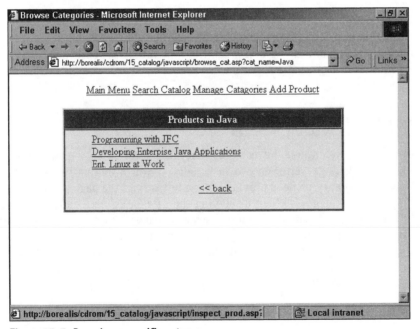

Figure 15-7: Browsing a specific category

The products on this page are listed as links to the inspect_prod.asp page. So the user can select a product and learn more about it. Start off the page with the standard language tag, as follows:

```
<%@ LANGUAGE="JAVASCRIPT" %>
<%
```

Declare the variables needed in the page. This includes two record sets, one for the categories and one for products. Also create a database Connection object.

```
var category;
var submit;
var recordSet = Server.CreateObject("ADODB.RecordSet");
var prodSet = Server.CreateObject("ADODB.RecordSet");
var database = Server.CreateObject("ADODB.Connection");
var sql;
var title;
```

Open the database connection. This connection will be shared by the various record sets used on this page.

```
database.Open("asp_devguide","asp_dev","");
```

Check if a category was provided in the query string, as follows:

```
category = Request.QueryString("cat_name");
if((""+category) == "undefined") category = null;
```

If there is a category, set up the title variable to include it; otherwise, initialize the title variable to request a category from the viewer.

```
if(category != null)
{
    title = "Products in "+category;
}
else
{
    title = "Choose a Category";
}
%>
```

Start the HTML page, menu, and formatting, as shown in Listing 15-4.

Listing 15-4: Starting the HTML for the browsing page

```
<html>
<head>
<title>Browse Categories</title>
</head>
<body link="006666" vlink="006666">


<center>
<a href="index.html">Main Menu</a>
<a href="search.asp">Search Catalog</a>
<a href="manage_cat.asp">Manage Categories</a>
<a href="insert_prod.asp">Add Product</a>
<br><br>
<table bgColor=006666 border=2 cellspacing=1
        cellpadding=4 width=450>
<tr><td align="center">
<font color="white"><b><%=title%></b></font>
</td></tr>
<tr bgColor=F0F0F0><td align="left">
<ul>
<%
```

Now, if a category was provided in the query string, display the products in that category, as follows:

```
if(category != null)
{
    var id,name;
```

Open a result set for the prodcat table and select all the records related to this category, as follows:

```
    recordSet.Open("select * from prodcat where catname='"
                            +category+"'",database);
```

Iterate through the records, getting the ID for each product in this category.

```
    while(! recordSet.EOF)
    {
        id = recordSet("prodid");
```

Perform another `select` statement, only this time access the products table. Use the product ID from the prodcat joining table as a restriction so that only one product's information is returned. We will have two record sets open, both using the same database connection.

```
prodSet.Open("select * from products where id='"
             +id+"'",database);
```

Make sure that the `select` succeeded and then print the link for the current product. Link the product's name to the inspect_prod.asp page with the appropriate query string.

```
if(!prodSet.EOF)
{
    Response.Write("<a href='inspect_prod.asp?id="+id+"'>");
    Response.Write(prodSet("name"));
    Response.Write("<a><br>");
}
```

Close the record set for the products database, and move to the next record in the prodcat selection. This will give us the next product in this category.

```
    prodSet.Close();
    recordSet.MoveNext();
}
```

Close the first record set, as follows:

```
recordSet.Close();
```

Provide a link back to the browse category page, without a query string. If users select this link, they will return to the list of categories.

```
Response.Write("<br><center><a href='browse_cat.asp'>");
Response.Write("&lt;&lt; back</a>");
}
```

Now handle the situation where there is no query string, as follows:

```
else
{
```

Open a record set containing a list of the categories in the database ordered by their name, as shown here:

```
recordSet.Open("select * from categories order by name;"
                ,database);
```

Iterate through this list, displaying a link for each category. Link the category's name back to the browse_cat.asp page, providing a query string that will focus the page on that category's products.

```
while(! recordSet.EOF)
{
    category = recordSet("name");
    Response.Write("<a href='browse_cat.asp?cat_name="
                                        +category+"'>");
    Response.Write(category);
    Response.Write("<a><br>");
    recordSet.MoveNext();
}
```

Close the record set when you are done with it, as follows:

```
recordSet.Close();
}
%>
```

End the HTML for the page, and close the database connection, as follows:

```
</ul>
</td></tr></table>
</form>
</center>
<%
database.Close();
%>
</body>
</html>
```

This browse page provides a different example of linking to yourself. In this case, the browser displays categories as links with query strings that let it focus on a particular category. If no query string is provided, the page displays the categories. If a query string is provided, then the appropriate products are displayed.

Displaying Product Information

When the catalog application wants to display information about a product, it uses the inspect_prod.asp page. This page takes a product ID in its query string and displays information about the given product. For example, when accessed from the category browser, this page may look like the one shown in Figure 15-8.

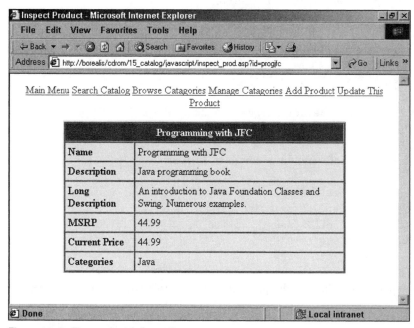

Figure 15-8: The product information page

Start the page off with the standard language tag, as follows:

```
<%@ LANGUAGE="JAVASCRIPT" %>
<%
```

Declare variables for the scripts on this page. A database connection and record set are used to retrieve data about a product.

```
var recordSet = Server.CreateObject("ADODB.RecordSet");
var database = Server.CreateObject("ADODB.Connection");
var sql;
var id,name,desc,lDesc,price,msrp;
var title;
```

Open the database connection, as follows:

```
database.Open("asp_devguide","asp_dev","");
```

Access the query string and try to find out if an ID was provided, as shown here:

```
id = Request.QueryString("id");
if((""+id) == "undefined") id = null;
```

If there is an ID, request the information about that product from the products table in the database, as follows:

```
if((id != null)&&((""+id)!= ""))
{
    recordSet.Open("select * from products where id='"
                                    +id+"'",database);
```

Store the product information in variables, like this:

```
    name = recordSet("name");
    desc = recordSet("description");
    lDesc = recordSet("longDescription");
    msrp = recordSet("msrp");
    price = recordSet("price");
```

Use a separate variable for the page header title; this will let you set a default header.

```
    title = name;
}
```

If no ID was provided in the query string, set the data to empty strings "" and the default title, as follows:

```
else
{
    title = "No Product Selected.";
    name = "";
    desc = "";
    lDesc = "";
    price = "";
    msrp = "";
}
%>
```

Begin the HTML, including the header, menu, and a table to contain the contents, as shown in Listing 15-5.

Listing 15-5: Beginning the HTML for the display product information page

```
<html>
<head>
<title>Inspect Product</title>
</head>
<body link="006666" vlink="006666">


<center>
<a href="index.html">Main Menu</a>
<a href="search.asp">Search Catalog</a>
<a href="browse_cat.asp">Browse Categories</a>
<a href="manage_cat.asp">Manage Categories</a>
<a href="insert_prod.asp">Add Product</a>
<a href="update_prod.asp?id=<%=id%>">Update This Product</a>
<br><br>

<table bgColor=006666 border=2
        cellspacing=1 cellpadding=4 width=450>
```

Display the title of the page. This is highlighted by color and will indicate if the page is accessed without an ID.

```
<tr><td align="center" colspan=2>
<font color="white"><b><%=title%></b></font></td></tr>
```

Display the data for the current product in rows of the table, as shown in Listing 15-6. Use the variables defined earlier.

Listing 15-6: Displaying product data in table rows

```
<tr bgColor=F0F0F0>
<td><b>Name</b></td><td><%=name%></td>
</tr>
<tr bgColor=F0F0F0>
<td><b>Description</b></td><td><%=desc%></td>
</tr>
<tr bgColor=F0F0F0>
<td><b>Long Description</b></td><td><%=lDesc%></td>
</tr>
<tr bgColor=F0F0F0>
<td><b>MSRP</b></td><td><%=msrp%></td>
</tr>
```

```
<tr bgColor=F0F0F0>
<td><b>Current Price</b></td><td><%=price%></td>
</tr>
<tr bgColor=F0F0F0>
<td><b>Categories</b></td>
<td>
<%
```

Use another script to display the categories for this product. First, close the recordSet, as follows:

```
var gotone = false;

recordSet.Close();
```

Next, perform a select on the prodcat table, limiting it to entries for this product ID. Order the results by the category name.

```
recordSet.Open("select * from prodcat where prodid='"
                +id+"' order by catname",database);
```

Iterate through the categories for this product, and display them in a comma-delimited list. Use the Boolean value of gotone to determine if this is the first category or one requiring a comma.

```
while(!recordSet.EOF)
{
    if(gotone) Response.Write(",");

    Response.Write(recordSet("catname"));
    gotone=true;
    recordSet.MoveNext();
}
%>
```

End the HTML and close the record set and database, as follows:

```
</td>
</tr></table>
</center>
<%
recordSet.Close();
database.Close();
%>
```

```
</body>
</html>
```

This is a pretty simple page. It does show how you can reuse a `RecordSet` object. Notice that we closed the record set before reusing it.

Managing Categories

The page for managing categories is called manage_cat.asp and is shown in Figure 15-9. This page displays a form for adding or removing categories. The page also acts as the target of the form and performs both the add and delete operations.

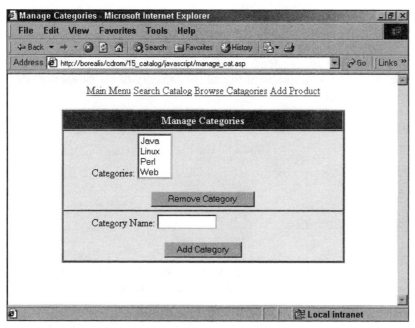

Figure 15-9: The managing categories page

A value on the `submit` button is used to distinguish between an add and delete in the form on this page. You can also use two forms and hidden fields to get the same results. Begin the page with the standard language tag, and declare the variables for the scripts, as follows:

```
<%@ LANGUAGE="JAVASCRIPT" %>
<%
var category;
var submit;
```

```
var recordSet = Server.CreateObject("ADODB.RecordSet");
var database = Server.CreateObject("ADODB.Connection");
var sql;
```

Open a connection to the database, as follows:

```
database.Open("asp_devguide","asp_dev","");
```

Get the value of the submit field in the form, and of the category field, as shown here:

```
submit = Request.Form("submit");
if((""+submit) == "undefined") submit = null;

category = Request.Form("cat_name");
if((""+category) == "undefined") category = null;
```

If the user is trying to add a category, and they provided the category name, execute the appropriate insert statement to add the category to the categories table, as follows:

```
if((category != null)&&(submit=="Add Category"))
{
    sql = "insert into categories values ('";
    sql += category;
    sql += "')";

    database.Execute(sql);
}
```

If the user is trying to remove a category, they should have selected it from the list. Get the selected item from the list and make sure it exists, like this:

```
category = Request.Form("category");
if((""+category) == "undefined") category = null;

if((category != null)&&(submit=="Remove Category"))
{
```

Delete the category from the categories table, as follows:

```
    sql = "delete from categories where name='";
    sql += category;
```

```
sql += "'";

database.Execute(sql);
```

Delete all references to the category from the prodcat table, as follows:

```
sql = "delete from prodcat where catname='";
sql += category;
sql += "'";

database.Execute(sql);
}
%>
```

Begin the HTML, including the page header, menu, and table for the form, as shown in Listing 15-7.

Listing 15-7: Beginning the HTML for the managing categories page

```
<html>
<head>
<title>Add Product</title>
</head>
<body link="006666" vlink="006666">


<center>
<a href="index.html">Main Menu</a>
<a href="search.asp">Search Catalog</a>
<a href="browse_cat.asp">Browse Categories</a>
<a href="insert_prod.asp">Add Product</a>
<br><br>
<table bgColor=006666 border=2 cellspacing=1
        cellpadding=4 width=450>
<tr><td align="center">
<font color="white"><b>Manage Categories</b></font>
</td></tr>
<tr bgColor=F0F0F0><td align="left">
<ul>
```

Point the form back to the manage_cat.asp page, as follows:

```
<form action="manage_cat.asp" method="post">
Categories:
```

Create the list of categories by performing a query on the categories table, as shown in Listing 15-8. Use the order by clause to sort the list.

Listing 15-8: Creating the list of categories

```
<%
recordSet.Open("select * from categories order by name;",database);

Response.Write("<select size=4 name='category'>");

while(! recordSet.EOF)
{
    category = recordSet("name");
    Response.Write("<option value='" + category);
    Response.Write("' >");
    Response.Write(category);
    Response.Write("</option>");
    recordSet.MoveNext();
}
```

Close the record set when you are done with it, as follows:

```
Response.Write("</select>");
recordSet.Close();
%>
</ul>
<center>
```

Use a value on the submit button to indicate that this part of the form was for removing a category, as follows:

```
<input type=submit name="submit" value="Remove Category">
</center>
</td></tr>
```

Define the fields and submit button for adding a category. This is pure HTML.

```
<tr bgColor=F0F0F0><td align="left">
<ul>
Category Name: <input name="cat_name" size=12>
</ul>

<center>
<input type=submit name="submit" value="Add Category">
</center>
</td></tr></table>
```

```
</form>
</center>
```

Close the database connection and the HTML page, as follows:

```
<%
database.Close();
%>
</body>
</html>
```

This page is a good example of how a complex program can include joins between tables that must be kept synchronized when adding or deleting data. How might you enhance this page to support renaming categories?

Adding Products

Perhaps the two most difficult pages in this example are the pages that add and update a product. These pages include some form validation and deal with numerous columns. To add a product, a user accesses the insert_prod.asp page. This page displays a form, as shown in Figure 15-10.

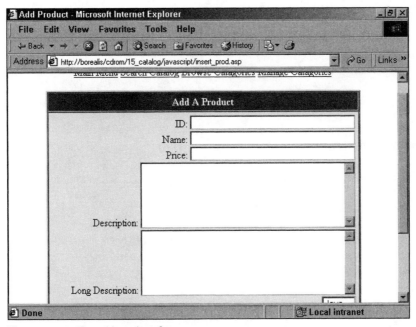

Figure 15-10: The add product form

When submitted, the form goes back to the insert_prod.asp page for handling. The ASP will make sure all the fields are filled in. You might also move this functionality to the client using JavaScript, but we didn't want to confuse the example with client and server-side scripting.

Start the page with the language tag, and by declaring the variables for the scripts. We will be using a variable called message to display an optional message to the user. For example, if all the fields are not filled in, a message asking the user to do so will be displayed above the form, as shown in Figure 15-11.

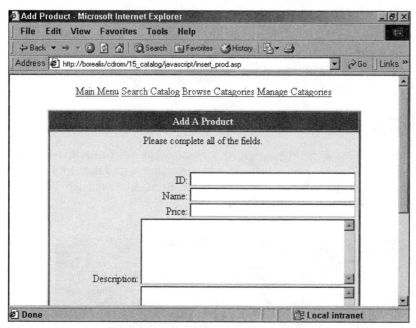

Figure 15-11: A message on the add product form

Normally, no message is displayed.

```
<%@ LANGUAGE="JAVASCRIPT" %>
<%
var category,id,name,desc,lDesc,price;
var recordSet = Server.CreateObject("ADODB.RecordSet");
var database = Server.CreateObject("ADODB.Connection");
var sql;
var message;
var i,max;
```

Open the database connection and initialize the `message` variable to `null`, as follows:

```
database.Open("asp_devguide","asp_dev","");
message = null;
```

See if an ID was included as part of a form submission. If not, then we will just display the form without trying to submit anything.

```
id = Request.Form("id");
if((""+id) == "undefined") id = null;

if((id != null)&&((""+id)!=""))
{
```

If there is an ID, get the values for the other fields and make sure that they are not undefined or empty, as shown here:

```
    name = ""+Request.Form("prodName");
    if((name == "undefined")||(name=="")) name = null;

    desc = ""+Request.Form("description");
    if((desc == "undefined")||(desc=="")) desc = null;

    lDesc = ""+Request.Form("longDescription");
    if((lDesc == "undefined")||(lDesc=="")) lDesc = null;

    price = ""+Request.Form("price");
    if((price == "undefined")||(price=="")) price = null;
```

If the form is not complete, set the `message` variable. Otherwise, we will perform an insert.

```
    if((name==null)||(desc==null)
        ||(price==null)||(lDesc==null))
    {
        message =
          "<center>Please complete all of the fields.</center>";
    }
    else
    {
```

Create the SQL to insert this product into the database, as shown in Listing 15-9.

Listing 15-9: Inserting the product into the database

```
sql = "insert into products values ('";
sql += id;
sql += "','";
sql += name;
sql += "','";
sql += desc;
sql += "','";
sql += lDesc;
sql += "',";
sql += price;
sql += ",";
sql += price;
sql += ")";
```

Insert the product. This will fail if the ID is not unique. In a commercial application, you should be able to use unique IDs generated by the database. However, that functionality is database dependent, so we have the user enter a unique value, as follows:

```
try
{
    database.Execute(sql);
}
catch(exp)
{
    message = "Failed to insert product, check id.";
}
```

Using the values from the category selection list, insert rows into the prodcat table to relate this new product to existing categories. Perform an execute for each insert statement, as follows:

```
max = Request.Form("category").Count;

for(i=1;i<=max;i++)
{
    sql = "insert into prodcat values ('";
    sql += Request.Form("category")(i);
    sql += "','";
    sql += id;
    sql += "')";

    database.Execute(sql);
}
```

Once the product is inserted, redirect the client to the inspect_prod.asp page. Notice that we perform this redirection before sending any HTML to the user. Redirection is part of the HTTP header, so it should come before any HTML is sent in the body. You can also use the new `Server.Transfer` method to perform this same task.

```
        Response.Redirect("inspect_prod.asp?id="+id);
    }
}
%>
```

Start the HTML for the page, including the menu and table for formatting, as shown in Listing 15-10.

Listing 15-10: Beginning the HTML for the adding products page

```
<html>
<head>
<title>Add Product</title>
</head>
<body link=006666>


<center>
<a href="index.html">Main Menu</a>
<a href="search.asp">Search Catalog</a>
<a href="browse_cat.asp">Browse Catgories</a>
<a href="manage_cat.asp">Manage Categories</a>
<br><br>

<table bgColor=006666 border=2 cellspacing=1 cellpadding=4
width=500>
<tr><td align="center">
<font color="white"><b>Add A Product</b></font></td></tr>
<tr bgColor=F0F0F0><td align="right">
```

If there is a value for the message variable, display the message, as follows:

```
<%
if(message != null)
{
%>
<%=message%><br><br>
<%
}
%>
```

Point the form back to the insert_prod.asp page, like this:

```
<form action="insert_prod.asp" method="post">
```

Provide a form element for each column in the products table, as shown in Listing 15-11.

Listing 15-11: Providing a form element for table columns

```
ID: <input type="text" name="id" size=40><br>
Name: <input type="text" name="prodName" size=40><br>
Price: <input type="text" name="price" size=40><br>
Description:
<textarea name="description" cols=40 rows=6
          wrap=virtual>
</textarea><br>
Long Description:
<textarea name="longDescription" cols=40 rows=6
          wrap=virtual>
</textarea><br>
Categories (Multiple ok):
<%
```

Use a select statement to get an ordered list of categories and display them in a select list, as shown in Listing 15-12. The user can use this list to select the categories for a new product when they create it.

Listing 15-12: Getting an ordered list of categories

```
recordSet.Open("select * from categories order by name;",database);

Response.Write("<select size=4 name='category' multiple>");

while(! recordSet.EOF)
{
    category = recordSet("name");
    Response.Write("<option value='" + category);
    Response.Write("' >");
    Response.Write(category);
    Response.Write("</option>");
    recordSet.MoveNext();
}

Response.Write("</select>");
```

```
recordSet.Close();
%>
<br><br>
```

Provide a `submit` button and close the HTML for this page. As always, close the database connection as well.

```
<input type="submit" value="Add Product">

</form>

</td></tr></table>
</center>
<%
database.Close();
%>
</body>
</html>
```

This adding products page introduces the new idea of having a message for errors that is optionally displayed with the HTML. This is a common mechanism for server-side error handling. However, for form validation it is much more responsive if you can use client-side JavaScript to immediately notify the user of missing information.

Updating Products

The last page in this example is the page for updating product information called update_prod.asp. This page is a mixture between the insert_prod.asp and the inspect_prod.asp. It provides a partial form for updating product information. However, as you can see in Figure 15-12, you cannot edit the ID of the product.

This page expects an ID to be provided in its query string or in a form post. If no ID is provided, the page will display a message indicating the error.

Start off with the language tag and variable declarations. On this page, the interesting variable is called catHolder. We are using a JavaScript object to hold the names of the categories for the current product so that we can select them in the list of all categories. You could use a Dictionary object in VBScript for the same purpose.

For more information on the Dictionary object, see the VBScript version of this application on the CD-ROM.

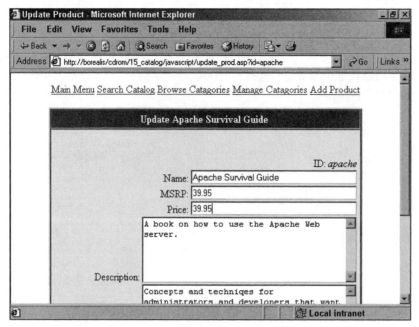

Figure 15-12: The update product page

```
<%@ LANGUAGE="JAVASCRIPT" %>
<%
var id,name="",desc="",lDesc="",price="",msrp="";
var recordSet = Server.CreateObject("ADODB.RecordSet");
var database = Server.CreateObject("ADODB.Connection");
var sql;
var message="";
var title="";
var catHolder=new Object();
var catName;
var submit;
```

Open the database connection, as follows:

```
database.Open("asp_devguide","asp_dev","");
```

See if there is an ID in the query string. This could happen when someone selects one of the links on the category browser or list of all products page.

```
id = Request.QueryString("id");
if((""+id) == "undefined") id = null;
```

If an ID is provided, perform a `select` to get the information for that product from the database, as shown here:

```
if((id != null)&&((""+id)!=""))
{
    recordSet.Open("select * from products where id='"
                                    +id+"'",database);
```

Store the product's attributes in variables. Use string concatenation to copy the data into a new string object. If you just do assignment, you are actually referencing an object in the record set. If the record set is closed, the data will become invalid. By using `""+` we are copying the data and can use it after the record set is closed, as shown here:

```
name = ""+recordSet("name");
desc = ""+recordSet("description");
lDesc = ""+recordSet("longDescription");
msrp = ""+recordSet("msrp");
price = ""+recordSet("price");
```

Again we are using a variable called `title` to dynamically create a header on the page. In this case, because we know the product's name, we will display it with the page.

```
title = "Update "+name;
```

Close the record set and then reuse it to get all the categories associated with this product ID, as follows:

```
recordSet.Close();

recordSet.Open("select * from prodcat where prodid='"
                                    +id+"'",database);
```

Store the name of each category as a property in the `catHolder` object. This object will act like a hash table or dictionary containing the categories for the current project. We will use these later to select items in the list of all categories.

```
while(!recordSet.EOF)
{
    catName = ""+recordSet("catname");
    catHolder[catName] = catName;
    recordSet.MoveNext();
}
```

Close the record set again, as follows:

```
recordSet.Close();
}
```

If the query string didn't contain a product ID, then the page is being accessed either because the form on it was submitted or it is in error.

```
else //see if this is a submission
{
```

See if there was a product ID in the form submission, as follows:

```
id = Request.Form("id");
if((""+id) == "undefined") id = null;
```

Also get the value of the submit button used. We will use this value to distinguish between updating and deleting a product.

```
submit = Request.Form("submit");
if((""+submit) == "undefined") submit = null;
```

If there is an ID, then we have a product to work with.

```
if((id != null)&&((""+id)!=""))
{
```

Get the new information for this product submitted with the form, as shown in Listing 15-13. Don't bother to copy the information, because we are going to use it to update the database and then redirect to the inspection page.

Listing 15-13: Getting the new information

```
name = Request.Form("prodName");
if((""+name) == "undefined") name = null;

desc = Request.Form("description");
if((""+desc) == "undefined") desc = null;

lDesc = Request.Form("longDescription");
if((""+lDesc) == "undefined") lDesc = null;

price = Request.Form("price");
if((""+price) == "undefined") price = null;
```

```
msrp = Request.Form("msrp");
if((""+msrp) == "undefined") msrp = null;
```

Check if the `Delete Product` button was pressed, as shown in Listing 15-14. If so, delete the product from the products table, and from the prodcat table. Then redirect the client to the main menu.

Listing 15-14: Checking whether the Delete Product button was pressed

```
if((""+submit) == "Delete Product")
{
    sql = "delete from products where id='";
    sql += id;
    sql += "'";
    database.Execute(sql);

    sql = "delete from prodcat where prodid='";
    sql += id;
    sql += "'";
    database.Execute(sql);

    Response.Redirect("index.html");
}
```

If the update form was not completed, initialize a message for the user, as follows:

```
else if((name==null)||(desc==null)
    ||(price==null)||(lDesc==null)||(msrp==null))
{
    message = "Please complete all of the fields.";
}
```

Otherwise, the form is complete, and we should update the products database, as follows:

```
else
{
```

Create a string containing the SQL to update the current product's `name`, `description`, `longdescription`, `price`, and `msrp`, as follows:

```
sql = "update products set name='";
sql += name;
sql += "',description='";
sql += desc;
sql += "',longdescription='";
```

```
sql += lDesc;
sql += "',price=";
sql += price;
sql += ",msrp=";
sql += msrp;
sql += " where id='";
sql += id;
sql += "'";
```

Execute the update as follows, storing a message if this fails:

```
try
{
    database.Execute(sql);
}
catch(exp)
{
    message = "Failed to update product.";
}
```

Delete all the entries in the prodcat table for this product, as follows:

```
sql = "delete from prodcat where prodid='";
sql += id;
sql += "'";
database.Execute(sql);
```

Then use the value selecting in the category list to add new entries to the prod-cat table. If the user didn't change the value in the selection list, then the database still will be accessed, but the results will be the same as if it wasn't changed.

```
max = Request.Form("category").Count;

for(i=1;i<=max;i++)
{
    sql = "insert into prodcat values ('";
    sql += Request.Form("category")(i);
    sql += "','";
    sql += id;
    sql += "')";

    database.Execute(sql);
}
```

Redirect the user to the inspect_prod.asp page to see the results of their update. Generate a query string based on the ID, so that the display page knows which product to show.

```
        Response.Redirect("inspect_prod.asp?id="+id);
    }
}
```

In case of an error, display a title indicating that no product was selected and then leave the form blank, as follows:

```
else
{
    title = "No Product Selected.";
    name = "";
    desc = "";
    lDesc = "";
    price = "";
    msrp = "";
}
}
%>
```

Now that the scripts are done and all redirections are complete, start the HTML, including the menu, as shown in Listing 15-15.

Listing 15-15: Beginning the HTML for the update products page

```
<html>
<head>
<title>Update Product</title>
</head>
<body link="006666" vlink="006666">


<center>
<a href="index.html">Main Menu</a>
<a href="search.asp">Search Catalog</a>
<a href="browse_cat.asp">Browse Categories</a>
<a href="manage_cat.asp">Manage Categories</a>
<a href="insert_prod.asp">Add Product</a>
<br><br>

<form action="update_prod.asp" method="post">

<table bgColor=006666 border=2
```

```
        cellspacing=1 cellpadding=4 width=500>
<tr><td align="center">
<font color="white"><b><%=title%></b></font></td></tr>
<tr bgColor=F0F0F0><td align="right">
```

Display the message if it was initialized, as follows:

```
<%
if(message != null)
{
%>
<%=message%><br><br>
<%
}
%>
```

Display the current product ID, as plain HTML, and include it in the form as a hidden field, as follows:

```
ID: <em><%=id%></em>
<input type="hidden" name="id" value="<%=id%>"><br>
```

Include the other product attributes as text fields, like this:

```
Name: <input type="text" name="prodName"
            size=40 value="<%=name%>"><br>
MSRP: <input type="text" name="msrp"
            size=40 value="<%=msrp%>"><br>
Price: <input type="text" name="price"
            size=40 value="<%=price%>"><br>
Description: <textarea name="description"
            cols=40 rows=6 wrap=virtual><%=desc%></textarea><br>
Long Description:
<textarea name="longDescription" cols=40 rows=6
          wrap=virtual>
<%=lDesc%></textarea><br>
Categories (Multiple ok):
<%
```

Dynamically generate a list of all the categories in the database, as follows:

```
recordSet.Open("select * from categories order by name;",database);

Response.Write("<select size=4 name='category' multiple>");
```

```
while(! recordSet.EOF)
{
```

For each category, create an `<option>` tag. Use the `catHolder` object to figure out if the current category is associated with the current object. If so, add the selected attribute to that `<option>` tag. This will ensure that the categories for the product are selected in the list by default.

```
    category = recordSet("name");
    Response.Write("<option value='" + category);
    Response.Write("' ");
    if(catHolder[category] != null) Response.Write("selected");
    Response.Write(">");
    Response.Write(category);
    Response.Write("</option>");
    recordSet.MoveNext();
}
```

Close the dynamic list, and record set, as follows:

```
Response.Write("</select>");
recordSet.Close();
%>
```

Define two buttons, one for deleting and one for updating, as follows:

```
<br><br>
<input type="submit" name="submit" value="Delete Product">
<input type="submit" name="submit" value="Update Product">
```

Close the HTML page and database, as follows:

```
</td></tr></table>
</form>
</center>
<%
database.Close();
%>
</body>
</html>
```

Like the other pages, this update page added a new twist. In this case, a generic object was used to store information so that it could be used during a later query. This technique made it really easy to select the appropriate items in our dynamic category list, without having to perform too many database queries.

Summary

Hopefully, this chapter's example will provide you with some good ideas for your own projects. Some basic lessons we have tried to demonstrate are

- Using an ASP to display and handle the same form
- Using generic objects, or dictionaries, to store data from the database
- Using variables to store optional messages to the user
- Server-side form validation
- Using multiple record sets on the same connection
- Copying data from a record set for use after the record set is closed

By combining these techniques and the others we've demonstrated, you will be well on your way to creating serious Active Server Page Web applications.

Chapter 16

Transactional Scripts

IN THIS CHAPTER

◆ What are transactions?

◆ Transactions and Active Server Pages

OFTEN WHEN DEVELOPING LARGE systems, you will encounter situations where you have multiple operations that need to be grouped together. For example, when a customer charges an order, the order needs to be sent to shipping for delivery and the customer's account charged. These two operations must be linked to ensure that they happen together, or they both fail.

Linking together operations in an ASP is performed with transactions. In Chapter 14, "Database Access in Active Server Pages," we discussed transactions in the context of a single database. In this chapter, we will look at transactions as they exist within an entire Active Server Page.

What Are Transactions?

Transactions rely on three basic concepts: the transaction scope, committing, and rolling back. A beginning and an end determine a transaction's scope. The programmer sets the beginning, or it is set automatically when a page is opened. The end is determined by committing or rolling back the transaction. Committing causes the changes in the scope to happen. Rolling back causes them to be ignored. This relationship is shown in Figure 16-1.

Transactions are used in situations where it is important that a set of operations are performed together or not at all. This concept of a group of operations that act in unison is called *atomicity*. The group of operations is treated as a single, atomic unit that must succeed or fail as a single unit. The classic example of atomicity is a bank transfer. In this case, the bank must ensure that both a withdraw operation and a deposit operation occur. If either fails, neither should succeed.

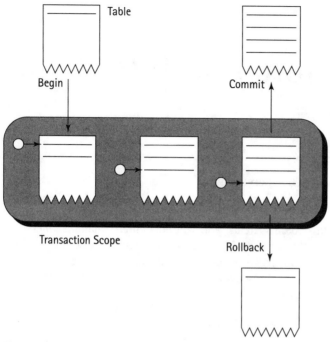

Figure 16–1: Transaction relationships

Transactions are also used to make sure that data or application state remains consistent throughout a set of operations. Because the operations in a transaction scope succeed or fail together, the programmer can be sure that some of the operations do not change state, while others fail. If the operations could succeed one by one, the data in an application could end up in the wrong state. For example, imagine that you are writing a program for an online video store that sells special collections of videos. When someone orders a collection, you remove each video from inventory and add it to his or her order. Without a transaction, the customer might receive two of the three videos in a collection, while being charged for the set.

When thinking about transactions, it is important to recognize that each transaction scope is isolated from the other transactions occurring in the system. For example, if two people sharing a joint checking account both try to remove money, the operations are independent and the account balance is reduced by both withdrawals. If they both try to withdraw $100 from an account containing $150, one will succeed and one will fail. They shouldn't both fail or both succeed. This independence is guaranteed by the transaction management software, so the developer should create their transactional code as if it will succeed or fail, independent of other operations in the system.

Finally, the effects of transactions are said to be *durable*. This means that the operations that you perform in a transaction scope will have an effect, and that effect will be seen by the entire system once the transaction is committed.

Transactions and Active Server Pages

Active Server Pages don't actually have support for transactional scripts in the broadest sense of the term. Rather, an ASP can interact with a transaction scope, and as a result, affect ActiveX components that the page is using. At a rough level, this is similar to the way an ASP can control transactions for the Active Data Objects (ADO). However, the general version of a transacted ASP script relies on the Microsoft Transaction Server, (MTS) and COM+ to manage transaction contexts for multiple components and operations.

An ASP that wants to participate in a transaction scope should contain the following processing directive:

```
<%@ TRANSACTION="trantype" %>
```

where `trantype` is one of the values listed in Table 16-1. These values are the same for all components that interact with MTS. Active Server Pages do not take advantage of all the values.

TABLE 16-1 TRANSACTION SCRIPT TYPES

Type	Description
Requires_New	Creates a new transaction context for this page.
Required	Uses an existing transaction context if possible, otherwise a new one is created. For ASPs, this is the same as Requires_New.
Supported	Indicates that something supports transactions but doesn't interact with them. For an ASP, no context is created when supported is used.
Not_Supported	For components, tells the system that they cannot be used in a transaction context. For an ASP, this flag simply means that a context will not be created.

When used with other processing directives, the transaction directive should appear in the same tag. For example, use this tag:

```
<%@ LANGUAGE="JavaScript" TRANSACTION="required" %>
```

for a JavaScripted ASP that requires a transaction scope.

If you use either the `Server.Execute` or `Server.Transfer` methods to access another ASP from the current one, the transaction scope for the *parent*, or calling page, will be used for the child. This allows you to break an application into multiple pages and maintain transactional integrity.

Transactions and components

The important concept for ASP developers is that for transactions to really work, you have to use ActiveX components that support them. These components can leverage transactions to ensure database integrity or any other goal that you have in mind. However, the ASP script isn't transactional itself. So operations performed in a script, like changing values of the Application object or performing database operations, are not parts of the context for a page. Rather the page is creating a context for the components it uses.

This means that you will need to work with the component developers and vendors to determine how they can support transactions and how the components can tell your ASPs about success and failure.

The ObjectContext object

To interact with the context, an ASP can use the `ObjectContext` object. This object is created automatically for pages that require transactions. The `ObjectContext` has two methods: `SetAbort` and `SetComplete`.

♦ The `SetAbort` method tells the current transaction context to perform a rollback, ignoring any changes that have been made. Remember that this abort applies to the components on the page, not to the page script itself.

♦ The `SetComplete` method tells the current transaction context that it succeeded. This will ensure that the operations performed by transactional contexts on the page are committed.

Transaction events

ASPs receive notification of commits and aborts for their transactions. This is important in situations where one component aborts a transaction and the ASP needs to notify the user that the operation failed. Notification of these transaction events is performed via two special subroutines defined in the ASP.

The ASP engine will call the `OnTransactionCommit` subroutine when the ASP's transaction is committed. If the transaction is aborted, the `OnTransactionAbort` subroutine is called.

To give you an idea how these two subroutines can be used, the page shown in Listing 16-1 indicates that it requires a transaction context, and defines both transaction event subroutines. Then the page aborts the transaction, causing the OnTransactionAbort routine to be called. This routine prints a message to the visitor notifying them of the problem with the page shown in Figure 16-2.

Listing 16-1: Defining transaction subroutines

```
<%@ LANGUAGE="JAVASCRIPT" TRANSACTION="REQUIRED"%>
<html>
<head>
<title>
    Using OnTransactionAbort
</title>
<%
function OnTransactionAbort()
{
    Response.Write("<h1>Transaction Was Aborted</h1>");
}

function OnTransactionCommit ()
{
    Response.Write("<h1>Transaction Was Committed</h1>");
}
%>
</head>
<body>

<%
ObjectContext.SetAbort();
%>

</body>
</html>
```

Now take the same page, and change the SetAbort to SetComplete (see Listing 16-2). This will cause the OnTransactionCommit routine to be called. This routine then displays the message shown in Figure 16-3.

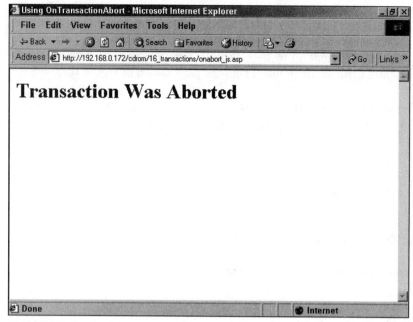

Figure 16-2: An abort message

Listing 16-2: Calling the OnTransactionCommit routine

```
<%@ LANGUAGE="JAVASCRIPT" TRANSACTION="REQUIRED"%>
<html>
<head>
<title>
    Using OnTransactionAbort
</title>
<%
function OnTransactionAbort()
{
    Response.Write("<h1>Transaction Was Aborted</h1>");
}

function OnTransactionCommit()
{
    Response.Write("<h1>Transaction Was Committed</h1>");
}
%>
</head>
<body>

<%
```

```
ObjectContext.SetComplete();
%>


</body>
</html>
```

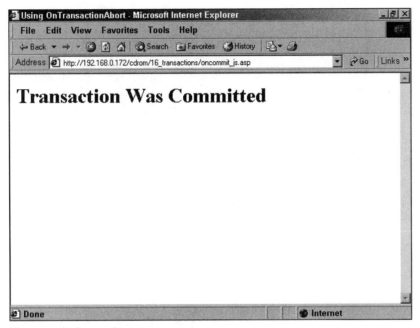

Figure 16-3: A commit message

By defining both of these routines, and coding your page to rely on them to provide user output, you can create pages that provide conditional results to the visitor based on the success or failure of your transacted operations.

Summary

As you can see, transactions from the ASP developer perspective are accessed via a small interface. However, in situations where you are performing operations that require atomicity, like e-commerce, transactions will be a core component of your applications. This means that you will either need to use the ADO transaction support, or create ActiveX components that support transaction contexts.

Chapter 17

Server Includes and Directives

IN THIS CHAPTER

- ◆ Server-side directives
- ◆ The #include directive
- ◆ HTML directives

SERVER-SIDE INCLUDES ARE a feature provided by the Internet Information Server (IIS) that allows files to be modularized. In the case of Active Server Pages, reusable code can be placed into a separate file rather than having to be copied and pasted into each ASP. For HTML files, a number of directives are provided to access information from the server that the HTML file otherwise would have no access to. In this chapter we will discuss both ASP includes and HTML directives. Keep in mind that some of the directives work as both and others only work in HTML pages.

Server-Side Directives

There are six directives, or server-side includes, supported in IIS. These are listed in Table 17-1. Of the directives, only the #include directive works in ASPs. The others are reserved for HTML pages. However, for the server to know that an HTML page contains these directives, you must use a special extension. Although these can be configured on the Web server, the commonly used default extensions that denote an HTML file containing server-side includes are .shtml and .shtm.

TABLE 17-1 HTML- AND ASP-SUPPORTED SERVER-SIDE DIRECTIVES

Directive	Description	Pages That Support It
#config	Configures the output of other includes.	HTML
#echo	Prints the value of a server variable.	HTML
#exec	Executes CGI scripts or shell commands.	HTML
#flastmod	Displays the date for the last time a file was modified.	HTML
#fsize	Displays the size of a file.	HTML
#include	Includes the contents of another file into the file containing the directive.	HTML and ASP

To use a directive, place it in an HTML comment. For example, to include a file you might use, place the directive as follows:

```
<!-- #include file="vb_include.inc" -->
```

Remember that these includes are processed on the server, and the client will see only the results of their execution.

The #include Directive

The #include directive is perhaps the most useful directive. It lets you include, verbatim, another file into the one containing the directive. This means that an HTML file can contain HTML from another file, or an ASP can contain variable and function definitions from another file. When used with ASPs, the #include directive is executed first so that scripts in the including page can rely on code in the included page. The #include directive uses the following syntax:

```
<!-- #include PathType = FileName -->
```

where the path type is either File or Virtual as described in Table 17-2. By providing both these options, IIS allows the programmer more flexibility in specifying the location of include files.

TABLE 17-2 #INCLUDE PATH TYPES

Path Type	Description
File	The filename should be a relative path from the directory containing the document using the #include directive. The included file can be in the same directory or a subdirectory but not in a directory above the current one.
Virtual	The filename should be a full virtual path for the Web server from the root directory to the file.

Notice that the File path type should limit files from being included if they are not within the correct directory structure relative to the including document.

HTML

To give you an idea of how an include works in HTML, the document shown in Listing 17-1 contains two include statements. One include file uses a relative link from the root directory, via the cdrom virtual directory. The other is a file in the same directory as this one on the CD-ROM. This file is called include.shtml, to indicate that the server should process it.

Listing 17-1: Using include files in HTML

```
<html>
<head>
<title>
    Using include
</title>
</head>
<body>
<h1>flastmod.shtml</h1>
<!-- #include file="flastmod.shtml" -->

<br><br>

<h1>fsize.shtml</h1>
<!-- #include virtual = "/cdrom/17_includes/fsize.shtml" -->

</body>
</html>
```

When viewed with a browser, not from the Web server, this page would look like the one shown in Figure 17-1. Without the Web server, the #include directives aren't processed, so the page has just the headers and comments in it.

Figure 17-1: Include.shtml when the includes are not processed

However, if you access the page using the Web server, the #include directives are processed, and the page looks like the one shown in Figure 17-2.

ASP

Includes can also be used in an ASP. This works basically like a copy and paste operation. So the code just "appears" as if you typed it into the page. The following two sections contain examples that show how an include can be used in VBScript and JavaScript. If you are using both languages, you will need to create the same include twice, one for each language. Because the process is like a copy and paste operation, there is no language conversion.

Normally, include files for ASPs will contain functions or constant definitions that can be reused in several circumstances. In fact, we used an include file in Chapter 14, "Database Access in Active Server Pages," to reuse some database constants. By convention, include files will often be labeled with a .inc extension to draw attention to them.

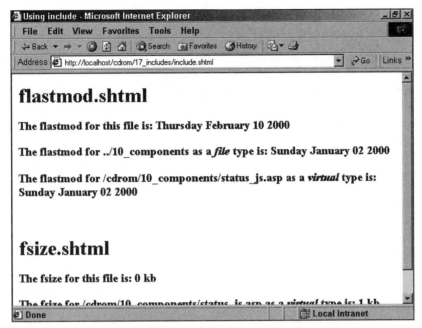

Figure 17-2: Include.shtml with the includes being processed

VBSCRIPT

The first file in the VBScript example is vb_include.inc. This file defines a constant called `message` and a function called `DoubleIt`. Note the `<%` and `%>` to demark code. Remember this is a copy and paste–style operation, so these characters are not assumed.

```
<%
const message = "Hello ASP Developers!"

Function DoubleIt(x)

    DoubleIt = x*2

End Function
%>
```

The other file in this example is called include_vb.asp. This file begins by indicating that it is a VBScript ASP, as follows:

```
<%@ LANGUAGE="VBSCRIPT" %>
<html>
<head>
<title>
```

```
    Using include
</title>
</head>
<body>
```

The include can be placed as follows anywhere above the code that uses it.

```
<!-- #include file="vb_include.inc" -->
```

Constants from the include can be used directly, as if they appeared in the file itself, as shown here:

```
<%=message%>
```

```
<br><br>
```

```
2 doubled is <%=DoubleIt(2)%>
```

```
</body>
</html>
```

When displayed from the server, this page should look like the one shown in Figure 17-3.

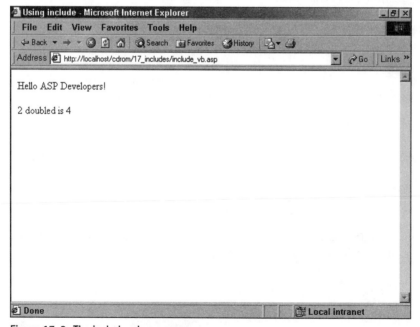

Figure 17-3: The include_vb.asp page

JAVASCRIPT

The first file in the JavaScript example is js_include.inc. This file defines a variable called message and a function called DoubleIt. Note the <% and %> to demark code. Remember this is a copy and paste–style operation, so these characters are not assumed.

```
<%
var message = "Hello ASP Developers!";

function doubleit(x)
{
    return x*2;
}
%>
```

The other file in this example is called include_js.asp. This file begins by indicating that it is a JavaScript ASP, as follows:

```
<%@ LANGUAGE="JAVASCRIPT" %>
<html>
<head>
<title>
    Using include
</title>
</head>
<body>
```

The include can be placed as follows anywhere above the code that uses it.

```
<!-- #include file="js_include.inc" -->
```

Constants from the include can be used directly, as if they appeared in the file itself, as you see here:

```
<%=message%>

<br><br>

2 doubled is <%=doubleit(2)%>

</body>
</html>
```

When displayed from the server, this page should look like the one shown in Figure 17-4.

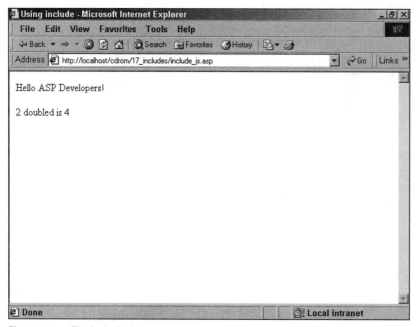

Figure 17-4: The include_js.asp page

HTML Directives

The remaining server-side #include directives work only in HTML files. Remember that you must indicate that a file contains server-side includes by naming it with an .shtm or .shtml extension. Of course, you also can configure the server to recognize other extensions as well.

The #echo directive

The #echo directive can be used to display server variables in an HTML page. These variables are already available to ASPs via the built-in objects, so this directive will not work in an ASP. The basic syntax for #echo is as follows:

```
<!-- #echo var=VariableName -->
```

where the variable name is one of the values listed in Table 17-3.

TABLE **17-3 #ECHO VARIABLES**

Variable	Description
ALL_HTTP	All HTTP headers that are not one of the other variables in this table.
AUTH_TYPE	The type of authentication used. The string will be "Basic" if basic authentication is used, and it will be "Integrated Windows Authentication" for integrated authentication.
AUTH_PASSWORD	The value entered in the client's authentication dialog box when basic authentication is used.
AUTH_USER	The user authenticated using the AUTH_TYPE authentication scheme.
CONTENT_LENGTH	The number of bytes that the script can expect to receive from the client.
CONTENT_TYPE	The content type of the information supplied in the body of a POST request.
DOCUMENT_NAME	The current filename.
DOCUMENT_URI	The virtual path to the current document.
DATE_GMT	The current date in Greenwich Mean Time (GMT).
DATE_LOCAL	The current date in the local time zone.
GATEWAY_INTERFACE	The revision of the CGI specification used by the Web server.

HTTP_ACCEPT	Data types that the client has said that it will accept in response to their query. Values of the HTTP accept header fields are concatenated, and separated by a comma (,). For example, if the following lines are part of the HTTP header:
	
	`accept: */*; q=0.1`
	`accept: text/html`
	`accept: image/jpeg`
	
	the HTTP_ACCEPT variable will have a value of
	
	`*/*; q=0.1, text/html, image/jpeg`

Continued

TABLE 17-3 #ECHO VARIABLES *(Continued)*

Variable	Description
LAST_MODIFIED	The date that the document was last modified.
PATH_INFO	Additional path information, as given by the client. This consists of the trailing part of the URL after the script name, but before the query string, if any. For example, in the following: http://www.pri.com/go.asp/over/there /over/there is the path information.
PATH_TRANSLATED	This is the value of PATH_INFO, but with any virtual path expanded into a directory specification.
QUERY_STRING	The information that follows the question mark (?) in the URL that referenced this script.
QUERY_STRING_UNESCAPED	The query string after it is URL-decoded.
REMOTE_ADDR	The IP address of the client. This may be the address of a firewall or proxy server, when one is used.
REMOTE_HOST	The host name of the client. This may be the name of a firewall or proxy server, when one is used. IIS 2.0 and 3.0 return an IP address for this parameter.
REMOTE_USER	The user name supplied by the client and authenticated by the server. The value is an empty string when the user is anonymous (but authenticated).
REQUEST_METHOD	The HTTP request method, usually GET for an HTML page.
SCRIPT_NAME	The name of the script program being executed.
SERVER_NAME	The server's host name, or IP address, as it should appear in self-referencing URLs.
SERVER_PORT	The TCP/IP port on which the request was received.
SERVER_PORT_SECURE	A string of either 0 or 1. If the request is being handled on the secure port, this will be 1. Otherwise, it will be 0.
SERVER_PROTOCOL	The name and version of the information retrieval protocol relating to this request. This usually is HTTP/1.0. The protocol is returned in the format name/version.

Variable	Description
SERVER_SOFTWARE	The name and version of the Web server answering the request. The server information is returned in the format name/version.
URL	The base URL for the current request.

As you can see, there are a lot of variables available. To give you an idea of how you might access these, the example shown in Listing 17-2 displays three variables and their values in a table. This file is provided on the CD-ROM as echo.shtml.

Listing 17-2: Using echo

```
<html>
<head>
<title>
    Using echo
</title>
</head>
<body>

<table border=1>
<tr>
<td>ALL_HTTP</td>
<td><!-- #echo var="ALL_HTTP"--></td>
<tr>
<tr>
<td>SERVER_SOFTWARE</td>
<td><!-- #echo var="SERVER_SOFTWARE"--></td>
<tr>
<tr>
<td>URL</td>
<td><!-- #echo var="URL"--></td>
<tr>
</table>
</body>
</html>
```

When displayed, this page should look something like the one shown in Figure 17-5.

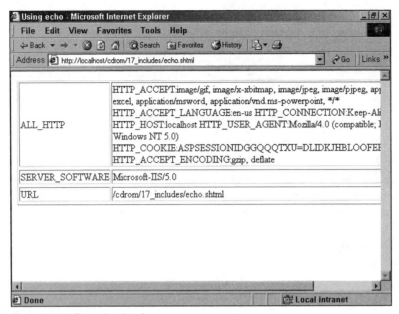

Figure 17-5: The echo.shtml page

The #exec directive

The #exec directive can be used to execute commands and place the results in an HTML page. The format of the #exec include is as follows:

```
<!-- #exec CommandType=Command -->
```

where CommandType is either CGI or CMD. CGI commands should be specified as a CGI script, ASP, or ISAPI application that you want to run. These commands can include a query string in the path following a question mark (?) so that parameters can be passed to the command.

The CMD type lets you execute shell commands. This feature normally is turned off and rarely should be activated, because it could allow a page to execute commands such as Format. Speak with your system administrator before activating regular command types.

The #flastmod directive

The #flastmod include will return the date that a file was last modified. This directive uses the following syntax:

```
<!-- # flastmod PathType=FileName -->
```

where the path type is either File or Virtual. as described in Table 17-4.

TABLE 17-4 #FLASTMOD PATH TYPES

Path Type	Description
File	The filename should be a relative path from the directory containing the document using the #include directive.
Virtual	The filename should be a full virtual path for the Web server from the root directory to the file.

For example, the page shown in Listing 17-3 displays the last modification time for itself, a directory, and another file.

Listing 17-3: Using flastmod

```
<html>
<head>
<title>
    Using flastmod
</title>
</head>
<body>

<h3>
The flastmod for this file is:
 <!-- #flastmod file="flastmod.shtml"-->
<br><br>

The flastmod for ../10_components
 as a <em>file</em> type is:
 <!-- #flastmod file="../10_components" -->
<br><br>

The flastmod for /cdrom/10_components/status_js.asp
 as a <em>virtual</em> type is:
 <!-- #flastmod virtual = "/cdrom/10_components/status_js.asp" -->
<br><br>

</h3>
</body>
</html>
```

When accessed via the server, this page will display results like those shown in Figure 17-6.

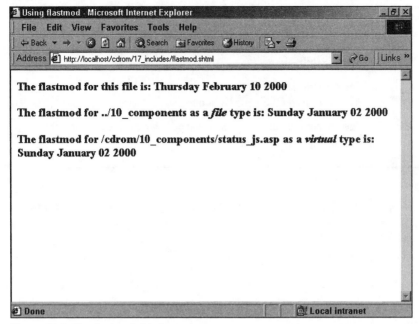

Figure 17-6: The flastmod.shtml page

The format for the date can be controlled using the #config include, which will be discussed later in the chapter.

The #fsize directive

The #fsize include will return the size of a file. This directive uses the following syntax:

```
<!-- # fsize PathType=FileName -->
```

where the path type is either File or Virtual, as described in Table 17-4.

For example, the page shown in Listing 17-4 displays its own size and the size of another file.

Listing 17-4: Using fsize

```
<html>
<head>
<title>
    Using fsize
</title>
</head>
<body>
```

```
<h3>
The fsize for this file is:
 <!-- #fsize file="fsize.shtml"--> kb
<br><br>

The fsize for /cdrom/10_components/status_js.asp
 as a <em>virtual</em> type is:
 <!-- #fsize virtual = "/cdrom/10_components/status_js.asp" --> kb
<br><br>

</h3>
</body>
</html>
```

When accessed via the server, this page will display results like those shown in Figure 17-7.

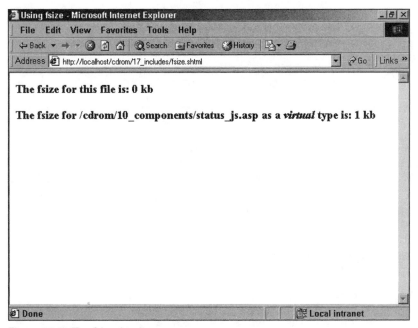

Figure 17-7: The fsize.shtml page

The size defaults to kilobytes, thus the zero size of one file. Using the #config include, you can change the units to bytes, as discussed in the next section.

The #config directive

The #config include can be used to set parameters for three output mechanisms: error messages, flastmod, and fsize. The syntax for #config is as follows:

```
<!-- #config output=string -->
```

where output is one of the values listed in Table 17-5.

TABLE 17-5 #CONFIG OUTPUT VALUES

Output Value	Description
ERRMSG	Controls the message returned to the client when an error occurs processing a server-side include. By default the error is useful to programmers, but is not visitor friendly. The String parameter should contain the new error message.
TIMEFMT	This string is used to format the time output from the flastmod include. Possible formats are discussed later in this section.
SIZEFMT	This value can be either ABBREV, which displays sizes in kilobytes, or BYTE, which displays sizes in bytes.

The values of the TIMEFMT field can be a combination of characters and special codes. For example, the code %m stands for month, and could be used to create a format like %m/%d/%y, which will display dates in the format 5/5/99. The valid codes are listed in Table 17-6. By combining the codes, you can create numerous date formats. These codes are case sensitive.

TABLE 17-6 TIMEFMT CODES

Code	Description
%a	Abbreviated name for the day of the week; for example, Mon.
%A	Complete name for the day of the week; for example, Monday.
%b	Abbreviated name of the month.
%B	Full month name.

Code	Description
%c	Date and time representation that is locale dependent, for example, 4/4/99 12:12:12.
%d	Day of the month as a number from 01 to 31.
%H	Hours in 24-hour format (00-23).
%I	Hours in 12-hour format (01-12).
%j	Day of the year as a number (001-366).
%m	Month as a number (01-12).
%M	Minutes as a number (00-59).
%p	Current locale's AM/PM indicator.
%S	Seconds as a number (00-59).
%U	Week of the year as a number (00-51). Sunday is the first day of the week for this calculation.
%w	Day of the week as a number (0-6).
%W	Week of the year as a number (00-51).Monday is the first day of the week for this calculation.
%x	Date representation for the current locale; for example, 5/5/99.
%X	Time representation for the current locale; for example, 12:05:33.
%y	Year without the century.
%Y	Year with the century.
%z or %Z	Time zone name and abbreviation; nothing if not appropriate.
%%	Percent sign character.

For example, the page shown in Listing 17-5 formats the time to month/day/year and the size to bytes.

Listing 17-5: Using config to affect the output of echo

```
<html>
<head>
<title>
```

```
    Using echo
</title>
</head>
<body>

Configuring timefmt to: %m/%d/%y<br>
Configuring sizefmt to: bytes<br>
<!-- #config timefmt="%m/%d/%y" -->
<!-- #config sizefmt="bytes" -->

<h3>
The fsize for this file is:
 <!-- #fsize file="fsize.shtml"--> bytes
<br><br>

The fsize for /cdrom/10_components/status_js.asp
 as a <em>virtual</em> type is:
 <!-- #fsize virtual = "/cdrom/10_components/status_js.asp" -->
bytes<br><br>

The flastmod for this file is:
 <!-- #flastmod file="flastmod.shtml"-->
<br><br>

The flastmod for ../10_components
 as a <em>file</em> type is:
 <!-- #flastmod file="../10_components" -->
<br><br>

The flastmod for /cdrom/10_components/status_js.asp
 as a <em>virtual</em> type is:
 <!-- #flastmod virtual = "/cdrom/10_components/status_js.asp" -->
<br><br>

</h3>
</body>
</html>
```

When accessed via the server, this page will display results like those shown in Figure 17-8.

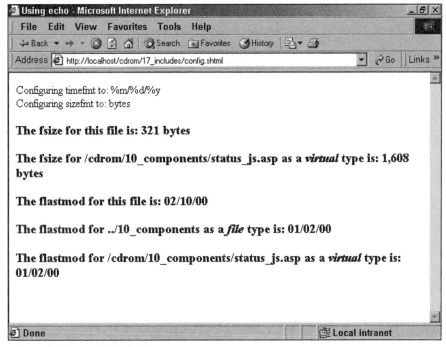

Figure 17-8: The config.shtml page

Summary

As you can see, server-side includes can be used in HTML to access information that normally is available only to ASPs and other programs. Includes can be used in both HTML and ASPs to create reusable components. In particular, a large Web site can store reusable code in include files, thus improving productivity and reducing maintenance costs. These includes do require the server to parse the HTML, so they shouldn't be used unless necessary. Also, they require a special extension, so that the server can return a plain HTML page without parsing.

Chapter 18

Access Control

IN THIS CHAPTER

◆ Web authentication mechanisms

◆ Integrated mechanisms to secure a page

◆ Custom authentication

RESTRICTING ACCESS TO CONTENT is an important aspect of securing information you publish on the Web. There are several options for securing your content, and some rely on different methods requiring the visitor to provide a login and a password. Another option requires the visitor to provide a cryptographic authentication.

Cryptographic authentication uses a digital certificate as a means of authenticating the identity of a user. A digital certificate is the equivalent of using an ID card to prove your identity. A digital certificate encodes several bits of information about the owner of the certificate and the organization that issued it. If you trust the certificate's issuer, you can trust the user presenting it (digital certificates are extremely hard to forge).

In this chapter, we'll introduce the various options that are available to you, as well as brew a simple solution that uses a database that you can use for authenticating visitors.

Web Authentication Mechanisms

In terms of user authentication, IIS provides several different ways you can implement an authentication policy. Some of these policies are either Windows centric or not widely supported by browsers that limit what you can really use for the type of deployment you need. Here's the five different supported authentication mechanisms:

◆ Anonymous Access

◆ Basic Authentication

◆ Digest Authentication

◆ Integrated Windows Authentication

◆ Certificate Authentication

This section discusses each of these user-authentication means.

Logins and passwords

All of IIS's login and password mechanisms (the first four mentioned previously) rely on Windows NT/2000 user accounts. By simply setting a set of permissions on the directory storing your files and enabling the requirement to use authentication, you can protect your content to valid users in the computer or NT domain. If the user has permission to access the files, then they will be able to access them over the Web. This simple mechanism works great for internal sites, since more than likely all users in your organization already have some sort of login or password assigned to them to access networked resources.

For public Internet use, this mechanism is not really feasible from an administrative point of view, as you would have to create and manage Windows user accounts for people you don't know or necessarily trust. Even under these conditions it is still desirable to authenticate people. To address this issue we have developed a trivial scheme that you can base your work on. Note that other authentication solutions are available from third parties. A quick search of the Web will provide you with current products from other vendors that may prove useful to you.

Keeping in mind the tight coupling between user accounts and the authentication mechanisms provided by IIS, let's take a look at what these different mechanisms offer.

Anonymous access

Anonymous access grants access to all public areas of your Web site without requiring any sort of login or password. The server automatically assigns the visitor the username IUSR_*computername* where *computername* is the name of the host where IIS is running.

All security for the IUSR_*computername* account is defined in that user account, which essentially assigns "guest" group privileges to the visitor. Guest privileges are fairly restricted; however, depending on the size of your organization and your security policy, it is possible that the guest mechanism has been disabled and that enabling it could present a security risk. Please check with your network administrator prior to enabling or disabling security policies.

When a visitor makes a request under the anonymous access scheme, IIS impersonates the IUSR_*computername* account, effectively accessing resources in your server as that user. It can do this because IIS knows the login and password for this account. Before returning a page to the visitor, it checks to ensure that given its current permissions, it can access the page. If it can, the page is returned. If it fails, IIS will attempt a different authentication mechanism. If no other mechanism is found, the server denies access to the resource by returning a "403 Access Denied" status. When anonymous authentication is enabled, the server always attempts to access the page under this mechanism first.

Basic authentication

If you have seen Web authentication by filling in the login information in a panel provided by the browser, more than likely you have seen basic authentication. Again, on IIS, the login and password you enter into this panel must be a valid Windows NT/2000 login name. The browser then encodes this information and sends it over the network to the server, which then intercepts this request and validates the login information. If it authenticates, the login and password work, and the request is fulfilled.

The drawback with basic authentication is that the login and password information is sent over the network in plain text format. This makes it very easy to compromise this information, especially if the user is contacting the server from the public Internet.

Digest authentication

To solve the problems with basic authentication, digest authentication was developed. Like basic authentication, digest authentication verifies the login and password without sending this information over the network. Using various pieces of information, including the URL that the visitor wants to access and an agreed-upon algorithm for generating a special value called a *hash* (a number), both the browser and the server generate a value that they can compare. If the values match, then the authentication information also matches, validating the visitor. One enhancement over basic authentication is that even if someone could generate a spoofed value that allowed access, only one URL would be accessible with that code. Also, because the hash is only "one-way" there is no way of extracting the password or any other information from the hash value. This alone makes it a much better and more secure solution than basic authentication.

To enable digest authentication on your system, you need to be running a Windows 2000 domain controller that has access to the passwords and accounts you want to use. This limits digest authentication to enterprise-type applications.

Integrated Windows authentication

Integrated Windows authentication uses a similar mechanism to digest authentication. Because the user's browser has knowledge of the user, there's no prompting for a login or password unless the user disables this feature or the authentication fails. The limitation with this mechanism is that it is only supported by Internet Explorer and this method doesn't work over HTTP proxy connections. This limits its use to internal networks.

Certificate authentication

Lastly, authentication can be provided by a digital certificate presented by the visitor when connecting to the server using Secure Sockets Layer (SSL). SSL validates that the information contained in the certificate has not been tampered with and that it comes from a trusted source. On the server side, the presented certificate information is mapped to some Windows user account that then tells the server who the visitor is. This mechanism is the most secure, but also the most complex to set up. For more information on certificate-based authentication, please consult your Web server's documentation.

Using the Integrated Mechanisms to Secure a Page

You can enable one or more of the previously discussed authentication methods for a virtual directory or file. To enable any of these methods:

1. Create a Windows user account. The user account should define the security you wish to assign to the user. Refer to your Windows documentation for information on how to add accounts.

2. Configure the NTFS permissions for the directory or file you want to share.

3. Using the Internet Services Manager, select the resource you want to share and open its property sheet by right-clicking the object and choosing Properties.

4. Select the Directory Security tab (or File Security if sharing a file). Under "Anonymous access and authentication control" click the Edit button.

5. On the Authentication Methods panel that appears, select the type of authentication you want to provide. Note that depending on the server or network configuration, you may have different options available to you. At the very least, you should be able to provide anonymous, basic, and integrated Windows authentication. By default, anonymous and integrated Windows authentication should be enabled.

Note that basic, digest, or integrated Windows authentication will only be used if anonymous access is not selected, anonymous access fails, or access to the resource is restricted by the NTFS permissions you assigned to the file or directory.

Custom Authentication

It is possible for you to develop an authentication component (a filter) that doesn't rely on Windows user accounts. However, there are several commercial and free products already available; one of these is Authetix from http://www.flicks.com. Another alternative is to code your own set of scripts to provide some authentication scheme.

The next few pages show you a simple custom authentication mechanism that uses a database to store login and password information. By no means should this code be used for protecting sensitive information, as it doesn't leverage any of the authentication mechanisms built into IIS. With that said, the goal of this is to provide a "hassle" to the visitor for accessing some resource you don't want them to easily get to. This could be used to allow visitors to access information after providing you with some information about themselves or something to that effect.

Our simple authentication helper relies on storing a property called isAuthenticated on the Session object. If the property is set to true, then the user is granted access to the files. If not, a login panel requiring the user to log in is displayed. The neat thing about this script is that it is ubiquitous to the page. All you need to do to provide the authentication is create a database and add users you want to grant access and then include the script into your other ASP pages.

 The custom authentication mechanism will only work for script-based pages. Static HTML pages or other resources won't be protected!!!

Authenticating against a database

The code to the script is provided in this section. The script was developed as an object, so you'll see several functions that are then mapped into methods. These functions provide the basic functionality you want; with them, you can add, delete, list, and authenticate users. The entire scheme works from a simple database table called users. The table only needs two columns: "login" to store the login name for the visitor and "password" to store the password. These tables were created as varchar(15) columns, allowing usernames and passwords that are a maximum of 15 characters long.

The function isSet() validates that the reference (object) provided has been initialized. If the value is undefined, null, or an empty string, the function returns false.

```
<%
function isSet(val)
{
  var tf = true;

  if(val == "undefined" || val == null || val == "")
  {
    tf = false;
  }
```

```
  return tf;
}
```

The next function, verifyLogin(), shown in Listing 18-1, validates the login and password entered by the visitor. It queries the database for a password matching a particular login. If the password returned by the database matches the one provided as an argument, the visitor is authenticated. Note that this assumes that the database will provide a constraint that requires all login names to be unique.

Listing 18-1: The login or password verification function

```
function verifyLogin(login, password)
{
  var isGood = false;
  var query = "SELECT password FROM users WHERE
login='" + login + "'";


  var records = this.dbc.Execute(query);
  var validation = records("password") + "";

  if(password == validation)
  {
    isGood = true;
  }


  return isGood;
}
```

The addLogin() and removeLogin() methods shown in Listing 18-2 provide an API that an administrative page can use to add or remove a login and password pair from the database. Many sites require the ability to allow users to add their own login and password as needed. These methods can be used for that.

Listing 18-2: Adding or removing login-password pairs

```
function addLogin(login, password)
{

  if(this.verifyLogin(login, password))
  {
    this.handleError("Login already exists.");
  }
  else
  {
    this.dbc.Execute("INSERT INTO users (login, password) " +
```

```
VALUES ('" + login + "', '" + password + "')");
  }


}


function removeLogin(login, password)
{
  this.dbc.Execute("DELETE FROM users where login='" + login +
      "' and password='" + password + "'");
}
```

The listLogins() method shown in Listing 18-3 returns an HTML table with a list of all the logins and passwords stored in the database.

Listing 18-3: Listing logins and passwords

```
function listLogins()
{

  var records = this.dbc.Execute("SELECT * FROM users");
  var login = records("login");
  var password = records("password");

  var html = "<TABLE BORDER=1><TR><TH>Login</TH>
    <TH>Password</TH></TR>";

  while(records.EOF == false)
  {
    html += "<TR><TD>" + login + "</TD><TD>" + password + "</TD>\n";
    records.MoveNext();
  }

  html += "</TABLE>";

  return html;
}
```

The finish() method that follows closes the database connection and releases the resources consumed by this object.

```
function finish()
{
  this.dbc.Close();
}
```

Finally, the constructor for the Authenticator object follows. As arguments the constructor expects information to access the user's database. It requires the name of the ODBC datasource, and the login and password to use when accessing the tables. It then makes a connection to the database and associates the method names with the functions that perform the actual work.

```
function Authenticator(odbc, login, password)
{
  this.dbc = Server.CreateObject("ADODB.Connection");
  this.dbc.open(odbc, login, password);

  this.verifyLogin = verifyLogin;
  this.addLogin = addLogin;
  this.removeLogin = removeLogin;
  this.finish = finish;
  this.listLogins = listLogins;
}
```

After defining the object, there are a few top-level scripts that execute for every page that includes this code. This code is what performs the basic checks for validating if the visitor is authenticated or not.

The first thing that it does is read some information from the Form collection. Since authentication will come from a form, a hidden field in the form provides a flag that we can test to see if this script was called by the form. If this test fails, the script will provide the HTML form that the visitor can use to log in. The script also tries to read the Session to see if there's a property called isAuthenticated.

```
var message = "";
var authenticationRequest =
Request.Form("authenticationRequest") + "";
var isAuthenticated = Session("isAuthenticated");
```

If the script was called from the form, we require authentication, so we create an instance of the Authenticator, and authenticate the values provided by the form. (See Listing 18-4.) If successful, the isAuthenticated flag is set to true; otherwise, it is set to false. Then the connection to the database is closed, and the user is redirected to a URL provided by the form. The target of this redirect is really the same document we are accessing. This URL was provided dynamically when the script generated the form.

Listing 18-4: Creating an instance of the Authenticator

```
if(isSet(authenticationRequest))
{
  var authenticator =
```

```
new Authenticator("asp_logins", "asp", "secret");

  if(authenticator.verifyLogin(
Request.Form("login"),
Request.Form("password")))
  {
    Session("isAuthenticated") = true;
  }
  else
  {
    Session("isAuthenticated") = false;
  }

  authenticator.finish();
  Response.Redirect(Request.Form("referer"));
}
```

If the isAuthenticated flag is not set, we initialize it to null to distinguish from a failed authentication, as shown in the following code. An enhancement to this code would be able to distinguish between these conditions and issue pertinent warnings accordingly.

```
if(isSet(isAuthenticated) == false)
{
    isAuthenticated = null;
}
```

Next we test to see if the authentication failed or was never done (null); if this is the case, we need to return a form to the browser so the visitor has the opportunity to authenticate. The trick in this code is determining the page that the user is visiting. We do this by examining the server variable "URL". This provides an absolute URL in this server to the page the visitor is viewing. This script assumes that its code is at the same level as the page the visitor accessed, so we find out the actual name of the file we are executing and eliminate any additional information.

```
if(isAuthenticated == null || isAuthenticated == false)
{

  // generate a form
  Response.Clear();

  var thisPage = Request.ServerVariables("URL") + "";
  var i = thisPage.lastIndexOf("/");
  i++;
  thisPage = thisPage.substring(i);
```

After this we are ready to print the form, as shown in Listing 18-5. Note that the URL for this document is saved in a hidden field called 'referer'. At this point the response is then terminated. This will prevent any content from the actual page from being sent to the visitor's browser.

Listing 18-5: Printing the form

```
Response.Write("<HTML><BODY>Please enter your password\n" +
  "<FORM action='" + thisPage + "' method='post'>\n" +
  "<B>Login: </B><INPUT type='text' name='login'><BR>\n" +
  "<B>Password: </B><INPUT type='password' name='password'>\n" +
  "<INPUT type='submit' value='Validate'>\n" +
  "<INPUT type='hidden' name='authenticationRequest' " +
    value='true'>\n" +
  "<INPUT type='hidden' name='referer' value='" +
    thisPage + "'>\n" +
  "</FORM></BODY></HTML>");

  Response.End();

}
%>
```

A client page

Following is a client page that makes use of our home-brewed authentication scheme:

```
<%@ LANGUAGE="JSCRIPT" %>

<!-- #include file="Authenticator.js" -->
<HTML>
<BODY>
This content is secured
<A HREF="another.asp">Go to here</A>
</BODY>
</HTML>
```

As you can see, it is very simple. To make use of the script, the only thing that is required is to have a server-side include to load the authentication code before any output is generated by the page. The included page will run its own scripts as described earlier. If authentication fails, the browser will never see any of the content for the page.

Summary

Authentication is tricky business. IIS security implementations are great for internal Web sites that your company may host; however, for external sites that are publicly accessible over the Internet the close relationship between Windows user accounts and Web server permissions leaves a lot to be desired. It would be very useful for Microsoft to provide a file-based or RDBMS authentication mechanism that could support digest and basic authentication schemes without requiring the development of a customized solution. For now, third-parties provide some of these options.

Chapter 19

A Simple BBS

IN THIS CHAPTER

◆ Basic architecture

◆ Database schema

◆ Managing message boards

NUMEROUS WEB SITES HAVE begun to include forums and bulletin board systems (BBS) that visitors can use to exchange and share information. You may want to add this feature to your Web sites as well. Of course, there are shareware and commercial BBS systems available that use ASP and other technologies, but we're including a simple system in this book so that you can learn from the basic structure and so that you have a version, with source code, that you can modify. The remainder of this chapter describes the architecture and code for our simple version.

Basic Architecture

The basic architecture for this BBS groups messages into message boards. Currently the messages are not organized further into threads, although you could add this feature. Each message board contains a set of messages that can be displayed. Visitors can read messages and post new messages. In an actual Web site, you might include a list of the message boards on your front page. For the purposes of the book, we have created a page that displays a list of all the available boards as links.

The boards for our system are defined in a database table. An administration page is provided to add and remove boards from the system. Removing a board should remove all of the messages associated with it.

The messages on our simple BBS contain a sender, their e-mail address, the date it was posted, a subject, and the content. All of this information is stored in a database discussed in the next section.

When a visitor selects a board, their browser will display a page containing a list of the messages on that board. Each message's subject will show up as a link. Selecting the link will display the message. Pages in the system also contain a menu that allows the user to move between them and potentially post messages to a particular board.

As you look at the ASPs you may notice that we designed the simple version so that there are no links to the administration page. This keeps visitors from administrating the site. In a production situation you might also add password protection to the administration pages. This protection would best be implemented at the Web server level.

Database Schema

Driving the BBS is a database containing two tables. The msgboards table contains a list of the boards. (See Table 19-1.) The msgs table contains the messages. Each message board and message is assigned a unique ID by the database.

TABLE 19-1 THE MSGBOARDS TABLE

Column Name	Description
id	The unique ID for this board
name	The name of the board

The msgs table contains several columns describing the elements of each message, which are described in Table 19-2. The msgs rows also contain a board ID to join them with the msgboards table. Each msg is assigned a unique ID by the database.

TABLE 19-2 THE MSGS TABLE

Column Name	Description
id	A unique ID for the message
boarded	The ID for the board that this message belongs to
postdate	The date the message was posted
sender	The sender's name
sendemail	The sender's e-mail address
subject	The subject of this message
message	The text of the message

This schema is created using the page build_db.asp. This page is available on the CD-ROM. To tell the database to generate IDs for each message the autoincrement datatype is used for the id field in each table. The ODBC datasource for this example will be called asp_devguide.

Managing Message Boards

We created a page called manage_boards.asp to manage the message boards. This page provides a list of the boards and a field for adding new boards by name. The ID for a new board is created automatically by the database. As you can see in Figure 19-1 the administrator can select boards from the list and delete them using this page.

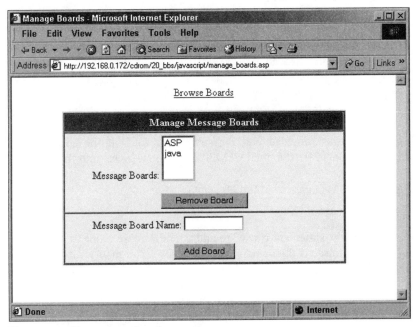

Figure 19-1: The manage_boards.asp page

As in other examples we have created this ASP to both display a form and respond to that form being submitted. The page starts off with some variable declarations. In particular, a recordSet and database object are created. There is also a variable called submit that will be used to determine which button was pressed to submit the form.

```
<%@ LANGUAGE="JAVASCRIPT" %>
<%
var board,boardid;
```

```
var submit;
var recordSet = Server.CreateObject("ADODB.RecordSet");
var database = Server.CreateObject("ADODB.Connection");
var sql;
```

Open the database. We are using the asp_devguide datasource found throughout the book, with a default username. You will need to modify this for your own site.

```
database.Open("asp_devguide","asp_dev","");
```

Next, check to see if there is a value for the submit field in the form. This value will be undefined if no form was submitted.

```
submit = Request.Form("submit");
if((""+submit) == "undefined") submit = null;
```

Also try to get the name of the message board that the administrator is trying to add. This may be undefined as well.

```
board = Request.Form("board_name");
if((""+board) == "undefined") board = null;
```

If a board name was provided and the submit button that the administrator pressed was the Add Board button, then we will insert a new board into the database.

```
if((board != null)&&(submit=="Add Board"))
{
```

A simple SQL insert statement is used to add the new board name to the system. We are not checking to see if the name is already in use. You may want to add this feature to a production system.

```
    sql = "insert into msgboards (name) values ('";
    sql += board;
    sql += "');";

    database.Execute(sql);
}
```

If the administrator wasn't trying to add a new board, they may have been trying to remove a board. See if there was a selection in the scrolling list.

```
board = Request.Form("boards");
if((""+board) == "undefined") board = null;
```

If a board was selected in the list and the Remove Board submit button was pressed, delete the board from the database.

```
if((board != null)&&(submit=="Remove Board"))
{
```

Use a delete statement to remove the board, including a where clause with the appropriate ID.

```
    sql = "delete from msgboards where id=";
    sql += board;

    database.Execute(sql);
```

Also delete any messages that are associated with the message board.

```
    sql = "delete from msgs where boardid=";
    sql += board;
    sql += "";

    database.Execute(sql);
}
%>
```

The next part of this ASP defines the HTML sent to the administrator, as shown in Listing 19-1. The page starts out with the basic HTML header and a menu to move to other pages.

Listing 19-1: Defining the HTML sent to the administrator

```
<html>
<head>
<title>Manage Boards</title>
</head>
<body link="006666" vlink="006666">


<center>
<a href="browse_boards.asp">Browse Boards</a>
<br><br>
<table bgColor=006666 border=2 cellspacing=1
    cellpadding=4 width=450>
<tr><td align="center">
<font color="white"><b>Manage Message Boards</b></font></td></tr>
<tr bgColor=F0F0F0><td align="left">
<ul>
```

The form on this page posts itself back to the page.

```
<form action="manage_boards.asp" method="post">
Message Boards:
<%
```

One element of the form is a selection list that displays a scrolling list of the existing boards so that the administrator can choose one to delete. This select list is named boards. A recordSet is used to get the names of all of the message boards and add them to the list (see Listing 19-2). Rather than identifying the boards by name, the ID is included as the value for each option, while their name is displayed to the administrator. This makes interacting with the database later easier.

Listing 19-2: Getting all the names of the message boards

```
recordSet.Open("select * from msgboards order by name;",database);

Response.Write("<select size=4 name='boards'>");

while(! recordSet.EOF)
{
    board = recordSet("name");
    boardid = recordSet("id");
    Response.Write("<option value='" + boardid);
    Response.Write("' >");
    Response.Write(board);
    Response.Write("</option>");
    recordSet.MoveNext();
}

Response.Write("</select>");
recordSet.Close();
%>
```

The remainder of the page contains the two submit buttons and a field for entering the name of a new message board. Once the page is complete, the database connection is closed and the HTML concluded. (See Listing 19-3.)

Listing 19-3: Two submit buttons and a field for new message board names

```
</ul>
<center>
<input type=submit name="submit" value="Remove Board">
</center>
</td></tr>

<tr bgColor=F0F0F0><td align="left">
```

```
<ul>
Message Board Name: <input name="board_name" size=12>
</ul>

<center>
<input type=submit name="submit" value="Add Board">
</center>
</td></tr></table>
</form>
</center>
<%
database.Close();
%>
</body>
</html>
```

This page should be starting to look familiar after the other examples. It displays a form generated from database data and responds to the administrator submitting the form.

Viewing the boards

The first page that a visitor might experience is called browse_boards.asp, which is shown in Figure 19-2. This page displays a list of the available message boards as links. Selecting the link for a board will display a list of messages on that board. The links will point to the page msgboard.asp, which expects the ID for a board to be passed in the query string. To get the list of board names and IDs, a database connection is opened and a record set is used. In a production system you might include this code as part of a different page, rather than having a special page to list message boards.

Start the page off by declaring needed variables and opening the database connection.

```
<%@ LANGUAGE="JAVASCRIPT" %>
<%
var board,boardid;
var submit;
var recordSet = Server.CreateObject("ADODB.RecordSet");
var database = Server.CreateObject("ADODB.Connection");
var sql;
var title;

database.Open("asp_devguide","asp_dev","");
%>
```

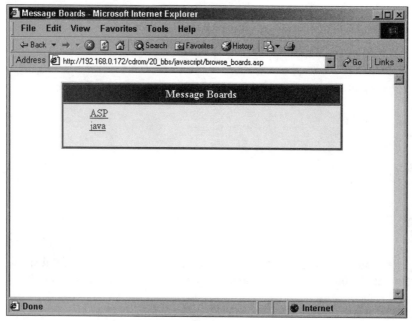

Figure 19-2: The browse_boards.asp page

Start the HTML off with the header and any other styling, as shown in Listing 19-4.

Listing 19-4: Displaying the list of boards

```
<html>
<head>
<title>Message Boards</title>
</head>
<body link="006666" vlink="006666">


<center>
<table bgColor=006666 border=2 cellspacing=1
    cellpadding=4 width=450>
<tr><td align="center">
<font color="white"><b>Message Boards</b></font></td></tr>
<tr bgColor=F0F0F0><td align="left">
<ul>
```

To display the message boards, open a record set using a select statement. Order the results of the select by name so that the message boards will be listed alphabetically.

```
<%
    recordSet.Open("select * from msgboards order by name;"
                        ,database);
```

For each board, display a link to msgboard.asp with the appropriate query string, as follows:

```
    while(! recordSet.EOF)
    {
        board = recordSet("name");
        boardid = recordSet("id");
        Response.Write("<a href='msgboard.asp?board_id="
                                            +boardid+"'>");
        Response.Write(board);
        Response.Write("<a><br>");
        recordSet.MoveNext();
    }
```

Close the record set when you are done, as follows:

```
    recordSet.Close();
%>
```

Conclude the HTML and close the database connection, like this:

```
</ul>
</td></tr></table>
</form>
</center>
<%
database.Close();
%>
</body>
</html>
```

Again, this type of page should be getting familiar. We connect to the database and load data to display HTML. Data, like IDs, can be used in links to other pages to control their appearance and behavior.

Viewing messages for a board

When a visitor selects a link on the previous page, they are presented with the msgboard.asp page. This page expects the ID for a message board as part of its query string. Using this ID, the page will display a list of the messages from that board. For example, Figure 19-3 shows a sample board we created during testing.

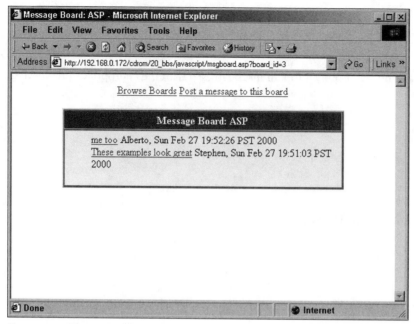

Figure 19-3: The msgboard.asp page

Like the previous pages, this page starts off by declaring variables and creating a database connection, as follows:

```
<%@ LANGUAGE="JAVASCRIPT" %>
<%
var board,boardid;
var recordSet = Server.CreateObject("ADODB.RecordSet");
var database = Server.CreateObject("ADODB.Connection");
var sql;

database.Open("asp_devguide","asp_dev","");
```

Next, check the query string for the board ID. Use this ID to get the name of the message board.

```
boardid = Request.QueryString("board_id");
if(((""+boardid) == "undefined") boardid = null;
```

Use a try-catch block to ensure that if the `boardid` is not set, the error generated by the database is handled.

```
try
{
    recordSet.Open("select * from msgboards where id="
                +boardid,database);

    board = recordSet("name");
    board = new String(board)//copy the name

    recordSet.Close();
```

Remember that the values in a record set are really objects, so when you assign them to a variable you aren't copying the data, just sharing it. To keep the data around after you close the record set, you need to copy the data into a new String object.

```
    board = new String(board)//copy the name
```

Then you can close the record set.

```
    recordSet.Close();
}
catch(e)
{
    board = null;
}
```

In the case that the board wasn't found, probably because the ID was bad, we will use the variable that was supposed to hold the name of the board as an error message.

```
if((board==null)
    ||((""+board) == "undefined"))
{
    board = "No such Board";
    boardid = -1;
}
%>
```

The HTML for this page uses the name of the board in the title and in the header for the table. (See Listing 19-5.)

Listing 19-5: Setting the title and header

```
<html>
<head>
<title>Message Board: <%=board%></title>
</head>
<body link="006666" vlink="006666">

<center>
<a href="browse_boards.asp">Browse Boards</a>
<a href="postmsg.asp?board_id=<%=boardid%>">
Post a message to this board
</a>
<br><br>
<table bgColor=006666 border=2 cellspacing=1
    cellpadding=4 width=450>
<tr><td align="center">
<font color="white">
<b>Message Board: <%=board%></b>
</font>
</td></tr>

<tr bgColor=F0F0F0><td align="left">
<ul>
```

The contents of the table are generated by performing a `select` statement on the `msgs` table, using the board ID to limit the results. (See Listing 19-6.) The results are also ordered by date, in descending order. This ensures that the newest messages are listed first. Each message is displayed in the form of a link to the `readmsg` page. The links include a query string with the ID of the message so that when the user clicks on one, the `readmsg` ASP can determine the message to display.

Listing 19-6: Performing a select statement on the msgs table

```
<%
if(boardid>=0)
{
    var recordSet = Server.CreateObject("ADODB.RecordSet");
    var id;

    recordSet.Open("select * from msgs where boardid="
                    +boardid+" order by postdate DESC"
                    ,database);


    while(!recordSet.EOF)
    {
```

```
        id = recordSet("id");

        Response.Write("<a href='readmsg.asp?id=");
        Response.Write(id);
        Response.Write("'>");
        Response.Write(recordSet("subject"));
        Response.Write("</a> ");
        Response.Write(recordSet("sender"));
        Response.Write(", ");
        Response.Write(recordSet("postdate"));
        Response.Write("<br>");

        recordSet.MoveNext();
    }

    recordSet.Close();
}
%>
```

Once the messages are displayed the HTML is concluded, as follows:

```
</ul>
</td></tr>
</table>
</center>
<%
database.Close();
%>

</body>
</html>
```

The new technique on this page of the example is the way data is copied from a record set to make it persist beyond the record set itself.

Viewing a message

When the user clicks on a link to readmsg.asp, they will see a page like the one shown in Figure 19-4. As you can see, this page displays the contents of a specific message.

The message to display is determined from the query string. If no message ID is passed to the page, it will display an error message instead, as shown in Figure 19-5.

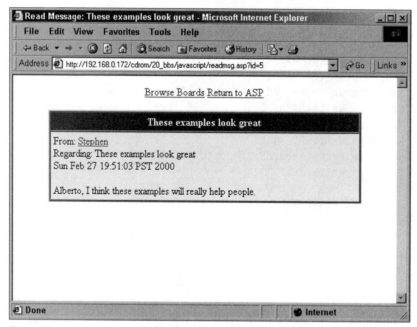

Figure 19-4: The readmsg.asp page

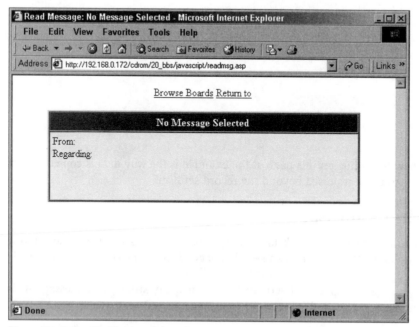

Figure 19-5: The No Message Selected error message

This page starts like the others, but contains a number of variables for storing the information from the message. A special variable called message is used to display an error message if an error occurs while retrieving the data for the message.

```
<%@ LANGUAGE="JAVASCRIPT" %>
<%
var msgid,boardid,board,date,sender,subject,email,content;
var dateObj;
var recordSet = Server.CreateObject("ADODB.RecordSet");
var database = Server.CreateObject("ADODB.Connection");
var sql;
var message;
var i,max;

database.Open("asp_devguide","asp_dev","");
message = null;
```

Start by trying to get the message ID from the query string, as follows:

```
msgid = Request.QueryString("id");
if((""+msgid) == "undefined") msgid = null;
```

If there is an ID, get the data for that message from the database. Use copies so that the record set can be reused to retrieve the name of the message board from the msgboards table.

```
if((msgid != null)&&((""+msgid)!=""))
{
    recordSet.Open("select * from msgs where id="+msgid,database);
    boardid = new String(recordSet("boardid"));
    date = new String(recordSet("postdate"));
    sender = new String(recordSet("sender"));
    email = new String(recordSet("sendemail"));
    subject = new String(recordSet("subject"));
    content = new String(recordSet("message"));
```

Later in the HTML we will use the message variable to indicate either the subject or an error. At this point the page is working, so set the message variable to the subject of the message.

```
    message = subject;
    recordSet.Close();
```

The msgs table contains the ID of the board associated with a message, but we need to query the msgboards table to get the name. (See Listing 19-7.) Again, use copies so that the data outlives the record set object.

Listing 19-7: Querying the msgboards table

```
recordSet.Open("select * from msgboards where id="
        +boardid,database);

board = recordSet("name");
board = new String(board)//copy the name

recordSet.Close();

if((board==null)
    ||((""+board) == "undefined"))
{
    board = "No such Board";
    boardid = -1;
}
}
```

If no ID is provided, set the message variable to indicate the problem, like this:

```
else
{
    message = "No Message Selected"
}


%>
```

Start the HTML for the page, including the subject in the page title, as follows:

```
<html>
<head>
<title>Read Message: <%=message%></title>
</head>
<body link=006666>


<center>
<a href="browse_boards.asp">Browse Boards</a>
<a href="msgboard.asp?board_id=<%=boardid%>">Return to
<%=board%></a>
<br><br>
```

Display the contents of the message in a table. Use a link to display the name, pointing it at the sender's e-mail address. (See Listing 19-8.) This way visitors can easily send e-mail to the person that posted the message.

Listing 19-8: Pointing a link at the sender's e-mail address

```
<table bgColor=006666 border=2 cellspacing=1
    cellpadding=4 width=500>
<tr><td align="center">
<font color="white"><b><%=message%></b></font></td></tr>
<tr bgColor=F0F0F0><td align="left">

From: <a href="mailto:<%=email%>"><%=sender%></a><br>
Regarding: <%=subject%><br>
<%=date%><br><br>
<%=content%><br>
</td></tr></table>
</center>
<%
database.Close();
%>
</body>
</html>
```

This page adds the technique of using data from one query to perform another query. You can also create a more complex query that performs this entire operation on the database. In many cases, it is preferable to minimize communications between the ASP and database, so you will probably use complex queries instead of this technique. However, there are situations where you need to perform the operation as shown and in those cases don't forget to copy data from the record set if you plan to reuse it.

Posting a message

When a visitor wants to post a message to a board, they use the postmsg.asp page. This page expects the ID for the board to post to as part of its query string. If the board is not provided, an error message is used to indicate the problem to the visitor. The form on postmsg.asp, shown in Figure 19-6, provides fields for entering your name, e-mail address, a subject, and the content of the message. The date is determined when the form is submitted, and the board ID is stored in a hidden field. Like the other pages in this example, the form is submitted back to the postmsg.asp itself.

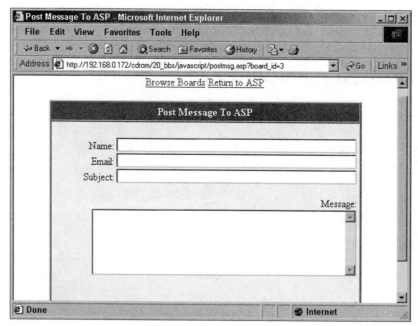

Figure 19-6: The postmsg.asp page

Like the other pages in this example, this one starts by declaring variables to hold the information from the form and creates a database connection, as follows:

```
<%@ LANGUAGE="JAVASCRIPT" %>
<%
var boardid,board,date,sender,subject,email,content;
var dateObj;
var recordSet = Server.CreateObject("ADODB.RecordSet");
var database = Server.CreateObject("ADODB.Connection");
var sql;
var message;
var i,max;

database.Open("asp_devguide","asp_dev","");
message = null;
```

The page can get the ID for a message board two ways. First it can come from the query string. Second, it can come from a hidden field in the form on the page itself. We check for the hidden field first, as follows:

```
boardid = Request.Form("id");
if((""+boardid) == "undefined") boardid = null;
```

If the page is being displayed because the form was submitted to it, then the data from the form is retrieved and checked to make sure it exists, as shown in Listing 19-9.

Listing 19-9: Retrieving data from the form

```
if((boardid != null)&&((""+boardid)!=""))
{
    sender = ""+Request.Form("sender");
    if((sender == "undefined")||(sender=="")) sender = null;

    email = ""+Request.Form("email");
    if((email == "undefined")||(email=="")) email = null;

    subject = ""+Request.Form("subject");
    if((subject == "undefined")||(subject=="")) subject = null;

    content = ""+Request.Form("content");
    if((content == "undefined")||(content=="")) content = null;
```

If any fields in the form were left blank, a message is displayed to the visitor, as follows:

```
if((sender==null)||(email==null)
    ||(subject==null)||(content==null))
{
    message =
        "<center>Please complete all of the fields.</center>";
}
```

Otherwise, a SQL `insert` statement is constructed to add the new message to the database. This statement includes the current date by creating a Date object and turning it into a string. (See Listing 19-10.) Notice that we are not performing any encoding on the message. In a production system you may want to encode the strings before sending them to the database to make sure that bad characters are not included in the SQL. One simple encoding is URL encoding. But that will expand the data. It is better to look at the database's documentation to determine the "bad" characters and if possible use the backslash escaping mechanism to encode them. In this scheme, you can use characters like "become \" to do this.

Listing 19-10: Adding a new message to the database

```
    else
    {
        dateObj = new Date();

        date = dateObj.toString();
```

```
sql = "insert into msgs (boardid,postdate,sender,"
sql += "sendemail,subject,message) values (";
sql += boardid;
sql += ",'";
sql += date;
sql += "','";
sql += sender;
sql += "','";
sql += email;
sql += "','";
sql += subject;
sql += "','";
sql += content;
sql += "')";
```

The insert statement is executed and if it succeeds, the poster is sent back to the message board page where they should see their new message. If there is a problem, an error message is displayed along with the form, as follows:

```
try
{
    database.Execute(sql);

    Response.Redirect("msgboard.asp?board_id="+boardid);
}
catch(exp)
{
    message = "Failed to insert message."+exp;
}
}
}
```

In the case that the page is not being accessed because the form on it was submitted, there will not have been an ID in the Form data. Check if there is an ID in the query string, like this:

```
else
{
    boardid = Request.QueryString("board_id");
    if((""+boardid) == "undefined") boardid = null;
```

If there is a board ID, use a record set to get the name of the message board. We will display this name on the page. In the case that no valid board ID is provided, we set the board name to an error message. (See Listing 19-11.)

Listing 19-11: Using a record set to get the message board's name

```
try
{
    recordSet.Open("select * from msgboards where id="
        +boardid,database);

    board = recordSet("name");
    board = new String(board)//copy the name

    recordSet.Close();
}
catch(e)
{
    board = null;
}

if((board==null)
    ||((""+board) == "undefined"))
{
    board = "No such Board";
    boardid = -1;
}
}

%>
```

The HTML for this page primarily defines a form, and formats it. The name of the message board is used in the title of the page, and the board ID is used in a menu link to jump the visitor back to the board they said they wanted to post a message to. (See Listing 19-12.)

Listing 19-12: Posting a message

```
<html>
<head>
<title>Post Message To <%=board%></title>
</head>
<body link=006666>


<center>
<a href="browse_boards.asp">Browse Boards</a>
<a href="msgboard.asp?board_id=<%=boardid%>">
Return to <%=board%>
</a>
<br><br>
```

```
<table bgColor=006666 border=2 cellspacing=1
    cellpadding=4 width=500>
<tr><td align="center">
<font color="white">
<b>Post Message To <%=board%></b>
</font>
</td></tr>
<tr bgColor=F0F0F0><td align="right">
```

The message variable is used throughout this page to indicate an error. If it is defined, display it, as follows:

```
<%
if(message != null)
{
%>
<%=message%><br><br>
<%
}
%>
```

Define the form, targeting it back to the current page. Include the board ID in a hidden field, so that when the form is submitted the page knows which board to associate with the message.

```
<form action="postmsg.asp" method="post">

<input type="hidden" name="id" value="<%=boardid%>"><br>
Name: <input type="text" name="sender" size=60><br>
Email: <input type="text" name="email" size=60><br>
Subject: <input type="text" name="subject" size=60><br><br>
Message:<br>
<textarea name="content" cols=50 rows=6 wrap=virtual></textarea><br>
<br><br>
<input type="submit" value="Submit Message">

</form>
```

Conclude the HTML and close the database, as follows:

```
</td></tr></table>
</center>
<%
database.Close();
```

```
%>
</body>
</html>
```

This page included the new technique of using redirection, and using the query string versus form collection to determine how it was accessed. Because ASPs have a limited set of inputs, it is important to use them as efficiently as possible, often encoding information in your choice of data transmission as much as the data itself.

Summary

Hopefully the example in this chapter will provide you with some good ideas for your own projects. Some basic lessons we have tried to demonstrate are as follows:

- Using an ASP to display and handle the same form
- Using variables to store optional messages to the user
- Using Server-side form validation
- Using multiple record sets on the same connection
- Copying data from a record set for use after the record set is closed
- Determining how a page was submitted by the way data was provided to it (query string vs. form)

By combining these techniques and the others demonstrated you will be well on your way to creating serious Active Server Page Web applications.

If you decide to add this message board system to your own site, you may want to think about extending it. Some ideas we had, but didn't want to muddy the example with, are adding the ability of the administrator to delete a message, threading messages using reply-to semantics, using a login instead of having the user type their name each time, categorizing boards, and providing preferences to control how many or how messages are displayed for a particular board. Each of these features offers a great opportunity for you to practice your ASP programming skills and adds a lot of value to the final system.

Chapter 20

A Simple Online Catalog Using DNA

IN THIS CHAPTER

◆ The basic architecture

◆ The database schema

◆ Browsing by category

◆ Displaying product information

◆ Managing categories

◆ Adding and updating products

CHAPTER 15, "A SIMPLE ONLINE CATALOG," used many of the methods introduced in earlier chapters to build a sample online catalog. To further demonstrate some of the application design and programming methods that make up the Windows Distributed interNet Applications (DNA) architecture, this chapter will rewrite the sample application first introduced in Chapter 15. See Appendix E for more information on Windows DNA architecture.

The overall goal of the application is to store basic information related to products and organize them into various categories. As in Chapter 15, the same product can exist within more than one category. Users can add and remove products and categories. Along with search capabilities, the sample application provides methods to update a product listing and list a single product or the entire catalog.

The entire sample application from Chapter 15 was provided by a series of ASP and HTML pages and a SQL Server database. In this chapter, we'll use the Windows DNA design approach to separate much of the business and data access logic from the ASP code and maintain it in a Visual Basic (VB) component along with a number of stored procedures maintained on the SQL Server database.

The Basic Architecture

The starting page for the sample application is an HTML page: index.html. From this page, users have access to all of the main functions of the application. Depending on the user's choice, they will receive a form or set of links that lead them to their next page. To ease the user navigation tasks, each page includes a menu at the top of the page that allows the user to either return to the main menu or navigate to another page.

Each of the pages is named to correspond with the function that the page provides. For example, insert_prod.asp handles the task of presenting the user a form to enter a new product's values and the logic to insert the product into the catalog. Figure 20-1 shows the relationship of all the pages within the sample application.

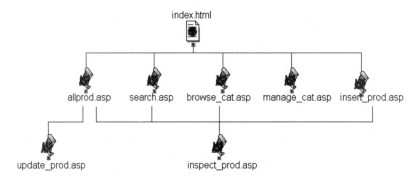

Figure 20-1: Sample application page relationships

Although the page relationships haven't changed from the original sample in Chapter 15, the overall architecture has. As shown in Figure 20-2, a COM component has been introduced in the Business Services tier. This component, written using Visual Basic, provides most of the hard-core programming that the sample application calls for. In fact, the ActiveX Data Objects (ADO) code used to communicate with the SQL Server database is entirely encapsulated in this component.

The Database Schema

As in Chapter 15, three tables in a SQL Server database support the catalog. For the sake of simplicity, this chapter's version of the sample application uses the same table structure. The products table stores information about the products in the database. It contains the columns described in Table 20-1.

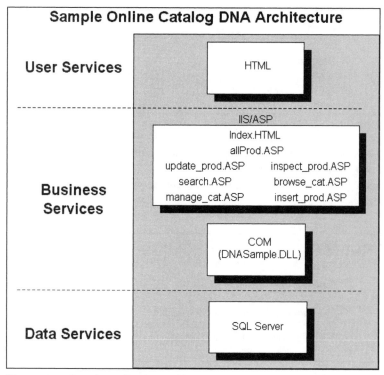

Figure 20-2: Sample application architecture

TABLE 20-1 PRODUCTS TABLE

Column Name	Description
id	A unique identifier for the product.
name	The product's name.
description	A short description of the product.
longdescription	A longer text description of the product.
msrp	The manufacturer's suggested retail price.
price	The actual current price of the product.

The categories table contains information about the categories defined for the catalog, as described in Table 20-2.

TABLE 20-2 CATEGORIES TABLE

Column Name	Description
name	The category's name.

The final table, called prodcat, joins the products and categories tables. This table contains two columns, which are listed in Table 20-3. These columns relate a product to its categories. Products in more than one category may appear in the table multiple times.

TABLE 20-3 PRODCAT TABLE

Column Name	Description
catname	The name of the category for this join.
prodid	The ID of the product being joined.

Stored procedures

All of the stored procedures follow a basic architecture. After the procedure `create` statement and any input parameter declarations, a local variable to hold a return value is defined and a transaction is started, as follows:

```
DECLARE @RetVal int
BEGIN TRAN Tran1
```

By encapsulating most of the logic for the stored procedure within a transaction, any inserts, updates, or deletes of the data can be rolled back if an error occurs. Next, each of the stored procedures performs one or more selects, inserts, updates, or deletes of the data followed by code to check the @@ERROR value.

```
SELECT  @RetVal = @@ERROR
```

SQL Server provides its error information in the @@ERROR variable. Therefore, after the code has stored any error information in the @RetVal local variable, the stored procedures check this value and either commit or rollback the transaction based on whether an error occurred. (See Listing 20-1.)

Listing 20-1: Committing or rolling back the transaction

```
IF (@retval <> 0)
BEGIN
        ROLLBACK TRAN Tran1

        IF @RetVal = 0
            SELECT @RetVal = -1
        GOTO ErrorMessage
        END
ELSE
    BEGIN
        COMMIT TRAN Tran1
        GOTO ExitSP
        END
```

As you can see, if an error occurred, the transaction is rolled back and control is passed to `ErrorMessage`. Otherwise, the transaction is committed and program control is passed to `ExitSP`. In a real-world application, code would properly handle errors. However, in this sample application, this is left up to you.

```
ErrorMessage:
    --TODO: build some type of error message for the user

ExitSP:
    --nothing
```

Table 20-4, lists all of the stored procedures used in the sample application.

TABLE 20-4 STORED PROCEDURES

Stored Procedure Name	Description
delCategory	Deletes a category from the categories and prodcat tables.
delProduct	Deletes a product from the products and prodcat tables.

Continued

TABLE **20-4 STORED PROCEDURES** *(Continued)*

Stored Procedure Name	Description
delProductCategory_ByProductID	Deletes a category from the prodcat table based on the product ID passed in.
getCategory_All	Gets all of the categories in the categories table.
getCategory_ByProductID	Gets all of the categories from the prodcat table associated with the product ID passed in.
getProduct_All	Gets all of the products in the products table.
getProduct_ByCategory	Gets all of the products that are associated with the category that is passed in.
getProduct_ByID	Gets the product identified by the product ID that is passed in.
insCategory	Inserts a category into the categories table.
insProduct	Inserts a product into the products table.
insProductCategory	Inserts a product-to-category association into the prodcat table.
searchProduct_ByCategory	Gets all of the products associated with the list of categories that is passed in.
searchProduct_ByKeyword	Gets all of the products that match the keyword string that is passed in.
searchProduct_ByPrice	Gets all of the products that are priced between the minimum and maximum prices that are passed in.
updProduct	Updates a product record.

As you can see, all of the SQL-related code that was included in the ASP pages from the Chapter 15 sample has been placed in stored procedures. By doing so, we have effectively removed the intricacies of the SQL database from the application itself. Therefore, in the event the database schema changed or a different database type was used, only the stored procedures and/or table structure would change—not any of the ASP code.

Main menu

The main menu, as shown in Figure 20-3, for the sample application is identical to the page already discussed in Chapter 15, "A Simple Online Catalog." Therefore, there's no reason to spend any more time going over it again.

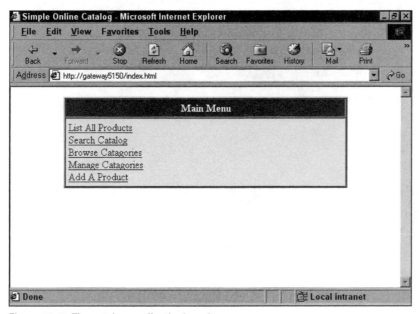

Figure 20-3: The catalog application's main menu

Complete catalog

The List All Products option provides a listing of all the products in the catalog using the allprod.asp page. The results of this page, shown in Figure 20-4, display a list of the products in the products table.

As before, in addition to each product's name, two links are provided: one to inspect the product using the inspect_prod.asp page, and the other to allow the user to update the properties for the product using the update_prod.asp page. Both of these ASPs accept a query string containing the ID of the product to display or update. The page begins with the typical HTML-required tags followed by a navigation menu, as shown in Listing 20-2.

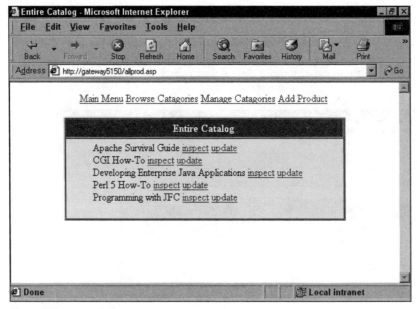

Figure 20-4: The allprod.asp page

Listing 20-2: Presenting a navigation menu

```
<%@ Language=VBScript %>
<%
Option Explicit

Dim objDNASample
Dim ID
Dim aProduct
Dim intProduct
%>
<html>
<head>
<title>Entire Catalog</title>
</head>
<body link="006666" vlink="006666">

<center>
<a href="index.html">Main Menu</a>
<a href="browse_cat.asp">Browse Categories</a>
<a href="manage_cat.asp">Manage Categories</a>
<a href="insert_prod.asp">Add Product</a>
<br><br>
```

This portion of the ASP page is similar on all the pages; therefore, it won't be covered on subsequent pages. The product listing is displayed in a table, so create the HTML for the table, as follows:

```
<table bgColor=006666 border=2 cellspacing=1
cellpadding=4 width=450>
<tr><td align="center">
<font color="white"><b>Entire Catalog</b></font></td></tr>

<tr bgColor=F0F0F0><td align="left">
<ul>
```

Next, we get a list of all the products. In the Chapter 15 sample, this was performed by creating an ADO `RecordSet` object. However, we'll use the COM component to get a list of all the products.

```
Set objDNASample = Server.CreateObject("DNASample.DNACatalog")

aProduct = objDNASample.getProduct_All

set objDNASample = nothing
```

As shown, we use the `Server.CreateObject` method to create an instance of the `DNASample.DNACatalog` COM component. Next, the `getProduct_All` method is called and the results are stored in the `aProduct` variable. Finally, the object is released.

One of the design goals for this sample was to abstract all of the ASP code from any type of ADO or data access tasks. Therefore, the result of the `getProduct_All` method returns a variant. In the event the variable type is a string, either no products exist in the database or an error occurred. In the event the variable type is an array, products were found and are stored in `aProduct` as a two-dimensional array. For now, we'll skip the details of how this was done via the COM component.

```
Select Case VarType(aProduct)

    Case 8 'string
        If aProduct = "" Then
            'no products found...not a problem
            Response.Write "No Products Found!"
        Else
'an error occurred and the error information is in 'the return
string
            Response.Write "<b>Error Occurred</b>:<br>" & aProduct
        End If
```

Notice that the `VarType` VBScript function is used to determine the datatype of the `aProduct` variable. As indicated by the comments in the code, if a string is returned, a message is provided to the user to indicate if an error occurred or if there simply aren't any products in the database.

In the event an array is returned, the `aProduct` is a two-dimensional array containing the data. To begin the product listing, an HTML table is created to format the data, as follows:

```
    Case 8204 'array
%>
        <table bgColor=006666 border=2 cellspacing=1 cellpadding=4
width=450>
        <tr><td align="center">
        <font color="white"><b>Entire Catalog</b></font></td></tr>
        <tr bgColor=F0F0F0><td align="left">
        <ul>
```

Next, the code iterates through the array using the `UBound` function to determine the maximum number of products to list. For each product, the name is shown to the user along with two links, `inspect` and `update`, to allow the user to further view and/or update the product, as shown in Listing 20-3.

Listing 20-3: Viewing or updating products

```
<%
        For intProduct = 0 To UBound(aProduct,2)

            id = aProduct(0, intProduct)

            Response.Write(aProduct(1, intProduct))
            Response.Write(" <a href='inspect_prod.asp?id=")
            Response.Write(id)
            Response.Write("'>inspect</a>")
            Response.Write(" <a href='update_prod.asp?id=")
            Response.Write(id)
            Response.Write("'>update</a><br>")

        Next
%>
```

Next, after iterating through the array, the table and the `Select Case` structures are completed, and then the HTML-required tags are completed to mark the end of the ASP page.

```
        </ul>
        </td></tr>
```

```
        </table>
        </center>
<%
    Case Else
        'nothing

End Select
%>
</body>
</html>
```

One of the things to note is that no ADO code was used. This basic structure is followed for each page within this sample. The primary reason is related to performance. By placing all of the ADO-related code in the compiled VB COM component, the connection and work times related to accessing the database are minimized. In addition, in the event the direction of the application changes and the data is no longer stored in a SQL Server database, the ASP code doesn't have to change. Therefore, code maintenance is simplified by limiting potential change points in the future.

The getProduct_All VB COM component method

Let's review the code in the VB COM component that provides the getProduct_All method. First, the function declaration shows that the return value is of type Variant, as follows:

```
Public Function getProduct_All() As Variant
```

This allows the flexibility to return a string containing the error information or a two-dimensional array containing the data. Next, an error handler is set up to trap any type of error that might occur and an ADO Connection is created that opens the connection specified in the g_connString variable.

```
    On Error GoTo errorHandler

    Dim conn As ADODB.Connection
    Dim rs As ADODB.Recordset

    'create and open an ado connection to the database
    Set conn = CreateObject("ADODB.Connection")
    conn.Open g_connString
```

With the connection open, we can use the Execute method to run the getProduct_All stored procedure. (See Listing 20-4.) The results are stored in an ADO RecordSet, rs. If no records exist, as indicated by rs.EOF being true, the return value of the function call is set to an empty string, "". Otherwise, the entire

RecordSet is assigned to the return value of the function call by using the ADO RecordSet `GetRows` method. The `GetRows` method gets the records in the RecordSet and formats the results in a two-dimensional array. The first dimension holds the columns and the second dimension holds the rows. For example, to access the third column of the fourth row, you would use `getProduct_All(2, 3)`. Note that both dimensions begin with zero.

Listing 20-4: Running the getProduct_All procedure

```
'create the recordset using the execute method
Set rs = conn.Execute("getProduct_All")

If Not rs.EOF Then

    'put the entire recordset in a two-dimensional
    'array and return it
    getProduct_All = rs.GetRows

Else

    'if no records found...set the return value to
    'an empty string
    getProduct_All = ""

End If
```

Finally, references to the ADO RecordSet and Connection objects are released and the function ends, as follows:

```
'clean up the ado stuff
rs.Close
Set rs = Nothing
conn.Close
Set conn = Nothing

Exit Function
```

In the event an error occurs, the ADO objects are released and the error information is returned from the function call, as follows:

```
Set rs = Nothing
Set conn = Nothing

getProduct_All = Err.Number & ":" & Err.Description
```

Although this function includes ADO-specific code, there is no dependency on the database schema, other than the name of the stored procedure. This further isolates the structure of the database from the application so that in the event database changes occur in the future, the VB COM component doesn't have to undergo code changes. In addition, many real-world applications use some type of data-caching mechanism in addition to simple databases. By abstracting the actual location of the data from the VB code, application architects can employ additional data storage strategies, such as persisted XML data.

Search page

The search page displays a form containing a number of criteria that can be used to limit the products found. These criteria include a keyword search, price limitations, and category limits. The keyword search looks for a word in the name, description, and longdescription of a product using the SQL-"like" syntax, while the price search only displays those products that have a price between the minimum and maximum prices entered by the user. Finally, a category search lists products associated with the category or categories selected by the user. Figure 20-5 shows a successful search.

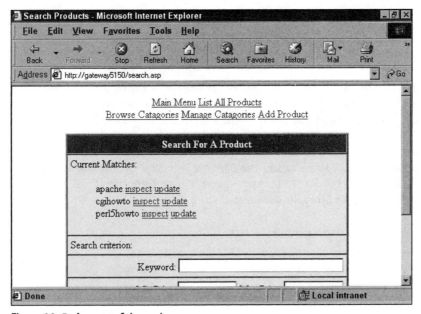

Figure 20-5: A successful search

When search results are displayed, links are provided to allow the user to further inspect or update a product. As with the previous page, all of the code to run the various searches and build an array of results is handled in the VB COM component. For keyword searches, the `searchProduct_ByKeyword` method is used, as shown here:

```
Set objDNASample = Server.CreateObject("DNASample.DNACatalog")

aProduct = objDNASample.searchProduct_ByKeyword("%" & _
    Replace(sKeyword,"'","''") & "%")

Set objDNASample = Nothing
```

Notice that the VBScript `Replace` function is used to make sure that any single quotes (') are changed to double quotes ("). This prevents SQL Server from balking at unterminated strings. Also, the keyword entered by the user is surrounded by percent signs (%) when the method call is made. Percent signs are special characters, wildcards, used by SQL Server to indicate that any character will match. The code to perform a search based on minimum and maximum prices is very similar.

```
Set objDNASample = Server.CreateObject("DNASample.DNACatalog")

aProduct = objDNASample.searchProduct_ByPrice(dMinPrice, dMaxPrice)

Set objDNASample = Nothing
```

In this case, the `searchProduct_ByPrice` method is called and the minimum and maximum prices that the user entered are passed into the method call.

Finally, if one or more categories were selected, a comma-delimited string is created that contains all of the categories selected. In addition, each category is surrounded with two single quotes to allow SQL Server to understand that this is a list of independent strings. Once again, the `DNASample` component is used to make a method call, `searchProduct_ByCategory`, that will perform the actual search and return the results in an array, as shown in Listing 20-5.

Listing 20-5: Returning search results in an array

```
ElseIf Request.Form("listCategory").Count > 0 Then
    intCategory = Request.Form("listCategory").Count

    For intX = 1 To intCategory
        If intX = 1 Then
            sCategory = "'" & _
Request.Form("listCategory").Item(intX) & "'"
```

```
        Else
            sCategory = sCategory & ",'" & _
        Request.Form("listCategory").Item(intX) & "'"
        End If
    Next

    Set objDNASample = Server.CreateObject("DNASample.DNACatalog")

    aProduct = objDNASample.searchProduct_ByCategory(sCategory)

    Set objDNASample = Nothing

End If
```

Once the particular search is performed, the variant result is evaluated to determine if an error occurred or if a two-dimensional array containing the resulting data was returned. As in the previous sample page, the results are displayed to the user by iterating the array.

One aspect of this example that could be improved is that each type of search is independent of the other. For example, the user can enter a keyword and select one or more categories. However, when the search is actually performed, only a keyword search will be done because it is the first evaluation in the ASP page. It's left up to you, the reader, to expand this sample page to include multiple search criteria.

The code contained in the VB COM component to support the search feature is very similar to the code that listed the entire product listing. The ADO method GetRows is used to read the entire RecordSet and place the data into a two-dimensional array. In the event an error occurs in the VB code, the function return value is set to the error number and description. Since this processing is exactly like that used for listing all of the products, it won't be covered again.

One thing to note about the form itself is that a VBScript procedure, showCategoryList, is used to build and display the list box of categories, as follows:

```
<%
showCategoryList "listCategory", Null
%>
```

This function is contained in the incCategoryList.asp and included at the bottom of the search.asp page, as you see here:

```
<!--#Include File="incCategoryList.asp"-->
```

The `showCategoryList` procedure supports two parameters: the name of the list box to create, and a list of categories, delimited by semicolons, to preselect or set up as defaults when the list box is created.

```
<%
Sub showCategoryList(ByVal sName, ByVal sDefault)
```

The first thing the procedure does is call the `getCategory_All` method of the VB COM component and stores the results in a local variable, as follows:

```
Set objDNASample =
Server.CreateObject("DNASample.DNACatalog")

    aCategory = objDNASample.getCategory_All

    set objDNASample = nothing
```

Similar to previous techniques, `aCategory` is a variant that either contains an empty string indicating that no categories exist, the error number and description if an error occurred, or a two-dimensional array of categories.

In the event an array was returned, the procedure uses a series of `Response.Writes` to build the list box, as shown in Listing 20-6.

Listing 20-6: Building the list box

```
Response.Write("<select size=4 name='" & sName & "' multiple>")

For intCategory = 0 To UBound(aCategory,2)

    sCategory = aCategory(0, intCategory)

    Response.Write("<option value='")
    Response.Write(sCategory)
    Response.Write("'")

    If Instr(";" & UCase(sDefault) & ";", ";" & _
UCase(sCategory) & ";") Then
    Response.Write(" selected")
    End If

    Response.Write(">")
    Response.Write(sCategory)
    Response.Write("</option>")
```

```
Next

Response.Write("</select>")
```

This process of creating a list box of categories is used in several ASP pages. Therefore, it is a perfect candidate for turning the process into a stand-alone VBScript procedure.

Browsing by Category

The browse_cat.asp page is used to allow the user to list the products associated with a particular category. When listed, each product name is shown and is displayed as a hyperlink to the inspect_prod.asp page. A QueryString value is used to indicate what category to list. In the event the QueryString does not exist, all of the categories are listed as links to the same page. Figure 20-6 shows the browse_cat.asp page as it looks when no category is included in the QueryString.

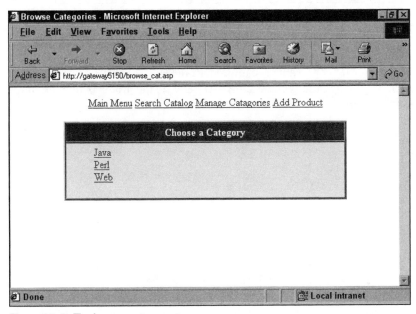

Figure 20-6: The browse category page

When you select a category, like Java, the products in that category are displayed, as shown in Figure 20-7.

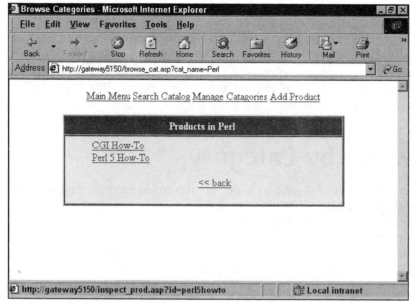

Figure 20-7: Browsing a specific category

After the typical declaration code – similar for all the ASP pages – is executed, the `cat_name` QueryString value is captured. In the event that it returns an empty string (`""`) only the categories will be shown. Otherwise, the products that are in the category included in the QueryString will be shown, as follows:

```
Category = Request.QueryString("cat_name")

If Category = "" Then
    Title = "Choose a Category"
Else
    Title = "Products in " & Category
End If
```

Given that `Category` is not an empty string, the `getProduct_ByCategory` method of the VB COM component is called, as shown here:

```
Set objDNASample = Server.CreateObject("DNASample.DNACatalog")

aProduct = objDNASample.getProduct_ByCategory(Category)

set objDNASample = nothing
```

At this point, this code is probably looking very similar to the previous examples. As was previously done, the result of the method call is stored in a variant type variable. In the case that products exist, the variable, aProduct, is a two-dimensional array of the product data. Otherwise, either an empty string is returned to indicate that no products exist or error information is returned.

In the case of no QueryString, a list of the categories is displayed using the getCategory_All method provided by the VB COM component, as follows:

```
Set objDNASample = Server.CreateObject("DNASample.DNACatalog")

aCategory = objDNASample.getCategory_All

set objDNASample = nothing
```

The remaining ASP code is exactly like that of the previous pages. If the returned value is of datatype string, the error information is shown or there were simply no products that were in the selected category. Otherwise, the return value is a two-dimensional array that is traversed and each product is listed.

Displaying Product Information

The inspect_prod.asp page is used to display information related to a particular product. The product ID to display is passed into the ASP page using a QueryString. Figure 20-8 shows a sample of what the page looks like when a product ID is found.

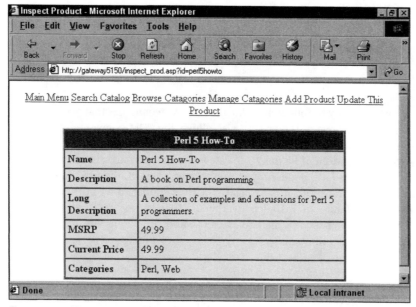

Figure 20-8: The product information page

As with the previous pages covered, the ASP code instantiates the DNASample object to gain access to the Business Services tier where the code resides to query the database and return the results in a variant. Notice that the `getProduct_ByID` method provided by the VB COM component is used, as follows:

```
Set objDNASample = Server.CreateObject("DNASample.DNACatalog")

aProduct = objDNASample.getProduct_ByID(ID)

set objDNASample = nothing
```

Although only one record is ever returned at a time, the `getProduct_ByID` method still uses the `GetRows` ADO method to return the information in a two-dimensional array. (See Listing 20-7.)

Listing 20-7: Returning information in a two-dimensional array

```
Set conn = CreateObject("ADODB.Connection")
conn.Open g_connString

Set rs = conn.Execute("getProduct_ByID '" & ProductID & "'")

If Not rs.EOF Then

    getProduct_ByID = rs.GetRows

Else

    getProduct_ByID = ""

End If
```

This is done primarily to follow the same data access techniques that are being used in all of the other ASP pages. However, it also allows the COM component to hide the ADO-specific code from the User Services tier code that resides on the ASP page.

As shown at the bottom of Figure 20-8, categories are listed as a comma-delimited list on the inspect_prod.asp page. As you might have guessed, the technique used to get the categories that a product is associated with is similar to all of the other data access techniques. First, an instance of the `DNASample` object is created. Then the `getCategory_ByProductID` method is called and the results are returned in a variant, `aCategory`, as follows:

```
Set objDNASample = Server.CreateObject("DNASample.DNACatalog")

aCategory = objDNASample.getCategory_ByProductID(ID)

set objDNASample = nothing
```

If the event, aCategory, is a two-dimensional array containing a list of categories that the product is associated with, the code iterates through the array, building a comma-delimited string that is displayed to the user.

```
For intCategory = 0 To UBound(aCategory,2)
    If intCategory = 0 Then
        Response.Write(aCategory(0, intCategory))
    Else
        Response.Write(", " & aCategory(0, intCategory))
    End If
Next
```

Managing Categories

Figure 20-9 shows the manage_cat.asp page that is used to manage the categories in the sample application. This page is actually made up of two sections. The top section is used to remove existing categories, while the section at the bottom is used to add a new category to the database.

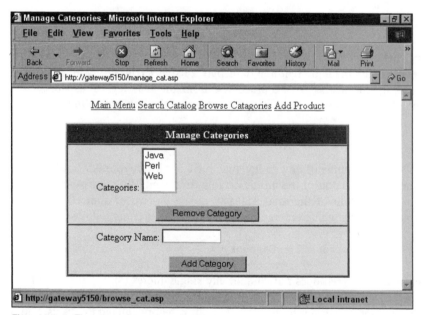

Figure 20-9: The managing categories page

Both sections are defined in the same HTML form. However, the value parameter defined for each submit button is used to distinguish between a request to delete a category or create a new one. (See Listing 20-8.)

Listing 20-8: Managing categories

```
<form action="manage_cat.asp" method="post">
Categories:
<%
showCategoryList "listCategory", NULL
%>
</ul>
<center>
<input type=submit name="submit" value="Remove Category">
</center>
</td></tr>

<tr bgColor=F0F0F0><td align="left">
<ul>
Category Name: <input name="insCategory" size=12 maxlength=80>
</ul>

<center>
<input type=submit name="submit" value="Add Category">
</center>
</td></tr></table>
</form>
```

Notice that the `showCategoryList` VBScript procedure, previously covered, is used to encapsulate the logic required to display a list box containing all of the categories. To provide access to the procedure from the manage_cat.asp page, the incCategoryList.asp page is included at the bottom of the page, as follows:

```
<!--#Include File="incCategoryList.asp"-->
```

This is a great example of how to leverage include files in your ASP code. At the completion of this version of the online catalog, this same VBScript procedure will have been used in four of the nine ASP pages. The process of adding a category starts by capturing the value entered in the form by the user, as follows:

```
Category = Request.Form("insCategory")
```

If the category entered does not contain any single quotes ('), an instance of the `DNASample` object is created and the `insCategory` method is called. The category entered by the user is passed into the method. If the category entered by the user does contain one or more single quotes ('), the insert into the database is not attempted and a message indicating that the category is invalid is displayed for the user.

```
If Category <> "" Then
    If Instr(Category,"'") = 0 Then
```

```
        Set objDNASample =
Server.CreateObject("DNASample.DNACatalog")

        objDNASample.insCategory(Category)

        set objDNASample = Nothing

    Else
        sMessage = "Invalid Category!<br>Category was not added."

    End If
End If
```

If the user selects the Remove Category button, the number of categories selected is stored in a local variable using the `Count` property of the list box, like this:

```
intCategory = Request.Form("listCategory").Count
```

Next, the selected categories are traversed. Each category is encapsulated with two single quotes and separated by a comma. This builds a comma-delimited list of category strings that can be used directly by the stored procedure.

```
For intX = 1 To intCategory
    If intX = 1 Then
        Category = "'" & _
Request.Form("listCategory").Item(intX) & "'"
    Else
        Category = Category & ",'" & _
Request.Form("listCategory").Item(intX) & "'"
    End If
Next
```

Finally, if the `Category` variable is not an empty string, the `DNASample` object is instantiated again and the `delCategory` method is called, with the comma-delimited list of categories as a parameter, as follows:

```
If Category <> "" Then
    Set objDNASample = Server.CreateObject("DNASample.DNACatalog")

    objDNASample.delCategory(Category)

    set objDNASample = Nothing

End If
```

In Chapter 15, deleting categories involved two different SQL statements: one to delete the categories from the categories table and another to delete the categories from the prodcat table. This approach creates a bit of a consistency problem. For example, what happens if the delete from the categories table succeeds, but the delete from the prodcat table fails? In essence, the prodcat table still associates products with a category that no longer exists.

One approach to resolve this issue would be to use a transaction in the ASP page. However, ASP-based transactions are notoriously slow and create a significant overhead burden on the IIS machine.

Another approach is to put both delete statements in the same stored procedure and use the transaction model built into SQL Server to provide the needed transaction to make sure data consistency is maintained. The delCategory stored procedure begins with the typical procedure declaration statement and an input variable definition. The @CatList variable holds the comma-delimited category strings. After defining a local variable to hold the error numbers, @SQLString is defined.

```
CREATE PROCEDURE delCategory
(
    @CatList varchar(1500) = null
)
As

SET NOCOUNT ON

--declare variable for error number
DECLARE @RetVal          int

--declare variable for the sql string
DECLARE @SQLString        varchar(5000)
```

The @SQLString local variable is used to hold the SQL string that will eventually be executed. Next, the transaction is created, as follows:

```
BEGIN TRAN Tran1
```

and then followed by the process of creating the SQL delete string to delete the categories, which are maintained in the @CatList variable, from the prodcat table, as follows:

```
    SELECT @SQLString = 'DELETE FROM ProdCat WHERE CatName  IN (' +
@CatList + ')'
```

Notice that because the @CatList variable is actually a comma-delimited list of category strings, a simple delete statement can't be used. Instead, a delete statement is built and stored in the @SQLString variable. Once the string is built, the execute method is used to actually execute the delete statement that is stored in @SQLString, as you see here:

```
EXEC (@SQLString)
```

Once the statement is executed, the @@ERROR value is stored and checked to see if an error occurred, as shown in Listing 20-9.

Listing 20-9: Checking for errors

```
--check @@ERROR for errors
SELECT  @RetVal = @@ERROR

--check for errors
IF (@retval <> 0)
    BEGIN
        --in case of errors, rollback current transaction
        ROLLBACK TRAN Tran1

        --if RetVal is 0, default to -1
        IF @RetVal = 0
            SELECT @RetVal = -1

        --branch to error message handler
        GOTO ErrorMessage
    END
```

If an error did occur, as indicated by @@ERROR not being equal to zero, the transaction, Tran1, is rolled back. This effectively reverses any change(s) made to the database. If no error occurred, a SQL string is built that will delete the same set of categories from the categories table using the same technique as the previous delete statement, as follows:

```
SELECT @SQLString = 'DELETE FROM Categories WHERE Name IN (' +
@CatList + ')'
    EXEC (@SQLString)
```

Once again, any error information is captured, and in the event an error occurred, the transaction is rolled back, as shown in Listing 20-10.

Listing 20-10: Rolling back a transaction

```
--check @@ERROR for errors
SELECT  @RetVal = @@ERROR

--check for errors
IF (@retval <> 0)
```

```
BEGIN
    --in case of errors, rollback current transaction
    ROLLBACK TRAN Tran1

    --if RetVal is 0, default to -1
    IF @RetVal = 0
        SELECT @RetVal = -1

    --branch to error message handler
        GOTO ErrorMessage
END
```

Since both delete statements are encapsulated in the same transaction, if the first delete was successful and the second delete failed, both delete statements would be reversed when the transaction is rolled back. This provides the level of data consistency required to keep both tables and any relationships between the two tables in sync.

If during the process of executing both delete statements no errors were generated, the transaction is committed. This essentially tells SQL Server to lock and save any changes made during the transaction.

```
BEGIN
    --in case of no errors, commit the current transaction
    COMMIT TRAN Tran1

    --branch to the exit point
    GOTO ExitSP
END
```

Another approach to providing this type of data consistency would be to separate the two delete statements into two stored procedures and wrap the separate execute statements in a transaction. This could easily be done in the VB COM component, however, when data access statements are closely related, as in this example. The general approach is to use a transaction-oriented stored procedure to ensure data consistency.

Adding and Updating Products

At this point, the code differences being used in each ASP have been negligible. Essentially, each page follows the same structure:

1. User-entered form values or query strings, if any exist, are stored in local variables.

2. An instance of the DNASample VB COM component is created.

3. The appropriate method, provided by DNASample, is used to make the change or request the data.

4. References to the DNASample object are released.

5. The variant returned from the method call is typed to determine if the method call was successful or not.

6. If not successful, a message is displayed to the user.

7. Otherwise, the two-dimensional array returned from the method call is traversed and the data is displayed to the user.

So, it shouldn't be too big of a surprise to find out that the ASP pages used to create a new product and update or delete an existing product don't have any new techniques to cover. Therefore, for the sake of brevity, and your sanity, we'll skip coverage of these last two pages of our sample application.

Summary

Chapter 15 provided a good example of how to create a traditional two-tier application using many of the techniques introduced earlier. This chapter focused on taking that same application and building it using an n-tier, or Windows DNA, approach.

The first step is isolating the data access code in stored procedures supported by the SQL Server database. Where needed, transactions were employed to provide assurances that data consistency would remain in the event of one or more failures. Next, the Business Services tier is expanded to include a Visual Basic COM component to actually call the appropriate stored procedure and perform the task requested. In addition, the VB code is used to hide the complexities of ADO-specific code by returning either a string with error information or a two-dimensional array containing the data requested.

The net effect of this approach simplifies the ASP code originally used in the Chapter 15 example . . . almost to the point of being monotonous. However, this does reinforce the idea that building Windows DNA applications is not necessarily more complicated than building two-tier applications. In fact, as was the case in this example, the ASP code is simplified and isolated from other aspects, or tiers, of the application.

This process of isolation effectively decouples the User Services tier from the code residing in the other tiers so that any changes made to the presentation of the data don't have the potential to introduce errors in other aspects of the application. In addition, now that the database and access techniques are isolated from the User Services code, the database can undergo any number of changes without affecting the ASP code.

Finally, by moving the data access code into a VB-compiled component, application performance is improved. This, along with the ASP code only creating references to a `DNASample` component and releasing these references as soon as possible, provides a more scalable architecture that will support many more concurrent users than the previous two-tier architecture outlined in Chapter 15.

Appendix A

What's On the CD-ROM

THIS BOOK'S **CD-ROM** includes the source code for all the complete examples in this book with solutions as well as some third-party products. The following sections explain how to access the solutions and third-party products and describe them.

Accessing the Solutions and Third-Party Products

The index.html file serves as the entry point to the solutions and any third-party demonstration products on the CD-ROM. To access the solutions and the products, use your favorite Web browser to open the index.html file.

To run the solutions, you must create a virtual root on your web server to host the solutions. For instructions on how to do this, refer to the introductory chapters in this book. Some of the more complex examples require their own virtual root and that you set up a database or some other component to properly run the Web application. For information on a specific configuration, refer to the appropriate chapter in this book.

For information on how to install, configure, and run the third-party products, refer to the vendor's documentation. If no documentation is included in the CD-ROM, visit the vendor's Web site for more information.

Source Code

Included in the CD-ROM is the source code to all complete examples presented in the book. You can use these samples as the basis for your own code or run them from your Web server to see the examples in action. The source files are organized by chapter. Solutions that require multiple files are stored in their own subdirectory, preserving any structure necessary for the application to find its resources.

Third-Party Products

Licensing information for the third-party products is as stated on the respective vendors' licensing agreements. We have recommended that these products be included on the CD-ROM to help you evaluate them. Some of these products require that you purchase a license to enable their full capabilities. Inclusion of the product does not imply that you have a license for these products.

Lastly, the software business moves more quickly than the publishing business. By the time you read this book, it is likely that new versions of these products will be available for download or purchase. Please visit each product's vendor's Web site prior to spending considerable time evaluating any of the "frozen" versions included on the accompanying CD-ROM.

 Third-party products are copyrighted/trademarked by their respective companies. Where a trademark symbol was displayed on a product name, we have diligently included it here too.

SA-FileUp(tm), evaluation version

SA-FileUp allows you to upload files from any browser to a Microsoft Internet Information Server. The software is fully scriptable via Active Server Pages. The software is available from Software Artisans. The Web address for this product is `http://www.softwareartisans.com/softartisans/saf.html`.

Caprock Dictionary

Caprock Dictionary provides an alternative to the built-in ASP Dictionary object that provides better performance when used from the Application or Session object. The built-in ASP Dictionary object is marked STA (single-threaded apartment) and cannot efficiently be stored in the Application or Session. Caprock Dictionary is available from Caprock Consulting. It can be found at `http://www.caprockconsulting.com/comsoftware.asp`.

ASP-db Pro, evaluation version

ASP-db Pro is a control that allows you to easily use a few lines of code. It provides a full-featured browsing interface to most popular databases. Major vendor databases are supported. ASP-db Pro is available at `ASP-db` at `http://www.aspdb.com/demo.asp`.

BrowserHawk(tm) 2000 Enterpise Edition

BrowserHawk 2000 Enterprise Edition (evaluation copy) accurately recognizes Web browses that visit your Web site and their capabilities. With BrowserHawk, you can easily create dynamic Web sites, which properly support the myriad of browsers in use. BrowserHack is available from cyScape at `http://www.cyscape.com/products/bhawk/intro.asp`.

Appendix B

ASP Primary Objects Reference

THIS REFERENCE PROVIDES A brief overview of the major ASP built-in objects: Application, Request, Response, Server, and Session. For additional detail and examples, please refer to the appropriate chapters where these objects are discussed.

Application Object Collections

This section provides the contents, methods, and events for the Application object.

Contents

The `Contents` collection stores all items added to the Application that have not been added using the `<OBJECT>` tag. The Application contents collection stores values that are accessible by all active sessions in the application. You can store all primitive types in the collection. Typically, unless an object has been designed and implemented in a way that it can be accessed from multiple threads, you cannot store it in the collection. You cannot store JavaScript arrays in the collection (for a workaround, see Chapter 9, "A Prototypical Application").

Values can be stored by name (key) or by index, as follows:

```
Application.Contents("aKey") = "hello";
Application.Contents(2) = "first";
```

To read a value, do this:

```
var str = Application.Contents("aKey");
var another = Application.Contents(2);
```

To find out how many items are stored in the collection, access the collection's Count property, like this:

```
var count = Application.Contents.Count;
```

The names of keys stored in the collection can be retrieved by finding out the number of elements in the Application, and then accessing the collection's Key property, as follows:

```
var keyCount = Application.Contents.Count;
for(int j=1; j <= keyCount; j++)
{
  Response.Write(Application.Contents.Key(j));
}
```

StaticObjects

The StaticObjects collection contains a reference to all objects created with the <OBJECT> tag using an Application scope. As with the Contents collection, the StaticObjects collection provides Item, Key, and Count properties that you can use to access these objects (see the previous "Contents" section).

Application object methods

Following is a list of methods for the Application object methods:

- ◆ Contents.Remove(key | index) – **Removes the specified item from the Application's contents collection. The item can be specified by name (String parameter) or by index (integer), as follows:**

  ```
  Application.Contents.Remove("aKey");
  ```

- ◆ Contents.RemoveAll() – **Removes all items stored in the Application's content collection, as follows:**

  ```
  Application.Contents.RemoveAll();
  ```

- ◆ Lock() – **Obtains an exclusive right on the Application object. Other scripts must wait until the lock is released or the script times out or finishes executing. While inside of the lock, the script may modify the Application object, as follows:**

  ```
  Application.Lock();
  ```

- ◆ Unlock() – **Releases a lock on the Application obtained through the Lock() method. Scripts should call Unlock as soon as they are done modifying the Application object, as follows:**

  ```
  Application.Unlock();
  ```

Application object events

Following is a list of events for the Application object:

♦ `Application_OnStart` – The `Application_OnStart` event occurs when the first Session is about to be created in an Application. The event is called prior to a Session being created. You can use this event to initialize your application before a visitor accesses it. The `Application_OnStart` event must be defined in the global.asa file for the application. You may only access the Application and Server objects from within your event handler.

♦ `Application_OnEnd` – The `Application_OnEnd` event occurs after the last Session on the application is destroyed. You can use this event to save state from your application before the server re-claims its resources. The `Application_OnEnd` event must be defined in the global.asa file for the application. You may only access the Application and Server objects from within your event handler.

Request Object Collections

This section provides reference information for the Request object collections.

ClientCertificate

The `ClientCertificate` collection provides information about the digital certificate used by the visitor for authentication purposes (the Web server must be configured to request this information). Available keys for the object are the following:

♦ Certificate – the entire certificate in binary format

♦ Flags – provides masks that you can use to test the certificate. To use the flags, you must include the files cerjavas.inc (JavaScript) or cervbs.inc (VBScript). Available flags are:

■ `ceCertPreset` (client certificate is present)

■ `ceUnrecognizedIssuer` (the issuer of the certificate is not recognized/valid)

♦ Issuer – returns the distinguished name for the issuer. To obtain specific fields instead of the entire string, append the appropriate subfield from the following:

■ `C` – country

■ `CN` – Common name

- GN – Given Name
- I – Initials
- L – Locality
- O – Organization name
- OU – Organizational unit
- S – State or province
- T – Title

To access the issuer common name, specify IssuerCN as a key.

◆ SerialNumber – returns the certificate serial number as a series of hexadecimal bytes.

◆ Subject – Returns the distinguished name for the owner of the certificate. To obtain specific fields instead of the entire string, append the appropriate subfield (see Issuer, previously).

◆ ValidFrom – Returns the date when the certificate becomes valid.

◆ ValidUntil – Returns the date the certificate expires.

Cookies(name)(key)

Allows you to read cookie values sent with the HTTP request. Cookie values may be nested; the HasKeys property is set to true if the cookie itself contains embedded properties.

```
var color = Request.Cookies("favoriteColor");
if(Request.Cookies.HasKeys == true)
{
    lastName = Request.Cookies("name")("lastname");
}
```

Form(elementName)[(index) | .Count]

Allows you to read values submitted via a form using the POST method. The ElementName property is the name of the form field, index is an optional parameter that allows you to access one of multiple values for the same name elements, or multiple value elements. Index count starts at 1. Count is the number of elements available for a particular elementName. If you do not use the index property to retrieve a particular element from the list, the entire list is returned as a comma delimited string.

QueryString(elementName)[(index) | .Count]

The QueryString collection is similar to the Form collection, except that values are retrieved from the query string on the request URL. Forms that are posted using the GET method must use this collection to read their values.

ServerVariables(variableName)

The ServerVariables collection is used to retrieve the HTTP server variables (see Chapter 8, The Server Object").

TotalBytes: Request object property

The TotalBytes property specifies the total number of bytes sent to the server in the body of the HTTP request. Typically, this information is used in conjunction with the BinaryRead() method.

BinaryRead(byteCount): Request object method

The BinaryRead method retrieves data sent to the server in the body of the HTTP request. This method returns a SafeArray. A SafeArray is an array that provides information about the number of dimensions and the number of elements contained in the array. Attempting to retrieve form data using the Form collection after calling this method results in an error. Calling this method after retrieving form data using the Form collection also results in an error. The SafeArray objects can be accessed using Microsoft's VBArray object.

Response Object Collections

This section provides reference information for the Response object collections.

Cookies(cookieName)[(keyName)|.attribute]

The Cookies collection allows you to set cookie values. Cookies are stored under the cookieName that you provide. In addition, a cookie may have additional values that are accessible via a keyName. In addition to cookie values that you need to store for your application, cookies have a set of properties that control the cookie visibility, expiration, or, if it should only be provided while under a secured connection, and most importantly, its expiration date. The possible attributes are as follows:

◆ Domain – Specifies the domain where cookies should be sent.

◆ Expires – Specifies the expiration date for the cookie. If not set, the cookie expires when the session ends or the user closes the browser window.

◆ HasKeys – Read-only property. Set to true if the cookie has subkeys (as in the case of the "name" cookie previously).

◆ Path – Specifies a path within the URL where the cookie should be sent. The default path is "/" or all pages under the server. If your cookies are not used by other applications within your site, limit the cookie by specifying a Path.

◆ Secure – Specifies that the cookie should be sent only when connection between the server and the browser is secure (SSL).

```
Response.Cookies("name")("firstName") = "Alberto";
Response.Cookies("name")("lastName") = "Ricart";

Response.Cookies("favoriteColor") = "blue";
Response.Cookies("favoriteColor").Expires = "January 1, 2001";
Response.Cookies("favoriteColor").Path = "/registrationApp/";
Response.Cookies("favoriteColor").Secure = true;
```

Response object properties

◆ Buffer – Specifies if page output is buffered. By default this property is set to true.

◆ CacheControl – Enables ASP-generated content to be cachable by a proxy server. By default this is set to false.

◆ Charset – Specifies the character set used on the content-type header.

◆ ContentType – Sets the content type of the response, typically this is determined by the file type returned by the Web server. If outputting binary data from an ASP script, this property should be set to indicate the data type being returned.

◆ Expires – Specifies how many minutes a browser should cache this information without reloading it from the server.

◆ ExpiresAbsolute – Specifies the date and time that a cached page should expire. Requests made after this date and time should be obtained by making a new request from the server.

◆ IsClientConnected – Set to true if the browser is still connected to the server, or false otherwise.

```
if(Response.IsClientConnected == false)
Response.End();
```

◆ `PICS(picsLabel)` – Sets the PICS (Platform for Internet Content Selection) label. The PICS label aids the rating of Web content. PICS is typically used to limit the type of content available to younger surfers.

 While `PICS(picsLabel)` is categorized as a property, it is really a method.

◆ `Status` – Sets the status line returned by the server when a request is fulfilled. Status values are defined by the HTTP specification. A status line is composed of a 3 digit status code and an explanation.

```
Response.Status = "200 OK";
```

Response object methods

The following is a list of Response Object methods:

◆ `AddHeader(headerName, value)` – Adds the specified by headerName and value specified by value to the HTTP response header. This method is useful to all HTTP header.

◆ `AppendToLog(message)` – Appends a message to the Web server's log entry of the current request.

◆ `BinaryWrite(binaryData)` – Returns `binaryData` without any character conversion. This method is useful if your application is reading binary data, like an image, from a database.

◆ `Clear()` – Clears the ASP buffer. This is useful when an error is detected, and your script must discard any generated output. For this method to work, the `Response.Buffer` property must be `true` (the default).

◆ `End()` – Stops processing of the current script and returns any HTML generated by the page.

◆ `Flush()` – Sends the contents of the ASP buffer to the browser.

◆ `Redirect(URL)` – Sets the Status line returned by the server to "302 Object Moved" and sets the Location header to point to URL. On receiving this status and header modern browsers will request the URL provided in the Location header.

◆ `Writes(String)` – Outputs `String` to the HTTP output. The output may be buffered as per `Response.Buffer`.

Server Object Properties

This section provides reference information for the properties of the Server object:

- ◆ `ScriptTimeout` – Specifies the maximum amount of time in seconds that a script can run before the server terminates it.

Server object methods

The following is a list of Server Object methods:

- ◆ `CreateObject(id)` – Creates an instance of a server component. The `id` for the component is provided by a string that has the following format: [Vendor.]Component[.Version]. Both the Vendor and Version of the component are optional.

  By default objects created using this method have a page scope. This means that whenever the current page finishes executing the object is destroyed unless you have assigned it to an Application or Session property.

- ◆ `Execute(URL)` – The `Execute` method calls an ASP page as if were part of the current script. The executed page has access to the Request object provided to the original page. The URL provided for the executed page must be in the same application as the original request.

- ◆ `GetLastError()` – Returns an ASPError object descrigbing the current error condition. This method is available before any content is returned to the client.

- ◆ `HTMLEncode(String)` – Replaces illegal characters in the provided String by their HTML counterparts and returns a new String with the properly converted values:

  ```
  var myString = "The <P> tag is used to define new
  paragraphs.";
  myString = Server.HTMLEncode(myString);
  myString == "The &lt;P&gt; tag is ued to define new
  paragraphs."
  ```

- ◆ `MapPath(URL)` – Provides the physical path to the provided URL. This method doesn't check to see if the provided URL is a valid file or path in the system.

- ◆ `Transfer(URL)` – Transfers execution from one page to another. The Session and Application properties are retained. This method is similar to `execute`, except that the call never returns control to the originally requested URL.

- URLEncode(String) – Converts characters illegal in a URL to their encoded counterparts. This method is useful if you are generating links that have a query string:

```
var favoriteGame = "Half Life";
favoriteGame = Server.URLEncode(favoriteGame);
favoriteGame == "Half+Life";
```

Session Object Collections

This section provides the contents and lists of properties, methods, and events for the Session object.

Contents

The Contents collection stores all items added to the sessions that have not been added using the <OBJECT> tag. The Session contents collection follows the visitor from page to page providing persistence to the visitor's session. You can store all primitive types in the collection. Typically, unless an object has been designed and implemented in a way that it can be accessed from multiple threads, you cannot store it in the collection. You cannot store JavaScript arrays in the collection (for a workaround, see Chapter 9, "A Prototypical Application").

Values can be stored by name (key) or by index, as follows:

```
Session.Contents("aKey") = "hello";
Session.Contents(2) = "first";
```

To read a value, do this:

```
var str = Session.Contents("aKey");
var another = Session.Contents(2);
```

To find out how many items are stored in the collection access the collection's Count property, like this:

```
var count = Session.Contents.Count;
```

The names of keys stored in the collection can be retrieved by finding out the number of elements in the Session, and then accessing the collection's Key property, as follows:

```
var keyCount = Session.Contents.Count;
for(int j=1; j <= keyCount; j++)
```

```
{
   Response.Write(Session.Contents.Key(j));
}
```

StaticObjects

The `StaticObjects` collection contains a reference to all objects created with the `<OBJECT>` tag using a Session scope. As with the Contents collection, the `StaticObjects` collection provides `Item`, `Key`, and `Count` properties that you can use to access the these objects (see the previous "Contents" section).

Session object properties

Following is a list of Session object properties.

- ◆ `CodePage` – This property can be read or set to the character set that will be used to display content generated by your scripts. Different languages and locales use different code page values. Code page 1252 is used for American English and most European languages. Code page 932 is used for Japanese Kanji.

- ◆ `LCID` – Specifies the location identifier, which is a standard international abbreviation that uniquely identifies a locale. This information is used to format currency, dates, and other types of data in their appropriate formats.

- ◆ `SessionID` – The `SessionID` is the numeric identifier assigned by the server to a session when the session was created. The `SessionID` value should not be used as a unique identifier as the server may generate duplicate IDs when it is restarted. To read the current `SessionID`:

  ```
  var id = Session.SessionID;
  ```

- ◆ `Timeout` – Specifies the number of minutes of inactivity before a Session is ended. The default value is 10 minutes. If a visitor starts a session and does not request pages from the application before the timeout is exceeded, the Session is discarded. To change the `Timeout`, do this:

  ```
  Session.Timeout = 1;
  ```

  To read the current `Timeout`, do this:

  ```
  var timeout = Session.Timeout;
  ```

Session object methods

Following is a list of Session object methods:

- `Abandon()` – Destroys the session releasing all referenced resources. The Session is destroyed when the current page has finished processing. This method is called automatically when the Session times out (`Session.Timeout`).

- `Contents.Remove(key | index)` – Removes the specified item from the Session's contents collection. The item can be specified by name (String parameter) or by `index` (integer).

- `Contents.RemoveAll()` – Removes all items stored in the Session's content collection.

Session object events

Following is a lsit of Session Object events:

- `Session_OnStart` – The `Session_OnStart` event occurs when the server creates a new Session. The server executes this event prior to executing any pages in the application, so it can be used for initialization purposes. The `Session_OnStart` event must be defined in the global.asa file for the application. You may access any ASP objects from within this script.

- `Session_OnEnd` – The `Session_OnEnd` event occurs when a script calls `Abandon()` or when the Session times out. You can use this event to save the user's state or update some application level property. The `Session_OnEnd` event must be defined in the global.asa file for the application. You may access any ASP objects from within this script, however, not all methods are available. When the `Session_OnEnd` handler runs, the server is not executing any application page, so methods like `MapPath` generate an error when called from the handler.

Appendix C

JavaScript Syntax

JAVASCRIPT IS EXECUTED FROM top to bottom. Unlike VBScript, JavaScript is case-sensitive. Your code will have to use uppercase and lowercase values consistently. JavaScript provides syntax for:

- Adding comments

- Performing operations on data

- Looping

- Branching

- Defining and calling functions

- Interacting with objects

 Each statement in JavaScript ends with a semicolon. Note the use of semicolons in the examples in this appendix.

Comments

Comments allow you to write notes without interfering with the code's functionality. JavaScript provides two types of comments. A // can be used to indicate a comment till the end of the line. The /* and */ can be used to surround a comment of any size. For example, the following code contains two comments:

```
var x = 8;
// This line is a comment
/*
This is a comment.
I love comments.
*/
```

The one restriction on comments is that you don't place a comment inside another comment.

JavaScript Data

JavaScript data is stored in variables. Variables are named holders that represent a value. A variable can store strings, Booleans, numbers, or objects. A variable's type is determined by its contents, so it will change type as necessary to fit what you put into it. Each variable in a script is "scoped" to the function or script it is defined in.

Variables are created with the keyword `var`. When you create a new variable, it will have the value null or undefined. You can also assign a value to a variable at declaration, as in:

```
var x= 3;
```

Variable names must begin with a letter or underscore (_). Subsequent characters may include digits (0-9). So both `myString1` and `_myFrame` are valid variable names, but `12foo` is not.

JavaScript Functions

A function in JavaScript is a collection of code. A function's statements are executed when it is invoked, not when it is defined. So you can define functions and call them several times to execute the same code several times. In an ASP, JavaScript can be used to define new functions or you can use existing functions. Using the `#include` directive, you can define functions in one file and use them in another.

New functions are defined using the `keyword` function. Each function must have a unique name in the document. Function names must begin with a letter or underscore (_). Subsequent characters may include digits (0-9). A function can accept data, called arguments or parameters. Functions can return a value. A function definition consists of the following:

- The function keyword

- The name of the function

- A set of parentheses ( ) with optional arguments separated by commas

- A set of curly braces { } containing the statements associated with the function

- An optional return value

Essentially, function definitions look like this:

```
function aFunction( arg1, arg2, ... )
{
    ...
}
```

For example, the following code contains two function definitions; both take arguments, but only one returns a value.

```
function greeting(str)
{
Response.Write(" Hello ", str);
}
function doubleIt(x)
{
return (2 * x);
}
```

Operators

JavaScript operators are used in calculations like 1+2. Each operator is represented by a one- or two-character symbol. When an operator is encountered, it is executed using the appropriate arguments, called *operands*. Perhaps the most important operator is the assignment operator. Assignment sets a variable's value.

```
var x = 4, y = 0;
y = x;
//y= 4
```

JavaScript provides the arithmetic operators listed in Table C-1.

TABLE C-1 ARITHMETIC OPERATORS

Symbol	Operation	Description
+	Addition	Add two numbers.
-	Subtraction	Subtract two numbers.
*	Multiplication	Multiply two numbers.
/	Division	Divide two numbers.
%	Modulo	Perform an integer division on two numbers and return the remainder.
++	Increment	Add one to a number.
--	Decrement	Subtract one from a number.

Many of the arithmetic operators have shortcut equivalents, as listed in Table C-2.

TABLE C-2 SHORTCUT OPERATORS

Expression	Shortcut
x = x + y	x += y
x = x - y	x -= y
x = x * y	x *= y
x = x / y	x /= y
x = x % y	x %= y

Strings can be appended with + or +=. Numeric values are automatically converted to strings when necessary. For example, the following:

```
var string = "& copy;" + 1997 + " Paradigm Research, Inc."
```

results in this:

```
"& copy; 1997 Paradigm Research, Inc."
```

Operators are provided for comparing two values, as listed in Table C-3.

TABLE C-3 COMPARISON OPERATORS

Symbol	Operator
==	Equal
!=	Not equal
<	Greater than
>	Less than
>=	Greater than or equal to
<=	Less than or equal to

Comparison operators return a Boolean value, either true or false. (See Table C-4.) These operators can be combined using logical operators to form other Boolean values. A ! can be used as an operator to invert the value of a Boolean.

TABLE C-4 LOGICAL OPERATORS

Symbol	Operator	To evaluate to true
&&	And	Both operands must be true.
||	Or	One operand must be true.
!	Not	Negates a Boolean value.

Conditional Statements

JavaScript provides several constructs for conditionally executing code. The if statement is used to conditionally execute code based on a Boolean value. An optional else statement can be used to provide an alternative if the Boolean value is not true. For example:

```
if(name == "alberto")
{
    Response.Write("Hello Al");
}
else
{
    Response.Write("Hello "+name);
}
```

The else is optional. You can also chain if-else statements, as in:

```
if(name == "alberto")
{
    Response.Write("Hello Al");
}
else if(name == "stephen")
{
    Response.Write("Hello Steve");
}
```

```
else
{
    Response.Write("Hello "+name);
}
```

Again, the final `else` is optional.

A conditional expression is used to perform an inline `if-else`. The conditional expression uses ? and : for syntax:

```
(condition) ? value for true : value for false
```

The condition is tested. If it is true, the value for true is inserted in place of the entire statement. If the condition is false, the value for false is used. For example:

```
Response.Write ( name == "me" ? "hello!" : "Bye");
```

If the name variable is "me," then this writes "hello!"; otherwise, it writes "Bye."

The switch allows you to implement nested `if-else` logic with a simpler syntax. Code between a case and break statements is executed if the value matches the contents of the switch expression. If no match is found, code after the default is executed. For example:

```
switch(exp)
{
case "Yes":
    ...
break;
case "No":
    ...
break;
default:
    ...
}
```

The break in this example is very important. The script will jump to the correct case and execute until a break or the end of the switch. So if there is no break, the first case will execute the entire switch.

Looping Statements

JavaScript supports the following four looping statements:

- ◆ for

- ◆ while

- ◆ do...while

- ◆ for...in (See the section below entitled "JavaScript Objects.")

A for loop repeats until a specified condition evaluates to false. The for loops have three control statements. An initializer is executed once, when the loop is encountered. An iterator is executed each time the loop completes. A test is used before the loop code is executed.

```
for(initializer;test;iterator)
{
    . . .
}
```

For example, to loop over a counter variable that goes from 0 to 9, use:

```
for(i=0;i<10;i++)
{
    . . .
}
```

A while loop repeats as long as the specified condition evaluates to true. If the condition is false when the loop is first encountered, the code inside the loop is never executed.

```
while(condition)
{
    . . .
}
```

A do...while loop executes the body of the loop at least once and repeats as long as the specified condition evaluates to true.

```
do
{
    . . .
}
while (condition)
```

The break statement can be used inside a loop. It terminates the current loop and continues execution on the statement following the terminated loop. The continue statement stops execution of the looping block and restarts execution at the top of the looping block.

JavaScript Objects

Objects allow you to package multiple properties together. Properties are either variables or functions. Properties by themselves can be objects. Functions associated with objects are called methods. Methods and properties associated with an object need to be referred to by the object's name. JavaScript provides both built-in and dynamic objects. The built-in objects for JavaScripted ASPs are the same as those for VBScript.

The Array object provides many useful array manipulation methods. The Date object provides methods for date and time manipulation. String objects contain text manipulation and formatting methods. The Math object contains number manipulation methods.

Some objects need to be created before they are used. To create a dynamic object you need to specify the keyword new and the name of the constructor method:

```
    . . .
var today = new Date();
today.getMonth();
    . . .
```

In this case, the constructor for the Date object returns a new Date object initialized to today's date.

Properties are accessed by name using a dot (.). Properties can also be accessed using [ ] and an index or the property. For example:

```
object.bgColor = "red";
object[bgColor]=" red";
object[0]= "Alberto";
```

Methods are accessed by name using ( ), and may have optional arguments. For example:

```
Response.Write("something");
```

If you access a property in an object, and the property doesn't exist, it will be added to the object.

A for...in statement iterates through all properties of an object. In the following example, the variable p is set to the name of each property in the document object:

```
for(p in document)
{
document.write(p, ": ", document[p], "<BR>");
}
```

The delete operator deletes an object's property or an element at a specific index in an array.

```
var obj = new Object();
obj.name = "test";
document.write(obj.name, "<BR><BR>"); // test
delete obj.name;
document.write(obj.name, "<BR><BR>"); // undefined
```

The objects listed in the remainder of this section are built into JavaScript and can be created at any time.

Array

Array objects are used to store a collection of values. Create arrays using:

```
new Array()
new Array(size)
new Array(element0, element1, ..., elementn)
```

Then access elements using the [ ] notation. For example:

```
var myArray = new Array();

for (i = 0; i < 10; i++)
{
myArray[i] = i;
}

var x = myArray[4];
```

Notice that spaces are added to the array as needed to fit new elements. Properties and methods for this object are listed in Tables C-5 and C-6, respectively.

TABLE **C-5 ARRAY OBJECT PROPERTIES**

Property	Description
Constructor	Specifies the function that creates an object's prototype.
Index	For an array created by a regular expression match, the zero-based index of the match in the string.

Continued

TABLE C-5 ARRAY OBJECT PROPERTIES *(Continued)*

Property	Description
Input	For an array created by a regular expression match, reflects the original string against which the regular expression was matched.
Length	Reflects the number of elements in an array.
Prototype	Allows the addition of properties to all objects.

TABLE C-6 ARRAY OBJECT METHODS

Method	Description
concat(array1, ... ,arrayN)	Joins two arrays and returns a new array.
join (separator)	Joins all elements of an array into a string.
pop()	Removes the last element from an array and returns that element.
push(element1, .. elementN)	Adds one or more elements to the end of an array and returns the new length of the array.
reverse()	Transposes the elements of an array: the first array element becomes the last and the last becomes the first.
shift()	Removes the first element from an array and returns that element.
slice(begin [,end])	Extracts a section of an array and returns a new array. If no end is provided, all elements until the end of the array are returned.
sort(compare Function)	Sorts the elements of an array. If no sort function is provided, the elements are sorted alphabetically.
toString()	Returns a string representing the array and its elements.
unshift (element1, .. elementN)	Adds one or more elements to the front of an array and returns the newlength of the array.

Date

Date objects are used to represent a time and date. Dates can be created in three ways:

```
var newDateObj = new Date()
var newDateObj = new Date(dateVal)
var newDateObj = new Date(year, month, date
                [, hours[, minutes[, seconds[,ms]]]])
```

By default a date will represent the date and time it is created. Properties and methods for the Date object are listed in Tables C-7 and C-8, respectively.

TABLE C-7 DATE OBJECT PROPERTIES

Property	Description
Constructor	Specifies the function that creates an object's prototype.
Prototype	Allows the addition of properties to a Date object.

TABLE C-8 DATE OBJECT METHODS

Method	Description
getDate()	Returns the day of the month.
getDay()	Returns the day of the week.
getFullYear()	Returns the year for the specified date.
getHours()	Returns the hours for the specified date.
getMilliseconds()	Returns the milliseconds in the specified date.
getMinutes()	Returns the minutes in the specified date.
getMonth()	Returns the month in the specified date.
GetSeconds()	Returns the seconds in the specified date.

Continued

TABLE C-8 DATE OBJECT METHODS *(Continued)*

Method	Description
getTime()	Returns the numeric value corresponding to the time for the specified date.
getTimezoneOffset()	Returns the timezone offset in minutes for the current locale.
getUTCDate()	Returns the day (date) of the month in the specified date according to universal time.
getUTCDay()	Returns the day of the week in the specified date according to universal time.
getUTCFullYear()	Returns the year in the specified date according to universal time.
getUTCHours()	Returns the hours in the specified date according to universal time.
getUTCMilliseconds()	Returns the milliseconds in the specified date according to universal time.
getUTCMinutes()	Returns the minutes in the specified date according to universal time.
getUTCMonth()	Returns the month in the specified date according to universal time.
getUTCSeconds()	Returns the seconds in the specified date according to universal time.
getYear()	Returns the year in the specified date according to local time.
parse(string)	Returns the number of milliseconds in a date string since January 1, 1970, 00:00:00, local time.
setDate(value)	Sets the day of the month for a specified date.
setFullYear(value)	Sets the full year for a specified date.
setHours(value)	Sets the hours for a specified date.
setMilliseconds(value)	Sets the milliseconds for a specified date.
setMinutes(value)	Sets the minutes for a specified date.
setMonth(value)	Sets the month for a specified date.

Method	Description
setSeconds(value)	Sets the seconds for a specified date.
setTime(value)	Sets the value of a Date object.
setUTCDate(value)	Sets the day of the month for a specified date according to universal time.
setUTCFullYear(value)	Sets the full year for a specified date according to universal time.
setUTCHours(value)	Sets the hour for a specified date according to universal time.
setUTCMilliseconds (value)	Sets the milliseconds for a specified date according to universal time.
setUTCMinutes(value)	Sets the minutes for a specified date according to universal time.
setUTCMonth(value)	Sets the month for a specified date according to universal time.
setUTCSeconds(value)	Sets the seconds for a specified date according to universal time.
setYear(value)	Sets the year for a specified date.
toGMTString(value)	Converts a date to a string, using the Internet GMT conventions.
toLocaleString(value)	Converts a date to a string, using the current locale's conventions.
toString(value)	Returns a string representing the specified Date object.
toUTCString(value)	Converts a date to a string, using the universal time convention.
UTC(value)	Returns the number of milliseconds in a Date object since January 1, 1970, 00:00:00, universal time.

Error

The object passed to a catch block to represent an exception is of type Error. An Error object has two properties listed in Table C-9.

TABLE C-9 ERROR OBJECT PROPERTIES

Property	Description
description	A string description of the error.
number	The error code for the problem.

Math

The Math object is created automatically by the JavaScript engine and is used to perform mathematical operations. Its properties and methods are listed in Tables C-10 and C-11, respectively.

TABLE C-10 MATH OBJECT PROPERTIES

Property	Description
E	Euler's constant and the base of natural logarithms, approximately 2.718.
LN10	Natural logarithm of 10, approximately 2.302.
LN2	Natural logarithm of 2, approximately 0.693.
LOG10E	Base 10 logarithm of E, approximately 0.434.
LOG2E	Base 2 logarithm of E, approximately 1.442.
PI	Ratio of the circumference of a circle to its diameter, approximately 3.14159.
SQRT1_2	Square root of 1/2; equivalently, 1 over the square root of 2, approximately 0.707.
SQRT2	Square root of 2, approximately 1.414.

TABLE C-11 MATH OBJECT METHODS

Method	Description
abs(number)	Returns the absolute value of a number.
acos(number)	Returns the arccosine (in radians) of a number.

Method	Description
asin(number)	Returns the arcsine (in radians) of a number.
atan(number)	Returns the arctangent (in radians) of a number.
atan2(number)	Returns the arctangent of the quotient of its arguments.
ceil(number)	Returns the smallest integer greater than or equal to a number.
cos(number)	Returns the cosine of a number.
exp(number)	Returns Enumber, where number is the argument, and E is Euler's constant, the base of the natural logarithms.
floor(number)	Returns the largest integer less than or equal to a number.
log(number)	Returns the natural logarithm (base E) of a number.
max(number1,number2)	Returns the greater of two numbers.
min(number1,number2)	Returns the lesser of two numbers.
pow(base,exponent)	Returns base to the exponent power.
random()	Returns a pseudo-random number between 0 and 1.
round(number)	Returns the value of a number rounded to the nearest integer.
sin(number)	Returns the sine of a number.
sqrt(number)	Returns the square root of a number.
tan(number)	Returns the tangent of a number.

String

Strings in JavaScript are stored in String objects. Each String object has a number of methods that can be used to access its data. One feature of a String object is that it is read-only. So methods that appear to change the data actually return new strings. The String object's properties and methods are listed in Tables C-12 and C-13, respectively.

TABLE C-12 STRING OBJECT PROPERTIES

Property	Description
constructor	Specifies the function that creates an object's prototype.
length	Reflects the length of the string.
prototype	Allows the addition of properties to a String object.

TABLE C-13 STRING OBJECT METHODS

Method	Description
charAt(index)	Returns the character at the specified index.
charCodeAt(index)	Returns a number indicating the Unicode value of the character at the given index.
concat(str1,str2)	Combines the text of two strings and returns a new string.
fromCharCode(code1, ... , codeN)	Returns a string created by using the specified sequence of Unicode values.
indexOf(str, startindex)	Returns the index within the calling String object of the first occurrence of the specified value, or -1 if not found.
lastIndexOf(str, startindex)	Returns the index within the calling String object of the last occurrence of the specified value, or -1 if not found.
match(regEx)	Used to match a regular expression against a string.
replace(regEx, replacement)	Used to find a match between a regular expression and a string, and to replace the matched substring with a new substring.
search(regEx)	Executes the search for a match between a regular expression and a specified string.
slice(start [,end])	Extracts a section of a string and returns a new string. The end is optional, as the end of the string will be used as a default.

Method	Description
split(str)	Splits a String object into an array of strings by separating the string into substrings.
substr(start [,length])	Returns the characters in a string beginning at the specified location through the specified number of characters. If no length is provided, the end of the string is used.
substring(start,end)	Returns the characters in a string between two indexes into the string, not included the character at index end.
toLowerCase()	Returns the calling string value converted to lowercase.
toString()	Returns a string representing the specified object.
toUpperCase()	Returns the calling string value converted to uppercase.

Note that many of these methods return a new string; they do not convert the existing string. So you use the following:

```
var str1,str2;
str1 = "lower";
str2 = str1.toUpperCase();
```

Or to change str1, use the following:

```
str1 = str1.toUpperCase();
```

VBArray

The VBArray object is used to access elements in a VBScript array. This object is created from the VBArray using the following:

```
var vbA = new VBArray(existingVBScriptArray);
```

Its methods are listed in Table C-14.

TABLE C-14 VBARRAY OBJECT METHODS

Method	Description
dimensions()	Returns the number of dimensions in the array.
getItem(dimension1[, dimension2, ...], dimension)	Returns an item at the specified location.
lbound(dimension)	Returns the lowest index used in the specified dimension of a VBArray.
toArray()	Creates a JavaScript array from the VBArray and returns it.
ubound(dimension)	Returns the highest index value used in the specified dimension of the VBArray.

Regular Expressions

A regular expression is a pattern definition. Patterns can be used for finding, matching, and extracting text. These are particularly useful when testing values in forms or searching through data. However, they constitute a programming language in their own right and are the subjects of books all their own. Please consider this a mini-primer and not a comprehensive reference. A string enclosed in slashes defines a regular expression:

```
var re = /abc/;
//matches anything containing the
//sequence "abc"
```

To make the pattern case-insensitive, add an i after the closing slash, as follows:

```
var re = /abc/i;
// matches anything containing
// "abc" or "ABC" or "aBc"
```

To match an a followed by any single character, except for a newline character, write the following:

```
var re = /a./;
// doesn't match "a\n"
```

To make a match between alternatives, separate them with a vertical bar |, as follows:

```
var re = /abc|def/;
// Matches anything containing
// the sequence "abc" or "def"
```

To make a match from one of several characters, do the following:

```
var re = /[abcdef]/;
// Matches anything containing
// "a","b","c","d","e","f"
// same as /a|b|c|d|e|f/
```

Options inside [ ] are called a character class. Some other character class examples follow:

```
/[abcABC]/
/[0123456789]/ - matches a single digit
/[0-9]/ - same thing
/[0-9\-]/ matches 0-9 or a '-'
/[a-z0-9]/ matches lowercase letters and numbers
/[a-zA-Z0-9_]/ letters, digits and '_'
```

To match the reverse, negate it with a ^, as follows:

```
/[^0-9]/ - match anything single but a digit
/[^\^]/ - match anything but the circumflex
```

There are a number of predefined character classes. These are listed in Table C-15.

TABLE C-15 CHARACTER CLASSES

Expression	Meaning
/[\d]/	Same as /[0-9]/
/[\w]/	Match words; same as /[a-zA-Z0-9_]/
/[\s]/	Match white space /[\r\t\n\f]/
/[\D]/	Same as /[^0-9]/
/[\W]/	Match words; same as /[^a-zA-Z0-9_]/
/[\S]/	Match words; same as /[^ \r\t\n\f]/

There are also patterns to multiply other patterns. These are listed in Table C-16.

TABLE **C-16 PATTERNS**

Multiplier	Usage
*	(Asterisk) Match zero or more of the previous character or character class.
+	(Plus) Match one or more of the previous character or character class.
?	(Question mark) Match zero or one of the previous character or character class.
{n}	Match exactly n count of the previous character or character class.
{n, [m]}	Match at least n count with a maximum of m (if provided) count of the previous character or character class.

If there are two or more multipliers, the one on the left is greediest. For example, using the string bill@msn.microsoft.com and the regular expression /\@.+\..+/, the matched values are @, msn.microsoft, ., and com. Notice how the first .+ was greedy and left the minimum number of characters for the last .+ to match.

Adding parentheses around any part of a pattern doesn't change the pattern, but causes the match to be memorized. Memorized portions can be processed afterwards using built-in variables named $1–$9. For example:

```
/(.+)(\@)(.+)/
```

sets these values to:

```
$1: 'bill'
$2: '@'
$3: 'msn.microsoft.com'
```

Anchoring a pattern specifies the context surrounding the match. The \b matches a word boundary so:

- /or\b/ matches or endings
- /\bor/ matches words starting in or to the end of the string
- /\bor\b/ matches the word or

The \b matches anything not in a word boundary, the ^ matches the beginning of a string, and the $ matches the end. Note the use of ^ here and in character classes; the meanings are vastly different.

Patterns can be made case-insensitive by appending an i after the pattern, as follows: /abc/i. Patterns can be made global by appending a g after the pattern, as follows: /abc/g. Global patterns can search for multiple occurrences of a pattern in a string. Both options can be combined: /abc/gi.

In JavaScript, regular expressions are represented by RegExp objects. A RegExp object provides methods for finding and replacing matches in strings. The predefined RegExp object has properties that are set whenever you use a regular expression.

Regular expression objects can be created using the constructor RegExp (patternString, flags). For example:

```
var re = new RegExp("ab+c", "i");
```

When you use the constructor, omit the / surrounding the pattern. Regular expressions can also be defined using literal notation, as follows:

```
var re = /ab+c/i;
```

The constructor version is useful if your program will determine the pattern at runtime.

Once you have a RegExp object, you can test for a match in two ways: The test() method or the exec() method, as follows:

```
var re = /abc/;
var hasIt = re.test("has abc in it");
// hasIt is a Boolean value
var re = /abc/;
var matches = re.exec("has abc in it");
// matches is an Array and updates
// properties of the global RegExp
// object
```

The test() method just returns a Boolean, while the exec() method returns an array. The first element (index 0) contains the matched string. Other elements are memory locations for parenthesized portions of the pattern ($1...$n). Unlike the RegExp object, there's no limit to the number of memories returned.

Error Handling

Errors during the execution of JavaScript are handled using the try-catch notation. Catch takes a single argument, which will be an object representing the error:

```
try
{
    //Code that may have an exception
```

```
}
catch(exp)
{
    //Code to execute if an exception occurred
}
```

If an exception occurs in the `try` block, flow moves to the `catch` block immediately, skipping part of the `try` block if necessary.

Appendix D

VBScript Syntax

THIS APPENDIX PROVIDES a brief VBScript reference. VBScript can be used to define the work that you want an Active Server Page to do, and it provides syntax for the following:

- Storing data in variables

- Performing operations, like arithmetic

- Branching to different code based on the value of some data

- Looping over the same code until a condition is true

- Grouping code into functions and subroutines

Comments

VBScript comments allow you to write notes without interfering with the code's functionality. VBScript provides the two comments tags ' and REM for comments until the end of the line.

For example:

```
DIM x ' a comment
x = 8; REM a comment
' This line is a comment
REM This is also a comment
```

VBScript Data

VBScript stores data in variables. Variables are named data holders. Names should be alphanumeric, starting with a character. Variables are scoped to the entire page or a single subroutine or function. Variables are declared using the keyword Dim.

```
Dim name
Dim address, phone
```

Variables can be initialized to a literal value:

- Strings in double quotes – "hello"

- Numbers – integer (45) or floating point (32.3)

- Booleans – True or False

- Nothing – Null

- Dates in hash marks – #6-1-97#

Use the equals sign to perform an assignment. For example:

```
Dim name
Dim salary, bday
name="Stephen"
bday=#6-6-66#
salary=15000
```

You cannot use assignment during declaration. Don't use `Dim name="stephen"`.

Constants

Constants can be declared using the `const` keyword. For example:

```
const message = "hello"
```

defines a constant called message with the value "hello." A number of constants are built into the VBScript language. Some of the more useful constants are listed in Tables D-1, D-2, and D-3.

TABLE D-1 DATE AND TIME CONSTANTS

Constant	Value	Description
VbSunday	1	Sunday
VbMonday	2	Monday
VbTuesday	3	Tuesday
VbWednesday	4	Wednesday
VbThursday	5	Thursday

Constant	Value	Description
VbFriday	6	Friday
VbSaturday	7	Saturday
VbFirstJan1	1	Use the week in which January 1 occurs (default)
VbFirstFourDays	2	Use the first week that has at least four days in the new year
VbFirstFullWeek	3	Use the first full week of the year

TABLE D-2 STRING CONSTANTS

Constant	Value	Description
VbCr	Chr(13)	Carriage return
VbCrLf	Chr(13) & Chr(10)	Carriage return–linefeed combination
VbFormFeed	Chr(12)	Form feed
VbLf	Chr(10)	Line feed
VbNewLine	Chr(13) & Chr(10)	Platform-specific newline character or Chr(10)
VbNullChar	Chr(0)	Character having the value 0
VbNullString	String having value 0	Not the same as a zero-length string ("")
VbTab	Chr(9)	Horizontal tab

TABLE D-3 FILE CONSTANTS

Constant	Value	Description
ForReading	1	Open a file for reading.
ForWriting	2	Open a file for writing. If the file already exists, overwrite it.
ForAppending	8	Open a file for appending.

Operators

Operators are used in calculations such as 1+2, 3*4, and so on. VBScript operators are represented by character symbols or keywords. When an operator is encountered, it is executed using the appropriate arguments (operands).

Assignment operator

Assignment sets a variable's value using the equals sign =. Variables can be assigned a value from the following:

◆ A literal

◆ Another variable

◆ The result of some operation

For example:

```
Dim x, y, z
x = 4
y = 0
y = x
z = y + 4
```

Arithmetic operators

VBScript provides a number of arithmetic operators, including one operator that connects two strings together. (See Table D-4.)

TABLE D-4 ARITHMETIC OPERATORS

Operator	Description
+	Addition
-	Subtraction
*	Multiplication
^	Exponentiation
/	Floating point division
\	Integer division

Operator	Description
&	String concatenation
MOD	Modulo

The following example shows how the & operator can be used to connect strings:

```
DIM first, last, full
first = "Mister"
last = 0 'A number
full = first & " " & last
REM full is "Mister 0"
```

Comparison operators

Comparison operators are used to compare two values. Comparison operators return a Boolean value of True or False. (See Table D-5.)

TABLE D-5 COMPARISON OPERATORS

Operator	Description
EQV	Compares operands for equivalency
IS	Determines if two objects are the same object
=	Equal to
<>	Not equal to
<	Less than
<=	Less than or equal to
>	Greater than
>=	Greater than or equal to

Logical operators

Logical operators allow you to build more complex comparisons. These are listed in Table D-6.

TABLE D-6 LOGICAL OPERATORS

Operator	Description
AND	True if both operands are True
OR	True if either operand is True
NOT	True if the operand is False
XOR	True if only one operand is True

For example, the following code will set the value of bool to True if x is greater than y and x is greater than 2:

```
Dim x, y
Dim bool
x = 4
y = 7
bool = (x > y) AND (x>2)
```

Conditional Execution

VBScript provides two constructs for conditionally executing code: the If-Then construct and the Select Case construct.

If-Then

The If-Then construct is used to conditionally execute code. If-Then evaluates an expression and executes the specified code if the expression is True. Else can be used with If-Then to execute alternate code if the expression is False. Elseif can be used to nest additional tests. The code for an If-Then statement is concluded with End If. Both the Elseif and Else statements are optional.

```
If condition Then
    [statements]
ElseIf condition-n Then
    [elseifstatements]
Else
    [elsestatements]
End If
```

You can use If statements to conditionally return HTML to the client.

```
<%
Dim name
name = "Fran"
If name="Stephen" Then %>
Hello Stephen
<% Else %>
Hello stranger, glad to meet you!
<% End If %>
```

Select Case

Select Case allows you to implement nested If-Then-Else logic with a simpler syntax. Code between Case statements is executed if the value matches. If no match is found, code after Case Else is executed.

```
Select Case exp
  Case "Yes"
    ...
  Case "No"
    ...
  Case Else
    ...
End Select
```

The following example uses a Select Case to display different HTML based on the test:

```
<%
Dim exp
exp = "Maybe"

Select Case exp
%>
<% Case "Yes" %>
Thank you for your interest!
<% Case "No" %>
Thank you for your interest. We hope you reconsider.
<% Case Else %>
We'll have one of our sales representatives
contact you for more information
<% End Select %>
```

Looping Constructs

VBScript supports several looping statements:

- ◆ For...Next
- ◆ Do... Loop
- ◆ While...Wend
- ◆ For Each...Next

Choose the loop you need based on the type of test and the test timing.

For...Next

A `For...Next` loop repeats until a specified expression evaluates to False. A counter can be used during the loop. By default the step is 1, but can be configured. If you want to use the default, the step portion of this construct can be left out. Otherwise you can use either a positive or negative value to control the iteration process. For example, you could use a step size of 2 to count every other number in a sequence, or –1 to count backwards:

```
For counter = start To end Step step
        [statements]
Next
```

The loop can be aborted with a call to Exit For. The following example uses a For...Next loop to display several lines of HTML:

```
<% For i = 0 To 10 Step 1 %>
Line: <%= i %> <BR>
<% Next %>
```

While...Wend

A `While...Wend` loop repeats as long as the specified expression evaluates to True. The While loop checks an expression at the top of the loop. If it is False at the start, the loop will never be executed.

```
<%
Dim i, words, charAt
i = 0
words = "Hello World"
while ((charAt <> " ") AND (i <= Len(words)))
%>
<%= charAt %><BR>
```

```
<%
    i = i+1
    charAt = Mid(words,i,1)
Wend
%>
```

Do...Loop

The Do...Loop is flexible. It will test a value before the loop, but can either be run while the value is True, or until the value is False.

```
Do [{While | Until} condition]
        [statements]
Loop
```

The Do...Loop can also perform the test at the end of the loop, allowing the loop to execute at least once. This type of loop is used when you need it to execute once, regardless of the tests value.

```
Do
    [statements]
Loop [{While | Until} condition]
```

For Each...Next

The For Each Next loop is used to iterate through the items in a collection or array.

```
For Each element In group
        [statements]
Next
```

For example, the following code creates an array of strings and loops over through all of the contents:

```
<%
Dim word, words
words = Array("One", "Two", "Three")

For Each word In words
%>
<%= word %>
<%
Next
%>
```

Exit statement

The Exit statement terminates the current loop and continues execution on the statement following the terminated loop:

- ◆ Exit Do - Exit a Do loop
- ◆ Exit For - Exit a For loop

Arrays

An Array is an ordered list of variables. Each element in the list is referenced by an index.

```
names(0) = "Fido"
```

Define them like this:

```
Dim arrayname(upperbound)
Dim names(5)
```

You can create multidimensional arrays like this:

```
Dim names(5,5)
```

Arrays can have up to 60 different dimensions. VBScript arrays always start at index 0. The upper index of an array is returned by the UBound() function. So the size of an array can be calculated like this:

```
size = UBound(arrayname) + 1
```

Arrays can be dynamically sized. To define an array that can be resized, declare it without specifying its size, as follows:

```
Dim names()
```

Before using, size the array with ReDim:

```
ReDim names(20)
```

To preserve the contents of the array while resizing, specify the Preserve option, as follows:

```
ReDim Preserve names(21)
```

Shrinking an array loses data in any slots that were cut off.

When used with multi-dimensional arrays only the last dimension can be re-dimensioned.

Functions

VBScript uses functions and subroutines to organize reusable code. Functions can be placed anywhere an expression is valid, can take parameters, and can return a single value. Subroutines are executed using the `Call` keyword (optional). Subroutines can take parameters but they return no values.

Subroutines are declared with the keyword `Sub`. They can accept data (arguments or parameters). A subroutine ends with the keywords `End Sub`.

Functions are defined using the keyword `Function`. Functions can accept data (arguments or parameters). They can also return a value. A function ends with the keywords `End Function`. To return a value, assign it to the name of the function as if it was a variable.

Both subroutines and functions should have names that begin with a letter or underscore (_). They must be defined before they are called. And the name should be unique within the document.

The following example shows how a subroutine can be declared and called:

```
<%
Dim results
Sub join(string1, string2, answer)
    answer = string1 & string2
End Sub
' Use of Call is optional
join "Hello ", "World", results
' If you want to use Call, arguments must
' be enclosed in ()s
Call join("Hello ", "World", results)
' result is in results
%>
```

The following example shows how to define and call a function that returns data:

```
<%
Function Join(string1, string2)
    Join = string1 & string2
End Function
%>
<%= Join("Basket","ball") %>
<BR>
<%= Join("Ruta","baga") %>
```

The Exit statement can be used to terminate a function or subroutine:

♦ `Exit Function` – Exit a function

♦ `Exit Sub` – Exit a subroutine

Built-in functions

Table D-7 contains a list of the functions built into VBScript. Square brackets [ ] are used to indicate optional arguments to the functions. Functions that include a comparison flag can have that flag set to one of two values: `vbBinaryCompare (0)` or `vbTextCompare (1)`.

TABLE D-7 BUILT-IN VBSCRIPT FUNCTIONS

Function	Description
Abs(number)	Returns the absolute value of a number
Array(size)	Returns a variant containing an array
Asc(string)	Returns the ANSI character code corresponding to the first letter in a string
Atn(number)	Returns the arctangent of a number
CBool(variable)	Converts a variable to a Boolean
CByte(variable)	Converts a variable to a byte
CCur(variable)	Converts a variable to currency
CDate(variable)	Converts a variable to a date
CDbl(variable)	Converts a variable to a double
Chr(variable)	Returns the character associated with the specified ANSI character code
CInt(variable)	Converts a variable to a integer
CLng(variable)	Converts a variable to a long
Cos(number)	Returns the cosine of an angle
CStr(variable)	Converts a variable to a string

Function	Description
Date()	Returns the current system date
DateAdd (interval, number, date)	Returns a date to which a specified time interval has been added
DateDiff(date1,date2)	Returns the number of intervals between two dates
DatePart(interval, date[, firstdayofweek[, firstweekofyear]])	Returns the specified part of a given date
DateSerial(year, month, day)	Returns a date for a specified year, month, and day
DateValue(string)	Returns a date from the provided string
Day(date)	Returns a whole number between 1 and 31, inclusive, representing the day of the month
Eval(string)	Evaluates an expression and returns the result
Exp(number)	Returns e raised to a power
Filter(InputStrings, Value[, Include[, Compare]])	Returns a zero-based array containing a subset of a string array based on a specified filter criteria
Fix(number)	Returns the integer portion of a number
FormatCurrency (Expression[, NumDigitsAfterDecimal [,IncludeLeadingDigit [,UseParensForNegativeNumbers [,GroupDigits]]]])	Returns an expression formatted as a currency value using the currency symbol defined in the system control panel
FormatDateTime(Date)	Returns an expression formatted as a date or time

Continued

TABLE D-7 BUILT-IN VBSCRIPT FUNCTIONS *(Continued)*

Function	Description
`FormatNumberFormatNumber (Expression [, NumDigitsAfterDecimal [,IncludeLeadingDigit [,UseParensForNegativeNumbers [,GroupDigits]]]])`	Returns an expression formatted as a number
`FormatPercentFormatPercent (Expression[, NumDigitsAfterDecimal [,IncludeLeadingDigit [,UseParensForNegativeNumbers [,GroupDigits]]]])`	Returns an expression formatted as a percentage (multiplied by 100) with a trailing % character
`GetRef`	Returns a reference to a procedure that can be bound to an event
`Hex(number)`	Returns a string representing the hexadecimal value of a number
`Hour(date)`	Returns a whole number between 0 and 23, inclusive, representing the hour of the day
`InStr([start, ]string1, string2[, compare])`	Returns the position of the first occurrence of one string within another
`InStrRev([start, ]string1, string2[, compare])`	Returns the position of an occurrence of one string within another, from the end of string
`Int(number)`	Returns the integer portion of a number
`IsArray(variable)`	Returns a Boolean value indicating whether a variable is an array
`IsDate(variable)`	Returns a Boolean value indicating whether an expression can be converted to a date
`IsEmpty(variable)`	Returns a Boolean value indicating whether a variable has been initialized

Function	Description
IsNull(variable)	Returns a Boolean value that indicates whether an expression contains no valid data (Null)
IsNumeric(variable)	Returns a Boolean value indicating whether an expression can be evaluated as a number
Join(list[, delimiter])	Returns a string created by joining a number of substrings contained in an array using the specified delimiter
LBound(array)	Returns the smallest available subscript for the indicated dimension of an array
LCase(string)	Returns a string that has been converted to lowercase
Left(string,num)	Returns a specified number of characters from the left side of a string
Len(string)	Returns the number of characters in a string or the number of bytes required to store a variable
Log(number)	Returns the natural logarithm of a number
LTrim(string)	Returns a copy of a string without leading spaces
Mid(string,num)	Returns a specified number of characters from a string
Minute(date)	Returns a whole number between 0 and 59, inclusive, representing the minute of the hour
Month(date)	Returns a whole number between 1 and 12, inclusive, representing the month of the year
MonthName(date)	Returns a string indicating the specified month
Now()	Returns the current date and time according to the setting of your computer's system date and time

Continued

TABLE D-7 BUILT-IN VBSCRIPT FUNCTIONS *(Continued)*

Function	Description
Oct(number)	Returns a string representing the octal value of a number
Replace(expression, find, replacewith[, start[, count[, compare]]])	Returns a string in which a specified substring has been replaced with another substring a specified number of times
Right(date)	Returns a specified number of characters from the right side of a string
Rnd()	Returns a random number
Round(number)	Returns a number rounded to a specified number of decimal places
Rtrim(string)	Returns a copy of a string without trailing spaces
Second(date)	Returns a whole number between 0 and 59, inclusive, representing the second of the minute
Sgn(number)	Returns an integer indicating the sign of a number
Sin(number)	Returns the sine of an angle
Space(number)	Returns a string consisting of the specified number of spaces
Split(expression[, delimiter[, count[, compare]]])	Returns a zero-based, one-dimensional array containing a specified number of substrings
Sqr(number)	Returns the square root of a number
StrComp(string1, string2[, compare])	Returns a value indicating the result of a string comparison
StringString(number, character)	Returns a repeating character string of the length specified
StrReverse(string)	Returns a string in which the character order of a specified string is reversed
Tan(number)	Returns the tangent of an angle

Function	Description
Time()	Returns a date indicating the current system time
Timer()	Returns the number of seconds that have elapsed since 12:00 AM (midnight)
TimeSerial(hour, minute, second)	Returns a date containing the time for a specific hour, minute, and second
TimeValue(string)	Returns a date containing the time indicated in the string
Trim(string)	Returns a copy of a string without leading or trailing spaces
TypeName(variable)	Returns a string that provides variant subtype information about a variable
UBound(array)	Returns the largest available subscript for the indicated dimension of an array
UCase(string)	Returns a string that has been converted to uppercase
Weekday(date, [firstdayofweek])	Returns a whole number representing the day of the week; the first day of the week can be specified as a number where 1 is Sunday, and the other days increase from 1
WeekdayName(date)	Returns a string indicating the specified day of the week
Year(date)	Returns a whole number representing the year

Objects

In VBScript, an object is assigned to a variable using the set keyword, as in the following:

```
Set conn = Server.CreateObject("ADODB.Connection")
```

Objects have attributes and procedures. Both of these are accessed using a dot notation. For example:

```
recordSet.EOF
```

accesses the EOF property of the object stored in `recordSet`, while the following:

```
Response.Write("<h2>Deleteted "&numRec&" row.</h2>")
```

calls the write procedure, or method, of the Response object.

Appendix E

Microsoft Windows Distributed interNet Applications Architecture

MOST DEVELOPERS ARE FAMILIAR with the traditional client/server application development model. However, with Microsoft's introduction of the Windows Distributed interNet Applications Architecture (Windows DNA), the recommended model for developing applications has changed. The fundamental concept of Windows DNA is the separation, or isolation, of application services. Typically, this includes at least three layers or tiers:

1. User Services, which handles the user interface

2. Business Services, which handles the majority of the application logic and business rules

3. Data Services, which handles the management and synchronization of data

Throughout the remainder of this chapter, we'll take a further look into each of these tiers. For further information, visit `http://www.microsoft.com/dna/`.

Looking Back At Two-Tier Development

Prior to the introduction of Web servers and middleware to handle business logic, most applications where divided into two tiers: a *user services* tier that resided on the user's or client's machine and a *data services* tier that usually resided on a centralized server. Hence, the name client/server applications. Depending on where the business logic resided, an application was considered to be either a fat-client or a thin-client solution.

As shown in Figure E-1, both approaches to two-tier development include a user interface in the User Services tier and some type of data store in the Data Services tier. What differs is where the application logic or business rules reside. A typical fat-client application maintains its set of business rules in the User Services tier, while thin-client applications maintain their set of business rules in the Data Services tier. To complicate matters, in practice, most two-tier applications actually spread the business rules in both tiers. The main drawback with this two-tier approach is scalability.

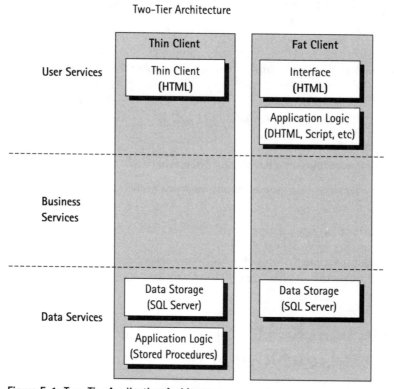

Figure E-1: Two-Tier Application Architecture

In the fat-client scenario, where the application logic resides on the client, the user's machine can quickly becomes the focus of application failures. Typically, these failures are caused by incompatibilities or inconsistencies with the client machine. Other times, failures are caused when large amounts of data must be transferred from the database server to the client to perform a particular task. In the Internet model, where many users are still using low-bandwidth dialup accounts to access applications, the performance hit is not acceptable.

For thin-client applications, the client machine capability is minimized. However, the issue then becomes performance problems related to an overworked database server. When the application logic resides on the database server, as the number of users increases, the requests against the database server increase. Therefore, the database server is spending less time serving data and more time performing application logic.

Code maintenance also becomes an issue in the two-tier model because the application logic is tightly coupled to either the User Services or Data Services tiers, depending on whether a fat- or thin-client approach was used. For example, for fat-clients, when a business logic change occurs, the application portion that resides on the client machine has to be updated. In the thin-client scenario, the business logic is tightly coupled with the Data Services tier. This presents a problem because oftentimes a database schema change is required to support a simple business rule change.

From this brief background in two-tier development, you can quickly see that a different approach was needed to support the growing demand for scalable and maintainable applications.

Windows DNA Architecture

The Windows DNA Architecture primarily focuses on providing a model for developing n-tier, or multitier, applications. Typically this includes the three tiers introduced earlier:

1. User Services

2. Business Services

3. Data Services

Figure E-2 shows two n-tier architecture approaches. As indicated, both solutions isolate the application logic and business rules from the User Services and Data Services tiers.

The key to building n-tier applications using the Windows DNA model is Microsoft's Component Object Model (COM). As shown in Figure E-3, COM provides the glue to integrate the family of technologies that make up Windows DNA. For extensive coverage of COM, take a look at *Essential COM* by Don Box. This is one of the best developer resources for learning about COM and how to properly use it.

One of the things you will probably notice about Figure E-3 is that the Business Services tier includes several layers itself. For example, for ASP applications, you will typically include code running on IIS, COM+, and MSMQ. Although, physically, this architecture includes more than three-layers, logically, it is still only three levels – one for each logical isolation of code. Therefore, you will also see DNA applications referred to as n-tier instead of three-tier.

N-Tier Architecture

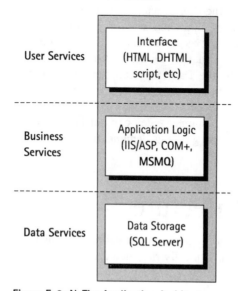

Figure E-2: N-Tier Application Architecture

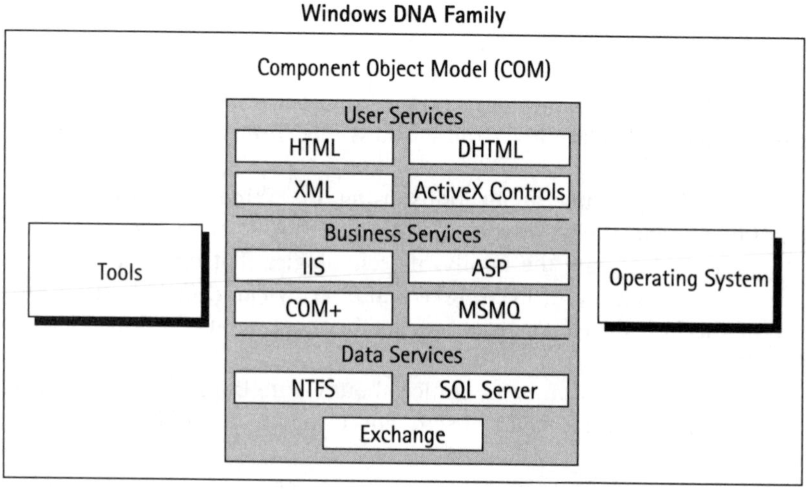

Windows DNA Family

Figure E-3: Windows DNA Family

Although at first look, the application architecture is more complicated for DNA applications than for traditional 2-tier applications, the payback comes from more scalable solutions and easier application maintenance. For example, Figure E-4 shows a block diagram of a simple DNA application.

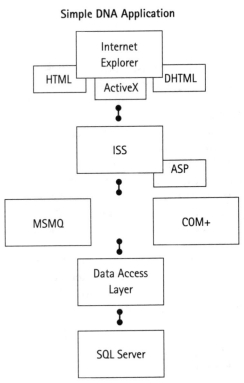

Simple DNA Application

Figure E-4: Simple DNA Application Architecture

One of the obvious things about this application is that the all database access is handled via the Data Access Layer (DAL) component. Taking this as an example, having only one set of code that accesses the database effectively isolates the database schema from the remainder of the application. Therefore, as changes are made to the database, only the DAL component requires updates. As long as the updates made do not include changes to the components interface(s), the Business Services tier code does not require any changes.

The scalability payback partly comes from the power of COM+. Because COM+ provides thread management and resource pooling, the performance cost of instantiating objects is limited. Basically, when a section of User Services code instantiates an object that is provided by COM+, COM+ checks to see if an instance is already available. If so, the instantiating process is not performed. There are many other services provided by COM+.

The remaining scalability improvement is a byproduct of the isolation process. By isolating processes or types of processes on their own hardware, the hardware platforms can be designed specifically for the task(s) that will be performed. In general, the application overhead is spread out over more machines which essentially means an application can handle more traffic/requests.

User Services Tier

As introduced earlier, the User Services tier handles the user interface. Presentation Services is another term used to describe this tier. In addition, to user interface issues, the User Services tier is also involved with tasks related to user authentication, client-machine platform differences, and so on.

The User Services tier is the where the application logic that deals with client machine differences is handled. Generally there are two approaches to browser-based applications. The easiest approach, from a User Services tier perspective, is to build applications that work across all browser versions or a large subset. In this case, basic HTML is used to build the client page. This approach usually involves using IIS/ASP, to some extent, to augment the User Services tier. Since only plain HTML is available on the client machine, ASP scripting is used to build the HTML and return the page to the client machine.

For browser-based applications that are enhanced or built for specific versions of a browser, the tools available expands greatly. For example, if Internet Explorer 5.0 was the target platform, the User Services tier could use DHTML, ActiveX Controls, XML, and so forth to build a powerful user interface.

Business Services Tier

As mentioned, the Business Services tier is where most of the application logic and business rules are placed and enforced. The general goal for this tier is to provide a link between the data and the presentation of that data. As shown in Figure E-3, the Business Services tier includes:

- ◆ Internet Information Server (IIS)
- ◆ Component Services/COM+
- ◆ Microsoft Message Queue Server (MSMQ)
- ◆ Custom COM+ Components

For ASP applications, IIS provides most of the interaction between the User Services and Business Services tiers. As shown throughout most of this book, developers can use any number of scripting languages to build ASP pages that are interpreted by the Internet Server Application Programming Interface (ISAPI). However, most large applications limit the use of ASP code and try to encapsulate the code in a custom COM+ component.

As introduced earlier, MTS provides management for process and threads along with maintaining object instances. However, MTS also exposes a transaction model. This transaction model is very similar to the one described in Chapter 16, "Transactional Scripts." In essence, developers can encapsulate a series of different steps in a single *transaction* so that if a step fails, all the previous steps are reversed or rolled back.

Microsoft Message Queue Server (MSMQ) provides applications with the ability to perform asynchronous communication between different components within a system. Basically, this allows developers to queue tasks or messages in the event a component or subsystem is unavailable. Once the targeted component or subsystem becomes available, it can check the queue and perform the series of tasks or messages that are waiting.

Chapter 10, "Extending ASP with ActiveX Components," described how to extend your ASP applications using some of the COM components available for IIS. However, most large ASP applications include a variety of COM+ components written to support specific application logic or business rules. Furthermore, the majority of the application development process is spent building these custom components and building the script contained in the ASP pages.

Data Services Tier

The Data Services tier focuses, almost entirely, on the storage and access of data. In the Windows DNA model, the core of the Data Services provided to an application are provided by SQL Server and/or Exchange.

SQL Server is a relational database management system that, for ASP applications, is usually accessed via ActiveX Data Objects (ADO). In addition to simply providing a place where data is stored, SQL Server also provides stored procedures that are actually pre-compiled Transact-SQL statements that are performed as a single unit of execution. In addition, SQL Server exposes a transaction model that is used to further encapsulate a series of different SQL statements and to either commit or rollback the entire series. The transaction model, is very similar to the transaction model described earlier. For more information, see http://www.microsoft.com/sql/.

Microsoft Exchange, while mostly known as a mail server, provides a very rich set of messaging and collaboration services. You access most of these services using the Messaging Application Programming Interface (MAPI), Collaboration Data Services (CDO), and Active Directory Service Interfaces (ADSI). For more information, see `http://www.microsoft.com/exchange/`.

A Simple Windows DNA Application

Since this is a developer's book, the best way to demonstrate the n-tier approach is by looking at a code sample. Figure E-5 shows the architecture of the sample application.

Hello World Architecture

Figuure E-5: HelloWorld Architecture

The application is browser-neutral at the User Services tier. (See Figure E-6.) The Business Services tier includes IIS/ASP and a custom COM component. The Data Services tier is supported by SQL Server.

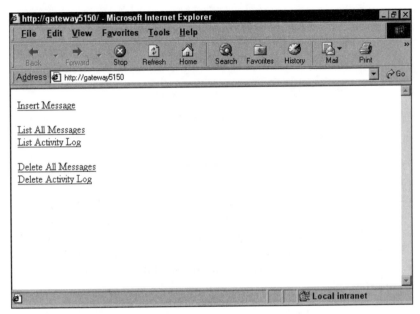

Figure E-6: HelloWorld Default Page

The applications default.asp page provides a simple menu. As shown, the application provides five options and each option is supported by its own ASP page.

Data Services tier

We'll begin by looking at the Data Services tier. A SQL Server database (HelloWorld) contains two tables; one to store messages (see Table E-1) and the other to store activity log information (see Table E-2).

TABLE E-1 THE STRUCTURE FOR THE MESSAGE TABLE

Column Name	DataType	Description
MessageID	INT (Identity)	Primary Key for table.
MessageText	VARCHAR(255)	Contains the message text.

TABLE E-2 THE STRUCTURE FOR THE ACTIVITYLOG TABLE

Column Name	DataType	Description
LogID	INT (Identity	Primary Key for table.
LogDateTime	DATETIME	Defaults to date/time when record is inserted.
LogText	VARCHAR(255)	Contains activity text.

In addition to the tables, store procedures are used to access the database. For example, to insert a record, use the insMessage stored procedure. To retrieve all the messages in the Message table, call the getMessage_All stored procedure. Finally, to delete all the messages in the Message table, call the delMessage_All stored procedure. There are similar insert, get, and delete stored procedures for interaction with the ActivityLog table.

Business Services tier

The Business Services tier of the sample application includes a custom COM component built with Visual Basic (VB). To begin, the component maintains the connection information for the database in a global value, as follows:

```
Public g_connString As String
```

When the component is initialized, the Class_Initialize procedure is called automatically by the VB runtime environment, as follows:

```
Private Sub Class_Initialize()
    g_connString = "HelloWord"

End Sub
```

This sets up the database connection information for the remainder of the COM component. Next, the COM component includes a function to insert a message; insMessage. This method requires the text of the message to insert to be passed into the function. The function returns either True or False based on the success or failure of the database insert.

The function first creates an ADO connection object and opens the connection to the database specified in the g_connString variable, like this:

```
Set conn = CreateObject("ADODB.Connection")
conn.Open g_connString
```

Next, the Execute method of the connection object is used to call the insMessage stored procedure. Notice that this line of code uses VB's Replace function to make sure that any single quotes (') are replaced with two quotes (") to ensure the string is inserted correctly.

```
conn.Execute "insMessage '" & Replace(sMessageText, "'", "''") & "'"
```

After the ADO Connection object is closed and released, the insActivityLog method is called to insert a record in the activity log, as follows:

```
insActivityLog "Inserted Message: " & sMessageText
```

Finally, the return information is set for the function and the function is exited. The insActivityLog function is very similar with the exception that the insActivityLog stored procedure is called to insert a record into the activity log.

The delete functions, delMessage_All and delActivityLog_All, have the same basic structure as the insert functions. So, we'll skip those and take a look at the functions used to retrieve information from the database.

The getMessage_All function is used to get all the messages in the Message table. The function returns a disconnected RecordSet containing all the records, as follows:

```
Public Function getMessage_All() As ADODB.Recordset
```

The ADO Command object is used to actually run the getMessage_All stored procedure on the SQL Server database, like this:

```
Set cmd = CreateObject("ADODB.Command")

cmd.ActiveConnection = g_connString
cmd.CommandText = "getMessage_All"
cmd.CommandType = adCmdStoredProc
```

To facilitate the use of a disconnected RecordSet, we need to specify that the cursor is a client-side cursor, as follows:

```
rs.CursorLocation = adUseClient
```

Next, the RecordSet is created as a forward-only, read-only RecordSet.

```
rs.Open cmd, , adOpenForwardOnly, adLockReadOnly
```

At this point, the RecordSet containing the data is created. Now, we can drop the connection to the database, which effectively *disconnects* the RecordSet from the database.

```
Set cmd.ActiveConnection = Nothing
Set cmd = Nothing
Set rs.ActiveConnection = Nothing
```

Before exiting the getMessage_All function, an activity log record is inserted to log that all the messages were viewed, and finally the RecordSet is set at the return code for the function, as follows:

```
insActivityLog "Viewed all messages"

Set getMessage_All = rs
```

The getActivityLog_All function is nearly identical to the getMessage_All function with the exception that the ActivityLog table is the target instead of the Message table.

The Business Services tier also uses ASP code to interface between the browser and the custom COM component. The insMessage.asp file, for example, contains a simple HTML form that is used to enter the text of the message to insert into the Message table.

```
<form method="post" action="insMessage.asp">
Enter your message:<br>
<input type="text" maxlength="255" name="MessageText">
<input type="submit" value="Submit" name="submit">
</form>
```

Figure E-7 shows what the insMessage.asp page looks like. When the form is submitted, the form is posted to the same page. At the top of the insMessage.asp page is the ASP code to determine if the Submit button was clicked, as follows:

```
If Request.Form("Submit") <> "" Then
```

If the Submit button was clicked, the custom COM component is instantiated, like this:

```
Set objSampleDNA = Server.CreateObject("SampleDNA.HelloWorld)
```

After the object is instantiated, the insMessage method is called and the message text the user submitted is passed into the function, as follows:

```
objSampleDNA.insMessage(Request.Form("MessageText"))
```

After cleaning up the object resources, the user is returned to the default page using the Server.Transfer method, like this:

```
Server.Transfer "default.asp"
```

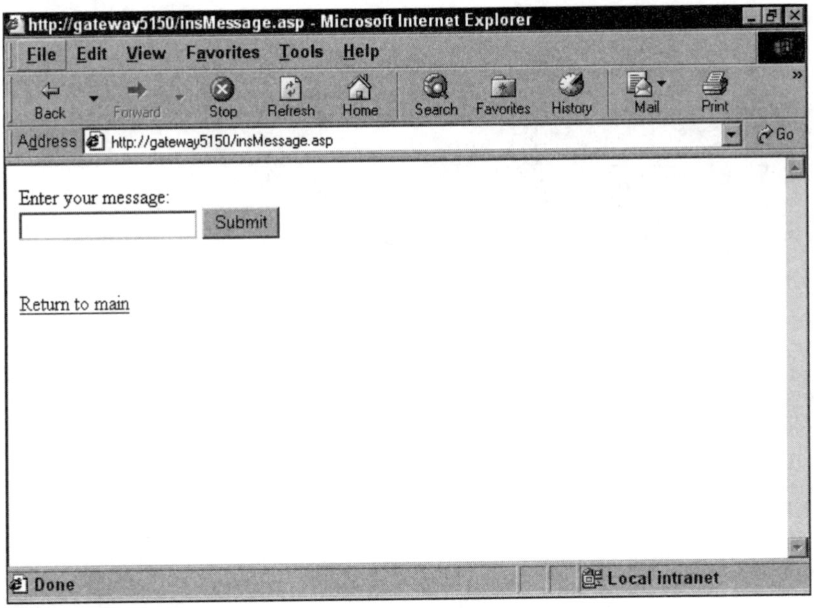

Figure E-7: The insMessage.asp page

As you can see, by encapsulating the ADO code in the custom COM component, the complexity of the ASP code is greatly diminished. The ASP pages used to delete the Message and ActivityLog records are very similar. So, there's no need to cover them here.

The ASP pages used to list the messages and activity log records are a little different. For example, to retrieve all of the records in the Message table, the getMessage_All method is called after instantiating the COM component, as follows:

```
Set rsMessage = objSampleDNA.getMessage_All
```

Notice that the return value of the method call creates a RecordSet: rsMessage. Once the RecordSet is created, the ASP code iterates through the RecordSet and prints out each message using the Response.Write method.

```
Do While Not rsMessage.EOF
    Response.Write rsMessage("MessageText") & "<br>"
    rsMessage.MoveNext
Loop
```

Finally, the RecordSet and COM component are closed and released, as follows:

```
rsMessage.Close
Set rsMessage = Nothing

Set objSampleDNA = Nothing
```

The result is displayed in Figure E-8.

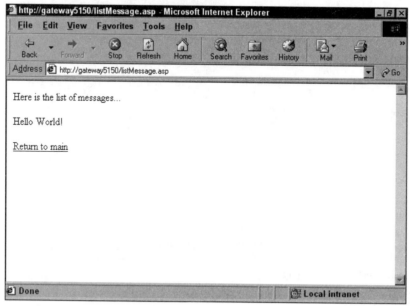

Figure E-8: The lstMessage.asp page

User Services tier

Because this is a simple application, all of the User Services tier code is simple HTML that was built using ASP. This brings up a good point about how the tiers relate to one another. As demonstrated in this example application, there is a fine line between the different tiers. In the case of this example, ASP was used to build the HTML and the browser was used to actually interpret the HTML code and display the results to the user. In most cases, the lines between the different components are pretty obvious. However, ASP tends to blur those lines when it's used to create a portion of the HTML.

Summary

Windows DNA is the predominant application model used today when building n-tier applications for the Microsoft Windows and BackOffice product families. By designing applications using this model, applications can successfully be scaled to support large numbers of clients and requests. In addition, because of the model of encapsulation used in Windows DNA applications, efforts related to code maintenance are minimized and code reuse is maximized.

Appendix F

IIS Status Codes

TABLE F-1 PROVIDES A LIST of the standard status codes and their associated messages returned by IIS.

TABLE F-1 STANDARD STATUS CODES AND MESSAGES

Name	Value	Description
HTTP_STATUS_CONTINUE	100	The request can be continued.
HTTP_STATUS_SWITCH_PROTOCOLS	101	The server has switched protocols in an upgrade header.
HTTP_STATUS_OK	200	The request completed successfully.
HTTP_STATUS_CREATED	201	The request has been fulfilled and resulted in the creation of a new resource.
HTTP_STATUS_ACCEPTED	202	The request has been accepted for processing, but the processing has not been completed.
HTTP_STATUS_PARTIAL	203	The returned meta information in the entity-header is not the definitive set available from the origin server.
HTTP_STATUS_NO_CONTENT	204	The server has fulfilled the request, but there is no new information to send back.

Continued

TABLE F-1 **STANDARD STATUS CODES AND MESSAGES** *(Continued)*

Name	Value	Description
HTTP_STATUS_RESET_CONTENT	205	The request has been completed, and the client program should reset the document view that caused the request to be sent to allow the user to easily initiate another input action.
HTTP_STATUS_PARTIAL_CONTENT	206	The server has fulfilled the partial GET request for the resource.
HTTP_STATUS_AMBIGUOUS	300	The server couldn't decide what to return.
HTTP_STATUS_MOVED	301	The requested resource has been assigned to a new permanent URI (Uniform Resource Identifier), and any future references to this resource should be done using one of the returned URIs.
HTTP_STATUS_REDIRECT	302	The requested resource resides temporarily under a different URI (Uniform Resource Identifier).
HTTP_STATUS_REDIRECT_METHOD	303	The response to the request can be found under a different URI (Uniform Resource Identifier) and should be retrieved using a GET method on that resource.
HTTP_STATUS_NOT_MODIFIED	304	The requested resource has not been modified.

Name	Value	Description
HTTP_STATUS_USE_PROXY	305	The requested resource must be accessed through the proxy given by the location field.
HTTP_STATUS_REDIRECT_KEEP_VERB	307	The redirected request keeps the same verb. HTTP/1.1 behavior.
HTTP_STATUS_BAD_REQUEST	400	The request could not be processed by the server due to invalid syntax.
HTTP_STATUS_DENIED	401	The requested resource requires user authentication.
HTTP_STATUS_PAYMENT_REQ	402	Not currently implemented in the HTTP protocol.
HTTP_STATUS_FORBIDDEN	403	The server understood the request, but is refusing to fulfill it.
HTTP_STATUS_NOT_FOUND	404	The server has not found anything matching the requested URI (Uniform Resource Identifier).
HTTP_STATUS_BAD_METHOD	405	The method used is not allowed.
HTTP_STATUS_NONE_ACCEPTABLE	406	No responses acceptable to the client were found.
HTTP_STATUS_PROXY_AUTH_REQ	407	Proxy authentication required.
HTTP_STATUS_REQUEST_TIMEOUT	408	The server timed out waiting for the request.
HTTP_STATUS_CONFLICT	409	The request could not be completed due to a conflict with the current state of the resource. The user should resubmit with more information.

Continued

TABLE F-1 STANDARD STATUS CODES AND MESSAGES *(Continued)*

Name	Value	Description
HTTP_STATUS_GONE	410	The requested resource is no longer available at the server, and no forwarding address is known.
HTTP_STATUS_LENGTH_REQUIRED	411	The server refuses to accept the request without a defined content length.
HTTP_STATUS_PRECOND_FAILED	412	The precondition given in one or more of the request header fields evaluated to false when it was tested on the server.
HTTP_STATUS_REQUEST_TOO_LARGE	413	The server is refusing to process a request because the request entity is larger than the server is willing or able to process.
HTTP_STATUS_URI_TOO_LONG	414	The server is refusing to service the request because the request URI (Uniform Resource Identifier) is longer than the server is willing to interpret.
HTTP_STATUS_UNSUPPORTED_MEDIA	415	The server is refusing to service the request because the entity of the request is in a format not supported by the requested resource for the requested method.
HTTP_STATUS_RETRY_WITH	449	The request should be retried after doing the appropriate action.
HTTP_STATUS_SERVER_ERROR	500	The server encountered an unexpected condition that prevented it from fulfilling the request.

Name	Value	Description
HTTP_STATUS_NOT_SUPPORTED	501	The server does not support the functionality required to fulfill the request.
HTTP_STATUS_BAD_GATEWAY	502	The server, while acting as a gateway or proxy, received an invalid response from the upstream server it accessed in attempting to fulfill the request.
HTTP_STATUS_SERVICE_UNAVAIL	503	The service is temporarily overloaded.
HTTP_STATUS_GATEWAY_TIMEOUT	504	The request was timed out waiting for a gateway.
HTTP_STATUS_VERSION_NOT_SUP	505	The server does not support, or refuses to support, the HTTP protocol version that was used in the request message.

Appendix G

Performance Considerations with ASP Applications

PERFORMANCE TUNING IS A huge subject that volumes have been written about. Full coverage of performance tuning is beyond the scope of this book. However, this chapter will cover some of the basics related to this topic. First we'll look at what makes up an HTTP request and some of the more important aspects of Web traffic. Then, we'll introduce two basic performance-tuning methodologies. This is followed by a section that covers how to use Microsoft's Web Application Stress tool, which is a free download from http://webtool.rte.microsoft.com. Finally, we'll cover a few Active Server performance killers and how to code more efficiently.

Anatomy of an HTTP Request

To begin understanding performance-related issues, it is necessary to have a thorough understanding of what happens when an HTTP request is made. Figure G-1 shows a simplified sequence of events that occur when a user requests a single HTML page with one image.

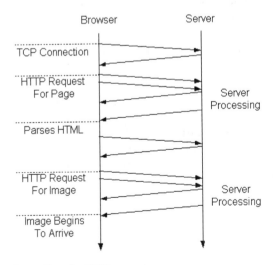

Figure G-1: An HTTP request sequence

As indicated, time increases from the top to the bottom of the browser and server process lines. First, the browser opens a TCP connection. This results in an exchange of synchronization and acknowledgement packets between the browser and the server, which is referred to as a three-way handshake, as follows:

1. Synchronization from browser to server

2. Synchronization from server to browser

3. Acknowledgment from browser to server

Once the connection is established, the browser sends an HTTP GET request to the server. The server receives the request, parses it, and performs any tasks required for returning the requested page. For simple static HTML pages, this might only involve reading the file from disk or memory cache. However, for an Active Server Page, this involves reading the file from disk, interpreting the file using the asp.dll that resides on the server, executing the code in the page, potentially reading from a database, and so forth.

Once the server processing is complete, the HTML is returned to the browser. At this point, the browser parses the HTML and begins rendering the code in the browser. When the browser gets to the image tag <img src=...>, a request is sent to the server for the image file.

Before the actual request can be sent, the process of exchanging synchronization and acknowledgment packets is performed again, and the HTTP GET request for the image file is sent to the server. The server receives the request, parses it, and pulls the image file from disk or memory cache. Finally, the server begins the process of sending the image file back to the browser.

Another aspect of HTTP traffic is that when a connection is established, TCP uses an approach referred to as *slow start*. This approach uses the first few data packets to determine the optimal transmission rate between the browser and server. Given that most objects that are used in Web applications are small in size, the page request is often complete before the slow start algorithm has completed. This makes for a very inefficient use of network bandwidth.

With the introduction of the 1.1 version of HTTP, the idea of a persistent connection was introduced. Simply stated, a *persistent connection* leaves a TCP connection open between consecutive HTTP requests. The performance benefits are obvious; the three-way handshake is not performed before each HTTP request. While HTTP 1.1 does address some of the performance issues inherent with HTTP transactions, a single HTTP request is required for each file, including images embedded in the originating HTML page.

Web Application Traffic Characteristics

Now that we've discussed the sequence of events for requesting an HTML page, we can spend time looking at two characteristics of Web traffic: burstiness and heavy tails.

Burstiness

The term *burstiness* refers to a characteristic of WWW traffic that indicates that data is transmitted randomly by both browsers and servers. The randomness of data traffic creates peaks of data traffic that exceed the average traffic rate by factors of eight to ten. For example, a typical Web page will have several images. Therefore, when a single page is requested, several other HTTP GETs are required to pull the image files from the server. Once the page request and all its image requests are complete, there is typically a delay before the next page request is sent from the browser to the server. Then when a new page is requested, the sequence of HTTP GETs is repeated. This, in essence, builds a number of peaks in Web traffic.

For example, let's assume we request a single HTML page with two images. The size of the HTML page is 600 bytes while the images are each 2,500 bytes. This makes for a total of 5,600 bytes of data that are transferred between the server and browser (for simplicity, we won't account for the bytes of overhead to actually make the data transfer work). Then the user waits a minute and makes another request for a page that totals another 5,600 bytes data. The total bytes transferred amount to 11,200 (minus the overhead). Average this out over the time frame of both requests, let's say 70 seconds, and the average data per second is 160 bytes.

Now, considering the same two-page requests, let's look at the burst rate. Suppose that for each page request, the total time to receive the completed page is 5 seconds with a minute delay between requests. Also, remember that each page totals 5,600 bytes (not counting overhead). This still matches the 70-second time frame and 11,200 total bytes considered in the first example. However, if we look at the burst rate for each page request – 5,600 bytes divided by 5 seconds – we see a burst rate of 1,120 bytes per second.

As you can see from this simple example, there is a significant difference between the two averages: 160 bytes versus 1,120 bytes. The idea of burstiness is very important when tackling performance bottlenecks. The most important thing to remember is that averages can be deceiving and should be looked at within a specific time window, not a simple average over many requests or large time frames.

Heavy tails

Heavy tails is another important concept to understand when looking at Web performance. Heavy-tailed distribution refers to file sizes. Generally, most HTTP GETs are for relatively small files. However, there are also requests for images that tend to be larger than simple HTML files and other media-type files.

For example, consider an example where during the span of an hour, a total of 1,000 HTTP GET requests are serviced by a server. The requested files are 250 HTML files totaling 750,000 bytes of data (3,000 bytes average). These HTML files have 700 image references totaling 5,600,000 bytes (8,000 bytes average). In addition, there are 50 requests for a ZIP file that contains a software installation. This ZIP file is 45,000 bytes totaling 3,600,000 bytes of data. If we total the number of bytes transferred (9,950,000) and compute the average from the total number of requests (1,000), we see that the average file size is 9,950 bytes. However, 95 percent of the file requests averaged less than 8,000 bytes of data.

As you can see from this example, the average is again misleading. Therefore, when looking at data transfer rates, it's best to place HTTP GET requests into classes that define a minimum and maximum file size. Then compute the averages, based on file class, to determine the file data transfer makeup of the server.

Performance-Tuning Methodologies

Performance tuning is more of an art than a science. However, with any approach, a performance baseline has to be determined before attempting any changes to the Web application. The Microsoft Web Application Stress tool, covered later in this chapter, is a great tool for performance testing. With it, you can simulate a large number of browsers hitting a Web server. Based on the performance information returned, that is, the number of requests serviced, time-out errors, and so forth, you can find where bottlenecks exist in a Web application.

Once the performance baseline is set, there are two basic approaches to improving performance: *most often* versus *worst performer*. The most often approach takes a look at the HTTP logs and determines which pages are requested most often. Then, performance-tuning efforts are focused on making these pages as efficient as possible. The problem is that these active pages may not have any performance bottlenecks, or the bottlenecks might be negligible. The worst performer approach takes a look at all the application's pages, determines the worst performing pages, and focuses the performance-tuning efforts on these pages. The problem with this approach is that the worst performing page might only be requested one percent of the time. Therefore, once the page is tuned, it will have a negligible effect on the overall performance of the Web application. In practice, it's best to use a combination of the two basic approaches.

Web applications are generally designed to support a wide variety of browsers and user requests simultaneously. However, when performance tuning, it's not the easiest task to get thousands of users hitting against a Web server. To help in this effort, there are many Web application stress tools available on the market today. The features of these products vary from vendor to vendor, along with price. However, the basic requirements for a stress tool are the following:

- Simulate many concurrent users

- Run a sequence of HTTP requests

- Support the common HTTP GET and POST commands

- Gather performance measurements

The general process of Web stress testing begins by determining a sequence of HTTP requests. This should include the page or pages you're trying to isolate but also a number of "wrapper" pages, such as menus, to break up the requests. Then isolate the server that is being tested from all traffic except your test requests. It's very difficult, if not impossible, to get accurate performance numbers if the server is servicing requests other than the HTTP requests your stress test is sending. Next, determine the test length. Most stress tools allow you to specify a length of time to run the test. During this time window, the test is repeated again and again until the time window has been exceeded. Generally, a good number to start with is 15 minutes.

Once the test plan has been determined, it's time to fire up the stress tool you'll use. As previously mentioned, there is a wide variety of tools available today — some full-featured and some with just the basics, with prices ranging from free to over $100,000 U.S. dollars. Currently, Microsoft's Web Application Stress tool is free and provides all of the basic features plus a few extras. Therefore, it's a great tool to use if you currently don't have a Web application stress tool.

The Microsoft Web Application Stress Tool

The Microsoft Web Application Stress (WAS) tool is an application used to perform stress testing for Web applications. Although it is capable of testing nearly any type of Web application, it was written by Microsoft to specifically support the testing of Active Server Pages–based Web applications. As with all Web stress-testing tools, its main purpose is to simulate multiple browsers requesting pages from a Web application. Here's a list of some of the more important features of the Web Application Stress tool:

- Supports HTML form posts and simple HTTP GETs

- Supports multiple users and passwords, cookies, and query strings

- Supports testing of non-authenticated and NTLM along with SSL

◆ Supports Domain Name Service (DNS) so clustered servers can be tested

◆ Performance counter tracking during tests

◆ Bandwidth throttling to simulate various modem throughputs

One of the most important features of WAS is that it doesn't require any type of software or hardware change on the server(s) where the Web application resides. This varies from many Web application stress tools where some type of software installation is required on the server. Many times this significantly changes the configuration of the Web application. However, with WAS, you only need to install the testing software on the client machines.

Setting up the Web Application Stress tool

When WAS is installed, the default test setup is also included. The defaults used for each stress test are shown in Figure G-2.

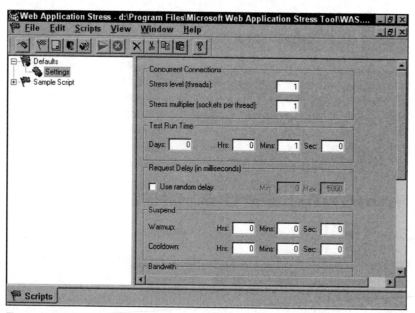

Figure G-2: WAS default test parameters

CONCURRENT CONNECTIONS

The Concurrent Connections section provides two values: Stress Level and Stress Multiplier. By default, both of these are set to 1. As mentioned previously, the point of a Web application stress tool is to simulate a large number of clients using a Web application. These two settings are used in conjunction with one another to determine the total number of concurrent requests hitting the targeted Web server.

Stress Level specifies the number of threads created and used by WAS. By default each thread uses one TCP/IP socket. However, the Stress Multiplier allows you to specify that more than one socket is to be used for each thread. In general, each socket is considered a single concurrent connection. Therefore, by multiplying Stress Level by Stress Multiplier, the total number of concurrent requests is determined.

Usually, you'll want to change the Stress Level value to the number of concurrent requests you'd like to test and leave the Stress Multiplier at 1. However, Windows NT has a limit of 2,000 active threads per machine and, generally, begins to perform poorly when more than 100 threads are active. Therefore, to simulate heavy loads, it is often better to set the Stress Level to 100 and increase the Stress Multiplier accordingly.

For example, to test the effects of 100 concurrent users, set the Stress Level to 100. However, to test with 200 concurrent users, set the Stress Level to 100 and the Stress Multiplier to 2.

TEST RUN TIME

The Test Run Time section of the Defaults Settings page is used to specify how long a stress test will perform. The default is 1 minute. However, you can specify nearly any value including a number of days. For practical purposes, setting the Test Run Time to 15 minutes is generally a good starting point.

REQUEST DELAY

The Request Delay section is probably the most misunderstood of all the WAS settings. Request Delay allows you to specify a limit on the size of data that WAS receives from each request. By default, WAS receives data in 1.2KB chunks. However, by selecting the Use random delay check box and setting the Min and Max values, you can, in essence, throttle the bandwidth to allow less than the 1.2KB default.

Request Delay is often mistaken for delays in requesting actual pages from the Web server. However, this option is controlled from the Script Item Editor that will be covered later in the chapter.

BANDWIDTH

Bandwidth throttling is used to simulate a particular model throughput value. By default, bandwidth throttling is not used. However, to simulate traffic from 28.8 connected users, for example, select the Throttle bandwidth check box and 28.8 Modem from the corresponding list box. Using bandwidth throttling is generally the best and easiest way to simulate large numbers of concurrent client connections.

As you can see, there are a number of different parameters used to control how WAS test scripts are performed. One thing to remember is that all of these options control how the client is used. From the perspective of the Web server, it's just a bunch of page requests. There isn't any knowledge, from the Web server's point of view, as to how the WAS client machine(s) are set up.

Creating Web Application Stress tool scripts

All testing done with WAS is done via a script. These scripts specify what pages within your application are tested, what query string parameters are passed into page requests, and so on. Although there are several ways to create scripts, one of the most useful is the Record method, as shown in Figure G-3.

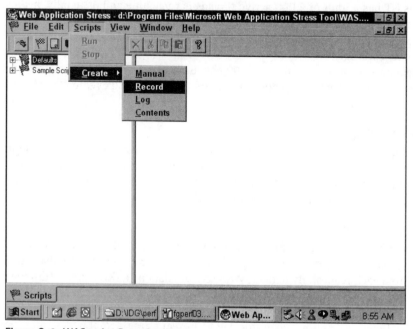

Figure G-3: WAS script Record method

After selecting the Record method for building a script, a dialog box, shown in Figure G-4, is displayed to allow you to specify options. Generally, only the Record browser cookies option should be selected.

Figure G-4: WAS script Record step one

Once the Record options are selected, click the Next button. This brings up the dialog box shown in Figure G-5.

Figure G-5: WAS script Record step two

Clicking the Finish button opens an instance of the default browser. From this point forward, every page request, post, and so forth is recorded and saved as a step in a WAS script. While the record process is being run, WAS displays the Recording tab, showing each action performed in the browser. (See Figure G-6.)

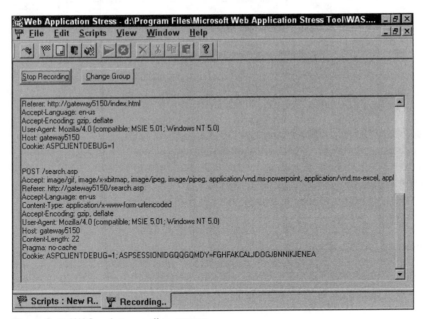

Figure G-6: WAS script recording process

As shown in Figure G-6, WAS records the type of request (for example, GET), the particular Web page being requested, and the HTTP header and cookie information. When you're done building the script, click the Stop Recording button on the WAS Recording tab. Once the script is recorded, WAS shows the new script listed in the Script Item Editor as "New Recorded Script."

As shown in Figure G-7, each page is shown in the order it was visited. The Verb column indicates the type of HTTP request that was received. WAS supports the GET, HEAD, and POST types of requests. The Path column lists the actual page that was requested.

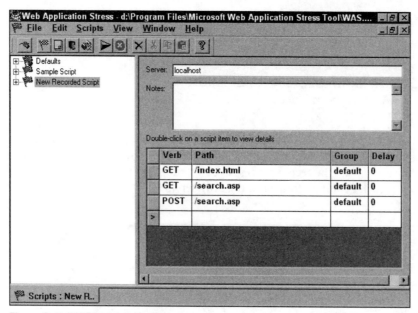

Figure G-7: WAS Script Item Editor

As previously mentioned, the Delay column is used to specify a delay, in milliseconds, between page requests. This is used to simulate delays between page requests that are similar to the delays that occur when an actual user is navigating a Web application. By default, Delay is always 0, indicating that no delay will occur. To specify a delay of 1 second, enter 1000.

To view the details associated with each script item, double-click on the placeholder on the left of each item. A new tab is added to the WAS tool giving you access to query string and form post values, HTTP header information, SSL, and RDS settings. For more information related to changing and controlling these values, take a look at the WAS online help.

Running Web Application Stress tool scripts

Prior to running a script, expand the script information by clicking the plus sign (+) next to the script name. This expands the Script Editor tree, as shown in Figure G-8.

Expand the tree for the script that was just created and select the Settings entry. This will show the settings for the test based on the Defaults Settings covered previously. At this point, we'll leave all of the settings just as they are and simply run the script for the 1 minute default by clicking the Run Script button, as shown in Figure G-9.

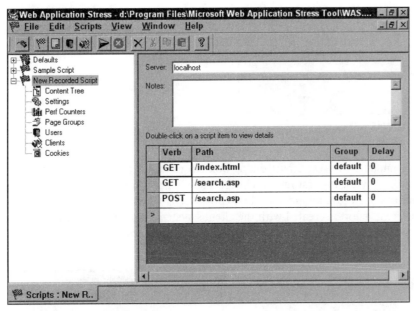

Figure G-8: WAS Script Editor tree

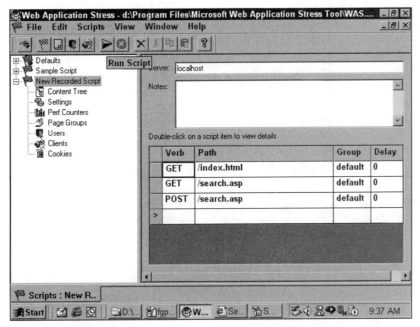

Figure G-9: WAS run script

While the script is running, the Test Status dialog box shown in Figure G-10 appears.

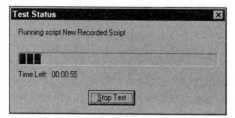

Figure G-10: WAS test status

When complete, the Test Status dialog box closes and the control returns to the Script Editor. To view the test report, choose View Reports from the menu. For each script that has been run, an entry in the Report tree is listed. For each instance of a test, a different report is created with the client's system Date and Time as the label. As shown in Figure G-11, the report lists a variety of information.

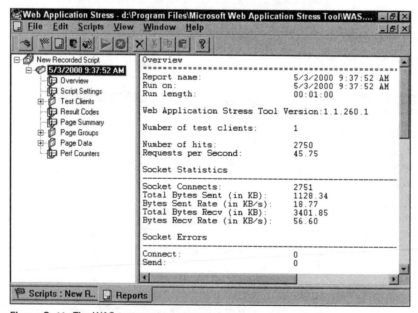

Figure G-11: The WAS test report

Although there is a variety of information provided, the most important information is the Number of Hits, Requests per Second, Socket Errors, and Result Codes. The Number of Hits gives the total number of hits performed for all the page requests during the test. The Requests per Second gives you the average number of requests the Web server was able to service each second during the test.

The Socket Errors and Result Codes listings are important for determining if any errors occurred during the test. Ideally, no socket errors would occur and the result codes would all be 200. The Result Codes correspond to the standard HTTP result codes. For example, 200 indicates the request was serviced while a 404 indicates that the requested page could not be found. Table G-1 lists many of the common HTTP result codes.

TABLE G-1 HTTP RESULT CODES

Result Code	Description
100	Continue
101	Switching protocols
200	OK
201	Created
202	Accepted
203	Non-authoritative information
204	No content
205	Reset content
206	Partial content
300	Multiple choices
301	Moved permanently
302	Moved temporarily
303	See other
304	Not modified
305	Use proxy
400	Bad request
401	Unauthorized
402	Payment required
403	Forbidden
404	Not found

Continued

TABLE G-1 HTTP RESULT CODES *(Continued)*

Result Code	Description
405	Method not allowed
406	Not acceptable
407	Proxy authentication required
408	Request time-out
409	Conflict
410	Gone
411	Length required
412	Precondition failed
413	Request entity too large
414	Request path too large
415	Unsupported media type
500	Internal server error
501	Not implemented
502	Bad gateway
503	Service unavailable
504	Gateway time-out
505	HTTP version not supported
NA	HTTP result code not given

Another important area of the report is the Page Summary section, which is shown in Figure G-12.

As shown, each page in the script is listed along with the number of hits for each. The TTFB Avg and TTLB Avg provide the average time for the first byte and the last byte, respectively, to be received by WAS. These averages are a good indication of how latency shows up between the actual page request, the point where the browser first begins to see the return of the request, and the point when the request is complete. Of all the information provided in the test reports, these two values are probably the best indication of what the end users of your Web application will experience with regard to performance.

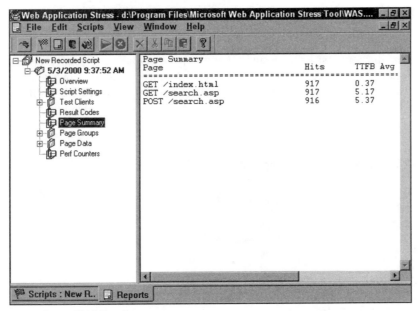

Figure G-12: WAS Test Report page summary

Gathering performance counter data

Another important aspect in performance testing is gathering actual performance counters on the server(s) that is being tested. This is another area where Microsoft's Web Application Stress tool excels. Figure G-13 shows the WAS Script Editor tree with Perf Counters selected.

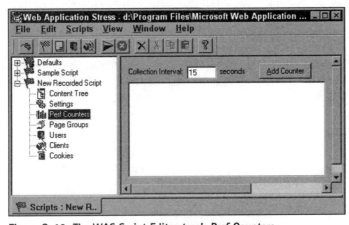

Figure G-13: The WAS Script Editor tree's Perf Counters

As shown, by default, no performance counters are selected and Collection interval is set to 15 seconds. A good starting point for the collection interval is 5 seconds. Keep in mind that gathering performance counter information creates overhead on the server(s) being tested. Therefore, the actual performance results will be negatively affected by adding these performance counters. However, the data is invaluable when doing performance tests and therefore the cost is justified. After selecting the Add Counter button, the Add counter to report dialog box opens, as shown in Figure G-14.

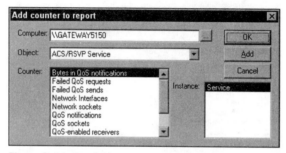

Figure G-14: The Add counter to report dialog box

If you have used the Performance Tool that comes with Windows 2000, this dialog box will look familiar. It is the same dialog box displayed when selecting performance counters to log when using the Performance Tool. There are literally hundreds of performance counters to choose from. However, the most common and useful counters are the following:

◆ **Active Server Pages\Requests Queued** – This counter indicates the number of requests waiting to be serviced by ASP. This value will ideally remain close to zero. If this value exceeds the number of processors on the server being tested, users' requests will begin receiving Server Too Busy errors for each request that is queued beyond the number of processors that are available. Values consistently more than the number of processors available indicate the page(s) being requested are too complicated to be completed when the server is at the current stress level.

◆ **Active Server Pages\Requests Rejected** – This counter provides the number of requests not executed because the queue is full. In addition, this counter is incremented when there are insufficient resources to satisfy the number of requests being received by the server. When this number is consistently above zero, the server is being stressed too heavily.

◆ **Processor(_Total)\% Processor Time** – This counter is by far the best indicator of stress level the server is experiencing. Generally, this value should not be more than 50 percent on a consistent basis. When the value is consistently above 80 percent, the level of stress is beyond the capability of the hardware. If this is the case, back off the number of concurrent users that are being tested until the value consistently dips below 80 percent. For minimum hardware configurations, you might find that this number never dips below 80 percent. In these cases, the only alternatives are to expand the hardware configuration by either adding processors, swapping slower processors for faster ones, or adding Web servers to a Web farm to spread the load between more machines.

◆ **System\Processor Queue Length** – All computers running Windows 2000 share a single processor queue, even computers with more than one processor. Processor Queue Length is the last observed number of threads in this processor queue. A value consistently beyond two threads indicates processor congestion. This is sometimes seen when objects that are not thread safe are stored in the Session object. Another problem that might be indicated is a slow-running ASP page. Finally, to complicate matters just a bit, a value consistently beyond two can also indicate that the Web server is overly stressed and not able to handle the level of traffic being requested.

Performance counters that are added to a test script are listed in the Perf Counters section of the WAS Script Editor tree, as shown in Figure G-15.

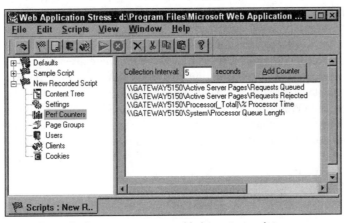

Figure G-15: Performance counters added to a test script

After running a WAS test script that includes performance counters, the counter results are included in the test report, as shown in Figure G-16.

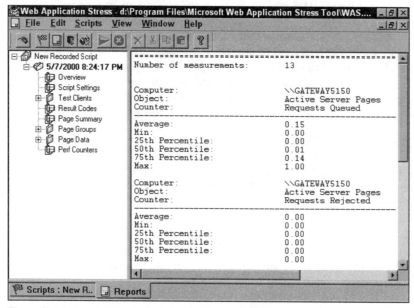

Figure G-16: Counter results included in the test report

As shown, the total number of measurements is listed along with results for each counter. The report provides minimum, maximum, and average values along with quarterly percentile values.

The four performance counters covered in this section are the most common and useful when performing stress tests on Web servers. However, there are many other counters that might be useful. More information regarding WAS and performance counters is available at http://webtool.rte.microsoft.com/tutor/perf.htm.

As shown, the Microsoft Web Application Stress tool is a fairly easy tool to use for testing Web applications under stress. WAS provides the tools to test nearly any Web application and provides information that is invaluable when developing serious Web applications. For the latest information regarding the Web Application Stress tool, visit http://webtool.rte.microsoft.com/.

Page-Level Timers

In the previous section, the Web Application Stress tool was used to perform stress testing in a Web server environment. However, there are times when you need to find out where a bottleneck exists in a single page. For example, the WAS test results might indicate a page is performing slowly. However, the page might instantiate several components using the Server.CreateObject call, or it might do disk I/O using the FileSystemObject. When only looking at the overall performance of a page, it would be difficult to pinpoint the exact section of an ASP page that is experiencing a bottleneck.

VBScript provides the Timer() function that provides near-millisecond time values. By simply calling the Timer() function before and after a section of code and calculating the difference, you can get timing values within your Active Server Pages, as shown in the following example:

```
<% SectionStart=Timer() %>

... (your code)

<% SectionEnd=Timer()

SectionElapsed = FormatNumber(SectionEnd-SectionStart,5)

Response.Write "Section took " & SectionElapsed & _
    " seconds to process."
%>
```

Using the Date() function, JavaScript provides similar information, as follows:

```
<% var start = new Date(); %>

... (your code)

<% var end = new Date();

var processing = end.valueOf() - start.valueOf();

Response.Write("Page took " + processing
  + " milliseconds to process.");
%>
```

By using this code section timing approach, you can quickly pinpoint bottlenecks in your code.

Performance Considerations with ASP Applications

There are a variety of techniques or rules to keep in mind when developing Active Server Pages applications. Over the next few pages, we'll cover some of the most significant techniques that you can use.

Non-ASP files

By default, files that exist in an ASP application with either asp, cer, cdx, or asa as a file extension are parsed, interpreted, and executed by asp.dll before they are returned to the user. There is a caching methodology used for popular pages. However, even when cached, the asp.dll is used to execute the pages. For Active Server Pages that contain script code that is to be parsed, interpreted, and executed, this is to be expected. For those pages that don't contain any type of script code, CPU cycles are unnecessarily wasted parsing and interpreting these pages.

For those pages where include files are used but no server-side script exists, rename the files to end with .stm. This extension is mapped to the ssinc.dll that does some limited pre-processing of the page before it is sent to the requesting browser. The ssinc.dll file simply looks for include files, pulls them from the disk, and inserts the contents in the requesting page at the location where the include statement exists.

For those files that don't contain any server-side includes or script, use a file extension of .htm. This extension doesn't require any additional processing, and Internet Information Server (IIS) returns the contents of these files very efficiently.

Application mappings

When IIS is installed, there are a variety of application mappings that are defined. Most Web applications only use a few of the available mappings. However, IIS has to maintain the entire list of mappings and verify each file against this list. Since this causes unnecessary overhead for IIS, obsolete application mappings should be deleted. To update the application mappings list, select the properties for the Web application, as shown in Figure G-17, by right-clicking the Web site in Internet Information Services Manager.

Select the Home Directory tab from the Properties dialog box, and click the Configuration button shown in Figure G-18.

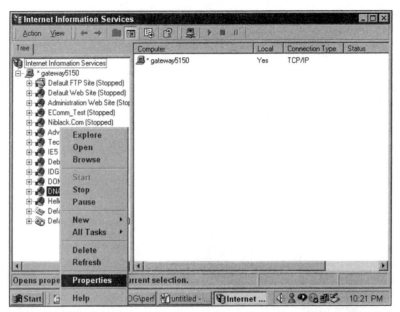

Figure G-17: Using Internet Information Services Manager to select a Web application's properties

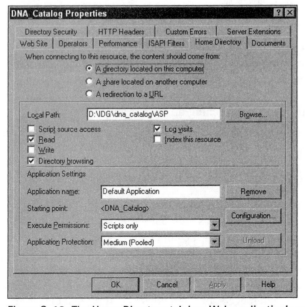

Figure G-18: The Home Directory tab in a Web application's properties dialog box

As shown in Figure G-19, the Application Configuration dialog box appears. The App Mappings tab lists all of the application mappings that are defined for the selected Web site.

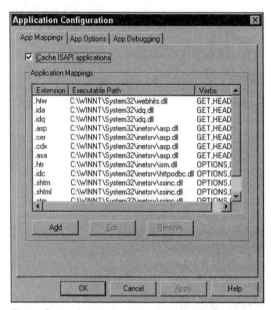

Figure G-19: Application mappings in the Application Configuration dialog box

Application mappings are based on the file extension. Therefore, for each file extension listed that is not used by your application, select it and click the Remove button. Be sure to verify that your Web site does not use any application mappings that you remove. This is easily done by searching all of the files that make up your Web site and verifying that the file extension that corresponds to the application mapping is not used.

Referencing variables

In general, locally scoped variables are more efficient to work with than globally defined variables. When a variable is defined as a global variable, its value must be stored in memory that is accessible throughout the application. When working with ASP, this is generally handled by defining Application or Session variables. While in some cases global variables are needed, in many cases they are not. Therefore, when defining variables at Application or Session level, verify that the variable is really going to be needed and referenced at a global level. If not, redefine the variable as a local variable to the particular ASP script.

When variables are used, be sure to use the DIM keyword for VBScript or the var keyword for JavaScript. In addition, Option Explicit should always be defined. When doing so, ASP is able to more easily manage the variable list and provide you with warnings when a referenced variable has not actually been explicitly defined using DIM or var keywords.

Another general guideline when working with ASP is that if a value in a collection is referenced more than once in a page, store the value in a local variable rather than explicitly referencing the Collection object. For example, in Listing G-1, the CustID column is referenced several times.

Listing G-1: Referencing the CustID column

```
<%
Do While Not RS.EOF
Response.Write RS("CustID") & ":" & RS("CustName")
    Select Case RS("CustID")
        Case < 100
            'do something
        Case >= 100
            'do something else
    End Select
Response.Write "That's all for CustomerID=" & RS("CustID")
RS.MoveNext
Loop
%>
```

Listing G-2 rewrites it to store the CustID value in a local variable.

Listing G-2: Storing the CustID value in a local variable

```
<%
Do While Not RS.EOF
    CustomerID = RS("CustID")
    Response.Write CustomerID & ":" & RS("CustName")
    Select Case CustomerID
        Case < 100
            'do something
        Case >= 100
            'do something else
    End Select
Response.Write "That's all for CustomerID=" & CustomerID
RS.MoveNext
Loop
%>
```

For the most part, the two code samples in Listings G-1 and G-2 are identical. However, the code sample in Listing G1-2 stores the CustID value in a local variable and then all future references to the CustID value are resolved using the local variable. While this technique does take an additional step, it actually performs better. The overhead associated with referencing a collection value is much higher than referencing a local variable. Therefore, in cases where you reference a collection value more than once in a code segment, always define a local variable and store the collection value in the local variable.

Using the global.asa file

The global.asa file is very useful when building ASP Web sites. However, it can also create unnecessary overhead if not maintained. For example, there are four events that are available in the global.asa file:

- ◆ Application_OnStart

- ◆ Application_OnEnd

- ◆ Session_OnStart

- ◆ Session_OnEnd

If these event handlers are defined in the global.asa file, the events are fired by IIS and any code within the handler is parsed and executed by ASP. This process occurs even when an event handler doesn't have any code to execute. For example, a Session_OnStart event handler defined as follows:

```
<SCRIPT LANGUAGE=VBScript RUNAT=Server>
    SUB Session_OnStart
    END SUB
</SCRIPT>
```

will still require IIS to fire the event and ASP to parse the code for every new session that is started. This unnecessary processing is easily stopped by simply deleting any event handlers defined in the global.asa file that don't contain code.

Sessions and the Session object

The Internet is an inherently stateless environment. More simply stated, Web servers simply return files that are requested. There is no concept of what happened prior to a request or what will happen in future requests. This differs from traditional application development where the state of a user's actions is known by the application.

Therefore, when ASP was first introduced, the Session object changed the way Web application development was approached. By using the Session object, as discussed in Chapter 7, "The Session Object," developers are able to maintain information that spans more than one page request. In theory, this was a huge step forward in Web development. However, as with most things, there is a cost associated with using the Session object.

For example, when sessions are enabled on a Web server, the state of every request is maintained. This history has to be maintained somewhere. In the case of IIS, this information is maintained on the Web server in memory. As the number of users increases and the amount of information being cached increases, valuable memory resources are dedicated to support the Session object.

In addition, if sessions are enabled on the Web server, IIS and ASP must process the various page requests differently. IIS and ASP must recognize that state information may or may not be used. Therefore, processing resources on the server are used again to help maintain this information.

The general rule for highly active ASP Web applications is to use the Session object very cautiously, if at all. In many cases, information being stored in the Session object can easily be passed from page to page via query strings or hidden form values or stored in cookies on the client's machine. However, these other approaches are not nearly as easy to use as the Session object is.

For Active Server Pages that do not require any type of Session support, include the `EnableSessionState` directive at the top of each page. For example, to specify that VBScript is the default scripting language used and to not support the Session object on a page, place the following at the top of the page:

```
<%@ Language = VBScript
EnableSessionState = False %>
```

For those Web applications that don't use the Session object anywhere in the application, it is more efficient to turn off the Enable Session State flag on the application configuration tab of the Web site Properties dialog box.

Buffering ASP output

Buffering is simply the process of storing ASP output on the server until the buffer is explicitly flushed or page processing is completed. With the introduction of IIS 5.0, buffering is enabled by default. However, you can control buffering at the page level by setting `Response.Buffer = True` to enable buffering or `Response.Buffer = False` to disable buffering. Keep in mind that once you set `Response.Buffer` on an ASP page, the setting cannot be changed. For example, the following ASP code would generate an error:

```
<%
Response.Buffer = True
...(your code here)
Response.Buffer = False
...(your code here)
%>
```

Generally, having buffering enabled will provide better utilization, and therefore performance, of an IIS server. However, from the client and browser point of view, performance might decrease because data is not returned immediately by the Web server while it's being buffered. Therefore, when using buffering, keep in mind that the `Response.Flush` method is available to write the entire contents of the buffer to the browser.

Using buffering and the `Response.Flush` method in conjunction with one another, you can fully control the process of writing data to the browser while maintaining maximum efficiency of Web server resources.

The Response.IsClientConnected property

In many cases, users will navigate away from a particular page before it is fully received from the Web server. However, the Web server is oblivious to this. Therefore, the Web server continues to process the page request and then tries to send the results back to the browser. Since the browser is no longer at the same page, the data sent by the Web server is refused by the user's browser. The user is never aware that anything happened with the exception that there might be a few modem light flashes when the server's response is first received. The server, however, has already wasted the CPU cycles.

The Response object provides a property that keeps track of the connection state of the user request. Essentially, when a browser cancels a request, a TCP packet is sent to the Web server to disconnect. This is recognized by IIS and ASP; however, for ASP requests that are already processing, there is not any type of event that fires in the ASP model to let currently running scripts abort processing.

By checking the status of the `Response.IsClientConnected` property, ASP script code can intermittently check to see if the user has canceled the request. Once again, in theory this sounds great but there is a cost. Checking the `Response.IsClientConnected` property is VERY expensive to process. It requires the Response object to hold the execution of an ASP script and send a synchronize request to the user. This is very similar to doing a three-way handshake when setting up a TCP connection.

Following is a VBScript code sample using the `Response.IsClientConnected` method:

```
<%
If Response.IsClientConnected Then
    ... (some bit of code)
Else
    'Client is not connected. Clear the response buffer...
    Response.Clear
    '...and end the processing
    Response.End
End If
%>
```

As you can imagine, the `Response.IsClientConnected` method is a huge performance loser, especially when used in loops. However, if used sparingly and before other expensive operations are performed on the server, it can save processing time. In general, this is a technique that should be used with caution and really only when you see trends where users commonly cancel a request for a particular page or when a particular process is requested.

The Server.Transfer method

Introduced with IIS 5.0, the `Server.Transfer` method, covered in Chapter 8, "The Server Object," is a huge performance improvement over previous redirection techniques. It's very common for a user to request a particular ASP. During the processing of the ASP, the script redirects the user to a different page using the `Response.Redirect` method. When this is done, an HTTP redirect message is actually sent to the browser and the browser parses this and then automatically requests the page that was redirected. It's pretty obvious that this is not the most efficient way to send a user from one page to another.

In addition, the `Response.Redirect` method does not maintain transaction or state information when the redirect is performed. Therefore, aside from using query strings or cookies, any information from the first page is lost when the user is redirected to the second page. Enter the `Server.Transfer` method. When the `Server.Transfer` method is called, all the state information for all the ASP intrinsic objects is included with the transfer. In addition, the current contents of the request collections (that is, `Request.Form`, `Request.QueryString`, and so on) are sent to the page being transferred.

The `Server.Transfer` method syntax is similar to the `Request.Redirect`. The only parameter is the path that the user is being transferred to. However, one significant difference is that `Server.Transfer` is available at any point during the server-side processing. The `Response.Redirect` method is not available after data has been sent to the browser unless the `Response.Clear` method is called first to erase any buffered HTML output.

For example, page1.asp is defined as follows:

```
<%
Response.Write "You're at the top of page 1...<br><br>"

Response.Write "Now, page 1 will use the Server.Transfer" & _
    " method to send you to page 2...<br><br>"

Server.Transfer "Page2.asp"

Response.Write "You're at the bottom of page 1...<br><br>"
%>
```

Notice that `Response.Writes` are used to display text to let you know what page is running. page2.asp is defined as follows:

```
<%
Response.Write "You're at the top of page 2...<br><br>"

Response.Write "Page1QS=" & Request.Querystring("Page1QS") & _
    "<br><br>"

Response.Write "You're at the bottom of page 2...<br><br>"
%>
```

It also uses `Reponse.Writes` to display text to indicate what page is being processed. Notice that a `QueryString` value (`Page1QS`) is referenced. Figure G-20 shows the browser output when page1.asp is invoked using `Page1.asp?Page1QS= testing`.

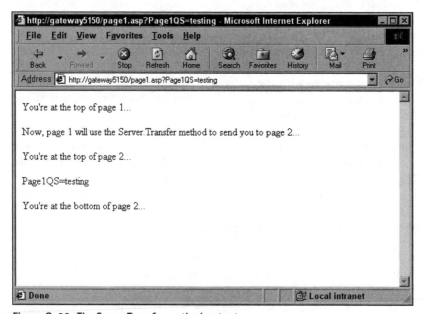

Figure G-20: The Server.Transfer method output

As shown, page2.asp is able to access the `QueryString` value that was actually passed to page1.asp. Also, notice that the "You're at the bottom of page 1..." message is not shown. This illustrates how the `Server.Transfer` method passes control from one page to another.

The Server.Execute method

The `Server.Execute` method, also covered in Chapter 8, is another new feature introduced with IIS 5.0. Basically, this method replaces the need for many server-side include files. As mentioned earlier, when the asp.dll parses and interprets a file, it stores a copy of that interpreted file in memory for future use. The management of this code cache is beyond the scope of this book. However, it's clear that this caching technique dramatically increases performance for IIS/ASP applications.

One flaw with using server-side includes is that multiple copies of the same include file are maintained in the cache if the include file is included in more than one Active Server Page. Essentially, a server-side include directive does nothing more than copy the contents of the include file and insert them into the ASP script. Therefore, when an include file is used by multiple Active Server Pages, multiple copies of the same include file are maintained in the cache. As you can see, the use of includes, while great for leverage code libraries, is not the most efficient when looking at how the script is processed.

The `Server.Execute` method uses a different approach to code reuse. The `Server.Execute` method is more like a procedure call used in other programming languages. When `Server.Execute` is called, the file that is specified in the path is executed without placing a copy of the code in the calling ASP. The effect of this is that script formerly cached multiple times is now stored only once in the cache. While this is a tremendous improvement over the previous server-side include method, there is now a different problem.

Using server-side includes, you could place any number of code functions and procedures in an include file. This made the code maintenance aspect fairly easy. With the `Server.Execute` method, however, the file is not included – it is executed. Therefore, you can't simply change all of your server-side includes to `Server.Execute` calls. First, you'll have to look at each include file and break them up into small executable units. This of course tends to make code maintenance more difficult. With that said, the performance benefits of using the `Server.Execute` method over the server-side include method is worth the effort.

To illustrate the use of `Server.Execute`, page1.asp is defined as follows:

```
<%
Response.Write "You're at the top of page 1...<br><br>"

Response.Write "Now, page 1 will use the Server.Execute" & _
    " method to send you to page 2...<br><br>"

Server.Execute "Page2.asp"

Response.Write "You're at the bottom of page 1...<br><br>"
%>
```

Notice that `Response.Writes` are used to display text to let you know what page is running. page2.asp is defined as follows:

```
<%
Response.Write "You're at the top of page 2...<br><br>"

Response.Write "Page1QS=" & Request.Querystring("Page1QS") & _
    "<br><br>"

Response.Write "You're at the bottom of page 2...<br><br>"
%>
```

It also uses `Reponse.Writes` to display text to indicate what page is being processed. Notice that a `QueryString` value (`Page1QS`) is referenced. Figure G-21 shows the browser output when page1.asp is invoked with `Page1.asp?Page1QS=testing`.

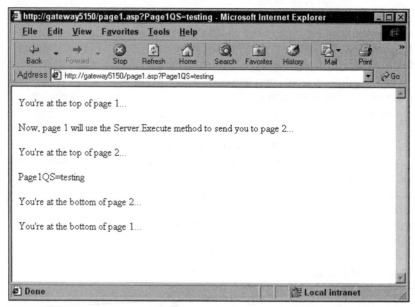

Figure G-21: Server.Execute method output

As shown, page2.asp is able to access the `QueryString` value that was actually passed to page1.asp. Also, notice that the "You're at the bottom of page 1..." message is now displayed. This illustrates how the `Server.Execute` method passes control from one page to another and then returns.

Using components

Using components to extend the functionality of IIS and ASP is very powerful. In fact, aside from the most simple of scripts, much of the ASP development effort is spent interacting with components. For example, ADO, which is provided by a component developed by Microsoft, is typically used for interacting with databases.

At the same time, if not used or managed appropriately, components can also create performance issues within ASP applications. Creating an instance of an object is generally very expensive from a performance perspective. Therefore, if a component is not necessary, don't create an instance of it. Generally, it's best to create an instance of an object right before it's needed. Along these same lines, once an object is no longer needed, release the instance of the object from memory.

Many objects are thread safe or thread aware. For these objects, you can define the object within the global.asa file using the `<OBJECT>` tag. For example, placing the following:

```
<object id="ListBox_xLKUP" progid="IISSample.LookupTable"
runat="Server" scope="Application"></object>
```

at the top of a global.asa file defines an instance of the `IISSample.LookupTable` component at the application level. Therefore, now Active Server Pages can reference the object directly using the value of `id` without having to use the `Server.CreateObject` method, as shown in this example:

```
<%
Response.Write ListBox_xLKUP.Key(nX) & ":" & ListBox_xLKUP.Value(nX)
%>
```

Defining objects using the `<OBJECT>` tag is a great way to circumvent the cost of instantiating the same object in various places throughout an application. However, this technique should only be used for thread-safe or thread-aware components. If you're not sure if a component meets this requirement, it's best not to use this technique.

The ADO MoveNext method

When using ActiveX Data Objects (ADO) to communicate with a database, the `MoveNext` method of the RecordSet object is the typical approach to navigating through a RecordSet. However, it is also the least efficient. Here's a typical segment of code that iterates through a RecordSet:

```
Set conn = Server.Createobject("ADODB.Connection")
Conn.Open "connectionstring"
Set rs = Conn.Execute("SELECT * FROM Users")
Do While Not rs.EOF
```

```
    Response.Write rs("UserName")
    rs.MoveNext
Loop
rs.Close
Set rs = Nothing
conn.close
Set conn = Nothing
```

A faster performing alternative is to use the GetRows method of the RecordSet object. The GetRows method pulls an entire RecordSet or a portion of the RecordSet at one time and places the results in a two-dimensional array. The first dimension is used to store column-based information while the second dimension is used to store row-based information. Also, each dimension is 0-based, meaning that the elements of each dimension start at 0 rather than 1. For example, if the GetRows method was used for a RecordSet that contained 4 columns with 100 rows of data, the first dimension would begin at 0 and end at 3 while the second dimension would start at 0 and end at 99. Listing G-3 shows the previous example rewritten to use the GetRows method.

Listing G-3: Iterating through the RecordSet

```
Set conn = Server.Createobject("ADODB.Connection")
Conn.Open "connectionstring"
Set rs = Conn.Execute("SELECT * FROM Users")
If Not rs.EOF
    aRS = rs.GetRows
Else
    aRS = ""
End If
rs.Close
Set rs = Nothing
conn.close
Set conn = Nothing
If VarType(aRS) = 8204 Then
    For intX = 0 To UBound(aRS,2)
        Response.Write aRS(0,intX)
    Next
End If
```

As you can see, the examples are very similar. However, the second example pulls the entire RecordSet in one line, one call. Then the ADO RecordSet and connection objects are released. From then on, the processing is done against the two-dimensional array that was created when the GetRows method was called.

This makes for very efficient use of the Web server resources. The expense of having the ADO objects instantiated on the Web server is minimized by setting up, using, and releasing the objects and the associated resources as quickly as possible.

In addition, iterating through an array is much more efficient than iterating through a RecordSet. The most obvious reason is that when the entire RecordSet was pulled from the database using the GetRows method, the overhead of setting up each data packet transfer was minimized and could potentially span records. Using the MoveNext method, by design, only pulls one record at a time. Therefore, more data transfer overhead is required.

While the GetRows technique is a great performance booster, it is not perfect. At some point, using GetRows to pull an entire RecordSet can kill server performance. Imagine a RecordSet with 20 columns totaling 800 bytes of data and 20,000 rows. Storing all this information in a two-dimensional array would take a huge amount of memory on the Web server. The MoveNext method, however, is only going to pull one record at a time. Therefore, in this case the MoveNext method would be much more efficient.

To help alleviate this problem, the GetRows method includes several parameters, as follows:

```
array = recordset.GetRows(rows, start, fields)
```

All of these parameters are optional. So, by default, when the GetRows method is called without any parameters, all of the rows, starting with the current record, and all the fields are copied to the array. However, for large RecordSets, it's best to buffer the data by pulling a small number of rows at one time. For each GetRows call made, the current location in the RecordSet is maintained. Therefore, repeated calls to GetRows will not pull the same set of records. For example, the first call to GetRows(100) pulls records 0-99. The next call to GetRows(100) pulls records 100–199, and so forth. If the number of records to pull exceeds the remaining number of records available in the RecordSet, the remaining records are pulled and the upper bounds of the second dimension are adjusted to reflect the last record. Therefore, it is important to always check the UBound of the second dimension to determine how many records actually exist in the array.

The starting record to pull is specified in the start parameter in the event the RecordSet supports bookmarks. The fields parameter allows you to specify a single column name or ordinal position or an array of column names or ordinal positions.

Listing G-4 provides an example showing how to only pull the UserName column in the previous example, 100 records at a time.

Listing G-4: Pulling 100 records at a time

```
Set conn = Server.Createobject("ADODB.Connection")
Conn.Open "connectionstring"
Set rs = Conn.Execute("SELECT * FROM Users")
Do While Not rs.EOF
    aRS = rs.GetRows(100,,Array("UserName"))
    If VarType(aRS) = 8204 Then
        For intX = 0 To UBound(aRS,2)
```

```
            Response.Write aRS(0,intX)
        Next
    End If
Loop
rs.Close
Set rs = Nothing
conn.close
Set conn = Nothing
```

Summary

Through this brief introduction of performance considerations to keep in mind when building ASP applications, there are a lot of issues to consider. Aside from the coding aspects of creating an application, you also must consider the performance cost of one method versus another.

To help determine performance bottlenecks in a Web application, stress testing is required. The Web Application Stress tool is a free and fully functional tool to perform many different types of stress tests to help identify potential bottlenecks.

Index

Symbols

A

Continued

Notes

_____

_____

_____

_____

_____

_____

_____

_____

_____

_____

_____

_____

_____

_____

_____

_____

_____

_____

_____

IDG Books Worldwide, Inc.—
End-User License Agreement

READ THIS. You should carefully read these terms and conditions before opening the software packet(s) included with this book ("Book"). This is a license agreement ("Agreement") between you and IDG Books Worldwide, Inc. ("IDGB"). By opening the accompanying software packet(s), you acknowledge that you have read and accept the following terms and conditions. If you do not agree and do not want to be bound by such terms and conditions, promptly return the Book and the unopened software packet(s) to the place you obtained them for a full refund.

1. <u>License Grant</u>. IDGB grants to you (either an individual or entity) a nonexclusive license to use one copy of the enclosed software program(s) (collectively, the "Software") solely for your own personal or business purposes on a single computer (whether a standard computer or a work-station component of a multiuser network). The Software is in use on a computer when it is loaded into temporary memory (RAM) or installed into permanent memory (hard disk, CD-ROM, or other storage device). IDGB reserves all rights not expressly granted herein.

2. <u>Ownership</u>. IDGB is the owner of all right, title, and interest, including copyright, in and to the compilation of the Software recorded on the disk(s) or CD-ROM ("Software Media"). Copyright to the individual programs recorded on the Software Media is owned by the author or other authorized copyright owner of each program. Ownership of the Software and all proprietary rights relating thereto remain with IDGB and its licensers.

3. <u>Restrictions On Use and Transfer</u>.

   (a) You may only (i) make one copy of the Software for backup or archival purposes, or (ii) transfer the Software to a single hard disk, provided that you keep the original for backup or archival purposes. You may not (i) rent or lease the Software, (ii) copy or reproduce the Software through a LAN or other network system or through any computer subscriber system or bulletin-board system, or (iii) modify, adapt, or create derivative works based on the Software.

   (b) You may not reverse engineer, decompile, or disassemble the Software. You may transfer the Software and user documentation on a permanent basis, provided that the transferee agrees to accept the terms and conditions of this Agreement and you retain no copies. If the Software is an update or has been updated, any transfer must include the most recent update and all prior versions.

4. <u>Restrictions on Use of Individual Programs</u>. You must follow the individual requirements and restrictions detailed for each individual program in Appendix A of this Book. These limitations are also contained in the individual license agreements recorded on the Software Media. These limitations may include a requirement that after using the program for a specified period of time, the user must pay a registration fee or discontinue use. By opening the Software packet(s), you will be agreeing to abide by the licenses and restrictions for these individual programs that are detailed in Appendix A and on the Software Media. None of the material on this Software Media or listed in this Book may ever be redistributed, in original or modified form, for commercial purposes.

5. <u>Limited Warranty</u>.

   (a) IDGB warrants that the Software and Software Media are free from defects in materials and workmanship under normal use for a period of sixty (60) days from the date of purchase of this Book. If IDGB receives notification within the warranty period of defects in materials or workmanship, IDGB will replace the defective Software Media.

   (b) IDGB AND THE AUTHORS OF THE BOOK DISCLAIM ALL OTHER WARRANTIES, EXPRESS OR IMPLIED, INCLUDING WITHOUT LIMITATION IMPLIED WARRANTIES OF MERCHANTABILITY AND FITNESS FOR A PARTICULAR PURPOSE, WITH RESPECT TO THE SOFTWARE, THE PROGRAMS, THE SOURCE CODE CONTAINED THEREIN, AND/OR THE TECHNIQUES DESCRIBED IN THIS BOOK. IDGB DOES NOT WARRANT THAT THE FUNCTIONS CONTAINED IN THE SOFTWARE WILL MEET YOUR REQUIREMENTS OR THAT THE OPERATION OF THE SOFTWARE WILL BE ERROR FREE.

   (c) This limited warranty gives you specific legal rights, and you may have other rights that vary from jurisdiction to jurisdiction.

6. <u>Remedies</u>.

   (a) IDGB's entire liability and your exclusive remedy for defects in materials and workmanship shall be limited to replacement of the Software Media, which may be returned to IDGB with a copy of your receipt at the following address: Software Media Fulfillment Department, Attn.: Active Server Pages 3 Developer's Guide, IDG Books Worldwide, Inc., 10475 Crosspoint Blvd., Indianapolis, IN 46256, or call 1-800-762-2974. Please allow three to four weeks for delivery. This Limited Warranty is void if failure of the Software Media has resulted from accident, abuse, or misapplication. Any replacement Software Media will be warranted for the remainder of the original warranty period or thirty (30) days, whichever is longer.

(b) In no event shall IDGB or the authors be liable for any damages whatsoever (including without limitation damages for loss of business profits, business interruption, loss of business information, or any other pecuniary loss) arising from the use of or inability to use the Book or the Software, even if IDGB has been advised of the possibility of such damages.

(c) Because some jurisdictions do not allow the exclusion or limitation of liability for consequential or incidental damages, the above limitation or exclusion may not apply to you.

7. **U.S. Government Restricted Rights**. Use, duplication, or disclosure of the Software by the U.S. Government is subject to restrictions stated in paragraph (c)(1)(ii) of the Rights in Technical Data and Computer Software clause of DFARS 252.227-7013, and in subparagraphs (a) through (d) of the Commercial Computer — Restricted Rights clause at FAR 52.227-19, and in similar clauses in the NASA FAR supplement, when applicable.

8. **General**. This Agreement constitutes the entire understanding of the parties and revokes and supersedes all prior agreements, oral or written, between them and may not be modified or amended except in a writing signed by both parties hereto that specifically refers to this Agreement. This Agreement shall take precedence over any other documents that may be in conflict herewith. If any one or more provisions contained in this Agreement are held by any court or tribunal to be invalid, illegal, or otherwise unenforceable, each and every other provision shall remain in full force and effect.

my2cents.idgbooks.com

Register This Book — And Win!

Visit **http://my2cents.idgbooks.com** to register this book and we'll automatically enter you in our fantastic monthly prize giveaway. It's also your opportunity to give us feedback: let us know what you thought of this book and how you would like to see other topics covered.

Discover IDG Books Online!

The IDG Books Online Web site is your online resource for tackling technology — at home and at the office. Frequently updated, the IDG Books Online Web site features exclusive software, insider information, online books, and live events!

10 Productive & Career-Enhancing Things You Can Do at www.idgbooks.com

- Nab source code for your own programming projects.

- Download software.

- Read Web exclusives: special articles and book excerpts by IDG Books Worldwide authors.

- Take advantage of resources to help you advance your career as a Novell or Microsoft professional.

- Buy IDG Books Worldwide titles or find a convenient bookstore that carries them.

- Register your book and win a prize.

- Chat live online with authors.

- Sign up for regular e-mail updates about our latest books.

- Suggest a book you'd like to read or write.

- Give us your 2¢ about our books and about our Web site.

You say you're not on the Web yet? It's easy to get started with IDG Books' *Discover the Internet*, available at local retailers everywhere.

CD-ROM Installation Instructions

The source files are organized by chapter. Solutions that require multiple files are stored in their own subdirectory, preserving any structure necessary for the application to find its resources.

The index.html file serves as the entry point to the solutions and any third-party demonstration products on the CD-ROM. To access the solutions and the products, use your favorite Web browser to open the index.html file. To run the solutions, you must create a virtual root on your web server to host the solutions.

For information on how to install, configure, and run the third-party products, refer to the vendor's documentation. If no documentation is included in the CD-ROM, visit the vendor's Web site for more information.

For more information, see Appendix A, "What's On the CD-ROM."